PLUNKETT'S SHARING & GIG ECONOMY, FREELANCE WORKERS & ON-DEMAND DELIVERY INDUSTRY ALMANAC 2023

Editor and Publisher:
Jack W. Plunkett

Executive Editor and Database Manager:
Martha Burgher Plunkett

Senior Editor and Researchers:
Isaac Snider

Editors, Researchers and Assistants:
Charles Bui
Bryant Huynh
Annie Paynter
Gina Sprenkel
Jason Suerte
S. Charith Vadla

Information Technology Manager:
Rebeca Tijiboy

Special Thanks to:
eMarketer
Federal Reserve Bank System
MBO Partners
Mastercard International
U.S. Census Bureau, Economics and Statistics
Administration

Plunkett Research®, Ltd.
P. O. Drawer 541737, Houston, Texas 77254 USA
Phone: 713.932.0000   Fax: 713.932.7080
www.plunkettresearch.com

Plunkett Research®, Ltd.
P. O. Drawer 541737
Houston, Texas 77254-1737
Phone: 713.932.0000, Fax: 713.932.7080 www.plunkettresearch.com

ISBN13 # 978-1-62831-664-3 (eBook Edition # 978-1-62831-989-7)

Limited Warranty and Terms of Use:

Users' publications in static electronic format containing any portion of the content of this book (and/or the content of any related Plunkett Research, Ltd. online service to which you are granted access, hereinafter collectively referred to as the "Data") or Derived Data (that is, a set of data that is a derivation made by a User from the Data, resulting from the applications of formulas, analytics or any other method) may be resold by the User only for the purpose of providing third-party analysis within an established research platform under the following conditions: (However, Users may not extract or integrate any portion of the Data or Derived Data for any other purpose.)

   a) Users may utilize the Data only as described herein. b) User may not export more than an insubstantial portion of the Data or Derived Data, c) Any Data exported by the User may only be distributed if the following conditions are met:

      i)   Data must be incorporated in added-value reports or presentations, either of which are part of the regular services offered by the User and not as stand-alone products.
      ii) Data may not be used as part of a general mailing or included in external websites or other mass communication vehicles or formats, including, but not limited to, advertisements.
      iii) Except as provided herein, Data may not be resold by User.

"Insubstantial Portions" shall mean an amount of the Data that (1) has no independent commercial value, (2) could not be used by User, its clients, Authorized Users and/or its agents as a substitute for the Data or any part of it, (3) is not separately marketed by the User, an affiliate of the User or any third-party source (either alone or with other data), and (4) is not retrieved by User, its clients, Authorized Users and/or its Agents via regularly scheduled, systematic batch jobs.

PLUNKETT'S SHARING & GIG ECONOMY, FREELANCE WORKERS & ON-DEMAND DELIVERY INDUSTRY ALMANAC 2023

The only comprehensive guide to the sharing & gig economy industry

Jack W. Plunkett

Published by:
Plunkett Research®, Ltd., Houston, Texas
www.plunkettresearch.com

PLUNKETT'S SHARING & GIG ECONOMY, FREELANCE WORKERS & ON-DEMAND DELIVERY INDUSTRY ALMANAC 2023

CONTENTS

Continued on next page

INTRODUCTION

PLUNKETT'S SHARING & GIG ECONOMY, FREELANCE WORKERS & ON-DEMAND DELIVERY INDUSTRY ALMANAC is designed to be used as a general source for researchers of all types.

The data and areas of interest covered are intentionally broad, ranging from the trends relating to sharing across the travel, retail, food and apparel industries, to emerging technology, to an in-depth look at the major for-profit firms (which we call "THE SHARING & GIG ECONOMY 150") within the many industry sectors that make up the sharing, gig economy and on-demand arena.

This reference book is designed to be a general source for researchers. It is especially intended to assist with market research, strategic planning, employment searches, contact or prospect list creation and financial research, and as a data resource for executives and students of all types.

PLUNKETT'S SHARING & GIG ECONOMY, FREELANCE WORKERS & ON-DEMAND DELIVERY INDUSTRY ALMANAC takes a rounded approach for the general reader. This book presents a complete overview of the entire sharing and gig economy industry (see "How To Use This Book"). For example, you will find trends in the hotel room, car, bicycle and aircraft sharing markets, along with easy-to-use charts and tables on all facets of sharing, gig economy and on-demand services in general, from the sales and profits of the providers to projected growth in the industry.

THE SHARING & GIG ECONOMY 150 is our unique grouping of the biggest, most successful corporations in all segments of the sharing & gig industry, including housing, transportation, food, apparel and related services. Tens of thousands of pieces of information, gathered from a wide variety of sources, have been researched and are presented in a unique form that can be easily understood. This section includes thorough indexes to THE SHARING & GIG ECONOMY 150, by geography, industry, sales, brand names, subsidiary names and many other topics. (See Chapter 4.)

Especially helpful is the way in which PLUNKETT'S SHARING & GIG ECONOMY, FREELANCE WORKERS & ON-DEMAND DELIVERY INDUSTRY ALMANAC enables readers who have no business background to readily compare the financial records and growth plans of large sharing and gig economy companies and major industry groups. You'll see the mid-term financial record of each firm, along with the impact of earnings, sales and strategic plans on each company's potential to fuel growth, to serve new markets and to provide investment and employment opportunities.

No other source provides this book's easy-to-understand comparisons of growth, expenditures, technologies, corporations and many other items of great importance to people of all types who may be studying this, one of the fastest growing industries in the world today.

By scanning the data groups and the unique indexes, you can find the best information to fit your personal research needs. The major companies in the sharing and gig economy field are profiled and then ranked using several different groups of specific criteria. Which firms are the biggest employers? Which companies earn the most profits? These things and much more are easy to find.

In addition to individual company profiles, an overview of sharing and gig economy markets and trends is provided. This book's job is to help you sort through easy-to-understand summaries of today's trends in a quick and effective manner.

Whatever your purpose for researching the sharing and gig economy field, you'll find this book to be a valuable guide. Nonetheless, as is true with all resources, this volume has limitations that the reader should be aware of:

- Financial data and other corporate information can change quickly. A book of this type can be no more current than the data that was available as of the time of editing. Consequently, the financial picture, management and ownership of the firm(s) you are studying may have changed since the date of this book. For example, this almanac includes the most up-to-date sales figures and profits available to the editors as of late 2022. That means that we have typically used corporate financial data as of the end of 2021.

- Corporate mergers, acquisitions and downsizing are occurring at a very rapid rate. Such events may have created significant change, subsequent to the publishing of this book, within a company you are studying.

- Some of the companies in THE SHARING & GIG ECONOMY 150 are so large in scope and in variety of business endeavors conducted within a parent organization, that we have been unable to completely list all subsidiaries, affiliations, divisions and activities within a firm's corporate structure.

- This volume is intended to be a general guide to a quickly evolving industry. That means that researchers should look to this book for an overview and, when conducting in-depth research, should contact the specific corporations or industry associations in question for the very latest changes and data. Where possible, we have listed contact names, toll-free telephone numbers and internet site addresses for the companies, government agencies and industry associations involved so that the reader may get further details without unnecessary delay.

- Tables of industry data and statistics used in this book include the latest numbers available at the time of printing, generally through the end of 2021. In a few cases, the only complete data available was for earlier years.

- We have used exhaustive efforts to locate and fairly present accurate and complete data. However, when using this book or any other source for business and industry information, the reader should use caution and diligence by conducting further research where it seems appropriate. We wish you success in your endeavors, and we trust that your experience with this book will be both satisfactory and productive.

Jack W. Plunkett
Houston, Texas
February 2023

HOW TO USE THIS BOOK

The two primary sections of this book are devoted first to the automotive industry as a whole and then to the "Individual Data Listings" for THE SHARING & GIG ECONOMY 150. If time permits, you should begin your research in the front chapters of this book. Also, you will find lengthy indexes in Chapter 4 and in the back of the book.

THE SHARING & GIG ECONOMY INDUSTRY

Chapter 1: Major Trends Affecting the Sharing & Gig Economy Industry. This chapter presents an encapsulated view of the major trends that are creating rapid changes in the sharing and gig economy industry today.

Chapter 2: Sharing & Gig Economy Industry Statistics. This chapter presents in-depth statistics on shared travel, food, apparel and retail revenues, the growth of on demand services and more.

Chapter 3: Important Sharing & Gig Economy Industry Contacts – Addresses, Telephone Numbers and Internet Sites.
This chapter covers contacts for important government agencies, sharing and on-demand organizations and trade groups. Included are numerous important internet sites.

THE SHARING & GIG ECONOMY 150

Chapter 4: THE SHARING & GIG ECONOMY 150: Who They Are and How They Were Chosen. The companies compared in this book were carefully selected from the sharing and gig economy industry, largely in the United States. Many of the firms are based outside the U.S. For a complete description, see THE SHARING & GIG ECONOMY 150 indexes in this chapter.

Individual Data Listings:
Look at one of the companies in THE SHARING & GIG ECONOMY 150's Individual Data Listings. You'll find the following information fields:

Company Name:
The company profiles are in alphabetical order by company name. If you don't find the company you are seeking, it may be a subsidiary or division of one of the firms covered in this book. Try looking it up in the Index by Subsidiaries, Brand Names and Selected Affiliations in the back of the book.

Industry Code:
Industry Group Code: An NAIC code used to group companies within like segments.

Types of Business:

A listing of the primary types of business specialties conducted by the firm.

Brands/Divisions/Affiliations:

Major brand names, operating divisions or subsidiaries of the firm, as well as major corporate affiliations—such as another firm that owns a significant portion of the company's stock. A complete Index by Subsidiaries, Brand Names and Selected Affiliations is in the back of the book.

Contacts:

The names and titles up to 27 top officers of the company are listed, including human resources contacts.

Growth Plans/ Special Features:

Listed here are observations regarding the firm's strategy, hiring plans, plans for growth and product development, along with general information regarding a company's business and prospects.

Financial Data:

Revenue (2022 or the latest fiscal year available to the editors, plus up to five previous years): This figure represents consolidated worldwide sales from all operations. These numbers may be estimates.

R&D Expense (2022 or the latest fiscal year available to the editors, plus up to five previous years): This figure represents expenses associated with the research and development of a company's goods or services. These numbers may be estimates.

Operating Income (2022 or the latest fiscal year available to the editors, plus up to five previous years): This figure represents the amount of profit realized from annual operations after deducting operating expenses including costs of goods sold, wages and depreciation. These numbers may be estimates.

Operating Margin % (2022 or the latest fiscal year available to the editors, plus up to five previous years): This figure is a ratio derived by dividing operating income by net revenues. It is a measurement of a firm's pricing strategy and operating efficiency. These numbers may be estimates.

SGA Expense (2022 or the latest fiscal year available to the editors, plus up to five previous years): This figure represents the sum of selling, general and administrative expenses of a company, including costs such as warranty, advertising, interest, personnel, utilities, office space rent, etc. These numbers may be estimates.

Net Income (2022 or the latest fiscal year available to the editors, plus up to five previous years): This figure represents consolidated, after-tax net profit from all operations. These numbers may be estimates.

Operating Cash Flow (2022 or the latest fiscal year available to the editors, plus up to five previous years): This figure is a measure of the amount of cash generated by a firm's normal business operations. It is calculated as net income before depreciation and after income taxes, adjusted for working capital. It is a prime indicator of a company's ability to generate enough cash to pay its bills. These numbers may be estimates.

Capital Expenditure (2022 or the latest fiscal year available to the editors, plus up to five previous years): This figure represents funds used for investment in or improvement of physical assets such as offices, equipment or factories and the purchase or creation of new facilities and/or equipment. These numbers may be estimates.

EBITDA (2022 or the latest fiscal year available to the editors, plus up to five previous years): This figure is an acronym for earnings before interest, taxes, depreciation and amortization. It represents a company's financial performance calculated as revenue minus expenses (excluding taxes, depreciation and interest), and is a prime indicator of profitability. These numbers may be estimates.

Return on Assets % (2022 or the latest fiscal year available to the editors, plus up to five previous years): This figure is an indicator of the profitability of a company relative to its total assets. It is calculated by dividing annual net earnings by total assets. These numbers may be estimates.

Return on Equity % (2022 or the latest fiscal year available to the editors, plus up to five previous years): This figure is a measurement of net income as a percentage of shareholders' equity. It is also called the rate of return on the ownership interest. It is a vital indicator of the quality of a company's operations. These numbers may be estimates.

Debt to Equity (2022 or the latest fiscal year available to the editors, plus up to five previous years): A ratio of the company's long-term debt to its shareholders' equity. This is an indicator of the overall financial leverage of the firm. These numbers may be estimates.

Address:

The firm's full headquarters address, the headquarters telephone, plus toll-free and fax numbers where available. Also provided is the internet address.

Stock Ticker, Exchange: When available, the unique stock market symbol used to identify this firm's common stock for trading and tracking purposes is indicated. Where appropriate, this field may contain "private" or "subsidiary" rather than a ticker symbol. If the firm is a publicly-held company headquartered outside of the U.S., its international ticker and exchange are given.

Total Number of Employees: The approximate total number of employees, worldwide, as of the end of 2022 (or the latest data available to the editors).

Parent Company: If the firm is a subsidiary, its parent company is listed.

Salaries/Bonuses:

(The following descriptions generally apply to U.S. employers only.)

Highest Executive Salary: The highest executive salary paid, typically a 2022 amount (or the latest year available to the editors) and typically paid to the Chief Executive Officer.

Highest Executive Bonus: The apparent bonus, if any, paid to the above person.

Second Highest Executive Salary: The next-highest executive salary paid, typically a 2022 amount (or the latest year available to the editors) and typically paid to the President or Chief Operating Officer.

Second Highest Executive Bonus: The apparent bonus, if any, paid to the above person.

Other Thoughts:

Estimated Female Officers or Directors: It is difficult to obtain this information on an exact basis, and employers generally do not disclose the data in a public way. However, we have indicated what our best efforts reveal to be the apparent number of women who either are in the posts of corporate officers or sit on the board of directors. There is a wide variance from company to company.

Hot Spot for Advancement for Women/Minorities: A "Y" in appropriate fields indicates "Yes." These are firms that appear either to have posted a substantial number of women and/or minorities to high posts or that appear to have a good record of going out of their way to recruit, train, promote and retain women or minorities. (See the Index of Hot Spots For Women and Minorities in the back of the book.) This information may change frequently and can be difficult to obtain and verify. Consequently, the reader should use caution and conduct further investigation where appropriate.

Glossary: A short list of sharing and gig economy industry terms.

Chapter 1

MAJOR TRENDS AFFECTING THE SHARING & GIG ECONOMY, FREELANCE WORKERS & ON-DEMAND DELIVERY INDUSTRY

Major Trends Affecting the Sharing & Gig Economy Industry:

1) Introduction to the Sharing & Gig Economy Industry
2) The Coronavirus' Effect on the Sharing & Gig Economy
3) The Sharing & Gig Economy's Effect on Employment, Work Life and Careers
4) Gig Workers'/Drivers' Rights & Employment Status Evolve
5) Repairs, Errand-Running, Pet Walking and Assembly-on-Demand Businesses Evolve
6) Sharing Economy Gains Market Share in Travel with Online Sites Like Airbnb, Vrbo and Many Global Competitors
7) Private Jet Sharing and Rentals Grow
8) Uber, Lyft and Didi Dominate the Car on Demand (Ride Hailing) Industry
9) Self-Driving, Autonomous Cars Receive Massive Investments in Research and Development Worldwide
10) Bicycle Sharing Grows in Major Cities, But Finances Are Challenging
11) Demand for Home Grocery Delivery Service Such as Instacart and Amazon Fresh Soars

12) Meal Kits from Firms like Blue Apron Make It Easy to Prepare Home-Cooked Meals
13) Grubhub, DoorDash and Others Deliver Restaurant Meals and Household Items to Homes
14) Fashion Rental Pioneered by Online Apparel Firm Rent the Runway
15) Shared Spaces for Co-Living and Co-Working Face Challenges
16) Gig Economy and Self-Driving Cars Pose Insurance Challenges and Underwriting Opportunities
17) The Future of the Sharing Economy and Gig Workforce: Regulation, Benefits, Licensing and Soaring Growth

1) Introduction to the Sharing & Gig Economy Industry

The penetration of digital technology into all aspects of life is no better represented than in the adjustment of work arrangements that is occurring through the sharing economy. A sometimes-misunderstood term, the "sharing economy" is a system of peer-to-peer services, exchanges or rentals facilitated through a digital intermediary (a platform dedicated to helping consumers find and purchase specific services). Often associated with the ride-sharing company Uber, many goods and services can be provided through similar platforms, such as delivery of restaurant meals; grocery shopping and delivery; personal assistants (such as dog walkers); specialty contractors (such as TaskRabbit workers who will assemble IKEA furniture); and internet-based scheduling of everything from restaurant reservations to heavy equipment rentals. Plunkett Research estimates the size of the global sharing economy at $280 billion for 2022.

There were mixed results for this sector due to the Coronavirus pandemic. Ride-sharing companies saw plummeting revenues because of the shelter-at-home, work-from home environment. Likewise, accommodation-sharing platforms such as Airbnb and Vrbo saw large drops in revenues at first, while people were in shelter-at-home mode, but later saw business return as travelers sought options to hotels. At the same time, meal and grocery delivery services like GrubHub and Instacart soared—they were the perfect answer to closed restaurants and COVID-conscious consumers.

Closely intertwined with the sharing economy is the expansion of "gig" and freelance work. While such short-term or one-time ("contingent") work arrangements are not new, today's digital platforms enable a far greater number of people who desire gig or freelance work to connect with consumers and businesses that want to hire them. These platforms allow increased access to services and workers in ways never seen before. This segment is often referred to as the "gig economy."

The sharing and gig economy is a truly disruptive development that was enabled through the rapid, worldwide deployment of the smartphone and through the ease of development of massive web-based services via databases and other systems hosted in the cloud. The nature of this industry is disruptive because the sharing economy offers very advanced solutions to everyday problems, saving time and effort for consumers, and often saving costs and creating efficiencies in the process, whether it's the ability to let graphic designers bid on a small job for a business, the ease of getting a restaurant meal ordered and delivered to the home or the convenience of getting a ride from an airport to a hotel.

Examples of how the Sharing and Gig Economy is Disrupting Business and Industry:

a. The traditional taxi business has been literally overwhelmed by competition from ride-hailing services such as Didi, Uber and Lyft. Taxi service, particularly in the United States, can be incredibly frustrating—there is nothing worse than waiting in the rain for an empty taxi to cruise by. In contrast, platforms like Uber have given consumers the power to hail a ride from their smartphones, watch on a digital map as the vehicle nears the pickup destination, and pay seamlessly via a saved credit card or other payment option such as PayPal once the ride is completed. This is such an advancement that the world's largest automobile manufacturers are now planning for the day when a massive segment of global consumers will opt to use ride-hailing as their everyday transportation, declining to purchase and own personal automobiles. A new descriptor has been coined to describe this trend: "mobility services." In the near future, self-driving vehicles will boost this trend.

b. Meanwhile, bicycle-sharing platforms, particularly the massive networks in China, are offering a highly popular mode of convenient, inexpensive, instant urban transportation for millions of consumers daily who are willing to pedal a bike. This is a global trend.

c. Equally frustrating to many consumers is the task of assembling furniture and cabinetry purchased in-the-box from retailers like Ikea. TaskRabbit will send a highly experienced agent to your home to quickly assemble that new purchase for you in a cost-effective manner. This is so vital an idea that Ikea acquired TaskRabbit.

d. While shopping online via ecommerce and then awaiting your purchase to be delivered via UPS or a similar courier or freight service is rapidly gaining global market share over traditional store-front retailing, there is still immense demand for items that will be used in the home on the same day as ordered. Groceries are the perfect example. Thus, shopping/rapid delivery services such as Instacart are changing the face the grocery industry. Instacart will let you select items that you want from your favorite store, send an agent to do the shopping or the pickup, and then deliver the goods promptly to your home. This is such a breakthrough idea that giant U.S. retailer Target acquired Instacart competitor Shipt, U.S. supermarket chain Kroger launched its own delivery service and a large number of the world's largest retailers have or will run their own delivery services. Amazon is a global leader in this regard with its same-day delivery (Amazon Fresh") of groceries and other staples.

e. Traditionally, the provision of hotel rooms and other overnight accommodations was managed by hotel, motel and resort companies, with minor market share going to inns, bed and breakfasts, and long-term furnished-apartment firms. The sharing economy has turned the hospitality industry in an entirely new direction as Airbnb makes millions of rooms, flats and houses available for nightly rental worldwide, and services like Vrbo and Onefinestay specialize in booking travelers into any of millions of vacation homes, condos and urban apartments. Suddenly, travelers can benefit from short-term rental of fully furnished and equipped accommodations, often with features such as multiple bedrooms and baths, laundry facilities and kitchens, and sometimes with fabulous views, swimming pools or gardens.

f. A U.S.-based firm called Rent the Runway grew quickly with its unique business model. This company rents clothing, shoes and accessories, focused on fashion-conscious women. Consumers choose what they want to wear online, and the company ships the items promptly via UPS. When the short-term rental is over, the customer simply puts the item into a special shipping bag and drops it off at a UPS store for easy return. Back at the company, the item is cleaned and restocked to the rental inventory. In fact, the firm has turned into the world's largest dry-cleaning operation.

2) The Coronavirus' Effect on the Sharing & Gig Economy

As with many business sectors, the Coronavirus had a profound effect on the sharing and gig economy, both negative and positive. On the negative side, early shelter-at-home mandates devastated on-demand ride services such as Uber and Lyft, as well as shared workspaces. On the positive side, online ordering and home delivery for groceries as well as prepared meal services skyrocketed.

While the early months of the Coronavirus saw plummeting demand for travel and for accommodations, short-term home rental sites such as Vrbo soon found booming business among travelers who wanted to avoid hotels once the shelter-at-home restrictions were relaxed. Travelers were often booking properties close to home and traveling with family members rather than friends.

Meanwhile, soaring numbers of travelers with means were soon flying privately, especially through charters and fractional ownership. Massachusetts-based Sentient Jets (www.sentient.com) reported that 50% of its business in June 2020 was first-time customers, up 127% over 2019. NetJets

(www.netjets.com) reported its best month for new customer business since 2007.

The onset of the Coronavirus pandemic rocked the car sharing industry, undermining ridership as people stayed home. With the gradual reopening of many businesses, Uber and Lyft later saw an uptick in ridership under stringent new safety and cleanliness policies, but they nonetheless had very disappointing revenues.

With regard to online grocery shopping, the virus escalated the practice exponentially. Data analytics firm Inmar found in a recent poll that 78.7% of respondents shopped online for groceries after the pandemic outbreak, up from 39% before. This was a boon for companies such as Instacart and Amazon, and it spurred virtually all supermarket chains to increase delivery options. In fact, Texas-based supermarket chain HEB acquired delivery company Favor and Target acquired Shipt in order to control their own home delivery systems and infrastructure.

The fundamentals of shared workspace business models such as WeWork were challenged by the Coronavirus. Problems included difficulty in social distancing in shared spaces, soaring unemployment and the rapid escalation of work-from-home, which hurts the market for office space of all types.

3) The Sharing & Gig Economy's Effect on Employment, Work Life and Careers

The sharing economy is disrupting the nature of work, employment and entrepreneurship. Most sharing/gig economy workers are working as independent, contract workers, not employees. This means that they do not qualify for company-provided benefits such as health coverage or retirement plans. Many of them conduct work for two or more sharing economy firms. That is, a worker might drive for Uber at night, do installations for TaskRabbit on weekends and shop for Instacart on weekdays. They may vary the schedule according to the demand level, which can be constantly monitored via smartphone.

In one-on-one interviews, Plunkett Research has found that many sharing/gig workers consider themselves to be "entrepreneurs." While they may not have created a new company that employs others or makes products, they nonetheless work for themselves, independently, using their own tools or vehicles and setting their own schedules. In that regard, they are literally running a business, in the same way that a one-man plumbing shop is a business.

Working independently in the sharing/gig economy generally requires no specialized education, and no licensing beyond a drivers' license. This type of work lends itself very well to people, such as retirees or students, who only want to work part-time, or who want a part-time sideline in addition to a regular job. One study (MBO Partners) found that 49% of part-time independent workers also had a full-time traditional job.

MBO Partners publishes an annual report "The State of Independence in America," that studies the independent worker market. MBO estimated the 2022 level of independent workers in the U.S. at 64.6 million, up 26% from 2021's 47.8 million. (Their total includes three categories of independent worker: full-time, part-time and occasional. Many of these people have multiple jobs.) For 2022, independent workers generated approximately $1.35 trillion in revenue, up from $1.30 trillion in 2021, according to Staffing Industry Analysts (SIA).

There is a significant debate underway in many nations as to whether or not people working as Uber drivers, Instacart shoppers and similar agents are actually employees, rather than contract workers. Legislative reform may well be attempted on large scale in this regard. In some cases, class action lawsuits have been filed by the contract workers. If governments rule that such workers are employees, it would have a massive effect on the business models of sharing economy firms. In the U.S., for example, it would mean that firms were subject to paying payroll taxes such as Social Security, and were subject to very high levels of labor, safety, health and anti-discrimination laws. This debate will likely continue for many years to come, and may well lead to legal reform in some nations. Another outcome may be the formation of contractor workers' unions or union-like organizations that might demand better pay or working conditions. The "Independent Drivers Guild" now exists in New York City, representing tens of thousands of local Uber drivers, but not quite acting as a true labor union.

Over time, there could conceivably be massive changes within gig-based companies of all types. Multiple laws and regulations that protect employees and regulate the ways in which firms must treat them could come into effect, such as minimum wage, unemployment coverage, employer's liability, OSHA, EEOC and a long list of additional rules. On the other hand, there is already intense competition among gig economy employers, such as Uber and Lyft, to find and hire new workers. Sign-on bonuses, incentives, perks and better revenue share for

workers are now common. Better treatment and pay may have the effect of neutralizing calls to turn contract workers into true employees.

4) Gig Workers'/Drivers' Rights & Employment Status Evolve

One of the perks for independent workers is choosing when and where to work. Uber reported that as of late 2019, 92% of its drivers worked less than 40 hours per week, and 45% work fewer than 10 hours per week. RBC Capital Markets conducted a survey of Uber and Lyft drivers in 2019 which found that 70% of respondents being "extremely" or "very" satisfied with their job experience.

There is a significant debate underway in many nations as to whether or not people working as Uber drivers, Instacart shoppers and similar agents are actually employees, rather than contract workers. Legislative reform may well be attempted on large scale in this regard. In some cases, class action lawsuits have been filed by the contract workers. If governments rule that such workers are employees, it would have a massive effect on the business models of sharing economy firms. In the U.S., for example, it would mean that firms were subject to paying payroll taxes such as Social Security, and were subject to very high levels of labor, safety, health and anti-discrimination laws. This debate will likely continue for many years to come and may well lead to legal reform in some nations. Another outcome may be the formation of contractor workers' unions or union-like organizations that might demand better pay or working conditions. The "Independent Drivers Guild" now exists in New York City, representing tens of thousands of local Uber drivers, but not quite acting as a true labor union.

In September 2019, the state of California passed landmark legislation, California Assembly Bill 5 (AB5), that requires firms that rely on gig (contract) workers to consider these workers to be classified as employees. Legislation of this type can create massive changes within gig-based companies of all types. Multiple laws and regulations that protect employees and regulate the ways in which firms must treat them is coming into play, such as minimum wage, unemployment coverage, employer's liability, OSHA, EEOC and a long list of additional rules. Unions are extremely excited at the prospect of unionizing the gig industry's hundreds of thousands of California workers. In late 2019, the Competitive Enterprise Institute released the results of a study in which it estimated that reclassifying Uber drivers as employees would cost the firm in excess of $21,000 per worker and increase fares between 30% and 50%. A California court ruled in early 2020 that the law does not apply to trucking companies. (Many other industries had successfully lobbied for an exemption from the law.)

Shortly after AB5 was signed, companies directly affected by it, such as Uber, Lyft, Instacart and Postmates, helped to raise what was the largest voter referendum funding campaign in California to-date, totaling $204 million dollars. The money was used to pay for massive petition signature drives, in order to get proposed legislation begun that would modify AB5, as well as advertising campaigns to encourage voters to support the new proposition.

The result, Proposition 22, was placed on the California ballot and approved by California voters, in November 2020. While Proposition 22 enables sharing and gig companies to continue to classify their people as contract workers, it also provides those workers with new levels of protection. For example, the proposition provides workers with minimum compensation levels, health insurance subsidies (to drivers who meet certain qualifications), medical costs for on-the-job injuries and a prohibition to keep drivers from working more than 12 hours in a 24-hour period for a single company. It also requires companies to develop sexual harassment policies, conduct criminal background checks and require safety training for drivers. Proposition 22 will have widely felt effects on the gig economy as a whole.

It can be very interesting to compare the rights of gig workers in other nations to those in the U.S. In the U.K., an officially commissioned review for the British government recommended stronger protection for gig economy workers. In March 2021, Uber was ruled against in its efforts to fight court decisions that require the firm to reclassify its U.K. drivers as workers, not as independent contractors. This "workers" status grants significant rights to drivers, but is a peg below true employees. Uber announced that it would grant minimum wages to these drivers, and the ruling will likely make Uber responsible for paid time-off and pensions. (Uber currently pays health insurance costs in many of its markets, as well.) However, considerable legal wrangling may continue between Uber and U.K. regulators over how to interpret and implement requirements going forward.

In March 2020, a French court ruled that a former Uber driver should be recognized as an employee, enabling the driver to seek severance and back pay from Uber. As of early 2021, gig economy companies in Europe were working to negotiate labor agreements with workers and unions as a way of averting rulings that would establish drivers as employees.

In China, the Beijing Jiaotong University and ecommerce giant Alibaba conducted a survey of gig economy workers and found that couriers for ecommerce deliveries number more than 1.2 million. As many as 25% of them work more than 12 hours per day, seven days per week, while a majority work eight hours per day each day of the week. Some work directly for retailers such as JD.com or for delivery services such as SF Express. Others work for a group of delivery companies, including ZTO Express, Best Express and STO Express. The Jiaotong survey further found that most couriers make between $300 and $600 per month, or about the same earned by migrant factory workers in China. The going rate for couriers is about 15 cents per package.

In late 2021, the Chinese government established new rules to protect ride-hailing drivers. The rules include time off, benefits such as insurance and guidelines for ride hailing companies to publicly disclose fees charged per fare.

5) Repairs, Errand-Running, Pet Walking and Assembly-on-Demand Businesses Evolve

Another sector in the flourishing gig economy prior to the Coronavirus pandemic capitalized on busy consumers simple "to-do list" needs such as repairs, running errands, walking pets, shopping and assembling furniture, appliances and toys. Major players in this area include TaskRabbit, which was acquired by Ikea in late 2017; Handy, offering furniture assembly, moving help, TV mounting and home cleaning; Thumbtack, which provides lists and reviews of professionals to accomplish a variety of tasks in all 50 U.S. states; and Porch, which focuses on home projects such as appliance installation, landscaping, gutter cleaning and art hanging.

6) Sharing Economy Gains Market Share in Travel with Online Sites Like Airbnb, Vrbo and Many Global Competitors

One of the most remarkable growth stories in ecommerce has been the advent of new ways to book non-traditional accommodations for travelers. This "sharing economy" (also known as collaborative consumption) affords consumers the ability to rent or borrow everything from hotel rooms to cars to private homes. As with all hospitality sectors, shared accommodation has been hard hit by the Coronavirus pandemic. Many travelers may feel safer in small independent properties, away from crowds, rather than in large hotels. While the early months of the Coronavirus saw plummeting demand for travel and for accommodations, short-term home rental sites such as Vrbo soon found popularity among travelers who wanted to avoid hotels.

Vrbo, which stands for Vacation Rental by Owner, is a site that allows property owners, especially owners of second homes and resort condos, to advertise their properties online to people seeking vacation accommodations. Vrbo was acquired by startup HomeAway, Inc., a firm that originated when venture capital firm Austin Ventures agreed to back entrepreneur Brian Sharples in this promising business sector. HomeAway also owns Travelmob, a sharing-economy accommodations site focused on Asia. HomeAway was acquired by Expedia in 2015 for $3.9 billion, and the HomeAway name was dropped in favor of Vrbo.

Internet platforms that focus primarily on hotel room reservations are also adding homes and apartments as alternative places to stay. For example, Booking.com, a major presence in online hotel room booking and a subsidiary of Priceline, is also offering shared-space and vacation property listings on its site.

The biggest disruptor to the hotel industry is San Francisco-based Airbnb, Inc., founded in 2008. Airbnb.com members who are willing to let travelers stay in their homes can post their information, including pricing and accommodation details. The accommodations range from a bedroom in an occupied house or apartment to a luxury apartment or condo reserved entirely for the guest. In turn, travelers may search in a given market for members who are willing to accommodate them. Airbnb offers more than 5.6 million accommodations in 220 countries. Members are encouraged to write reviews describing the positive and/or negative aspects of their stays. These reviews are partially encouraged so that renters and travelers may view profiles and feedback before staying in homes or letting others stay in their homes, thereby reducing the risk of danger or other negative situations. The Airbnb network is also connected to Facebook, allowing members to search the social networking platform for additional information regarding certain hosts and guests. Airbnb charges room owners a 3% host fee and an additional fee of 6% to 12% per guest.

The average commission is about 12% of total revenues. The typical guest stays longer, on average, than a guest in a traditional hotel.

Airbnb has expanded to offer local-led activities in cities around the world. Activities are varied and may include bike rides, walking tours or fishing trips, to name a few, and are typically provided by Airbnb hosts. The company offers Airbnb Plus, a luxury service that matches higher-paying guests with quality-inspected home or apartment rentals.

Airbnb is establishing new standards for hosts with regard to cleanliness, communication and cancellations, and offers a mobile app to facilitate communication between hosts and guests. Hosts are encouraged to earn badges for "business travel ready" listings that offer such amenities as Wi-Fi and hairdryers. In growing numbers of cities, hosts are now required to purchase short-term rental licenses and collect and remit municipal taxes.

Literally hundreds of competitors and imitators have sprung up around the world. Some are focused on particular locales, travelers or types of accommodations. For example, OneFineStay.com (which was acquired by AccorHotels) is focused on renting a curated collection of better homes and condos in major cities, including New York, Paris, Los Angeles and London as well as resort destinations in the Caribbean, Hawaii and Central America, among others.

Despite their wide popularity, room- and home-sharing sites face multiple challenges. Fraud has been a problem, with unscrupulous site members collecting fees for rentals of properties that they claim to own but are in fact owned by others. Guest safety is a serious issue. There have been accidents, dog bites, even a guest locked into his room by a host seeking sexual favors. At most sites, there are no room inspections and no way to enforce room standards. Guest room rentals may not be covered under a homeowner's insurance policy. Likewise, such rentals may not be allowed under homeowner's association rules and municipal law. Last, but not least, the market may become saturated, with only a limited number of properties available to add to inventory.

Nonetheless, the traditional hotel industry sees room-sharing as a significant competitive threat that is already taking market share. The long-term result may be hotel chains creating their own branded sharing sites, listing both their own hotel properties and rooms or condos owned by others. Hotels may build hybrid properties as well, with apartment towers for room sharing next door to traditional hotel properties. The hotels could run the apartments to high standards, and could build oversized pools, spas and other common area facilities to be shared with guests from the apartments next door.

Marriott International offers a vacation property-sharing venture called Homes & Villas by Marriott International. The division offers 2,000 luxury properties worldwide with options ranging from one-bedroom homes to a castle in Ireland. Marriott is partnering with LaCure and Lloyd & Townsend Rose to vet and manage unique properties.

SPOTLIGHT: Short Term Apartment Rentals Compete with Hotels

Travelers are finding furnished apartments in cities around the world available for short term rentals. In some cases, large buildings built especially for this apartment-hotel purpose are springing up. Similar to an Airbnb stay, the apartments offer kitchens and washers and dryers for about 20% to 30% lower nightly rates than hotels. Management companies typically lease a few floors in a condo or apartment building, although Sonder Corp. (www.sonder.com) manages all 270 units in the Butler Brothers building in downtown Dallas. Another company that is active in this segment is Domio, Inc. (www.staydomio.com).

---

7) Private Jet Sharing and Rentals Soar

Prior to the Coronavirus pandemic, many wealthy travelers could not justify the expense of private air travel. The latest business jets can cost $75 million or more for the largest long-range aircraft—airplanes that can travel 7,000+ miles nonstop on intercontinental flights. Small to mid-size jets cost $10 million to $50 million, depending on size and range.

A pre-pandemic McKinsey study found that 90% of those who could afford to fly privately chose not to do so. During the onset of Covid in 2020, soaring numbers of affluent travelers began flying privately, especially through charters and fractional ownership plans. Massachusetts-based Sentient Jets (www.sentient.com) reported that 50% of its business in June 2020 was first-time customers, up 127% over 2019. NetJets (www.netjets.com) saw a boom as well and increased its fleet by more than 50 new jets in 2021 with plans to add 60 more in 2022.

Under the fractional concept, users commit to fly a given number of hours yearly. They pre-purchase the right to use one or more types of aircraft for those

hours. Fractional ownership management firms then acquire, staff, maintain and operate the aircraft, keeping them ready and waiting for their user base.

Leading companies in this field include NetJets (owned by conglomerate Berkshire Hathaway), Sentient Jet, Flight Options (www.flightoptions.com) and Flexjet (www.flexjet.com). NetJets is especially dominant in the fractional niche. Customers wanting to make only a modest commitment are typically sold "membership" cards. These cards are generally priced in prepaid amounts of $50,000 to $350,000. They allow the card holder to call upon aircraft on an as-needed basis, with the cost deducted from the balance remaining on the card.

Flexjet, offers a JetCard available in 25-hour increments. Fractional ownership and lease options are also available in 50-hour increments.

A few companies are offering aircraft membership plans that operate in a similar manner to scheduled airlines. The most notable is California's Surf Air (www.surfair.com), flying Pilatus turboprops around the San Francisco area, Los Angeles area and Las Vegas, with newer routes to Texas and the Florida panhandle. Reasonable monthly fees enable members to fly as often as they want.

Wheels Up (wheelsup.com) uses its growing membership to provide better prices on hourly charter. It offers membership pricing for family and corporate levels. Fees include a one-time initiation cost plus annual dues and hourly charges. The fleet includes King Air turboprops and Cessna Citation jets.

A new twist to private flight is startup XO Global (flyxo.com), formerly JetSmarter, Inc., which offers empty seats on private jets available through a smartphone app to its members. Flights include scheduled shuttle flights on major routes or empty-leg trips, which utilize planes being flown empty from one airport to another in preparation for a scheduled flight.

8) Uber, Lyft and Didi Dominate the Car on Demand (Ride Hailing) Industry

Uber, Inc. is a California-based creator of the Uber mobile app which connects drivers and ridesharing services with passengers. Uber operates in hundreds of cities worldwide. Upon receiving a ride request, Uber sends the closest driver to fulfill it. Riders can rate their experiences with drivers for other riders to view. The company retains a fee from each ride that it books and then passes the balance of the fare to the drivers. Uber's major U.S. competitor is Lyft.

Uber has expanded very aggressively on a worldwide basis, although it merged its operations in China with local competitor Didi Chuxing, after Uber incurred massive losses in China. This enabled the firm to concentrate its expansion efforts and cash in other markets, including the vast market in India where it is investing heavily. Uber is a major competitor in India, where it has been purchasing cars and leasing them out to local drivers who want to work with the firm.

UberEATS is a restaurant-prepared meal delivery service that is available in dozens of cities worldwide. Uber, through its cutting-edge technologies and industry-leading experience base, is in a position to potentially revolutionize the freight trucking dispatch industry.

Meanwhile, China's Didi Chuxing is working to push into new markets and invest in developing driverless technology. It recently expanded into Japan and Latin America.

Other ride hailing services include India's Ola, Korea's Kakao Taxi, Singapore's Grab (which acquired Uber's Southeast Asia ride sharing and food delivery business in March 2018) and the EU's Gett.

According to Lyft in its "2021 Economic Impact Report," a survey of its customers found that 45% of Lyft riders do not own or lease a personal vehicle, and because riders are able to use ride-hailing services, own more than 9 million fewer vehicles.

9) Self-Driving, Autonomous Cars Receive Massive Investments in Research and Development Worldwide

The U.S. National Highway Traffic Safety Administration (NHTSA)announced a 15-point safety assessment guideline to be used by manufacturers planning to produce self-driving vehicles. The list covers data sharing, data privacy, safety systems, crashworthiness and consumer education, among other things. A car's systems must be able to easily switch from machine driving to human driving when needed. All features must be submitted to the NHTSA for certification.

The Levels of Self-Driving Technologies

Level 0: The driver is always in total control, with no assistance. However most new cars today come with automated safety features that may adjust traction and braking under certain circumstances.

Level 1: Very simple driver assistance, such as cruise control and parking assist. The driver always controls the direction of the car on the road.

Level 2: The car can steer itself under certain situations, such as a slow-moving traffic jam. Requires constant monitoring by the driver.

Level 3: The car can largely steer, brake and adjust speed by itself. However, the car realizes its own limitations and may ask the driver to retake control at any moment. Technologies employed may include such items as adaptive cruise control and automatic lane centering.

Level 4: This is the lowest level of truly autonomous driving. The car is able to perform all driving tasks under most driving conditions.

Level 5: This is full automation, as no driver is required at all. The vehicle may be operated unoccupied.

Today, self-driving technology is largely a reality, although it will require continuous refinement to make it capable of meeting the demands of day-to-day transportation in a safe manner. Armed with sensors, cameras and cutting-edge software, these vehicles can navigate themselves completely. Machine learning and artificial intelligence are key to the development and operation of reasonably safe, practical autonomous vehicles. The more that such vehicles are tested on the road, the greater the ability of their systems to learn the endless variations of road conditions, traffic flow, pedestrian activities and highway hazards. Ford Motor Co. acquired Argo AI, an artificial intelligence research and development firm. GM has invested in Cruise Automation, a similar firm. In June 2022, Cruise Automation became the first company to operate a commercial driverless ride-hail service when it was granted a permit for use in San Francisco by the California Public Utilities Commission. This allows the firm to carry passengers who pay a fare.

Driverless technology also relies on maps that are constantly updated as roads and conditions change. A company called HERE Technologies (originally owned by Nokia but acquired by BMW, Mercedes-Benz and Audi) is mapping roads in the U.S. and Europe using data acquired from truckers equipped with scanners. Google is also working on precise mapping using technology that uses lasers transmitted from specially outfitted cars that create images of roads and their surroundings. Another company, Mobileye, makes camera systems that enable vehicles to detect obstacles and apply the brakes to avoid collisions. Volkswagen and BMW are equipping models with Mobileye and will gather and analyze the images to create maps in a crowdsourcing model.

Google's self-driving effort has been placed into a special subsidiary named Waymo. It has been conducting tests of self-driving cars for several years. Passengers have the use of buttons to start the vehicle, pull the vehicle over, lock or unlock doors and contact a call center. Waymo has been partnering with Lyft to offer rides in the Phoenix metro area in 10 driverless Waymo One vehicles (with human safety observers onboard). In July 2019, the firm received permission from California legislators to transport passengers as part of the state's Autonomous Vehicle Passenger Service pilot. In October 2020, Waymo began offering rides in fully driverless vehicles in the Phoenix area. Thousands of driverless rides have been provided since then without incident.

Uber instituted a test program for driverless vehicles in Pittsburgh, Pennsylvania in September 2016, and later launched tests in the Phoenix, Arizona area. Tragically, in March 2018, an Uber self-driving car (while under minimal supervision by an observer riding in the car) struck and killed a woman who was pushing a bicycle in a street in Arizona. Uber has realigned its effort by agreeing to work with Toyota in the self-driving field. Toyota announced that it would invest $500 million in Uber and that technology from both firms will be integrated into Toyota vehicles to be built for use on Uber's ride-sharing platform.

Taking the driver out of the vehicle would save as much as two-thirds of the cost of ride-sharing trips. It's no surprise that Uber, Lyft and Didi Chuxing (in addition to Google and Chinese search engine firm Baidu) are all investing in driverless technology.

Proponents of driverless cars argue that they are infinitely safer than traditional vehicles. Such automated cars may be able to react to potential crashes and safety hazards much more quickly and effectively than human drivers. In addition, their constant communication with nearby vehicles would enable more cars to be safely moving at a steady speed on a given stretch of road at one time, cutting traffic jams and enhancing transportation efficiency. McKinsey & Co. estimated that a widespread

adoption of self-driving cars and trucks could eliminate 90% of all auto accidents in the U.S. and prevent up to $190 billion in damages and health care costs yearly.

A $6.5 million, 23-acre testing site opened at the University of Michigan where AVs are tested in simulated congested urban conditions. Robotic pedestrians and cyclists dart into traffic while vehicles navigate any number of potentially hazardous conditions including traffic circles, bridges, tunnels, gravel roads and obstructed views.

Texas A&M University's Transportation Institute oversees the Center for Transportation Safety, an organization that conducts research and outreach programs funded at approximately $5 million per year. The school has recently launched its new RELLIS campus on 2,000 acres for research, testing, training and development related to advanced transportation.

Driverless trucks (18-wheelers) are also on the horizon. Although truckers and the firms they drive for tend to be slow to adopt new technologies, some are using automation to enable "platooning," or a caravan of two to three trucks equipped with video cameras, advanced cruise control systems and radar-based braking systems. The lead truck on a convoy controls acceleration and braking for all trucks in the line which are precisely spaced at distances as close as 30 feet. A real-time video camera beams a feed to the following truck drivers so that they can see the road ahead. Traveling single file affords aerodynamic drag reduction resulting in fuel savings of up to 10%.

The U.S. Postal Service (USPS) tested self-driving trucks on five 1,000-mile routes between Phoenix and Dallas in May 2019. The trucks were provided by TuSimple, an autonomous trucking firm. TuSimple also has an agreement with UPS and Ryder. Another driverless truck provider is Aurora, which has partnerships with FedEx and Werner Enterprises. Both TuSimple and Aurora hope to offer fully autonomous trucking services as soon as late 2023.

Driverless vehicles raise significant safety concerns. The software necessary to run the vehicles is vulnerable to hacking.

10) Bicycle Sharing Grows in Major Cities, But Finances Are Challenging

Cycling, both as a means of recreation and as a means of transportation, has grown dramatically. Cyclists who pedal to work are also proliferating. Bicycle sharing systems are responsible for part of this growth, both in the U.S. and in other parts of the world, but many of these new services are off to a shaky start financially. In some cases, operating costs have been higher than expected, in others equipment losses have been high or ridership has been low. Nonetheless, local governments are generally very supportive of encouraging this emissions-free, exercise-inducing form of transportation.

Advertising firm JCDecaux backs a bicycle-sharing program in Paris. Sturdy, comfortable bikes called Vélíbs are currently available at hundreds of rental stations throughout the city. Riders can rent bikes by the day or the week, but there are also annual subscriptions that allow unlimited 30-minute maximum rides for a modest yearly fee. Members create an account using their credit cards, which includes permission for the company to charge them if a bike is not returned.

Bike sharing has spread to cities including London, San Francisco and Singapore. Mexico City has a bike rental service called Ecobici with hundreds of pickup stations.

The City of New York launched its own bike share program in 2013, with sturdy bikes maintained by Alta Bicycle Share of Portland, Oregon. The program includes thousands of bikes. Called Citibike, it is sponsored by banking giant Citigroup. More than 1 million miles were traveled on its bikes in the first month of operation.

The history of the most popular bike sharing system is complicated. Bixi, a Canadian firm that designed and manufactured both bicycles and related technology for bike sharing systems, was originally formed by the City of Montreal, and later spun-off as a free-standing company, eventually supported through a large loan from the city. Bixi's technology is highly advanced, utilizing solar power for the pickup stations (called "docking stations"), as well as wireless communication networks for management. These features make it possible to install a new docking station virtually anywhere, without wiring or power.

In addition to developing the technology and bikes, Bixi operated the sharing systems in Montreal, Ottawa and Toronto. The company eventually sold the international rights to its system to a third party, PBSC Urban Solutions, which is headquartered in Quebec, Canada. PBSC systems are in operation in cities around the world. However, while PBSC sells the equipment, the systems themselves are typically operated by yet another firm, Alta Planning + Design. Alta specializes in design, planning and

implementation of bicycle systems, as well as pedestrian, greenway, park and trail corridors. PBSC also sells equipment to companies other than Alta.

One of the largest bike systems in the world is the bike program in Hangzhou, China, with tens of thousands of bikes. Competition among bike sharing firms is fierce in Beijing where firms including Mobike, raised substantial capital and worked to attract riders.

Bicycle Sharing, a Logical Solution for Global Problems:

Bicycle sharing networks are a perfect fit with many of the world's dominant trends. With relatively low capital costs and the ability to rapidly launch new bicycle sharing networks with little new infrastructure, the trend is likely to continue to grow very rapidly around the world. It is a logical response to the following global conditions:

- Obesity (bicycles are a practical means of exercise that can be used by almost anyone)
- Traffic congestion (commuters on bicycles can speed past traffic jams)
- Air pollution (no emissions)
- Growing need of transportation in urban centers in emerging nations (as more and more workers move into crowded metro areas like Beijing and Mumbai, bicycles are a logical way for them to have inexpensive access to transportation)

Source: Plunkett Research, Ltd.

Greater consumer convenience was enabled in bike sharing with the "dockless" station. Bikes are activated by smartphones, eliminating the need to build central parking and pickup stations. Consequently, the bikes can be dropped off anywhere, at the convenience of the rider, and then picked up by the next user. However, this also enables consumers to simply dump bicycles anywhere, often in poor condition, leading to massive losses for bicycle firms.

Bicycle safety will be a growing issue as more cyclists take to the roads. In the U.S., approximately 800 deaths and more than 500,000 emergency room trips related to cycling happen each year. Head injuries typically account for two-thirds of hospitalizations, according to the University of Wisconsin. However, accidents might lessen as drivers become more aware of cyclists. For example, in the Netherlands, where cycling has long been a part of urban living, drivers are encouraged to open their car doors with their right hands, therefore forcing them to look back, over their left shoulders, for oncoming cyclists before opening doors. In Boston, stickers alerting taxi passengers and drivers to look before opening doors were installed in 2013, with similar stickers appearing in all cabs in Chicago. The National Association of City Transportation Officials created an urban bikeway design guide for implementing bike safety plans, including buffered bike lanes, intersection signals and more.

11) Demand for Home Grocery Delivery Service Such as Instacart and Amazon Fresh Soars

Food retailing, with its highly perishable inventory, is a low-profit-margin enterprise—one in which consumers tend to make multiple trips to the market each month to select and purchase first-hand. The Coronavirus pandemic escalated online grocery shopping exponentially. Data analytics firm Inmar found in a recent poll that 78.7% of respondents shopped online for groceries after the pandemic outbreak, up from 39% before. A lasting, post-Coronavirus trend has been consumer demand in ordering groceries online and picking up completed orders at special supermarket parking spots.

One of the most closely watched online grocers is FreshDirect LLC, a unique business launched in 2001. FreshDirect is an online retail grocery business serving customers in New York City and the surrounding areas. It offers fresh food and grocery items, including fruits and vegetables, meat, seafood, deli items, cheese, dairy, coffee, tea, bakery goods, pasta and frozen food as well as kosher, gluten free, local and organic produce, health and beauty items and wine. It also provides catering services and a full line of ready-to-heat meals prepared by its on-staff chefs. FreshDirect owns and operates a 300,000-square-foot state-of-the-art processing facility, which enables the company to process and ship fresh meats, produce and dairy products quickly and efficiently. The company is also sometimes able to offer lower prices than traditional retail grocers, due to the lack of the need to operate expensive retail stores. Customers can also pick up their orders at the distribution facility. The firm served select counties in New York, New Jersey, Connecticut, Pennsylvania and Delaware. FreshDirect customers have the ability to shop by lifestyle, by clicking on gluten-free, kosher, organic or other groups. Satisfaction is 100% guaranteed. In late 2020, FreshDirect was acquired by Ahold Delhaize NV, which owns a number of supermarket chains including Giant and Stop & Shop. This may lead to fast expansion for FreshDirect.

Peapod, an aggressive home grocery delivery service that has been in business since 1989, has built a base of online shoppers slowly but surely. Peapod has a presence in a number of major cities and suburban areas, including cities in Massachusetts, Virginia, Maryland, Wisconsin, Washington, D.C., Connecticut, New York, Rhode Island, Illinois, Indiana and New Jersey. Peapod entered the New York City market for the first time in 2011, where it must compete directly against FreshDirect. Customers order online via Peapod.com and, for a fee, receive home delivery of their groceries, which are packed at warehouses near participating supermarkets. Despite its lengthy history and wealth of experience, Peapod struggled financially at first. It was acquired in 2001 by one of the world's largest supermarket chains, European-based Royal Ahold, through its Ahold USA unit. In February 2020, Ahold USA shut down the stand-alone Peapod online grocery operation in Illinois, Wisconsin and Indiana. However, the onset of the Coronavirus spurred new growth in the company, with supermarket chains Giant Food and Stop & Shop announcing the integration of Peapod's ecommerce technology and services into their businesses in 2020.

Amazon has been getting deeper into the grocery sector for many years, both through internal development and through acquisition. In late 2014, Amazon launched Prime Now, which delivers groceries and consumer goods in as little as one to two hours. Amazon has been aggressively rolling out warehouses in major cities all over the U.S. to serve its growing Prime Now business. In late 2016, Amazon opened its first brick and mortar grocery store called Amazon Go in Seattle, Washington. The 1,800 square-foot store offers prepared foods and grocery staples and requires shoppers to scan a smartphone app linked to an Amazon account upon arrival. The app maintains a virtual cart of the items selected by the shopper and charges the related account accordingly when the shopper leaves the store, without any interaction with a human cashier. Initially open only to Amazon employees for testing, the company opened the store to the public in 2017. In addition, Amazon had opened 44 stores under its Amazon Fresh brand, focusing on urban grocery stores, by August 2022, in eight U.S. states and Washington D.C.

In 2017, the firm acquired specialty supermarket firm Whole Foods Market, Inc. for $13.7 billion, sending shockwaves through the grocery industry. This is an extension of Amazon's grocery strategy. In

September 2020, Whole Foods opened its first online-only store in Brooklyn, New York.

Brick and mortar grocers are scrambling to fulfill the shift in consumers' shopping habits that was spurred by the Coronavirus. Walmart offers Walmart Grocery, a pickup and delivery service in which online orders can be picked up at store drive-through lanes, often on the same day. The firm also offers same day delivery in most U.S. markets.

Online grocery shopping is rapidly becoming commonplace at major supermarket chains, with consumers' options ranging from ordering online and picking up curbside, to delivery to the home. For example, the massive grocery firm Kroger offers a click and collect service called ClickList in stores nationwide, including many of its subsidiary brands such as Fred Meyer and Smith's.

Another twist on grocery shopping online is Instacart, a San Francisco-based company that models online shopping, somewhat on the same business model as Uber. Customers use an app to enter a list of groceries and other items they want, and nearby shoppers pick up the items and deliver them using their own cars, bikes or other transportation. Shoppers are independent contractors. This work may be attractive to people like students or stay-at-home parents who want to control their own schedules while making extra money. Instacart charges a delivery fee and marks up store prices for each item delivered. Demand for Instacart's services soared during the Coronavirus pandemic. In December 2017, Target Corporation announced its $550 million acquisition of grocery delivery startup Shipt, an Instacart competitor.

Grocery delivery in China has become commonplace. Dozens of startup companies, including Quick Bee, New Dada and Dianwoda, employ couriers on electric motorbikes who pick up orders from supermarkets, convenience stores and independent shops for quick delivery. The firms charge for each delivery (starting at about five yuan or 72 cents U.S. per package) and receive commissions from retailers. Retail giants Alibaba Group Holding and JD.com are investing heavily in these startups. Alibaba spent nearly 1 billion yuan ($150 million) on Dianwoda in 2016, and New Dada is 40% owned by JD.com. Alibaba's Freshippo concept combines a grocery store with a restaurant and a delivery app, which together utilize robotics and facial recognition to speed logistics and payment.

SPOTLIGHT: Micro-Fulfillment Centers

The Coronavirus brought sweeping changes to the retail sector—basically a rapid restructuring of the entire sector. Retail foot traffic slumped while ecommerce soared for everything from groceries to household items to apparel. These changes have significant implications for supply chain and distribution. Since consumers frequently demand same-day (and often two-hour) availability of goods that they have ordered online, a superior level of rapid distribution may, in many cases, only be provided by creating "micro-fulfillment centers." These centers are small, local warehousing, packing and distribution areas that may be only a few hundred square meters in size. They may be located in a special area within a retail store, or they may be free-standing facilities, often near the store. Thus, the centers are typically within dense population areas. (This is a sharp contrast to traditional fulfilment centers that typically are of massive size and often located a significant drive-time away from densely populated markets.) Micro-Fulfillment works best when coupled with systems and equipment designed especially for this purpose, and specialized robotics and related software are a great tool for this strategy.

---

12) Meal Kits from Firms like Blue Apron Make It Easy to Prepare Home-Cooked Meals

Firms such as Blue Apron and HelloFresh have gained a reasonable level of popularity in home kitchens throughout the U.S., the UK, much of Asia/Pacific and the EU. Customers subscribe to these services, which provide pre-portioned meal ingredients and recipes, and promise fresh, high-quality meats and produce that average about $10 per meal. Consumers order their meal kits online, which are delivered by UPS or similar ground services in high-tech packaging that keeps raw ingredients chilled and fresh. Demand was greatly spurred by the Coronavirus pandemic.

Supermarkets are responding aggressively to the meal kit trend. For example, Walmart, HEB Grocery Company and Kroger are offering meal kits. Reach-in coolers filled with attractively packaged, modestly-priced meal kits are in high traffic areas in such stores. Shoppers can grab and go, and quickly put together a fresh meal at home using recipe cards that are inside of the packages. Alternately, shoppers can order these meal kits online, and then pick them up at curbside—a highly convenient way to organize tonight's dinner without entering the store. HelloFresh has sold its branded meal kits to Giant

Food & Stop and Shop stores, and Blue Apron Holdings has sold meal kits at Costco stores. A firm called Plated has offered its kits through Safeway and Albertson stores, among others.

Consumers using these complete meal kits want to create fresh, home-cooked meals that do not require a shopping trip to the supermarket. At the same time, however, they want innovative menus and recipes that they can enjoy cooking and serving.

HelloFresh SE is the world's leader in this sector, with headquarters in Berlin, Germany and distribution centers in many nations worldwide. One of its brands, Factor75, delivers fully cooked meals, a wide departure from the traditional raw ingredients kits offered by HelloFresh's other brands. HelloFresh boosts it appeal by offering meal kits to fit a broad variety of dietary interests. For example, its Green Chef unit offers selections that are vegan, keto and paleo diet appropriate.

13) Grubhub, DoorDash and Others Deliver Restaurant Meals and Household Items to Homes

Apps that enable users to order restaurant meals for home delivery are now popular in cities around the world. Users create accounts on these apps, with payment card information as well as home address. Nearby restaurants appear on the smartphone app including complete menu information. Users make their choices; the app sends the order to the selected restaurant and dispatches a delivery courier. Delivery fees and driver/courier tips are added to the price of the food and charged to the credit card, PayPal or digital wallet account on file. Meal delivery services were a savior for many restaurants during the Coronavirus crisis. Major players in this niche include Grubhub, Seamless (which is part of Grubhub), DoorDash and Uber Eats in the U.S.; Delivery Hero and Takeaway.com in the EU; Just Eat in the U.K. and Deliveroo in the U.K, the EU, Asia and Australia. Uber's meal delivery unit saw soaring growth during the Coronavirus, helping to offset a decline in its traditional car service.

Restaurants pay very substantial fees, usually about 15% to 30% of the total per order to the meal delivery firms. Some restaurants may elect to hire their own dedicated drivers, but this can be challenging to manage, and a well-run system would include the cost and effort of implementing order-taking technology along with hiring delivery drivers. At least 25% to 30% of a restaurant's orders need to be for delivery in order to cover the expense, according to analysts at Boston Consulting Group.

Many restaurants are opting to outsource deliveries to firms such as Grubhub, DoorDash and Uber Eats. Often, these restaurants raise their prices on meals sold through the apps in order to recoup the costs.

During the Coronavirus pandemic, more than 70 U.S. cities and states temporarily capped fees charged by delivery apps and paid by restaurants. In New York City, permanent caps were set. However, in September 2021, DoorDash, Grubhub and Uber Technologies' Eats division filed suit against the city, stating that a permanent cap would necessitate rewriting contracts with restaurants, reduce marketing efforts and raise prices for customers.

Cheaper alternatives are providing competition for these firms such as Spread, a Manhattan food order and delivery website for that charges $1 per order and no commissions are paid by the restaurants. The big apps themselves are also taking steps to give restaurants a break. DoorDash is building websites for small restaurants, charging them a flat fee for delivery rather than a commission. The firm is also allowing restaurants to choose from three fee rates (15%, 25% or 30% in the U.S.), with varying degrees of marketing and product support. Uber Eats offers a similar flat fee service as does Grubhub.

The food delivery business model is cost intensive, and companies in this sector are innovating to increase order size. DoorDash, Uber and others are offering delivery of groceries, alcohol and a variety of household goods in addition to restaurant fare. Conversely, Grubhub, which was acquired by Just Eat Takeaway.com in June 2021, plans to focus on online marketing and delivery for restaurants exclusively. Notably, Grubhub announced plans in mid-2021 to roll out food delivery robots on college campuses in the U.S. in partnership with Yandex NV.

Starship Technologies (www.starship.xyz) has small, wheeled units in testing around the world. Starship Technologies' robots maneuver along sidewalks at speeds of up to four miles per hour with a range of two miles, making them applicable for the last-mile delivery stage of consumer or business shipping. When the units reach a delivery address, the addressee is alerted and uses a smartphone app to unlock the knee-high robot and remove the package(s) inside. The robots can carry up to 40 pounds. By early 2023, 4 million autonomous deliveries had been completed. The company's founders also started online telephony firm Skype.

SPOLIGHT: Restaurants with No Seats

The preponderance of delivery apps and services are fueling a new concept in restaurants: those with no seats for customers. In fact, customers aren't allowed in. These kitchen-only establishments do not have the overhead that comes with seating areas, waitstaff, signage, high-traffic real estate and related costs. Instead, the kitchen cooks to orders taken by app and needs only a central pickup counter or window where interactions with delivery service runners take place.

Delivery service Grubhub invested $1 million in Green Summit Group, a startup in Chicago, Illinois, to build a central kitchen which produces dishes for nine different "virtual restaurants." Each appears as a separate establishment with unique menus but is prepared in the same kitchen by the same staff. Former Uber CEO Travis Kalanick has launched a well-funded firm called CloudKitchens that buys relatively inexpensive commercial real estate and converts it into locations where entrepreneurs can rent delivery-only kitchen space. His firm has also launched its own delivery-only restaurant brands, such as Excuse My French Toast.

CloudKitchens' investments are global, ranging from China and India to the U.S. and UK. Walmart's Canada division is partnering with Ghost Kitchen Brands to offer online ordering and delivery. Creating Culinary Communities (C3) operated 800 "ghost kitchens" in mid-2022 and hoped to grow very aggressively. C3 investors include Simon Property Group and Accor S.A.

14) Fashion Rental Pioneered by Online Apparel Firm Rent the Runway

Rent the Runway, an online site that rents dresses, jewelry and accessories, makes luxury affordable to its 134,240 subscribers (as of July 2022), up from 95,245 in mid-2020. The site offers tens of thousands of dresses, tops, pants, skirts, as well as accessories and jewelry (many from top designers such as Badgley Mischka, Herve Leger and Vera Wang) which members rent for a few days and return in prepaid and addressed folding garment bags. The company's warehouse operations are housed in a 160,000-square-foot facility. In addition to packing and shipping, the facility has been carefully designed to incorporate dry-cleaning and sterilization of returned apparel, making Rent the Runway the largest dry-cleaning operation, in one building, in the U.S. Members may also purchase clothing and accessories, rather than rent.

Starting in 2017, Rent the Runway varied its offerings from one-time, one—item rentals to monthly subscriptions, including RTR Unlimited which allows the rental of unlimited numbers of pieces on rotation with no return dates. Rent the Runway also opened a small number of brick-and-mortar stores. The company reported that most people wear only 20% of their closets. This indicates that a continual stream of rented attire may have great appeal to certain consumers.

The Coronavirus pandemic hit Rent the Runway hard. Much of its business focused on clothing for the office or for parties, proms, weddings and other social gatherings and special events. By mid-2020, the firm had closed its brick-and-mortar stores permanently, and instituted layoffs. It also expanded its drop-off and pickup locations for online orders, utilizing some of its former stores. Business rebounded by late 2021, and the company conducted a successful IPO in late October of that year.

There are a number of fashion rental web sites, each with a particular focus. For example, Gwynnie Bee offers plus-size subscribers access to clothing in U.S. sizes 10-32, while Style Lend offers subscribers designer clothing from members' closets, generally in sizes 0, 2 or 4. Taelor offers men's clothing to monthly subscribers.

Top Fashion Rental Companies:
Gwynnie Bee, closet.gwynniebee.com
Le Tote, www.letote.com
Rent the Runway, www.renttherunway.com
Style Lend, www.stylelend.com
Taelor, taelor.style

15) Shared Spaces for Co-Living and Co-Working Face Challenges

While WeWork became famous for offering hip, shared office and workspaces, spawning many imitators both large and small, this innovative firm faced dismal news during 2019 and 2020, including huge financial losses and a cancelled stock IPO. (In 2021, the company successfully completed an IPO after reducing expenses and generally revamping operations.) The office sharing trend also led to a boom in shared apartment space, with common kitchens and social spaces. The fundamentals of these business models were challenged by the Coronavirus, including the obvious problems of difficulty in social distancing in shared spaces, soaring unemployment and the rapid escalation of work-from-home, which hurts the market for office space of all types.

Living Space Sharing: In major U.S. cities such as New York and San Francisco, apartment rents are so high that developers have been testing "co-living" spaces where tiny apartments share kitchens, lounges and communal atmospheres. The Coronavirus pandemic took a toll on many co-living companies, with several closing or consolidated. In mid-2020, WeWork shut down its WeLive program.

Common (www.common.com) had buildings in 10 U.S. cities including New York, New York; Los Angeles and San Francisco, California; Chicago, Illinois; Philadelphia, Pennsylvania; and Washington, D.C. as of 2023. Common acquired Starcity's 7,500 units (which were part of the branded Ollie co-living spaces in New York, New York; Pittsburgh, Pennsylvania; and Los Angeles, California) in mid-2021. Manhattan-based Outpost Club (outpost-club.com), which offers apartments and houses in Manhattan, Brooklyn and Philadelphia, took over Stoop, Bedly and Quarters.

Other startups are focusing on leasing furnished and unfurnished apartments with short-term flexible leases. For example, Sentral (www.sentral.com) offers a network of 3,000 apartments in seven U.S. cities, that allows renters to book units for any length of stay. Sonder Corp. (www.sonder.com) and Mint House, Inc. (minthouse.com) offer similar leasing options. This can be particularly useful to renters who are on short-term work assignments who are not sure of how long the work will last, as well as people who want to try out a new city temporarily before they make a commitment to move there.

In China, co-living has been popular with millennials. Unlike co-living arrangements in the U.S., China's renters have been willing to share bedrooms in addition to bathrooms, kitchens and living areas. You+ offers co-living spaces in Beijing, Shanghai and Guangzhou for about $300 per month. Buildings offer amenities including gyms and bars. Although primarily focused on young, single Millennials, married couples are welcome at You+ as are pets, but children are not allowed. Residents over age 45 are discouraged.

Workspace Sharing: A leader in this niche is WeWork. The company leases large offices, such as entire floors or buildings, divides the space and then sublets to other companies. The company had more than 800 locations in 39 countries as of late 2022. Work spaces are provided in two ways: On-Demand and All Access. On-Demand is a pay-as-you-go product that offers customers access to workspace on an as-needed basis. All Access is a subscription-based model that provides members with the ability

to work from any WeWork location. Partnerships are available for brokers, landlords and event planners, among others. The firm also offers Business Solutions, a professional services platform in partnership with VensureHR, offering single-point access to a suite of human resource services.

WeWork also offers the WeWork Services Store, an integrated hub for business services. The Services Store is a software platform that is much like an app store. It allows users to find, manage and purchase services with recommendations from members and special offers for WeWork members.

Starting in late 2019, WeWork was changing its methods and attempting to stem operating losses, after a failed effort to IPO the firm's stock. The firm announced plans to cut thousands of employees and to close several new business experiments that were draining funds.

Low demand during the Coronavirus pandemic led some firms to file for bankruptcy, including Knotel (which took bankruptcy in early 2021), once a very large operator, and Serendipity Labs. Several business entities linked to IWG PLC's office suite rental business also took bankruptcy.

As an alternative to signing long-term leases for space, there is a growing tendency for shared workspace operators to sign management agreements. These agreements allow for the operators to apply their expertise, marketing and digital platforms, while providing the building's owners with a share of the revenue, as opposed to a guaranteed rental payment.

16) Gig Economy and Self-Driving Cars Pose Insurance Challenges and Underwriting Opportunities

Transportation industry analysts believe that, over the mid- to long-term, more and more consumers will forgo car ownership in favor of ride-hailing services (such as Uber, Didi and Lyft). This has profound implications for the future of the automobile insurance industry, in the same way that it will deeply affect the automobile manufacturing sector.

Consequently, insurers are scrambling to devise policy options that cover drivers (or riders, which may include paying passengers) in a wide variety of transportation scenarios. Allstate subsidiary Arity is working to analyze staggering amounts of telematics (digital automobile trip records) data on personal driving habits to help develop such insurance options for the future. Arity says it has access to more than 1 billion miles of new driver information per month on top of 10 years of archival data from Drivewise, another Allstate subsidiary. Analysis of this data may help Allstate form a benchmark for future rates in emerging mobility services trips.

The Holy Grail for insurance companies will be the ability to sell more expensive and more comprehensive policies to these drivers for Uber and similar firms. However, Uber and similar drivers are on limited budgets and may be resistant to higher operating costs.

There are business opportunities for insurance startups that hope to serve the ride-hailing market. Zego, for example, brokers third-party liability insurance for food and package couriers working in the UK, Ireland, France and Spain, including those carrying orders for firms ranging from Deliveroo to Amazon.

While ride-hailing poses challenges to insurers, self-driving vehicles are even more complicated to insure. Some experts believe that self-driving cars will reduce accidents, citing data that indicates that as much as 94% of all accidents are caused by human error. This may create significant drops in revenues for insurance underwriters. For example, there may be fewer automobile-related wrecks, fatalities and personal injuries in the future, not to mention fewer individual car owners. It is possible that insurance premiums will become much more competitive and drop if accidents become rarer. This will drive insurance industry innovation and force insurance firms to create new types of products aimed at multiple types of consumers: traditional car owners, makers of self-driving vehicles and the software and other technologies that guide them, ride-hailing firms such as Uber, and individual consumers who want better personal coverage when they are riding in vehicles that they do not own.

17) The Future of the Sharing Economy and Gig Workforce: Regulation, Benefits, Licensing and Soaring Growth

There is a significant debate underway in many nations as to whether or not people working as Uber drivers, Instacart shoppers and similar agents are actually employees, rather than contract workers. Legislative reform has already been attempted on a large scale in this regard. In some cases, class action lawsuits have been filed by the contract workers. If governments rule that such workers are employees (rather than independent contract workers), it would have a massive effect on the business models of sharing economy firms. Such regulations may evolve

in different ways in various regions of the world. The EU and UK may be more likely to force firms to consider such workers as actual employees, at least to some extent. The U.S. is less likely to rush into such changes after a 2020 proposition approved by voters in the state of California took much of the power out of the state legislature's efforts to require most contract workers to become recognized as employees. However, the proposition did provide for better protections for contract workers, including medical assistance for accidents that occur while on duty, and minimum compensation requirements.

Meanwhile, the question of liability for accidents and other losses will continue to evolve. Who is responsible if a ride-sharing service car has an accident? Who is responsible if a contract personal service person commits a crime once in the home? The best answer may be for high levels of insurance to be offered by the sharing platforms, on top of individual policies maintained by owners of cars, homes and other equipment owned by people who are selling gig or sharing services. One of the most widely discussed liability problems arose when a tree branch (that was holding up a yard swing) fell on the head of a home-sharing guest, killing the guest. Who is responsible—the homeowner? The home-booking service? Both?

Additionally, governments at the state, province and city level will become more involved in regulating sharing and gig services. Many cities worldwide have already begun regulating ride-sharing companies such as Uber and Didi. What types of background checks should drivers undergo? How will such services be allowed to compete with highly regulated taxi services? Home and room-rental sharing platforms are raising massive questions in city governments. Should Airbnb renters pay the same hotel occupancy taxes that guests at Marriott or Hilton pay? Should homes that are rented to travelers have the same safety features required of hotels? What about people who are hired to provide minor home repairs through gig platforms? Should they have a plumber's license before they can fix a leaky faucet? The regulatory debate has only begun. Eventually, model regulation may evolve that will be widely adapted by many states or cities at once.

Meanwhile, several vital factors will continue to drive the sharing and gig economy forward:
1) The rapid growth of this sector has been enabled to a large extent by the global adoption of the smartphone. The number of consumers worldwide who own smartphones will continue to expand rapidly. At the same time, wireless

networks will become much faster reliable when 5G networks are perfected.

2) The investment community will remain interested in the sharing economy, and growth capital will remain readily available.

3) Sharing economy platforms will be easier and less expensive to launch thanks to the growing capabilities of cloud computing and related, open-source or low-cost software applications.

4) The population in many of the world's largest and most developed economies is aging rapidly, from China to the US and Canada, to Europe, Japan and Southeast Asia. Surveys show that a very significant portion of people turning 65 years of age want to continue to work and earn money. The flexible, part-time nature of gig economy work is ideally suited for many older workers.

5) There is no end the possible ways in which sharing economy entrepreneurs can invent new ways to solve distribution challenges, improve consumer satisfaction and convenience, and increase cost-efficiencies via new services.

6) Over the long-term, significant portion of transportation needs will be served by on-demand "mobility services" rather than by traditional, personal vehicle ownership. This is potentially a massive, global market that will be boosted by the development of autonomous cars.

7) The potential of self-driving cars to reduce costs by replacing drivers in the car-sharing sector is considerable.

Chapter 2

SHARING & GIG ECONOMY INDUSTRY STATISTICS

Contents:

Sharing and Gig Economy Industry Statistics and Market Size Overview

Category	Quantity	Unit	Date	Source
Global				
Estimated Revenue of Sharing Economy Companies	280.0	Bil. US$	2022	PRE
Global Freelance Workers	915	Mil.	2023	Mastercard
Global Gig Workers	78	Mil.	2023	Mastercard
Mobile-broadband Connections	9.1	Bil. US$	2022	PRE
U.S.				
Number of Independent Workers	64.6	Mil.	2022	MBO
Ride Sharing Users (Uber, etc.), Estimate	60.0	Mil.	2022	eMarketer
Number of Wireless Connections*	498.0	Mil.	2022	PRE

*The actual number of individuals who subscribe to wireless connections is substantially lower, as some people own more than one "subscription."

PRE = Plunkett Research Estimate

eMarketer = eMarketer.com

Mastercard = Mastercard International

MBO = MBO Partners

Persons Not in the Labor Force and Multiple Jobholders by Sex, U.S.: 2021-2022

(Seasonally Adjusted; In Thousands; Latest Year Available)

	Total		Men		Women	
	Nov. 2021	Nov. 2022	Nov. 2021	Nov. 2022	Nov. 2021	Nov. 2022
Not in the Labor Force, 16 Years and over						
Total not in the labor force	99,930	100436	40,986	41542	58,944	58894
Persons who currently want a job[1]	5,491	5211	2,523	2750	2,968	2642
Marginally attached to the labor force[2]	1,594	1501	780	751	814	751
Discouraged over job prospects[3]	471	430	288	298	183	133
Reasons other than discouragement	1,123	1071	492	453	631	618
Multiple Jobholders, 16 Years and over						
Total multiple jobholders[4]	7,180	7782	3,535	3702	3,645	4080
Percent of total employed	4.6	4.9	4.3	4.4	5.0	5.5
Primary job full time, secondary job part time	3,946	4507	2,130	2409	1,816	2089
Primary and secondary jobs both part time	1,750	1866	556	599	1,194	1267
Primary and secondary jobs both full time	333	336	185	191	148	146
Hours vary on primary or secondary job	1,107	1017	630	491	477	526

[1] Includes some persons who are not asked if they want a job.

[2] Persons "marginally attached to the labor force" are those who want a job, have searched for work during the prior 12 months, and were available to take a job during the reference week, but had not looked for work in the past 4 weeks.

[3] Discouraged workers are persons marginally attached to the labor force who did not actively look for work in the prior 4 weeks for reasons such as thinks no work available, could not find work, lacks schooling or training, employer thinks too young or old, and other types of discrimination.

[4] Includes a small number of persons who work part time on their primary job and full time on their secondary job(s), not shown separately.

Source: U.S. Census Bureau

Plunkett Research,® Ltd.

www.plunkettresearch.com

Share of U.S. Adults Performing Gig Work: 2021

(% of Adults who Participated in a Gig Activity in the Month Before the Survey)

Activities	2021
Gig Activities	
Selling items	11%
Offering short-term rentals	1%
Freelance or gig work	6%
Any gig activity	16%
Share performing gig activities	
Hard to get by	25%
Just getting by	17%
Doing okay	16%
Living comfortably	13%

Note: Respondents can select multiple answers.

Source: Board of Governors of the Federal Reserve System

Plunkett Research, ® Ltd.

www.plunkettresearch.com

Chapter 3

IMPORTANT SHARING & GIG ECONOMY, FREELANCE WORKERS & ON-DEMAND DELIVERY INDUSTRY CONTACTS

Addresses, Telephone Numbers and Internet Sites

Contents:

1) Careers-First Time Jobs/New Grads
2) Careers-General Job Listings
3) Careers-Job Reference Tools
4) Consulting Industry Associations
5) Continent & Country Guides & Information
6) Corporate Information Resources
7) Economic Data & Research
8) Hotel/Lodging Associations
9) Industry Research/Market Research
10) Internet Industry Associations
11) MBA Resources
12) Real Estate Industry Associations
13) Sharing Economy Associations
14) Trade Associations-General
15) Trade Associations-Global
16) Transportation Industry Associations
17) Travel & Health
18) Travel Business & Professional Associations
19) Travel Industry Associations
20) Travel Reservations & Tickets Online
21) Travel Resources
22) Traveling for People with Disabilities
23) Travel-Local Transportation, Bus & Car Rental

24) Travel-Vacation Home Rental & Exchange
25) U.S. Government Agencies
26) U.S. Government Travel Sites
27) Youth Travel Associations

1) Careers-First Time Jobs/New Grads

CollegeGrad.com, Inc.
950 Tower Ln., Fl. 6
Foster City, CA 94404 USA
E-mail Address: info@quinstreet.com
Web Address: www.collegegrad.com
CollegeGrad.com, Inc. offers in-depth resources for college students and recent grads seeking entry-level jobs.

National Association of Colleges and Employers (NACE)
62 Highland Ave.
Bethlehem, PA 18017-9085 USA
Phone: 610-868-1421
E-mail Address: customerservice@naceweb.org
Web Address: www.naceweb.org
The National Association of Colleges and Employers (NACE) is a premier U.S. organization representing

college placement offices and corporate recruiters who focus on hiring new grads.

2)   Careers-General Job Listings

CareerBuilder, Inc.
200 N La Salle Dr., Ste. 1100
Chicago, IL 60601 USA
Phone: 773-527-3600
Fax: 773-353-2452
Toll Free: 800-891-8880
Web Address: www.careerbuilder.com
CareerBuilder, Inc. focuses on the needs of companies and also provides a database of job openings. The site has over 1 million jobs posted by 300,000 employers and receives an average 23 million unique visitors monthly. The company also operates online career centers for 140 newspapers and 9,000 online partners. Resumes are sent directly to the company, and applicants can set up a special e-mail account for job-seeking purposes. CareerBuilder is primarily a joint venture between three newspaper giants: The McClatchy Company, Gannett Co., Inc. and Tribune Company.

CareerOneStop
Toll Free: 877-872-5627
E-mail Address: info@careeronestop.org
Web Address: www.careeronestop.org
CareerOneStop is operated by the employment commissions of various state agencies. It contains job listings in both the private and government sectors, as well as a wide variety of useful career resources and workforce information. CareerOneStop is sponsored by the U.S. Department of Labor.

LaborMarketInfo (LMI)
Employment Development Dept.
P.O. Box 826880, MIC 57
Sacramento, CA 94280-0001 USA
Phone: 916-262-2162
Fax: 916-262-2352
Web Address: www.labormarketinfo.edd.ca.gov
LaborMarketInfo (LMI) provides job seekers and employers a wide range of resources, namely the ability to find, access and use labor market information and services. It provides statistics for employment demographics on both a local and regional level, as well as career searching tools for California residents. The web site is sponsored by California's Employment Development Office.

Recruiters Online Network
E-mail Address: rossi.tony@comcast.net
Web Address: www.recruitersonline.com
The Recruiters Online Network provides job postings from thousands of recruiters, Careers Online Magazine, a resume database, as well as other career resources.

USAJOBS
USAJOBS Program Office
1900 E St. NW, Ste. 6500
Washington, DC 20415-0001 USA
Phone: 818-934-6600
Web Address: www.usajobs.gov
USAJOBS, a program of the U.S. Office of Personnel Management, is the official job site for the U.S. Federal Government. It provides a comprehensive list of U.S. government jobs, allowing users to search for employment by location; agency; type of work; or by senior executive positions. It also has special employment sections for individuals with disabilities, veterans and recent college graduates; an information center, offering resume and interview tips and other information; and allows users to create a profile and post a resume.

3)   Careers-Job Reference Tools

Vault.com, Inc.
132 W. 31st St., Fl. 16
New York, NY 10001 USA
Fax: 212-366-6117
Toll Free: 800-535-2074
E-mail Address: customerservice@vault.com
Web Address: www.vault.com
Vault.com, Inc. is a comprehensive career web site for employers and employees, with job postings and valuable information on a wide variety of industries. Its features and content are largely geared toward MBA degree holders.

4)   Consulting Industry Associations

International Society of Hospitality Consultants (ISHC)
411 6th St. S., Ste. 204
Naples, FL 34102 USA
Phone: 239-436-3915
E-mail Address: abelfanti@ishc.com
Web Address: www.ishc.com
The International Society of Hospitality Consultants (ISHC) is a society dedicated to promoting the

highest quality of professional consulting standards and practices for the hospitality industry.

5) Continent & Country Guides & Information

Africa Guide (The)
Web Address: www.africaguide.com
The Africa Guide provides travel information about hotels, tours, employment, travel documents, charities and cultural facts for the African continent.

Asia Travel Tips
E-mail Address: webmaster@asiatraveltips.com
Web Address: www.asiatraveltips.com
Asia Travel Tips is devoted to information about hotels and travel throughout Asia.

Countries of the World (InfoPlease)
501 Boylston St., Ste. 900
Boston, MA 02116 USA
Toll Free: 800-498-3264
Web Address: www.infoplease.com/countries.html
Countries of the World (InfoPlease) provides maps, history, politics, statistics and other information on countries around the world.

Countryreports.org
P.O. Box 430
Pleasant Grove, UT 84062-0430 USA
Fax: 866-300-3985
Toll Free: 866-689-0542
Web Address: www.countryreports.org
Countryreports.org offers a vast array of information on countries around the world.

IndTravel.com
E-mail Address: admn@indtravel.com
Web Address: www.indtravel.com
IndTravel.com offers valuable resources for travelers to India, including tips, maps, hotel discounts, links and information on history, culture, wildlife and cities.

VirtualTourist.com, Inc.
801 Parkview Dr. N., Ste. 200
El Segundo, CA 90245 USA
E-mail Address: feedback@virtualtourist.com
Web Address: www.virtualtourist.com
VitualTourist.com, Inc. offers information for locations around the world, posted and described by its members.

World Factbook (The)
Central Intelligence Agency
Office of Public Affairs
Washington, DC 20505 USA
Phone: 703-482-0623
Fax: 571-204-3800
Web Address:
www.cia.gov/library/publications/resources/the-world-factbook/
Published by the CIA, The World Factbook provides an array of information on every country in the world.

World Time Zones
Web Address: www.worldtimezone.com
The World Time Zones web site contains maps of the world that illustrate the various time zones. The site also has tools such as a sun clock, a world clock, a call planer, an interactive map and lists of time abbreviations.

World66.com
E-mail Address: info@world66.com
Web Address: www.world66.com
World66.com offers information on countries around the world from local editors and travelers.

6) Corporate Information Resources

Business Journals (The)
120 W. Morehead St., Ste. 400
Charlotte, NC 28202 USA
Toll Free: 866-853-3661
E-mail Address: gmurchison@bizjournals.com
Web Address: www.bizjournals.com
Bizjournals.com is the online media division of American City Business Journals, the publisher of dozens of leading city business journals nationwide. It provides access to research into the latest news regarding companies both small and large. The organization maintains 42 websites and 64 print publications and sponsors over 700 annual industry events.

Business Wire
101 California St., Fl. 20
San Francisco, CA 94111 USA
Phone: 415-986-4422
Fax: 415-788-5335
Toll Free: 800-227-0845
E-mail Address: info@businesswire.com
Web Address: www.businesswire.com

Business Wire offers news releases, industry- and company-specific news, top headlines, conference calls, IPOs on the Internet, media services and access to tradeshownews.com and BW Connect On-line through its informative and continuously updated web site.

Edgar Online, Inc.
35 W. Wacker Dr.
Chicago, IL 60601 USA
Phone: 301-287-0300
Fax: 301-287-0390
Toll Free: 800-823-5304
Web Address: www.edgar-online.com
Edgar Online, Inc. is a gateway and search tool for viewing corporate documents, such as annual reports on Form 10-K, filed with the U.S. Securities and Exchange Commission.

PR Newswire Association LLC
200 Vesey St., Fl. 19
New York, NY 10281 USA
Fax: 800-793-9313
Toll Free: 800-776-8090
E-mail Address: mediainquiries@cision.com
Web Address: www.prnewswire.com
PR Newswire Association LLC provides comprehensive communications services for public relations and investor relations professionals, ranging from information distribution and market intelligence to the creation of online multimedia content and investor relations web sites. Users can also view recent corporate press releases from companies across the globe. The Association is owned by United Business Media plc.

---

7)   Economic Data & Research

Centre for European Economic Research (The, ZEW)
L 7, 1
Mannheim, 68161 Germany
Phone: 49-621-1235-01
Fax: 49-621-1235-224
E-mail Address: empfang@zew.de
Web Address: www.zew.de/en
Zentrum fur Europaische Wirtschaftsforschung, The Centre for European Economic Research (ZEW), distinguishes itself in the analysis of internationally comparative data in a European context and in the creation of databases that serve as a basis for scientific research. The institute maintains a special library relevant to economic research and provides

external parties with selected data for the purpose of scientific research. ZEW also offers public events and seminars concentrating on banking, business and other economic-political topics.

Economic and Social Research Council (ESRC)
Polaris House
North Star Ave.
Swindon, SN2 1UJ UK
Phone: 44-01793 413000
E-mail Address: esrcenquiries@esrc.ac.uk
Web Address: www.esrc.ac.uk
The Economic and Social Research Council (ESRC) funds research and training in social and economic issues. It is an independent organization, established by Royal Charter. Current research areas include the global economy; social diversity; environment and energy; human behavior; and health and well-being.

Eurostat
5 Rue Alphonse Weicker
Joseph Bech Bldg.
Luxembourg, L-2721 Luxembourg
Phone: 352-4301-1
E-mail Address: eurostat-pressoffice@ec.europa.eu
Web Address: ec.europa.eu/eurostat
Eurostat is the European Union's service that publishes a wide variety of comprehensive statistics on European industries, populations, trade, agriculture, technology, environment and other matters.

National Bureau of Statistics (China)
57, Yuetan Nanjie, Sanlihe
Xicheng District
Beijing, 100826 China
Fax: 86-10-6878-2000
E-mail Address: info@gj.stats.cn
Web Address: www.stats.gov.cn/english
The National Bureau of Statistics (China) provides statistics and economic data regarding China's economy and society.

Organization for Economic Co-operation and Development (OECD)
2 rue Andre Pascal, Cedex 16
Paris, 75775 France
Phone: 33-1-45-24-82-00
Fax: 33-1-45-24-85-00
E-mail Address: webmaster@oecd.org
Web Address: www.oecd.org
The Organization for Economic Co-operation and Development (OECD) publishes detailed economic,

government, population, social and trade statistics on a country-by-country basis for over 30 nations representing the world's largest economies. Sectors covered range from industry, labor, technology and patents, to health care, environment and globalization.

Statistics Bureau, Director-General for Policy Planning (Japan)
19-1 Wakamatsu-cho
Shinjuku-ku
Tokyo, 162-8668 Japan
Phone: 81-3-5273-2020
E-mail Address: toukeisoudan@soumu.go.jp
Web Address: www.stat.go.jp/english
The Statistics Bureau, Director-General for Policy Planning (Japan) and Statistical Research and Training Institute, a part of the Japanese Ministry of Internal Affairs and Communications, plays the central role of producing and disseminating basic official statistics and coordinating statistical work under the Statistics Act and other legislation.

Statistics Canada
150 Tunney's Pasture Driveway
Ottawa, ON K1A 0T6 Canada
Phone: 514-283-8300
Fax: 514-283-9350
Toll Free: 800-263-1136
E-mail Address: STATCAN.infostats-infostats.STATCAN@canada.ca
Web Address: www.statcan.gc.ca
Statistics Canada provides a complete portal to Canadian economic data and statistics. Its conducts Canada's official census every five years, as well as hundreds of surveys covering numerous aspects of Canadian life.

8) Hotel/Lodging Associations

Alberta Hotel and Lodging Association (AHLA)
2707 Ellwood Dr. SW
Edmonton, AB T6X 0P7 Canada
Phone: 780-436-6112
Fax: 780-436-5404
Toll Free: 800-436-6112
Web Address: www.ahla.ca
The Alberta Hotel and Lodging Association (AHLA) seeks to provide an effective voice for approved travel accommodations in Alberta to both the government and the public.

American Hotel and Lodging Association
1250 I St., NW, Ste. 1100
Washington, DC 20005-3931 USA
Phone: 202-289-3100
Fax: 202-289-3199
E-mail Address: informationcenter@ahla.com
Web Address: www.ahla.com
The American Hotel and Lodging Association is a federation of state lodging associations throughout the U.S.

Asian American Hotel Owners Association (AAHOA)
1100 Abernathy Rd., Ste. 1100
Atlanta, GA 30328 USA
Phone: 404-816-5759
Fax: 404-816-6260
E-mail Address: info@aahoa.com
Web Address: www.aahoa.com
The Asian American Hotel Owners Association (AAHOA) provides an active forum in which Asian American hotel owners can communicate, interact and secure their position within the hospitality industry. Its membership consists of over 15,000 members who own more than 20,000 properties across the U.S.

Australian Hotels Association
24 Brisbane Ave., Fl. 4
Barton, ACT 2600 Australia
Phone: 61-2-6273-4007
E-mail Address: admin@aha.org.au
Web Address: www.aha.org.au
The Australian Hotels Association seeks to protect and develop the interests of Australia's hotel industry.

Bahamas Hotel & Tourism Association
Hotel's House
East Bay St., P.O. Box N-7799
Nassau, Bahamas
Phone: 242-502-4200
Fax: 242-502-4221
E-mail Address: bha@bahamashotels.org
Web Address: www.bhahotels.com
The Bahamas Hotel & Tourism Association seeks to promote, increase and regulate tourism through the cooperation, understanding and close association among hotel owners and operators in the Bahamas.

Belgium Hotel Association
Blvd. Anspachlaan 111, B 1
Brussels, B-1000 Belgium
Phone: 32-2-513-78-14

Fax: 32-2-503-57-17
E-mail Address: y.roque@fedhorecabruxelles.be
Web Address: www.horecabruxelles.be
The Belgium Hotel Association represents members
of the hotel and catering industry in Belgium.

British Hospitality Association
Augustine House
6a Austin Friars
London, EC2N 2HA UK
Phone: 44-207-404-7744
E-mail Address: bha@bha.org.uk
Web Address: www.bha.org.uk
The British Hospitality Association represents the
hotel, restaurant and catering industry in the United
Kingdom. It promotes the interests of operators,
brands and owners across hotels, restaurants and food
service, serviced apartments, clubs and visitor
attractions.

Caribbean Hotel & Tourism Association (CHTA)
2655 Le Jeune Rd., Ste. 910
Coral Gables, FL 33134 USA
Phone: 305-443-3040
Fax: 305-675-7977
E-mail Address:
events@caribbeanhotelandtourism.com
Web Address: www.caribbeanhotelandtourism.com
The Caribbean Hotel &Tourism Association (CHTA)
is dedicated to excellence in hospitality, leadership in
marketing and sustainable growth in tourism, to the
benefit of its members and the wider Caribbean
community.

eHotelier.com
Web Address: www.ehotelier.com
eHotelier.com is an online portal dedicated to
meeting the needs of the international hoteliers'
community. Its site offers in-depth lists of industry
organizations, professional development
opportunities and industry news and insights.

German Hotel Association
Keithstrasse 6
Berlin, 10787 Germany
Phone: 49-30-318048-0
Fax: 49-30-318048-28
E-mail Address: info@dehoga-berlin.de
Web Address: www.dehoga-berlin.de
The German Hotel Association is an organization that
represents the economic, social and professional
interests of the entire German hospitality industry.

Global Hotel Alliance
11819 Miami St., Fl. 3
Omaha, NE 68164 USA
Phone: 402-952-6668
Toll Free: 800-790-2200
E-mail Address: admin.corporate@gha.com
Web Address: www.gha.com
The Global Hotel Alliance is the world's largest
alliance of independent hotel groups, with 32 brands
and over 500 hotels across the world. The group's
web site provides destination information and tools
for customers and travel agents to book flights and
make hotel reservations.

Hotel Association of Canada (HAC)
130 Albert St., Ste. 1206
Ottawa, ON K1P 5G4 Canada
Phone: 613-237-7149
Fax: 613-237-8928
E-mail Address: info@hotelassociation.ca
Web Address: www.hotelassociation.ca
The Hotel Association of Canada (HAC) is a national
organization representing the hotel and lodging
industry in Canada, with membership comprising of
8,100 hotels, motels and resorts.

Hotel Association of India (HAI)
B-212-214 Somdutt Chamber 1
Bhikaji Cama Pl.
New Delhi, 110 066 India
Phone: 91-11-2617-1110
E-mail Address: info@hotelassociationofindia.com
Web Address: www.hotelassociationofindia.com
The Hotel Association of India (HAI) represents the
hospitality industry in India with over 300 hotels as
its members. The web site has information on the
whole spectrum of hotels and hotel groups in the
country.

Hotel Technology Next Generation
650 E. Algonquin Rd., Ste. 207
Schaumburg, IL 60173 USA
Phone: 847-303-5560
Web Address: www.htng.org
Hotel Technology Next Generation is a non-profit
trade association that facilitates the development of
next-generation, customer-centric technologies to
better meet the needs of the global hotel community.

**Hotels, Restaurants and Cafes in Europe
(HOTREC)**
111 Blvd. Anspach, Ste. 4
Brussels, B-1000 Belgium

Phone: 32-2-513-63-23
Fax: 32-2-502-41-73
E-mail Address: hotrec@hotrec.eu
Web Address: www.hotrec.eu
Hotels, Restaurants and Cafes in Europe (HOTREC) brings together 42 national hospitality associations in 28 countries across Europe. The organization monitors EU policies and brings the industries concerns to EU decision-makers.

International Hotel and Restaurant Association (IHRA)
42 Ave. General Guisan, Pully
Lausanne, 1009 Switzerland
Phone: 41-21-711-4283
E-mail Address: admin@ih-ra.com
Web Address: www.ih-ra.com
The International Hotel and Restaurant Association (IHRA) serves the needs of the international hospitality industry by monitoring issues that are raised by major international organizations involved in tourism.

Irish Hotels Federation (IHF)
13 Northbrook Rd.
Dublin, 6 Ireland
Phone: 353-1-497-6459
Fax: 353-1-497-4613
E-mail Address: info@ihf.ie
Web Address: www.ihf.ie
The Irish Hotels Federation (IHF) is the national organization of the hotel industry in Ireland. It represents over 1000 hotels and guesthouses and promotes and defends the interests of its members.

Japan Hotel Association (JHA)
Web Address: www.j-hotel.or.jp
The Japan Hotel Association (JHA) represents roughly 244 leading Japanese hotels and works to promote and develop the hotel industry in Japan.

Malaysian Association of Hotels
1 Ampang Ave.
C5-3, Wisma MAH, Jalan Ampang Utama 1/1,
Ampang Selangor, 68000 Malaysia
Phone: 603-4251-8477
Fax: 603-4252-8477
E-mail Address: info@hotels.org.my
Web Address: www.hotels.org.my
The Malaysian Association of Hotels seeks to unite Malaysian hotels into one representative body. The organization maintains partnership with both private

and government sectors and has more than 700 members under 13 chapters.

Singapore Hotel Association (SHA)
17 Cantonment Rd.
Singapore, 089740 Singapore
Phone: 65-6513-0233
Fax: 65-6438-7170
E-mail Address: secretariat@sha.org.sg
Web Address: www.sha.org.sg
The Singapore Hotel Association's (SHA) mission is to promote the interest of its members within the hotel industry. Its membership consists of 148 hotels. The organization manages Hotel Reservations Pte Ltd., which operates the hotel reservation counters at the airport.

Thai Hotels Association (THA)
203-209/3 Ratchadamnoen Klang Ave.
Bowonniwet, Pranakorn
Bangkok, 10200 Thailand
Phone: 66-2282-5277
Fax: 66- 2282-5278
E-mail Address: info@thaihotels.org
Web Address: www.thaihotels.org
The Thai Hotels Association (THA) is an organization of leading hotels aimed at promoting hotel industry in Thailand. It offers news, insights, latest business information to its 848 members.

9)   Industry Research/Market Research

Forrester Research
60 Acorn Park Dr.
Cambridge, MA 02140 USA
Phone: 617-613-5730
Toll Free: 866-367-7378
E-mail Address: press@forrester.com
Web Address: www.forrester.com
Forrester Research is a publicly traded company that identifies and analyzes emerging trends in technology and their impact on business. Among the firm's specialties are the financial services, retail, health care, entertainment, automotive and information technology industries.

MarketResearch.com
6116 Executive Blvd., Ste. 550
Rockville, MD 20852 USA
Phone: 240-747-3093
Fax: 240-747-3004
Toll Free: 800-298-5699

E-mail Address:
customerservice@marketresearch.com
Web Address: www.marketresearch.com
MarketResearch.com is a leading broker for
professional market research and industry analysis.
Users are able to search the company's database of
research publications including data on global
industries, companies, products and trends.

NPD Group (The)
900 W. Shore Rd.
Port Washington, NY 11050 USA
Phone: 516-625-0700
Toll Free: 866-444-1411
Web Address: www.npd.com
The NPD Group is one of the world's leading market
research firms covering the retailing and related
sectors. NPD covers industries including automotive,
beauty, technology, entertainment, fashion, food &
beverage, home, software, toys and wireless.

Plunkett Research, Ltd.
P.O. Drawer 541737
Houston, TX 77254-1737 USA
Phone: 713-932-0000
Fax: 713-932-7080
E-mail Address:
customersupport@plunkettresearch.com
Web Address: www.plunkettresearch.com
Plunkett Research, Ltd. is a leading provider of
market research, industry trends analysis and
business statistics. Since 1985, it has served clients
worldwide, including corporations, universities,
libraries, consultants and government agencies. At
the firm's web site, visitors can view product
information and pricing and access a large amount of
basic market information on industries such as
financial services, InfoTech, ecommerce, health care
and biotech.

10) Internet Industry Associations

Asia & Pacific Internet Association (APIA)
P.O. Box 1908
Milton, 4064 Australia
E-mail Address: apiasec@apia.org
Web Address: www.apia.org
Asia & Pacific Internet Association (APIA) is a
nonprofit trade association whose aim is to promote
the business interests of the Internet-related service
industry in the Asia Pacific region. The site contains
a list of organizations, standards, regional Internet
registries and related Asia Pacific organizations.

Internet Association
Phone: 202-869-8680
E-mail Address: info@internetassociation.org
Web Address: https://internetassociation.org
The Internet Association is a trade association that
exclusively represents leading global internet
companies on matters of public policy. It offers posts,
reports and resources relating to election advertising,
patents, net neutrality, trade, privacy, data security,
sharing economy and global internet governance.

11) MBA Resources

MBA Depot
Web Address: www.mbadepot.com
MBA Depot is an online community and information
portal for MBAs, potential MBA program applicants
and business professionals.

12) Real Estate Industry Associations

Corporate Housing Providers Association (CHPA)
9100 Purdue Rd., Ste. 200
Indianapolis, IN 46268 USA
Phone: 317-328-4631
Web Address: www.chpaonline.org
The Corporate Housing Providers Association
(CHPA) is a trade association dedicated to supporting
those in the corporate housing industry. The
corporate housing industry, a segment of the lodging
industry, provides a furnished apartment,
condominium or house for rent on a short term basis,
typically lasting 30 days or more. Corporate housing
is usually used by those traveling for business, those
relocating to a new area or those temporarily
displaced.

13) Sharing Economy Associations

Sharing Economy Association Singapore (SEAS)
E-mail Address: info@sharingeconomy.org.sg
Web Address: www.sharingeconomy.org.sg
The Sharing Economy Association (Singapore)
(SEAS) is a business association for companies and
organizations involved in the sharing economy. It
aims to be the regional hub for companies and
organizations involved in the sharing or collaborative
economy. It plays a proactive role in representing the
interests of the local business community and
contributing to the economic, educational, and
community development and build Singapore as a
Sharing City.

14) Trade Associations-General

Associated Chambers of Commerce and Industry of India (ASSOCHAM)
5, Sardar Patel Marg
Chanakyapuri
New Delhi, 110 021 India
Phone: 91-11-4655-0555
Fax: 91-11-2301-7008
E-mail Address: assocham@nic.in
Web Address: www.assocham.org
The Associated Chambers of Commerce and Industry of India (ASSOCHAM) has a membership of more than 300 chambers and trade associations and serves members from all over India. It works with domestic and international government agencies to advocate for India's industry and trade activities.

BUSINESSEUROPE
168 Ave. de Cortenbergh 168
Brussels, 1000 Belgium
Phone: 32-2-237-65-11
Fax: 32-2-231-14-45
E-mail Address: main@businesseurope.eu
Web Address: www.businesseurope.eu
BUSINESSEUROPE is a major European trade federation that operates in a manner similar to a chamber of commerce. Its members are the central national business federations of the 34 countries throughout Europe from which they come. Companies cannot become direct members of BUSINESSEUROPE, though there is a support group which offers the opportunity for firms to encourage BUSINESSEUROPE objectives in various ways.

15) Trade Associations-Global

World Trade Organization (WTO)
Centre William Rappard
Rue de Lausanne 154
Geneva 21, CH-1211 Switzerland
Phone: 41-22-739-51-11
Fax: 41-22-731-42-06
E-mail Address: enquiries@wto.og
Web Address: www.wto.org
The World Trade Organization (WTO) is a global organization dealing with the rules of trade between nations. To become a member, nations must agree to abide by certain guidelines. Membership increases a nation's ability to import and export efficiently.

16) Transportation Industry Associations

National Association of City Transportation Officials (NACTO)
120 Park Ave., Fl. 23
New York, NY 10017 USA
Phone: 929-276-2286
E-mail Address: nacto@nacto.org
Web Address: www.nacto.org
The National Association of City Transportation Officials (NACTO) is a non-profit association that represents large cities on transportation issues of local, regional and national significance.

17) Travel & Health

International Travel and Health
Ave. Appia 20
Geneva, CH-1211 Switzerland
Phone: 41-22-791-2111
Fax: 41-22-791-3111
E-mail Address: hartlg@who.int
Web Address: www.who.int/ith
The International Travel and Health section of the World Health Organization web site provides information about health and international travel.

18) Travel Business & Professional Associations

Hotel Booking Agents Association (HBAA)
Chestnut Ste. Office 9
Guardian House
Godalming, Surrey GU7 2AE UK
Phone: 0845-603-3349
E-mail Address: executiveoffice@hbaa.org.uk
Web Address: www.hbaa.org.uk
The Hotel Booking Agents Association (HBAA) represents industry specialists for hotel and conference bookings in the U.K. and throughout the world, in all grades and classifications of hotels, lodges, apartments, suites and bed and breakfasts, as well as all types of conference and meeting venues.

National Concierge Association (NCA)
2920 Idaho Ave. N.
Minneapolis, MN 55427 USA
Phone: 612-317-2932
E-mail Address: info@ncakey.org
Web Address: www.ncakey.org

The National Concierge Association (NCA) strives to provide networking, educational and promotional opportunities to concierges throughout the world.

19) Travel Industry Associations

Association for Tourism and Leisure Education (ATLAS)
Travit
P.O. Box 3042
Arnhem, 6802-DA The Netherlands
Phone: 31-26-4452699
Fax: 31-26-4452932
E-mail Address: admin@atlas-euro.org
Web Address: www.atlas-euro.org
The Association for Tourism and Leisure Education (ATLAS) seeks to develop transnational educational initiatives in tourism and leisure.

Canadian Tourism Commission (CTC)
1055 Dunsmir St., Four Bentall Ctr., Ste. 1400
Vancouver, BC V7X 1L2 Canada
Phone: 604-638-8300
E-mail Address: pean.chantal@ctc-cct.ca
Web Address: www.corporate.canada.travel
The Canadian Tourism Commission (CTC) is a national organization whose purpose is the promotion of the Canadian tourism industry, as well as acting as a liaison between tourism companies and the Canadian government.

Central European Countries Travel Association (CECTA)
Barn Farm, Milcombe
Banbury, Oxfordshire OX15 4RU UK
Phone: 44-1295-724404
Fax: 44-1295-720089
E-mail Address: info@cecta.org
Web Address: www.cecta.org
The Central European Countries Travel Association (CECTA) brings together the collective interests of Austria, the Czech Republic, Germany, Hungary, Slovakia and Poland and their travel industries.

International Tourism Partnership
60 Gray's Inn Rd.
London, WC1X 8AQ UK
Phone: 44-20-7467-3600
E-mail Address: itp@iblf.org
Web Address: www.tourismpartnership.org
The International Tourism Partnership seeks to encourage the hospitality industry to make a valuable

contribution to the countries and cultures in which they operate.

OpenTravel Alliance (OTA)
1740 Massachusetts Ave.
Boxborough, MA 01719 USA
Phone: 978-263-7606
Fax: 978-263-0696
E-mail Address: valyn.perini@opentravel.org
Web Address: www.opentravel.org
The OpenTravel Alliance (OTA) is a nonprofit organization comprised of major airlines, hoteliers, car rental companies, leisure suppliers, travel agencies, global distribution systems, technology providers and other interested parties working to create and implement industry-wide, open e-business specifications.

Pacific Asia Travel Association (PATA)
Pathumwan, 989 Rama I Rd.
Siam Twr., 28th Fl., Unit B1
Bangkok, 10330 Thailand
Phone: 66-2-658-2000
Fax: 66-2-658-2010
E-mail Address: communications@pata.org
Web Address: www.pata.org
The Pacific Asia Travel Association (PATA) is the recognized authority on Asia-Pacific travel and tourism.

Philippine Travel Agencies Association (PTAA)
12-1G EGI-Rufino Pl.
Taft cor. Sen Gil Puyat Ave.
Pasay City, 1300 Philippines
Phone: 632-552-0026
Fax: 632-552-0030
E-mail Address: ptaa@pldtdsl.net
Web Address: www.ptaa.org.ph
The Philippine Travel Agencies Association (PTAA) is the national travel association founded to foster unity in the travel industry in the Philippines and promote the welfare of its members and the traveling public.

Travel and Tourism Research Association (TTRA)
5300 Lakewood Rd.
Whitehall, MI 49461 USA
Phone: 248-708-8872
Fax: 248-814-7150
E-mail Address: info@ttra.com
Web Address: www.ttra.com

The Travel and Tourism Research Association (TTRA) is a professional organization of providers and users of travel and tourism research, serving as a primary resource to the travel and tourism industry.

Travel Technology Initiative (TTI)
22 Green Ct., The Green
Southwick, West Sussex BN42 4GS UK
Phone: 44-871-244-0747
Fax: 44-871-244-0747
E-mail Address: admin@tti.org
Web Address: www.tti.org
The Travel Technology Initiative (TTI) seeks to develop open standards for the exchange of electronic data between tour operators, airlines, ferries, hotels and rail operators.

U.S. Travel Association
1100 New York Ave. NW, Ste. 450
Washington, DC 20005-3934 USA
Phone: 202-408-8422
Fax: 202-408-1255
E-mail Address: feedback@ustravel.org
Web Address: www.ustravel.org
The U.S. Travel Association is the result of a merger between the Travel Industry Association (TIA) and the Travel Business Roundtable. It is a nonprofit association that represents and speaks for the common interests and concerns of all components of the U.S. travel industry.

Vacation Rental Managers Association (VRMA)
9100 Purdue Rd., Ste. 200
Indianapolis, IN 46268 USA
Phone: 317-454-8315
Fax: 317-454-8316
E-mail Address: vrma@vrma.com
Web Address: www.vrma.com
The Vacation Rental Managers Association (VRMA) is a professional trade association for the short-term property management industry.

World Tourism Organization (UNWTO)
Capitan Haya 42
Madrid, 28020 Spain
Phone: 34-91-567-8100
Fax: 34-91-571-3733
E-mail Address: omt@unwto.org
Web Address: www2.unwto.org
The World Tourism Organization (UNWTO) is a special agency of the UN that serves as a global forum for tourism policy issues and as a practical source of tourism knowledge and experience.

World Travel and Tourism Council (WTTC)
The Harlequin Bldg.
65 Southwalk St.
London, SE1 OHR UK
Phone: 44-20-7481-8007
Fax: 44-20-7488-1008
Web Address: www.wttc.org
The World Travel and Tourism Council (WTTC) is a forum for global business leaders in the travel and tourism industries.

20) Travel Reservations & Tickets Online

Expedia.com
333 108th Ave. NE
Bellevue, WA 98004 USA
Phone: 404-728-8787
Toll Free: 800-397-3342
E-mail Address: Press@expedia.com
Web Address: www.expedia.com
Expedia.com is a world leader in online travel service, through its travel products and research and planning capabilities.

Hotels.com
10440 N. Central Expy., Ste. 400
Dallas, TX 75231 USA
Phone: 214-361-7311
Toll Free: 800-246-8357
Web Address: www.hotels.com
Hotels.com is a specialized provider of discount accommodations worldwide.

Hotwire.com
655 Montgomery St., Ste. 600
San Francisco, CA 94111 USA
Phone: 415-520-1680
Toll Free: 866-468-9473
Web Address: www.hotwire.com
Hotwire.com offers travelers a quick and easy way to get better deals on airline tickets, hotel reservations and car rentals.

Kayak
55 N. Water St., Ste. 1
Norwalk, CT 06854 USA
Phone: 203-899-3100
Fax: 203-899-3125
E-mail Address: privacy-officer@kayak.com
Web Address: www.kayak.com
Kayak is a travel search engine. It searches hundreds of travel sites from all over the world to provide the information in an easy-to-use display that enables the

user to refine and choose the exact result he or she wants. The user is then sent directly to the source to make a purchase.

Orbitz.com
500 W. Madison St., Ste. 1000
Chicago, IL 60661 USA
Phone: 312-894-5000
Fax: 312-894-5001
Toll Free: 888-656-4546
E-mail Address: privacy@orbitz.com
Web Address: www.orbitz.com
Orbiz.com provides access to a variety of low fares and rates on airline tickets, rental cars, hotels, vacation packages and other travel products to be booked online.

Priceline.com
800 Connecticut Ave.
Norwalk, CT 06854 USA
Phone: 212-444-0022
Toll Free: 800-774-2354
Web Address: www.priceline.com
Priceline.com is an online travel center that allows users to name their own prices on airfare, hotels, rental cars, vacations and cruises.

Travelocity.com
3150 Sabre Dr.
Southlake, TX 76092 USA
Phone: 682-605-1000
Toll Free: 888-872-8356
Web Address: www.travelocity.com
Travelocity.com provides consumers with online tools and information for booking flights, hotels and other travel plans.

21) Travel Resources

Citysearch
8833 W. Sunset Blvd.
W. Hollywood, CA 90069 USA
Toll Free: 800-611-4827
E-mail Address: cscs@citysearch.com
Web Address: www.citysearch.com
Citysearch offers information on hotels, retail, professional services, restaurants, events and night life in cities around the world.

CNN, Travel
One CNN Ctr.
Atlanta, GA 30303 USA
Phone: 404-827-1500

E-mail Address: privacy.cnn@turner.com
Web Address: www.cnn.com/travel
CNN's travel site offers travel tips, columns and news stories.

Fodors, LLC
Web Address: www.fodors.com
The Fodor's web site, which is powered by Expedia.com and is from the popular travel-guide publisher, offers numerous travel resources and online guides. Fodor's is a registered trademark of Penguin Randon House.

Hong Kong Tourism Board
9-11/F Citicorp Ctr.
18 Whitefield Rd.
North Point, Hong Kong Hong Kong
Phone: 852-2807-6543
Fax: 852-2806-0303
E-mail Address: info@hktb.com
Web Address: www.discoverhongkong.com
The Hong Kong Tourism Board promotes Hong Kong as a travel destination. The site contains information for travelers including how to plan the trip, The site also lists attractions and events, as well as conventions and exhibition facilities.

Journal of Travel Research (JTR)
2455 Teller Rd.
Thousand Oaks, CA 91320 USA
Phone: 805-410-7763
Fax: 805-499-8096
Toll Free: 800-818-7243
E-mail Address: journals@sagepub.com
Web Address: jtr.sagepub.com
The Journal of Travel Research (JTR), a segment of SageJournals Online, comments on the latest developments in travel research and marketing that reflect the worldwide importance of tourism both economically and socially.

Travel Industry Indicators
P.O. Box 9009
St. Augustine, FL 32085 USA
Phone: 850-559-0012
E-mail Address: brianlondon@travelindicators.com
Web Address: www.travelindicators.com
Travel Industry Indicators is a monthly executive newsletter that monitors the rapidly changing travel marketplace.

22) Traveling for People with Disabilities

Society for Accessible Travel and Hospitality (SATH)
347 5th Ave., Ste. 605
New York, NY 10016 USA
Phone: 212-447-7284
Fax: 212-447-1928
E-mail Address: sathinfo@sath.org
Web Address: www.sath.org
The Society for Accessible Travel and Hospitality (SATH) is a nonprofit educational organization that actively represents travelers with disabilities.

23) Travel-Local Transportation, Bus & Car Rental

American Automobile Association (AAA)
1000 AAA Dr., Box 28
Heathrow, FL 32746 USA
Phone: 407-44-7000
Fax: 407-444-8030
Toll Free: 800-222-1134
Web Address: www.aaa.com
The American Automobile Association (AAA) offers members roadside assistance, financial services, car rental, a travel agency and a variety of other services.

International Automobile Driver's Club (IADC)
55 Grymes Hill Rd.
Staten Island, NY 10301 USA
Phone: 718-238-0623
Fax: 718-238-0623
E-mail Address: iadc.club2010@gmail.com
Web Address: www.iadc-club.com
The International Automobile Driver's Club (IADC) allows visitors to apply for an international driver's license online.

24) Travel-Vacation Home Rental & Exchange

Airbnb
888 Brannan St.
San Francisco, CA 94103 USA
Phone: 415-800-5959
Web Address: www.airbnb.com
Airbnb connects travelers with hosts in private homes as well as commercial properties including hotels, motels and hostels. The firm has listings in more than 220 countries and regions.

Intervac International
30 Corte San Fernando
Tiburon, CA 94920 USA
Toll Free: 800-756-4663
E-mail Address: info@intervacus.com
Web Address: www.intervac-homeexchange.com
Intervac International offers the world's largest online home exchange service, allowing members to temporarily swap lifestyles with families from over fifty countries.

Vrbo
1011 W. 5th St., Ste. 300
Austin, TX 78703 USA
Phone: 512-782-0845
Web Address: www.vrbo.com
Vrbo connects homeowners and property managers with travelers who seek vacation rental homes as an alternative to hotels. The site has the largest and most diverse selection of homes around the world, with more than 2 million bookable rentals. Vrbo is owned by Expedia Group.

25) U.S. Government Agencies

Bureau of Economic Analysis (BEA)
4600 Silver Hill Rd.
Washington, DC 20233 USA
Phone: 301-278-9004
E-mail Address: customerservice@bea.gov
Web Address: www.bea.gov
The Bureau of Economic Analysis (BEA), is an agency of the U.S. Department of Commerce, is the nation's economic accountant, preparing estimates that illuminate key national, international and regional aspects of the U.S. economy.

Bureau of Labor Statistics (BLS)
2 Massachusetts Ave. NE
Washington, DC 20212-0001 USA
Phone: 202-691-5200
Fax: 202-691-7890
Toll Free: 800-877-8339
E-mail Address: blsdata_staff@bls.gov
Web Address: stats.bls.gov
The Bureau of Labor Statistics (BLS) is the principal fact-finding agency for the Federal Government in the field of labor economics and statistics. It is an independent national statistical agency that collects, processes, analyzes and disseminates statistical data to the American public, U.S. Congress, other federal agencies, state and local governments, business and

labor. The BLS also serves as a statistical resource to the Department of Labor.

Bureau of Transportation Statistics (BTS)
1200 New Jersey Ave. SE
Washington, DC 20590 USA
Phone: 202-366-3282
Toll Free: 855-368-4200
E-mail Address: RITAinfo@dot.gov
Web Address: www.bts.gov
The Bureau of Transportation Statistics (BTS), part of the Research and Innovative Technology Administration (RITA) of the U.S. Department of Transportation (US DOT), provides comprehensive statistics on all aspects of the transportation industry.

Federal Aviation Administration (FAA)
800 Independence Ave. SW
Washington, DC 20591 USA
Phone: 202-267-3333
Toll Free: 866-835-5322
Web Address: www.faa.gov
The Federal Aviation Administration (FAA) is the U.S. Government agency with primary responsibility for the safety of civil aviation. It regulates the airline industry as well as private aviation.

Federal Highway Administration (FHWA)
1200 New Jersey Ave. SE
Washington, DC 20590 USA
Phone: 202-366-4000
Toll Free: 800-424-9071
E-mail Address: hotline@oig.dot.gov
Web Address: www.fhwa.dot.gov
The Federal Highway Administration (FHWA) is the division of the Department of Transportation that provides federal financial resources and technical assistance to state and local governments for constructing, preserving and improving the national highway system.

National Transportation Safety Board (NTSB)
490 L'Enfant Plz. SW
Washington, DC 20594 USA
Phone: 202-314-6000
E-mail Address: Hollowk@ntsb.gov
Web Address: www.ntsb.gov
The National Transportation Safety Board (NTSB) is an independent federal agency charged by Congress with investigating every civil aviation accident in the United States and significant accidents in other modes of transportation and issuing safety recommendations aimed at the prevention of future accidents.

U.S. Census Bureau
4600 Silver Hill Rd.
Washington, DC 20233-8800 USA
Phone: 301-763-4636
Toll Free: 800-923-8282
E-mail Address: pio@census.gov
Web Address: www.census.gov
The U.S. Census Bureau is the official collector of data about the people and economy of the U.S. Founded in 1790, it provides official social, demographic and economic information. In addition to the Population & Housing Census, which it conducts every 10 years, the U.S. Census Bureau conducts numerous other surveys annually.

U.S. Department of Commerce (DOC)
1401 Constitution Ave. NW
Washington, DC 20230 USA
Phone: 202-482-2000
E-mail Address: publicaffairs@doc.gov
Web Address: www.commerce.gov
The U.S. Department of Commerce (DOC) regulates trade and provides valuable economic analysis of the economy.

U.S. Department of Labor (DOL)
200 Constitution Ave. NW
Washington, DC 20210 USA
Phone: 202-693-4676
Toll Free: 866-487-2365
E-mail Address: m-DOLPublicAffairs@dol.gov
Web Address: www.dol.gov
The U.S. Department of Labor (DOL) is the government agency responsible for labor regulations. The Department of Labor's goal is to foster, promote, and develop the welfare of the wage earners, job seekers, and retirees of the United States; improve working conditions; advance opportunities for profitable employment; and assure work-related benefits and rights.

U.S. Department of Transportation (DOT)
1200 New Jersey Ave. SE
Washington, DC 20590 USA
Phone: 202-366-4000
Web Address: www.dot.gov
The U.S. Department of Transportation (DOT) is the Government agency in charge of all aspects of the U.S. transportation system. It has agencies dealing with all aspects of transportation, including

highways; hazardous materials transportation; pipelines; railroads; marine transportation; aviation; and public transit systems, such as buses and subways. It also has agencies researching transportation statistics, new transportation technologies and even the eventual impact of environmental change on transportation. The DOT web site has links to citizen traveler resource, as well as resources for transportation businesses and mainly transportation-related government grants.

U.S. Department of Transportation (US DOT)-Intelligent Transportation Systems (ITS)
1200 New Jersey Ave. SE, HOIT
Washington, DC 20590 USA
Toll Free: 866-367-7487
E-mail Address: ITSHelp@dot.gov
Web Address: www.its.dot.gov
The U.S. Department of Transportation's (US DOT) Intelligent Transportation System (ITS) program was established to support the development of intelligent transportation systems through the integration of intelligent vehicles and an intelligent infrastructure. The Federal ITS program supports the overall advancement of ITS through investments in major initiatives, exploratory studies and a crosscutting core program.

U.S. Securities and Exchange Commission (SEC)
100 F St. NE
Washington, DC 20549 USA
Phone: 202-942-8088
Fax: 202-772-9295
Toll Free: 800-732-0330
E-mail Address: help@sec.gov
Web Address: www.sec.gov
The U.S. Securities and Exchange Commission (SEC) is a nonpartisan, quasi-judicial regulatory agency responsible for administering federal securities laws. These laws are designed to protect investors in securities markets and ensure that they have access to disclosure of all material information concerning publicly traded securities. Visitors to the web site can access the EDGAR database of corporate financial and business information.

26) U.S. Government Travel Sites

Bureau of Consular Affairs-Travel Publications
Office of Inspector General
P.O. Box 9778
Arlington, VA 22219 USA
Phone: 202-647-3320

Toll Free: 800-409-9926
E-mail Address: oighotline@state.gov
Web Address:
travel.state.gov/travel/travel_1744.html
Bureau of Consular Affairs-Travel Publications web site, managed by the U.S. State Department, offers various documents covering topics ranging from crises abroad to tips for women traveling alone.

27) Youth Travel Associations

GoAbroad.com
2850 McClelland Dr., Ste. 2700
Ft. Collins, CO 80525 USA
Phone: 720-570-1702
Fax: 720-570-1703
E-mail Address: info@goabroad.com
Web Address: www.goabroad.com
Goabroad.com helps visitors find study abroad programs, internships, language schools, college degrees, jobs and teaching programs around the world. It also provides a newsletter, travel guides and assistance with TEFL certification.

World Youth Student & Educational Travel Confederation (WYSET)
Keizersgracht 174-176
Amsterdam, DW 1016 The Netherlands
Phone: 31-20-421-2800
Web Address: www.wysetc.org
The World Youth Student & Educational Travel Confederation (WYSET) is a leading global membership association and trade forum dedicated to the youth travel industry.

Chapter 4

THE SHARING & GIG ECONOMY 150: WHO THEY ARE AND HOW THEY WERE CHOSEN

Includes Indexes by Company Name, Industry & Location

The companies chosen to be listed in PLUNKETT'S SHARING & GIG ECONOMY, FREELANCE WORKERS & ON-DEMAND DELIVERY INDUSTRY ALMANAC comprise a unique list. THE SHARING & GIG ECONOMY 150 were chosen specifically for their dominance in the many facets of the sharing and gig economy industry in which they operate. Complete information about each firm can be found in the "Individual Profiles," beginning at the end of this chapter. These profiles are in alphabetical order by company name.

THE SHARING & GIG ECONOMY 150 includes leading companies from all parts of the United States as well as many other nations, and from all sharing, gig, freelance, on-demand delivery industries and related industry segments: hotel and room rental; car sharing services; delivery services; and many others.

Simply stated, the list contains the largest, most successful, fastest growing firms in the sharing and gig economy and related industries in the world. To be included in our list, the firms had to meet the following criteria:

1) Generally, these are corporations based in the U.S., however, the headquarters of many firms are located in other nations.

2) Prominence, or a significant presence, in sharing and gig economy, freelance, delivery on demand

and supporting fields. (See the following Industry Codes section for a complete list of types of businesses that are covered).

3) The companies in THE SHARING & GIG ECONOMY 150 do not have to be exclusively in the sharing and gig field.

4) Financial data and vital statistics must have been available to the editors of this book, either directly from the company being written about or from outside sources deemed reliable and accurate by the editors. A small number of companies that we would like to have included are not listed because of a lack of sufficient, objective data.

INDEX OF COMPANIES WITHIN INDUSTRY GROUPS

The industry codes shown below are based on the 2012 NAIC code system (NAIC is used by many analysts as a replacement for older SIC codes because NAIC is more specific to today's industry sectors, see www.census.gov/NAICS). Companies are given a primary NAIC code, reflecting the main line of business of each firm.

Industry Group/Company	Industry Code	2021 Sales	2021 Profits
Automobile (Car) Manufacturing (incl. Autonomous or Self-Driving)			
Argo AI	336111		
Nuro Inc	336111	0	
Automobile (Car) Rental			
ADA SA	532111	112,922,928	1,576,301
Avis Budget Group Inc	532111	9,313,000,448	1,284,999,936
eHi Car Services Limited	532111	300,000,000	
Enterprise Holdings Inc	532111	23,900,000,000	
Getaround Inc	532111		
Hertz Global Holdings Inc	532111	7,336,000,000	366,000,000
Imperial Logistics Limited	532111	3,242,104,576	59,056,872
Localiza Rent A Car S/A	532111	1,989,839,616	373,035,872
Share Now GmbH	532111		
Sixt SE	532111	2,584,136,800	354,441,200
Turo Inc	532111	170,000,000	
Zipcar Inc	532111	275,000,000	
Automobile (Car) Reservations (e.g., Uber), Car Sharing, Sharing Economy, Ticket Offices, Time Share and Vacation Club Rentals and Specialty Reservation Services			
99 Technology Limited	561599	30,709,600	-1,095,260
ANI Technologies Pvt Ltd (Ola)	561599	94,029,904	12,241,837
Cabify Espana SLU	561599	51,600,000	
Careem Networks FZ LLC	561599		
DiDi Global Inc	561599	25,140,998,144	-7,136,671,744
Full Truck Alliance Co Ltd (Manbang Group)	561599	673,553,856	-528,550,080
Gojek	561599		
Grab Holdings Inc	561599	675,000,000	-3,448,999,936
HopSkipDrive Inc	561599		
Lyft Inc	561599	3,208,323,072	-1,062,144,000
Uber Technologies Inc	561599	17,454,999,552	-496,000,000
UZURV Holdings Inc	561599		
Wingz Inc	561599		
Yandex NV	561599	4,878,052,352	-19,720,000
Automotive (Car and Truck) Exhaust System Repair			
YourMechanic Inc	811112		
Beauty Salons			
GLAMSQUAD Inc	812112	20,000,000	
Chartered Airlines (Nonscheduled Passenger Air Transportation)			
NetJets IP LLC	481211	4,900,000,000	
Wheels Up Experience Inc	481211	1,194,258,944	-190,020,000

Industry Group/Company	Industry Code	2021 Sales	2021 Profits
Commercial Real Estate Investment and Operations, Including Office Buildings, Shopping Centers, Industrial Properties and Related REITs			
CloudKitchen (City Storage Systems LLC)	531120		
IWG plc	531120	2,666,738,432	-245,140,288
Knotel Inc	531120	78,000,000	
Ucommune International Ltd	531120	16,594,500	-33,939,600
WeWork	531120	2,570,127,104	-4,439,027,200
Computer Programming and Custom Software Development and Consulting			
HelloTech Inc	541511		
Computer Software: Supply Chain & Logistics, (may incl. Artificial Intelligence, AI)			
Convoy Inc	511210A	650,000,000	
Consumer Electronics and Appliances Rental			
Rent-A-Center Inc	532210	4,583,451,136	134,940,000
Consumer Goods Rental			
Bestway Rental Inc	532299	298,488,645	
Rentah Inc	532299		
Equipment Rental and Leasing, Commercial and Industrial Machinery			
Brambles Limited	532490	5,209,800,192	526,100,000
Connell Company (The)	532490		
Herc Holdings Inc	532490	2,073,100,032	224,100,000
United Rentals Inc	532490	9,715,999,744	1,386,000,000
Formal Wear and Costume Rental			
Bag Borrow or Steal Inc	532220		
Heavy Equipment and Machinery Rental and Leasing Services, Including Construction Equipment and Cranes			
Custom Truck One Source Inc	532412	1,167,154,048	-181,500,992
Ramirent plc	532412		
Toromont Industries Ltd	532412	2,842,261,760	243,314,032
Interior Design Services			
Decorilla Inc	541410		
TurningArt.com	541410		
Internet Search Engines, Online Publishing, Sharing, Gig and Consumer Services, Online Radio, TV and Entertainment Sites and Social Media			
9flats PTE Ltd	519130		
Breather Products Inc	519130		
Care.com Inc	519130		
EatWith Media Ltd	519130		
Fancy Hands Inc	519130		
Fiverr International Limited	519130	297,662,016	-65,012,000
Freelancer Limited	519130		
Gigwalk	519130		
Graphite Solutions Inc	519130		
Handy Technologies Inc	519130	357,976,000	
Honor Technology Inc	519130		

Industry Group/Company	Industry Code	2021 Sales	2021 Profits
Hubstaff Talent (Netsoft Holdings LLC)	519130		
Kakao Corporation	519130	4,933,370,000	132,337,000
Lifealike Limited (onefinestay)	519130		
LiquidSpace Inc	519130		
Meituan Dianping	519130	25,907,636,224	-3,404,402,432
Postmates Inc	519130	875,000,000	
Roadie Inc	519130		
Rover Inc	519130	109,837,000	-64,049,000
Schlep Inc	519130		
Skillshare Inc	519130		
Social Travel Club Limited (Love Home Swap)	519130		
Soothe Inc	519130		
SpotHero Inc	519130		
StyleSeat Inc	519130		
TakeLessons	519130		
TaskEasy	519130		
TaskRabbit Inc	519130		
Thumbtack Inc	519130		
Upwork Inc	519130	502,796,992	-56,240,000
Urban Massage Ltd	519130		
UrbanSitter Inc	519130		
Vrbo	519130		
Wimdu	519130		
Zeel Networks Inc	519130		
Landscaping Services			
Lawn Love Inc	561730		
Local Messengers and Food Delivery, Gig Economy			
Amazon Flex	492210		
Caviar Inc	492210		
Deliveroo plc	492210	221,778,000	-369,631,000
DoorDash Inc	492210	4,888,000,000	-468,000,000
Gopuff (GoBrands Inc)	492210		
Grubhub Inc	492210	1,910,981,049	
Instacart	492210	1,825,000,000	
Just Eat Takeaway.com NV	492210	4,740,811,264	-1,071,560,448
NeighborFavor Inc (Favor)	492210		
ReserveBar Express Corp (Minibar Delivery)	492210		
Saucey	492210		
Shipt Inc	492210	3,150,000,000	
Swiggy (Bundl Technologies Private Ltd)	492210	311,032,000	
Waitr Holdings Inc	492210	182,194,000	-5,229,000
Wonder Distribution LLC	492210		
Zomato Limited	492210	295,328,000	-9,970,000
Market Research, Business Intelligence and Opinion Polling			
Observa Inc	541910		
Moving Services			
Bellhop Inc	484210		
Dolly Inc	484210		

Industry Group/Company	Industry Code	2021 Sales	2021 Profits
Offices of Lawyers			
Lawtrades Inc	541110		
LegalShield (Pre-Paid Legal Services Inc)	541110		
LegalZoom.com Inc	541110		
UpCounsel Technologies Inc	541110		
Online Sales, B2C Ecommerce, Sharing Economy Platforms			
Blue Apron Holdings Inc	454111	470,376,992	-88,381,000
FreshDirect LLC	454111	1,100,000,000	
Freshly Inc	454111		
Gwynnie Bee (CaaStle Inc)	454111		
HelloFresh SE	454111	6,321,151,488	270,104,960
Le Tote Inc	454111		
Ocado Group PLC	454111	2,990,400,000	-267,164,608
Rent the Runway Inc	454111	157,500,000	-171,100,000
Pet Care (except Veterinary) Services			
Wag! Group Co	812910	27,500,000	
Physicians (except Mental Health Specialists)			
Doctor On Demand Inc	621111		
Recreational Goods Rental			
Beijing Mobike Technology Co Ltd (Mobike)	532292		
Boatsetter Inc	532292		
Motivate LLC	532292	60,000,000	
Neutron Holdings Inc (Lime)	532292		
Sailo Inc	532292		
Spinlister LLC	532292		
Temporary Staffing, Help and Employment Agencies			
Adecco Group AG	561320	22,094,606,336	618,045,696
Allegis Group	561320	12,300,000,000	
Allied Healthcare International Inc	561320	500,000,000	
AMN Healthcare Services Inc	561320	3,984,235,008	327,388,000
BGSF Inc	561320	239,027,184	14,109,478
GEE Group Inc	561320	148,880,000	6,000
Healthcare Locum Limited	561320		
HireQuest Inc	561320	22,759,792	11,849,934
Innova Solutions Inc	561320	112,200,000	
Kelly Services Inc	561320	4,909,700,096	156,100,000
Kforce Inc	561320	1,579,922,048	75,177,000
ManpowerGroup Inc	561320	20,724,400,128	382,400,000
Mastech Digital Inc	561320	222,012,000	12,221,000
Randstad Holding NV	561320	25,982,177,280	809,998,464
RGF Staffing BV	561320	11,300,000,000	
Robert Half International Inc	561320	6,461,444,096	598,625,984
Staffing 360 Solutions Inc	561320	197,770,000	8,158,000
Staffmark Group	561320	1,300,000,000	
Trueblue Inc	561320	2,173,622,016	61,634,000
TSR Inc	561320	68,821,216	-600,974
Volt Information Sciences Inc	561320		
Wonolo Inc	561320		

Industry Group/Company	Industry Code	2021 Sales	2021 Profits
Transportation Equipment Rental and Leasing Services, Including Aircraft, Engines, Shipping Containers and Pallets			
First Ship Lease Trust (FSL Trust)	532411	24,975,000	-1,522,000
Travel Agencies and Room or Accommodation Sharing Services			
Airbnb Inc	561510	5,991,759,872	-352,033,984
FlipKey LLC	561510		
Homestay Technologies Limited	561510		
Rent Like A Champion Inc	561510		
Tujia Online Information Technology (Beijing) Co Ltd	561510		
Vacasa LLC	561510	889,057,984	-142,032,992
Truck, Utility Trailer and RV (Recreational Vehicle) Rental and Leasing			
AMERCO (U-Haul)	532120	4,541,984,768	610,856,000
CanaDream Corporation	532120	39,483,499	
Penske Corporation Inc	532120	33,000,000,000	
Redde Northgate plc	532120	1,547,662,345	106,334,752
RVshare LLC	532120		
Ryder System Inc	532120	9,662,953,472	519,040,992

ALPHABETICAL INDEX

Ryder System Inc
Sailo Inc
Saucey
Schlep Inc
Share Now GmbH
Shipt Inc
Sixt SE
Skillshare Inc
Social Travel Club Limited (Love Home Swap)
Soothe Inc
Spinlister LLC
SpotHero Inc
Staffing 360 Solutions Inc
Staffmark Group
StyleSeat Inc
Swiggy (Bundl Technologies Private Ltd)
TakeLessons
TaskEasy
TaskRabbit Inc
Thumbtack Inc
Toromont Industries Ltd
Trueblue Inc
TSR Inc
Tujia Online Information Technology (Beijing) Co Ltd
TurningArt.com
Turo Inc
Uber Technologies Inc
Ucommune International Ltd
United Rentals Inc
UpCounsel Technologies Inc
Upwork Inc
Urban Massage Ltd
UrbanSitter Inc
UZURV Holdings Inc
Vacasa LLC
Volt Information Sciences Inc
Vrbo
Wag! Group Co
Waitr Holdings Inc
WeWork
Wheels Up Experience Inc
Wimdu
Wingz Inc
Wonder Distribution LLC
Wonolo Inc
Yandex NV
YourMechanic Inc
Zeel Networks Inc
Zipcar Inc
Zomato Limited

INDEX OF U.S. HEADQUARTERS LOCATION BY STATE

To help you locate the firms geographically, the city and state of the headquarters of each company are in the following index.

ALABAMA
Shipt Inc; Birmingham

CALIFORNIA
Airbnb Inc; San Francisco
Caviar Inc; San Francisco
CloudKitchen (City Storage Systems LLC); Los Angeles
Doctor On Demand Inc; San Francisco
DoorDash Inc; San Francisco
Getaround Inc; San Franscisco
Gigwalk; San Francisco
Graphite Solutions Inc; San Francisco
HelloTech Inc; Los Angeles
Honor Technology Inc; San Francisco
HopSkipDrive Inc; Los Angeles
Instacart; San Francisco
Lawn Love Inc; San Diego
Le Tote Inc; San Francisco
LegalZoom.com Inc; Glendale
LiquidSpace Inc; San Mateo
Lyft Inc; San Francisco
Neutron Holdings Inc (Lime); San Francisco
Nuro Inc; Mountain View
Postmates Inc; San Francisco
Robert Half International Inc; Menlo Park
Saucey; Los Angeles
Soothe Inc; West Hollywood
Spinlister LLC; Los Angeles
StyleSeat Inc; San Francisco
TakeLessons; San Diego
TaskRabbit Inc; San Francisco
Thumbtack Inc; San Francisco
Turo Inc; San Francisco
Uber Technologies Inc; San Francisco
Upwork Inc; Santa Clara
UrbanSitter Inc; San Francisco
Wag! Group Co; San Francisco
Wingz Inc; San Francisco
Wonolo Inc; San Francisco
YourMechanic Inc; Mountain View

CONNECTICUT
United Rentals Inc; Greenwich

FLORIDA
Boatsetter Inc; Fort Lauderdale
GEE Group Inc; Jacksonville
Herc Holdings Inc; Bonita Springs
Hertz Global Holdings Inc; Estero

Kforce Inc; Tampa
Ryder System Inc; Miami

GEORGIA
Innova Solutions Inc; Duluth
Roadie Inc; Atlanta

ILLINOIS
Grubhub Inc; Chicago
Rent Like A Champion Inc; Chicago
Schlep Inc; Chicago
SpotHero Inc; Chicago

INDIANA
Custom Truck One Source Inc; Fort Wayne
Hubstaff Talent (Netsoft Holdings LLC); Indianapolis

LOUISIANA
Waitr Holdings Inc; Lafayette

MARYLAND
Allegis Group; Hanover

MASSACHUSETTS
FlipKey LLC; Boston
TurningArt.com; Boston
Zipcar Inc; Boston

MICHIGAN
Kelly Services Inc; Troy
Penske Corporation Inc; Bloomfield Hills

MISSOURI
Enterprise Holdings Inc; St. Louis

NEVADA
AMERCO (U-Haul); Reno
UpCounsel Technologies Inc; Yerington

NEW JERSEY
Avis Budget Group Inc; Parsippany
Connell Company (The); Berkeley Heights

NEW YORK
Blue Apron Holdings Inc; New York
Breather Products Inc; New York
Decorilla Inc; New York
Fancy Hands Inc; New York
FreshDirect LLC; Bronx
Freshly Inc; New York
GLAMSQUAD Inc; New York
Gwynnie Bee (CaaStle Inc); New York
Handy Technologies Inc; New York
Knotel Inc; New York
Lawtrades Inc; Long Island City
Motivate LLC; New York

Rent the Runway Inc; New York
Rentah Inc; Brooklyn
ReserveBar Express Corp (Minibar Delivery); New York
Sailo Inc; New York
Skillshare Inc; New York
Staffing 360 Solutions Inc; New York
TSR Inc; Hauppauge
Volt Information Sciences Inc; Uniondale
WeWork; New York
Wheels Up Experience Inc; New York
Wonder Distribution LLC; New York
Zeel Networks Inc; New York

OHIO
NetJets IP LLC; Columbus
RVshare LLC; Akron
Staffmark Group; Cincinnati

OKLAHOMA
LegalShield (Pre-Paid Legal Services Inc); Ada

OREGON
Vacasa LLC; Portland

PENNSYLVANIA
Argo AI; Pittsburgh
Gopuff (GoBrands Inc); Philadelphia
Mastech Digital Inc; Moon Township

SOUTH CAROLINA
HireQuest Inc; Goose Creek

TENNESSEE
Bellhop Inc; Chattanooga

TEXAS
AMN Healthcare Services Inc; Dallas
Bestway Rental Inc; Dallas
BGSF Inc; Plano
Care.com Inc; Austin
NeighborFavor Inc (Favor); Austin
Rent-A-Center Inc; Plano
Vrbo; Austin

UTAH
TaskEasy; Salt Lake City

VIRGINIA
UZURV Holdings Inc; Richmond

WASHINGTON
Amazon Flex; Seattle
Convoy Inc; Seattle
Dolly Inc; Seattle
Observa Inc; Seattle
Rover Inc; Olympia

Trueblue Inc; Tacoma

WISCONSIN
Bag Borrow or Steal Inc; Middleton
ManpowerGroup Inc; Milwaukee

KOREA
Kakao Corporation; Jeju-si Jeju-do

SINGAPORE
9flats PTE Ltd; Singapore
First Ship Lease Trust (FSL Trust); Singapore
Grab Holdings Inc; Singapore

SPAIN
Cabify Espana SLU; Madrid

SOUTH AFRICA
Imperial Logistics Limited; Bedfordview

SWITZERLAND
Adecco Group AG; Zurich
IWG plc; Zug

THE NETHERLANDS
Just Eat Takeaway.com NV; Amsterdam
Randstad Holding NV; Diemen
RGF Staffing BV; Almere
Yandex NV; Schiphol

UNITED ARAB EMIRATES
Careem Networks FZ LLC; Dubai

UNITED KINGDOM
Allied Healthcare International Inc; Stafford
Deliveroo plc; London
Healthcare Locum Limited; London
Lifealike Limited (onefinestay); London
Ocado Group PLC; Hatfield
Redde Northgate plc; Darlington
Social Travel Club Limited (Love Home Swap); Kettering
Urban Massage Ltd; London

Individual Profiles
On Each Of
THE SHARING & GIG ECONOMY 150

99 Technology Limited

NAIC Code: 561599

www.99tech.com/en

TYPES OF BUSINESS:

Car Ride Dispatch Service, Mobile App-Based
Marketing Solutions
Mobile Technology Products
Loyalty Management Tools
Marketing Mobile App
Mobile and Online Marketing Campaigns
Customer Engagement Strategies

BRANDS/DIVISIONS/AFFILIATES:

Didi Chuxing Technology Company
99 Marketplace

GROWTH PLANS/SPECIAL FEATURES:

99 Technology Limited is a loyalty technology service provider for the financial sector. The firm offers loyalty management tools and services for enterprise clients to increase customer acquisition and retention. Products and services include the 99 Marketplace mobile app, which offers access to other applications, entertainment, marketing services, online-to-offline (O2O) commerce and more; virtual and digital product portfolios for business procurement to improve efficiency and reduce costs; and loyalty technology, which comprises comprehensive and modularized loyalty management solutions for creating loyalty programs, creating and managing membership platforms, and enabling the redemption of membership rewards. 99 Technology offers a range of marketing campaigns that clients can personalize for their business purposes. 99 Technology is a subsidiary of Didi Chuxing Technology Company.

CONTACTS: *Note: Officers with more than one job title may be intentionally listed here more than once.*

Scott Sheng, CEO
Henry Chen, CFO
Ross Benson, Chmn.

FINANCIAL DATA: *Note: Data for latest year may not have been available at press time.*

In U.S. $	2021	2020	2019	2018	2017	2016
Revenue	30,709,600	35,502,800	27,065,600	18,433,700	18,787,400	44,450,700
R&D Expense						
Operating Income						
Operating Margin %						
SGA Expense						
Net Income	-1,095,260	4,835,070	1,878,160	-1,333,130	-2,615,720	-633,160
Operating Cash Flow						
Capital Expenditure						
EBITDA						
Return on Assets %						
Return on Equity %						
Debt to Equity						

CONTACT INFORMATION:

Phone: 86 021 23099177   Fax:
Toll-Free:
Address: Fl. 3, No. 763 Mengzi Rd., HK Prosperity Tower, Shanghai, 04553-900 China

STOCK TICKER/OTHER:

Stock Ticker: NNT   Exchange: ASX
Employees: Fiscal Year Ends: 12/31
Parent Company: Didi Chuxing Technology Company

SALARIES/BONUSES:

Top Exec. Salary: $ Bonus: $
Second Exec. Salary: $ Bonus: $

OTHER THOUGHTS:

Estimated Female Officers or Directors:
Hot Spot for Advancement for Women/Minorities:

9flats PTE Ltd

www.9flats.com

NAIC Code: 519130

TYPES OF BUSINESS:

Online Vacation Rental Services
Home-Sharing Rental Services
Book-a-Home Online Platform
Guest Rooms and Housing
Payment Solutions
Reservation Booking Technology

BRANDS/DIVISIONS/AFFILIATES:

9flats.com

CONTACTS: *Note: Officers with more than one job title may be intentionally listed here more than once.*

Stephan Uhrenbacher, Chmn.

GROWTH PLANS/SPECIAL FEATURES:

9flats PTE Ltd. operates the 9flats.com book-a-home platform, offering rental service for private apartments, vacation homes, guest houses or rooms. This alternative to hotels provides a variety of affordable rental opportunities offered by individuals throughout the world. Guests search for a place and send a booking request to the host. Hosts are expected to reply within 24 hours. Guests can also choose an instant booking option, from which payments are immediately taken upon confirmation. This payment is transferred to the host 24 hours after guests check in. Before arriving, guests and hosts arrange a time and place to meet and pick up keys. 9flats insurance covers guests against accidental damages. For hosts, it takes just a few minutes to list a place, add pictures, descriptions, addresses and prices. Booking requests are sent as emails or text messages. If hosts accept bookings quickly, have good reviews and keep calendars up to date, they can be considered as an instant booking host. Hosts must make sure rental spaces are clean and tidy, and stocked with clean towels and bedding. 9flats takes care of all payments online. In addition, the site also offers the option of choosing a rental with a host who will guide guests through local sites and activities. These hosts have been previously evaluated and selected by 9flats. The platform offers more than 6 million locations.

FINANCIAL DATA: *Note: Data for latest year may not have been available at press time.*

In U.S. $	2021	2020	2019	2018	2017	2016
Revenue						
R&D Expense						
Operating Income						
Operating Margin %						
SGA Expense						
Net Income						
Operating Cash Flow						
Capital Expenditure						
EBITDA						
Return on Assets %						
Return on Equity %						
Debt to Equity						

CONTACT INFORMATION:

Phone: 49 30-983216799   Fax:
Toll-Free:
Address: 111 N. Bridge Rd., #08-19 Peninsula Plaza, Singapore, 179098 Singapore

STOCK TICKER/OTHER:

Stock Ticker: Private   Exchange:
Employees: 40   Fiscal Year Ends:
Parent Company:

SALARIES/BONUSES:

Top Exec. Salary: $ Bonus: $
Second Exec. Salary: $ Bonus: $

OTHER THOUGHTS:

Estimated Female Officers or Directors:
Hot Spot for Advancement for Women/Minorities:

Sales, profits and employees may be estimates. Financial information, benefits and other data can change quickly and may vary from those stated here.

ADA SA

NAIC Code: 532111

www.ada.fr

TYPES OF BUSINESS:

Automobile Rental
Vehicle Rental Services
Car Rental
Van Rental
Bike Rental
Motorcycle Rental
Payment Solutions
Map Route Planner

BRANDS/DIVISIONS/AFFILIATES:

Rousselet Group

CONTACTS: *Note: Officers with more than one job title may be intentionally listed here more than once.*

Nicolas Rousselet, Chmn.

GROWTH PLANS/SPECIAL FEATURES:

ADA SA is a franchise car-rental company based in France and the French islands. ADA offers economy-class cars, electric cars, wagons and minivans. Some agencies additionally offer commercial vehicles, such as moving vans, dump trucks, all-terrain vehicles and weight-bearing porters. Through ADA's partnership with Holiday Bikes, it also offers two-wheeled vehicles such as bicycles, motorcycles and scooters for rent at most agencies. The company's other partnerships include Homebox, which rents out storage boxes that are located within the company's facility. In addition, most of the firm's agencies offer special equipment, such as baby and child seats, boosters, GPS systems and snow chains. The company offers supplemental insurance. ADA provides car and scooter rental service to people without a license, with the possibility to book and pay directly online or by contacting an ADA agency. The company operates in-terminal locations in nearly all of the major airports in France, including Ajaccio, Bastia, Bordeaux, Brest, Lorient, Lyon, Marseille, Montpellier, Nantes, Nice, Paris Orly, Paris Roissy Charles de Gaulle, Perpignan, Toulouse, Guadeloupe, Guyana and La Reunion. ADA also has agencies at all major railway stations in France. ADA customers can locate the agency of their choice through the company's partnership with Via Michelin, a map, route planner and travel guide service for the U.S. and Europe. ADA is a subsidiary of the Rousselet Group, a global holding company with several subsidiaries. These include Europe's largest taxi company, a software company and numerous real estate holdings.

FINANCIAL DATA: *Note: Data for latest year may not have been available at press time.*

In U.S. $	2021	2020	2019	2018	2017	2016
Revenue	112,922,928	107,852,000	110,604,000	62,509,400	57,092,600	46,887,600
R&D Expense						
Operating Income						
Operating Margin %						
SGA Expense						
Net Income	1,576,301	1,852,190	4,823,240	3,414,220	3,948,160	2,920,470
Operating Cash Flow						
Capital Expenditure						
EBITDA						
Return on Assets %						
Return on Equity %						
Debt to Equity						

CONTACT INFORMATION:

Phone: 41-27-46-00   Fax: 47-39-17-65
Toll-Free:
Address: 22-28 rue Henri Barbusse, Clichy, 92585 France

STOCK TICKER/OTHER:

Stock Ticker: ALADA   Exchange: Paris
Employees: 97   Fiscal Year Ends: 12/31
Parent Company: Rousselet Group

SALARIES/BONUSES:

Top Exec. Salary: $ Bonus: $
Second Exec. Salary: $ Bonus: $

OTHER THOUGHTS:

Estimated Female Officers or Directors:
Hot Spot for Advancement for Women/Minorities:

Adecco Group AG

www.adeccogroup.com

NAIC Code: 561320

TYPES OF BUSINESS:

Outsourced Staffing
Human Resources
Outsourcing
Staffing
Executive Search
Leadership Development

GROWTH PLANS/SPECIAL FEATURES:

Adecco is the largest recruitment provider globally, with just over 4,000 branches in over 60 countries. The company is listed in Switzerland and came about through the merger of two large staffing companies, Adia and Ecco, in 1996. Adecco provides both temporary and permanent staffing in addition to HR systems outsourcing, career transition counselling, and restructuring consulting services.

BRANDS/DIVISIONS/AFFILIATES:

Adecco
Modis
Badenoch + Clark
LHH
pontoon
Spring Professional
Vettery

CONTACTS: *Note: Officers with more than one job title may be intentionally listed here more than once.*

Alain Dehaze, CEO
Ralf Weissbeck, CIO
Coram Williams, CFO
Valerie Beaulier, CMO
Gordana Landen, Chief Human Resources Officer
Teppo Paavola, Chief Digital Officer
Alain Dehaze, Head-France
Martin Alonso, Head-Northern Europe
Robert P. (Bob) Crouch, Head-North America
Federico Vione, Head-Italy, Eastern Europe & India
Jean-Christophe Deslarzes, Chmn.
Christophe Duchatellier, Head-Japan & Asia

FINANCIAL DATA: *Note: Data for latest year may not have been available at press time.*

In U.S. $	2021	2020	2019	2018	2017	2016
Revenue	22,094,606,336	19,947,585,536	24,708,116,480	26,954,047,488	25,575,059,456	26,803,273,728
R&D Expense						
Operating Income						
Operating Margin %						
SGA Expense						
Net Income	618,045,696	-99,936,776	766,756,352	517,239,424	851,781,376	853,389,376
Operating Cash Flow						
Capital Expenditure						
EBITDA						
Return on Assets %						
Return on Equity %						
Debt to Equity						

CONTACT INFORMATION:

Phone: 41 448788888   Fax:
Toll-Free:
Address: Bellerivestrasse 30, Zurich, CH-8008 Switzerland

STOCK TICKER/OTHER:

Stock Ticker: AHEXF
Employees: 32,625
Parent Company:

Exchange: PINX
Fiscal Year Ends: 12/31

SALARIES/BONUSES:

Top Exec. Salary: $ Bonus: $
Second Exec. Salary: $ Bonus: $

OTHER THOUGHTS:

Estimated Female Officers or Directors: 1
Hot Spot for Advancement for Women/Minorities: Y

Airbnb Inc

NAIC Code: 561510

www.airbnb.com

TYPES OF BUSINESS:

Travel Agencies
Online Homestay Reservations
Room Rental Reservations
Tour Booking Online
Restaurant Reservations
Luxury Accommodations Booking
Insurance Protection

BRANDS/DIVISIONS/AFFILIATES:

Airbnb.com
Airbnb for Business
Airbnb Experiences
Beyond by Airbnb
Airbnb Plus
Airbnb Citizen
AirCover

GROWTH PLANS/SPECIAL FEATURES:

Started in 2008, Airbnb is the world's largest online alternative accommodation travel agency, also offering booking services for boutique hotels and experiences. Airbnb's platform offered 6 million active accommodation listings in 2021. Listings from the company's 4 million hosts are spread over 220 countries and 100,000 cities and towns. In 2021, 54% of revenue was from the North American region, 32% from Europe/Middle East/Africa, 7% from Asia-Pacific, and 7% from Latin America. Transaction fees for online bookings account for all its revenue. About 41% of employees are women.

CONTACTS: Note: Officers with more than one job title may be intentionally listed here more than once.

Brian Chesky, CEO
David Stephenson, CFO
Joseph Gebbia, Chairman, Divisional
David Bernstein, Chief Accounting Officer
Nathan Blecharczyk, Chief Strategy Officer
Aristotle Balogh, Chief Technology Officer
Catherine Powell, Other Corporate Officer

FINANCIAL DATA: Note: Data for latest year may not have been available at press time.

In U.S. $	2021	2020	2019	2018	2017	2016
Revenue	5,991,760,000	3,378,199,000	4,805,239,000	3,651,985,000	2,561,721,000	
R&D Expense	1,425,048,000	2,752,872,000	976,695,000	579,193,000	400,749,000	
Operating Income	542,166,000	-3,438,792,000	-501,543,000	18,744,000	-81,362,000	
Operating Margin %	.09%	-1.02%	- .10%	.01%	- .03%	
SGA Expense	2,021,656,000	2,310,176,000	2,318,700,000	1,580,814,000	1,198,905,000	
Net Income	-352,034,000	-4,584,716,000	-674,339,000	-16,860,000	-70,046,000	
Operating Cash Flow	2,189,694,000	-629,732,000	222,727,000	595,557,000	251,225,000	
Capital Expenditure	25,322,000	37,371,000	125,452,000	90,624,000	100,204,000	
EBITDA	275,711,000	-4,384,374,000	-287,573,000	155,577,000	36,646,000	
Return on Assets %						
Return on Equity %						
Debt to Equity	.49%	0.774				

CONTACT INFORMATION:

Phone: 415-510-4027   Fax:
Toll-Free:
Address: 888 Brannan St., San Francisco, CA 94103 United States

STOCK TICKER/OTHER:

Stock Ticker: ABNB   Exchange: NAS
Employees: 6,132   Fiscal Year Ends: 12/31
Parent Company:

SALARIES/BONUSES:

Top Exec. Salary: $600,000   Bonus: $218,000
Second Exec. Salary: Bonus: $18,000
$600,000

OTHER THOUGHTS:

Estimated Female Officers or Directors:
Hot Spot for Advancement for Women/Minorities: Y

Allegis Group

www.allegisgroup.com

NAIC Code: 561320

TYPES OF BUSINESS:

Staffing & Recruitment Services
Outsource Staffing Services
Managed Services
Recruitment Services
Online Platforms and Applications
Talent Advisory Services
Work Search Platforms
Digital Transformation Innovation

BRANDS/DIVISIONS/AFFILIATES:

Aerotek
TEKsystems
Aston Carter
Allegis Global Solutions
Major Lindsey & Africa
MarketSource
Actalent
QuantumWork

CONTACTS: Note: Officers with more than one job title may be intentionally listed here more than once.

Jay Alvather, Pres.

GROWTH PLANS/SPECIAL FEATURES:

Allegis Group is a staffing and managed services outsource company with 500 locations across the globe. The group provides businesses with a comprehensive suite of talent solutions through a network of specialized staffing and recruiting companies, each focusing on a different industry sector and its unique needs. The firm's company brands include: Aerotek, offering engineering, scientific, professional and industrial skills; TEKsystems, offering technology solutions, strategic planning and implementation; Aston Carter, offering accounting, finance and professional skills; Allegis Global Solutions, offering managed service provider (MSP), recovery point objective (RPO) and integrated talented solutions; Major, Lindsey & Africa, offering legal recruiting and talent management services; Allegis Partners, offering executive search services; MarketSource, offering sales outsourcing solutions; Actalent, offering global services and solutions in engineering and sciences; Getting Hired, offering a disability recruitment solution; QuantumWork, a cloud-based intelligent sourcing platform; QuantumWork Advisory, offering workforce design and advisory services; and CareerCircle, a digital workforce development platform. Together the group offers staffing and recruiting services, talent advisory services, workforce management services, search services and managed delivery services. Allegis Group provides matches for customers through its digital transformation innovations, including embedded personalization features.

FINANCIAL DATA: Note: Data for latest year may not have been available at press time.

In U.S. $	2021	2020	2019	2018	2017	2016
Revenue	12,300,000,000	11,223,900,000	13,282,500,000	12,650,000,000	12,300,000,000	11,200,000,000
R&D Expense						
Operating Income						
Operating Margin %						
SGA Expense						
Net Income						
Operating Cash Flow						
Capital Expenditure						
EBITDA						
Return on Assets %						
Return on Equity %						
Debt to Equity						

CONTACT INFORMATION:

Phone: 443 492-2410   Fax:
Toll-Free: 800-927-8090
Address: 7437 Race Rd., Hanover, MD 21076 United States

STOCK TICKER/OTHER:

Stock Ticker: Private   Exchange:
Employees: 19,000   Fiscal Year Ends:
Parent Company:

SALARIES/BONUSES:

Top Exec. Salary: $ Bonus: $
Second Exec. Salary: $ Bonus: $

OTHER THOUGHTS:

Estimated Female Officers or Directors:
Hot Spot for Advancement for Women/Minorities:

Allied Healthcare International Inc   www.alliedhealthcare.com

NAIC Code: 561320

TYPES OF BUSINESS:

Temporary Staffing
Home Care
Live-In Care
Clinical Care
End-of-Life Care
Re-enablement Support
Learning Disability Support

BRANDS/DIVISIONS/AFFILIATES:

Cera

CONTACTS: *Note: Officers with more than one job title may be intentionally listed here more than once.*

Narinder Singh, CEO

GROWTH PLANS/SPECIAL FEATURES:

Allied Healthcare International, Inc. provides various types of health care, as well as other related services including children and family services and payment services. Types of care include home care, live-in care, clinical care, end-of-life care, re-enablement, and care services for those with learning disabilities. Home care offers help around the house such as cooking, cleaning and shopping for daily necessities. It offers personal care such as bathing/showering, getting dressed, shaving or taking medication. It also offers companion services such as being taken to medical appointments or social outings, or offering companionship at home. Live-in care offers help around the house, personal care, companionship and being on-hand at night for extra support. Clinical care includes 24/7 support in the home environment and offers tailored care such as nutrition, breathing, airway management, spinal care, medication, diabetes and epilepsy. End of life care offers support for the individual and family, including medication management, feeding through tubes, managing symptoms, managing continence, and home ventilation and respiratory services. Re-enablement helps individuals learn new skills or re-learn existing ones. It also helps people with dementia or physical difficulties. Various levels of care and support is offered for individuals with learning disabilities and associated needs, including communication difficulties, autism, epilepsy and physical disabilities. Children and family services provide support regarding respite care, be-friending, holiday support, play and social support, arts and crafts, outside activities, tube feeding and care, school and homework support, chaperone and transport, contact supervision, and those with substance misuse, among other support services. Last, the company offers information and support regarding living in an assisted community apartment that offers tailored on-site care, support and clinical services Allied Healthcare is owned by Cera, a homecare provider based in the U.K.

FINANCIAL DATA: *Note: Data for latest year may not have been available at press time.*

In U.S. $	2021	2020	2019	2018	2017	2016
Revenue	500,000,000	483,787,500	509,250,000	485,000,000	462,000,000	440,000,000
R&D Expense						
Operating Income						
Operating Margin %						
SGA Expense						
Net Income						
Operating Cash Flow						
Capital Expenditure						
EBITDA						
Return on Assets %						
Return on Equity %						
Debt to Equity						

CONTACT INFORMATION:

Phone: 44 844-736-0254   Fax:
Toll-Free: 800-542-1078
Address: Cavendish House, Lakhpur Court, Staffordshire Tech, Stafford, ST18 0FX United Kingdom

STOCK TICKER/OTHER:

Stock Ticker: Subsidiary   Exchange:
Employees: 8,000   Fiscal Year Ends: 12/31
Parent Company: Cera

SALARIES/BONUSES:

Top Exec. Salary: $ Bonus: $
Second Exec. Salary: $ Bonus: $

OTHER THOUGHTS:

Estimated Female Officers or Directors:
Hot Spot for Advancement for Women/Minorities: Y

Amazon Flex

flex.amazon.com

NAIC Code: 492210

TYPES OF BUSINESS:

Local Delivery Service
Delivery App
Driver and Delivery Services
Package Delivery

BRANDS/DIVISIONS/AFFILIATES:

Amazon.com Inc

CONTACTS: *Note: Officers with more than one job title may be intentionally listed here more than once.*

Andy Jassy, CEO-Amazon.com

GROWTH PLANS/SPECIAL FEATURES:

Amazon Flex, a subsidiary of Amazon.com, Inc., operates a delivery app, enabling delivery persons to create their own working hours. Delivery workers must have a smartphone, download the Amazon Flex app, select a delivery region, confirm they are at least 21 years old, have a valid U.S. driver's license and register the type of vehicle they will be driving. Trucks must have an enclosed bed, protected from weather, for the safe delivery of packages. The app is the primary source of communication between Amazon and the independent deliverer. On the app, deliverers choose what hours they will be working, pick up packages from local Amazon hubs, scan them through the app and load them into their vehicles. The app then displays where to deliver each package, and may even suggest directions. Earnings are displayed on the app. Deliverers have the capability of making between $18 to $25 per hour delivering the packages. Amazon Flex is active in most large and medium U.S. cities, including Atlanta, Austin, Chicago, Denver, Houston, Los Angeles, New York, San Diego, San Francisco, Seattle, Tampa and Washington DC.

FINANCIAL DATA: *Note: Data for latest year may not have been available at press time.*

In U.S. $	2021	2020	2019	2018	2017	2016
Revenue						
R&D Expense						
Operating Income						
Operating Margin %						
SGA Expense						
Net Income						
Operating Cash Flow						
Capital Expenditure						
EBITDA						
Return on Assets %						
Return on Equity %						
Debt to Equity						

CONTACT INFORMATION:

Phone: Fax:
Toll-Free: 877 212-6150
Address: 410 Terry Ave. N., Seattle, WA 98109 United States

STOCK TICKER/OTHER:

Stock Ticker: Subsidiary
Employees:
Parent Company: Amazon.com Inc

Exchange:
Fiscal Year Ends: 12/31

SALARIES/BONUSES:

Top Exec. Salary: $ Bonus: $
Second Exec. Salary: $ Bonus: $

OTHER THOUGHTS:

Estimated Female Officers or Directors:
Hot Spot for Advancement for Women/Minorities:

AMERCO (U-Haul)

www.amerco.com

NAIC Code: 532120

TYPES OF BUSINESS:

Truck Rental & Leasing Services
Moving & Storage Services & Supplies
Property & Casualty Insurance
Life Insurance
Annuities
Self-Storage Properties
Propane Tank Refilling
Car Sharing Services

BRANDS/DIVISIONS/AFFILIATES:

U-Haul International Inc
Amerco Real Estate Company
Repwest Insurance Company
Oxford Life Insurance Company
Uhaul.com
Safemove
Safetow
Safestor

GROWTH PLANS/SPECIAL FEATURES:

Amerco Inc is an American provider of rental trucks to household movers. The company operates a fleet of trucks, trailers, and towing devices under the U-Haul brand. The service is targeted at do-it-yourself household movers. Amerco offers its products and services through a network of retail moving stores and independent U-Haul dealers. The company also offers self-storage solutions for household and commercial goods, as well as insurance products covering loss on goods in storage, medical, life, and cargo protection. It operates in three segments: Moving and Storage, Property and Casualty Insurance, and Life Insurance. The company's geographical segments are the United States and Canada.

CONTACTS: Note: Officers with more than one job title may be intentionally listed here more than once.

Edward Shoen, CEO
Jason Berg, CFO
Maria Bell, Chief Accounting Officer
Samuel Shoen, Director
Laurence De Respino, General Counsel
Mark Haydukovich, President, Subsidiary
John Taylor, President, Subsidiary
Matthew Braccia, President, Subsidiary
Douglas Bell, President, Subsidiary

FINANCIAL DATA: Note: Data for latest year may not have been available at press time.

In U.S. $	2021	2020	2019	2018	2017	2016
Revenue	4,541,984,768	3,978,867,968	3,768,707,072	3,601,114,112	3,421,766,912	3,275,655,936
R&D Expense						
Operating Income						
Operating Margin %						
SGA Expense						
Net Income	610,856,000	442,048,000	370,856,992	790,582,976	398,424,000	489,000,992
Operating Cash Flow						
Capital Expenditure						
EBITDA						
Return on Assets %						
Return on Equity %						
Debt to Equity						

CONTACT INFORMATION:

Phone: 775-688-6300   Fax: 775 688-6338
Toll-Free:
Address: 5555 Kietzke Ln., Ste. 100, Reno, NV 89511 United States

STOCK TICKER/OTHER:

Stock Ticker: UHAL   Exchange: NAS
Employees: 32,200   Fiscal Year Ends: 03/31
Parent Company:

SALARIES/BONUSES:

Top Exec. Salary: $ Bonus: $
Second Exec. Salary: $ Bonus: $

OTHER THOUGHTS:

Estimated Female Officers or Directors: 1
Hot Spot for Advancement for Women/Minorities:

AMN Healthcare Services Inc

www.amnhealthcare.com

NAIC Code: 561320

TYPES OF BUSINESS:
Temporary Medical Staffing
Employment Placement Agencies
Recruiting and Placement
Vendor Management

GROWTH PLANS/SPECIAL FEATURES:
AMN Healthcare Services is the largest healthcare staffing company in the United States. In 2021, it offered almost 15,000 nurses and allied healthcare full-time workers with provider clients nationwide. About two thirds of its business is generated from its temporary nursing division; the other third is generated from its physician placement and technology-backed workplace solutions divisions.

BRANDS/DIVISIONS/AFFILIATES:
American Mobile
Nursefinders
NursesRx
HealthSource Global Staffing
Med Travelers
Onward Healthcare
AMN Revenue Cycle Solutions
Stratus Video

CONTACTS: Note: Officers with more than one job title may be intentionally listed here more than once.
Susan Salka, CEO
Christopher Schwartz, CFO
Douglas Wheat, Chairman of the Board
Mark Hagan, Chief Information Officer
Denise Jackson, Chief Legal Officer

FINANCIAL DATA: Note: Data for latest year may not have been available at press time.

In U.S. $	2021	2020	2019	2018	2017	2016
Revenue	3,984,235,000	2,393,714,000	2,222,107,000	2,136,074,000	1,988,454,000	1,902,225,000
R&D Expense						
Operating Income	477,998,000	149,265,000	176,915,000	202,828,000	212,440,000	191,632,000
Operating Margin %	.12%	.06%	.08%	.09%	.11%	.10%
SGA Expense	730,451,000	549,747,000	508,030,000	452,318,000	399,700,000	398,472,000
Net Income	327,388,000	70,665,000	113,988,000	141,741,000	132,558,000	105,838,000
Operating Cash Flow	305,356,000	256,826,000	224,862,000	226,993,000	160,518,000	133,909,000
Capital Expenditure	53,663,000	39,102,000	36,458,000	36,386,000	26,529,000	21,956,000
EBITDA	581,695,000	243,452,000	235,435,000	244,065,000	244,719,000	221,252,000
Return on Assets %						
Return on Equity %						
Debt to Equity	.74%	1.142	0.961	0.69	0.569	0.799

CONTACT INFORMATION:
Phone: 866 871-8519   Fax:
Toll-Free:
Address: 8840 Cypress Waters Blvd., Dallas, TX 75019 United States

STOCK TICKER/OTHER:
Stock Ticker: AMN   Exchange: NYS
Employees: 3,800   Fiscal Year Ends: 12/31
Parent Company:

SALARIES/BONUSES:
Top Exec. Salary: $1,030,000   Bonus: $
Second Exec. Salary: $90,000   Bonus: $900,000

OTHER THOUGHTS:
Estimated Female Officers or Directors:
Hot Spot for Advancement for Women/Minorities:

ANI Technologies Pvt Ltd (Ola)   www.olacabs.com

NAIC Code: 561599

TYPES OF BUSINESS:

Car Ride Dispatch Service, Mobile App-Based
Taxi Mobile App
Ride Sharing Mobile App
Bicycle Rental

BRANDS/DIVISIONS/AFFILIATES:

Ola
Ola Electric
Ola Fleet Technologies
Ola Skilling
Ola Money
Ola Corporate
Ola Cars

CONTACTS: *Note: Officers with more than one job title may be intentionally listed here more than once.*

G.R. Arun, COO
Bhavish Aggarwal, Dir.-Engineering & Product

GROWTH PLANS/SPECIAL FEATURES:

ANI Technologies Pvt. Ltd. operates a mobile technology platform called Ola (also referred to as Ola Cabs), which connects passengers to a variety of transportation modes within India, as well as other countries. ANI Technologies' network has more than 1.5 million driver-partners across 250+ cities across India, Australia, New Zealand and the U.K. Through the app, passengers can book a ride by taxicab, auto-rickshaw, bike or car; and even connect with a shuttle or city bus or hire a corporate travel service. There are automobile rides available for every budget, from micro cars to superior luxury cars. The Ola mobile application is available on Windows, Android and iOS platforms. Ola's core mobility offering is supplemented by its electric-vehicle arm, Ola Electric; India's largest fleet management business, Ola Fleet Technologies; and Ola Skilling, which aims to enable millions of livelihood opportunities for India's youth. In addition, ANI Technologies' Ola Money is a seamless payment app; Ola Corporate enables businesses to book and manage employee travel; and Ola Cars, a vehicle commerce platform for purchasing new and used vehicles via mobile app.

FINANCIAL DATA: *Note: Data for latest year may not have been available at press time.*

In U.S. $	2021	2020	2019	2018	2017	2016
Revenue	94,029,904	361,696,147	427,087,500	341,670,000	212,730,000	114,364,000
R&D Expense						
Operating Income						
Operating Margin %						
SGA Expense						
Net Income	12,241,837	-81,100,854	-372,696,000	-436,918,000	-754,625,000	-348,870,000
Operating Cash Flow						
Capital Expenditure						
EBITDA						
Return on Assets %						
Return on Equity %						
Debt to Equity						

CONTACT INFORMATION:

Phone: 91 80-67350900   Fax: 91-80-67350904
Toll-Free:
Address: #414, Fl. 3, 4th Block, 17th Main, 100 Feet Rd., Koramanagala, Bengaluru, 560034 India

STOCK TICKER/OTHER:

Stock Ticker: Private   Exchange:
Employees: 7,000   Fiscal Year Ends: 03/31
Parent Company:

SALARIES/BONUSES:

Top Exec. Salary: $ Bonus: $
Second Exec. Salary: $ Bonus: $

OTHER THOUGHTS:

Estimated Female Officers or Directors:
Hot Spot for Advancement for Women/Minorities:

Argo AI

www.argo.ai

NAIC Code: 336111

TYPES OF BUSINESS:

Autonomous Driving Technology
Self-Driving Technology
Robotics
Artificial Intelligence
3D Mapping
Sensors
Self-Driving Testing
Dispatch Management Software

BRANDS/DIVISIONS/AFFILIATES:

Argo Autonomy Platform
Argo Lidar
Argo Hub

CONTACTS: Note: Officers with more than one job title may be intentionally listed here more than once.

Bryan Salesky, CEO
Peter Rander, Pres.
Wesley Ford, VP-Systems Engineering
Kate Kozlowski, Chief Compliance Officer
Brett Browning, CTO
Cynthia Kwon, VP-Strategy and Bus. Dev.

GROWTH PLANS/SPECIAL FEATURES:

Argo AI is a technology platform company that works with automakers to deliver a fully-integrated, self-driving system. The firm specializes in robotics and artificial intelligence (AI), which complements its partnerships with vehicle manufacturers Ford and Volkswagen for building self-driving technology. The Argo Autonomy Platform includes the software, hardware, high-definition maps and backend support to power full-service self-driving operations at scale. The platform is presently (late-2022) integrated into two vehicles with custom-built hardware and safety systems, the Ford Escape hybrid-electric autonomous vehicle for commercial services in U.S. cities, and the Volkswagen ID. Buzz all-electric autonomous van for commercial services in European cities. Technology-wise, Argo's 3D maps offer safety redundancy and street-level knowledge such as speed limits and traffic signs. Its sensors (lidar, radar and camera) provide a view of surroundings in all directions, and the sensor data predicts and plans vehicle actions. Argo Lidar is a proprietary laser sensor built specifically for safe self-driving, offering more than 400 meters (0.25 miles) of sensing range at highway speeds and 360-degree rotation for full coverage, among other features. Argo Hub is for commercial operations that require technology beyond the vehicle, and includes a flexible cloud infrastructure for dispatch and fleet management systems that can connect to existing operations. Argo Hub can deploy ride-hail and delivery services at scale. Argo's testing occurs in the laboratory, in simulated environments, closed courses and public roads. Headquartered in Pennsylvania, USA, the firm has engineering and development and fleet testing locations throughout the country, as well as in Munich and Hamburg, Germany.

FINANCIAL DATA: Note: Data for latest year may not have been available at press time.

In U.S. $	2021	2020	2019	2018	2017	2016
Revenue						
R&D Expense						
Operating Income						
Operating Margin %						
SGA Expense						
Net Income						
Operating Cash Flow						
Capital Expenditure						
EBITDA						
Return on Assets %						
Return on Equity %						
Debt to Equity						

CONTACT INFORMATION:

Phone: 412-525-3483   Fax:
Toll-Free:
Address: 2545 Railroad St., Pittsburgh, PA 15222 United States

STOCK TICKER/OTHER:

Stock Ticker: Private   Exchange:
Employees: Fiscal Year Ends:
Parent Company:

SALARIES/BONUSES:

Top Exec. Salary: $ Bonus: $
Second Exec. Salary: $ Bonus: $

OTHER THOUGHTS:

Estimated Female Officers or Directors:
Hot Spot for Advancement for Women/Minorities:

Avis Budget Group Inc

www.avisbudgetgroup.com

NAIC Code: 532111

TYPES OF BUSINESS:
Automobile Rental
Franchising
Truck Rental

BRANDS/DIVISIONS/AFFILIATES:
Avis
Budget
ZipCar
Payless
Apex
Maggiore
FranceCars
Turiscar

GROWTH PLANS/SPECIAL FEATURES:
Avis Budget Group Inc is a provider of automotive vehicle rental and car-sharing services. Its brands include Avis, Budget, and Zipcar. Avis is targeted to serve the premium commercial and leisure segments of the travel industry, while Budget is focused on value-conscious customers. The company operates its own network of rental locations and licenses its brands to franchisees. Zipcar is a car-sharing service that allows members to use the company-owned Zipcar fleet at an hourly rate. The company's largest region by revenue is the Americas.

CONTACTS: Note: Officers with more than one job title may be intentionally listed here more than once.
Joseph Ferraro, CEO
Brian Choi, CFO
Bernardo Hees, Chairman of the Board
Cathleen DeGenova, Chief Accounting Officer
Jean Sera, Chief Compliance Officer
Jagdeep Pahwa, Director
Izilda Martins, Executive VP, Geographical
Veresh Sita, Executive VP
Edward Linnen, Executive VP
Keith Rankin, President, Divisional

FINANCIAL DATA: Note: Data for latest year may not have been available at press time.

In U.S. $	2021	2020	2019	2018	2017	2016
Revenue	9,313,000,000	5,402,000,000	9,172,000,000	9,124,000,000	8,848,000,000	8,659,000,000
R&D Expense						
Operating Income	1,770,000,000	-752,000,000	485,000,000	468,000,000	528,000,000	575,000,000
Operating Margin %	.19%	-.14%	.05%	.05%	.06%	.07%
SGA Expense	1,145,000,000	703,000,000	1,237,000,000	1,220,000,000	1,120,000,000	1,134,000,000
Net Income	1,285,000,000	-684,000,000	302,000,000	165,000,000	361,000,000	163,000,000
Operating Cash Flow	3,491,000,000	691,000,000	2,586,000,000	2,609,000,000	2,648,000,000	2,640,000,000
Capital Expenditure	10,162,000,000	5,495,000,000	13,137,000,000	12,820,000,000	11,735,000,000	12,651,000,000
EBITDA	4,406,000,000	1,836,000,000	3,607,000,000	2,685,000,000	2,605,000,000	2,612,000,000
Return on Assets %						
Return on Equity %						
Debt to Equity			25.341	33.237	22.328	54.851

CONTACT INFORMATION:
Phone: 973 496-4700   Fax: 212 413-1924
Toll-Free:
Address: 6 Sylvan Way, Parsippany, NJ 07054 United States

STOCK TICKER/OTHER:
Stock Ticker: CAR   Exchange: NAS
Employees: 21,000   Fiscal Year Ends: 12/31
Parent Company:

SALARIES/BONUSES:
Top Exec. Salary: $500,000   Bonus: $500,000
Second Exec. Salary: Bonus: $
$1,000,000

OTHER THOUGHTS:
Estimated Female Officers or Directors: 2
Hot Spot for Advancement for Women/Minorities:

Bag Borrow or Steal Inc

www.bagborroworsteal.com

NAIC Code: 532220

TYPES OF BUSINESS:

Formal Wear Rental
Ecommerce Marketplace
Luxury Fashion Accessories

BRANDS/DIVISIONS/AFFILIATES:

CONTACTS: *Note: Officers with more than one job title may be intentionally listed here more than once.*

Robert Treves, CEO

GROWTH PLANS/SPECIAL FEATURES:

Bag Borrow or Steal, Inc. is an online boutique where women and men borrow, buy or sell luxury accessories. The site offers authentic handbags, shoes, jewelry, sunglasses and small accessories. No membership is required and there are no hidden fees; the displayed price includes everything except for sales tax, where applicable. Items of interest can be leased in one-month periods, and if not returned, the rental process automatically renews for another month. Merchandise can also be purchased, which includes free shipping. Sale returns must occur within four days of receipt for a merchandise credit, except for items marked as Final Sale. Those wanting to sell items have two options: consignment or immediate sell. Selling via consignment receives 70% of the earned sale, and payments are made weekly by the firm, not monthly (as many e-consignors do). Payments are transacted through PayPal, by check or in store credit. Immediate sell items must be pre-inspected and approved as genuine by the company, and payments can either be transacted through PayPal or via Bag Borrow or Steal store credit (which includes an additional 10% when paid with store credit). Bag Borrow or Steal handles all transactions, from photography to returns. Owners of merchandise take pictures of the items and fill out a submission form along with the pictures. Helpful pictures include date or serial codes, damage or imperfections, original receipts and packaging materials. Shipping is free using the company's pre-paid shipping label. For items not accepted, the firm promptly returns them at its own expense. Throughout the process, Bag Borrow or Steal emails owners with updates.

FINANCIAL DATA: *Note: Data for latest year may not have been available at press time.*

In U.S. $	2021	2020	2019	2018	2017	2016
Revenue						
R&D Expense						
Operating Income						
Operating Margin %						
SGA Expense						
Net Income						
Operating Cash Flow						
Capital Expenditure						
EBITDA						
Return on Assets %						
Return on Equity %						
Debt to Equity						

CONTACT INFORMATION:

Phone: 608 831-0899   Fax:
Toll-Free: 866 922-2267
Address: 2114 Eagle Dr., Middleton, WI 53562 United States

STOCK TICKER/OTHER:

Stock Ticker: Private   Exchange:
Employees: Fiscal Year Ends: 12/31
Parent Company:

SALARIES/BONUSES:

Top Exec. Salary: $ Bonus: $
Second Exec. Salary: $ Bonus: $

OTHER THOUGHTS:

Estimated Female Officers or Directors:
Hot Spot for Advancement for Women/Minorities:

Beijing Mobike Technology Co Ltd (Mobike)   mobike.com/global
NAIC Code: 532292

TYPES OF BUSINESS:
Bike Sharing Service
Bike Sharing
Bike Sharing App

BRANDS/DIVISIONS/AFFILIATES:
Meituan
Mobike

GROWTH PLANS/SPECIAL FEATURES:
Beijing Mobike Technology Co., Ltd. developed, owns and runs Mobike, a station-free bike sharing system based in China. Through the Mobike app, riders locate a nearby bike, tap the unlock button and scan the barcode, which automatically unlocks the bike. Users then ride the bike to their destination, legally park it as if it was personally owned by them and manually lock the bike, which automatically ends the trip. These features are made capable through Mobike's efforts in innovate and Internet of Things (IoT) technologies. The rental fee is usually charged per the half-hour. The bike sharing program provides a short distance transportation solution. Beijing Mobike Technology is wholly-owned by Meituan.

CONTACTS: Note: Officers with more than one job title may be intentionally listed here more than once.
Liu Yu, CEO

FINANCIAL DATA: Note: Data for latest year may not have been available at press time.

In U.S. $	2021	2020	2019	2018	2017	2016
Revenue						
R&D Expense						
Operating Income						
Operating Margin %						
SGA Expense						
Net Income						
Operating Cash Flow						
Capital Expenditure						
EBITDA						
Return on Assets %						
Return on Equity %						
Debt to Equity						

CONTACT INFORMATION:
Phone: 86 10-5825-1718   Fax:
Toll-Free:
Address: Gate 1, Ste. B, Chuangyi Park 5 Xueqing Rd., Fl. 3, Beijing, Beijing 100089 China

STOCK TICKER/OTHER:
Stock Ticker: Subsidiary
Employees:
Parent Company: Meituan

Exchange:
Fiscal Year Ends: 12/31

SALARIES/BONUSES:
Top Exec. Salary: $ Bonus: $
Second Exec. Salary: $ Bonus: $

OTHER THOUGHTS:
Estimated Female Officers or Directors:
Hot Spot for Advancement for Women/Minorities:

Bellhop Inc

NAIC Code: 484210

www.getbellhops.com

TYPES OF BUSINESS:

On-Demand Moving Services
Moving Business
Booking App
Local Moving Services
Long-Distance Moving Services
Loading and Unloading Services

BRANDS/DIVISIONS/AFFILIATES:

GROWTH PLANS/SPECIAL FEATURES:

Bellhop, Inc. is an on-demand moving business. The Tennessee-based firm operates in more than 70 cities across the U.S., with more than 100 trucks. Bellhop hand-picks hardworking and courteous college students and trains them to be exceptional at moving, whether locally, across the country or helping to rearrange furniture or other. The firm's instant online estimates and booking process takes mere minutes. Users enter what needs to be moved, how many Bellhop are needed and the date and time of service preferred. Bellhop offers office moving and self-storage services. Bellhop's local moving prices include a moving truck and professional driver, moving help, dollies, blankets and straps, and fuel and mileage. Long distance service includes loading and unloading at each destination, with the customer providing and driving the loaded moving vehicle. Bellhop can also help load or unload at a single location within a service area.

CONTACTS: Note: Officers with more than one job title may be intentionally listed here more than once.

Luke Marklin, CEO
Harrison Stevens, VP-Mktg.

FINANCIAL DATA: Note: Data for latest year may not have been available at press time.

In U.S. $	2021	2020	2019	2018	2017	2016
Revenue						
R&D Expense						
Operating Income						
Operating Margin %						
SGA Expense						
Net Income						
Operating Cash Flow						
Capital Expenditure						
EBITDA						
Return on Assets %						
Return on Equity %						
Debt to Equity						

CONTACT INFORMATION:

Phone: 423 805-9574   Fax:
Toll-Free: 888 836-3939
Address: 1110 Market St., Ste. 502, Chattanooga, TN 37402 United States

STOCK TICKER/OTHER:

Stock Ticker: Private   Exchange:
Employees: 200   Fiscal Year Ends: 12/31
Parent Company:

SALARIES/BONUSES:

Top Exec. Salary: $ Bonus: $
Second Exec. Salary: $ Bonus: $

OTHER THOUGHTS:

Estimated Female Officers or Directors:
Hot Spot for Advancement for Women/Minorities:

Bestway Rental Inc

www.bestwayrto.com

NAIC Code: 532299

TYPES OF BUSINESS:

Rent-to-Own Stores
Furniture Rental
Electronics, Audio & Appliances Rental
Household Goods Rental
Lease & Purchase Plans

BRANDS/DIVISIONS/AFFILIATES:

Bestway Rent-To-Own
Bestway Rental Inc

CONTACTS: *Note: Officers with more than one job title may be intentionally listed here more than once.*

David A. Kraemer, Pres.
Beth Durrett, CFO
Beth A. Durrett, Corp. Sec.

GROWTH PLANS/SPECIAL FEATURES:

Bestway Rental, Inc. is a rent-to-own firm that owns and operates 77 rental-purchase stores in Alabama, Arkansas, Indiana, Kentucky, Mississippi, North Carolina, South Carolina, Tennessee and Texas. Bestway Rent-To-Own stores are operated through wholly-owned subsidiary, Bestway Rental, Inc. The company's rental program allows customers to rent products under a flexible rental-purchase agreement. The rental agreements typically have a 12-to-30-month term with weekly or monthly payment options. Throughout the rental period, customers may elect to purchase the product rather than continuing to rent. Bestway offers a wide variety of brands, styles and models of television sets, audio equipment, computers and DVD players. In addition, it offers major home appliances such as washers, dryers, refrigerators and freezers as well as furniture. The company sells products under a full-service rental agreement, which requires the customer to pay the charge for each rental period in advance, but requires no additional advance payments or security deposits. Bestway also offers lease agreements that include purchase options. The firm markets its products and services by selecting prominent store locations in retail shopping areas on main traffic thoroughfares, and advertises mainly through direct mail channels. Bestway primarily serves customers in the low- to middle-income sector. The firm offers brand name products by Ashley, GE, LG, Whirlpool, Apple, and HP, among many others.

Bestway offers its employees comprehensive health benefits, 401(k), disability and life insurance and an employee purchase program.

FINANCIAL DATA: *Note: Data for latest year may not have been available at press time.*

In U.S. $	2021	2020	2019	2018	2017	2016
Revenue	298,488,645	287,008,313	294,367,500	280,350,000	267,000,000	250,000,000
R&D Expense						
Operating Income						
Operating Margin %						
SGA Expense						
Net Income						
Operating Cash Flow						
Capital Expenditure						
EBITDA						
Return on Assets %						
Return on Equity %						
Debt to Equity						

CONTACT INFORMATION:

Phone: 479-890-5941   Fax:
Toll-Free: 800-316-4567
Address: 310 S. Arkansas Ave., Dallas, TX 75251 United States

STOCK TICKER/OTHER:

Stock Ticker: Private   Exchange:
Employees: 40   Fiscal Year Ends: 07/31
Parent Company:

SALARIES/BONUSES:

Top Exec. Salary: $ Bonus: $
Second Exec. Salary: $ Bonus: $

OTHER THOUGHTS:

Estimated Female Officers or Directors: 1
Hot Spot for Advancement for Women/Minorities:

BGSF Inc

NAIC Code: 561320

www.bgsf.com

TYPES OF BUSINESS:

Temporary Help Services
Staffing Services
Real Estate
Professional
Light Industrial

BRANDS/DIVISIONS/AFFILIATES:

BG Staff Services Inc
BG Personal LP
BG Finance and Accounting Inc
BG California Multifamily Staffing Inc
EdgeRock Technology Holdings Inc
BG Talent
Extrinsic
InStaff

GROWTH PLANS/SPECIAL FEATURES:

BGSF Inc is engaged in providing temporary staffing services. The company has expertise in Real Estate, Professional, and Light Industrial sectors. The majority of its revenue comes from the Professional segment that provides skilled field talent on a nationwide basis for information technology & finance, accounting, legal and human resource client partner projects on a national basis. The services offered by the company include Staffing and Recruiting, Executive Search, Project & Consulting, and Onsite Management.

BG Staffing offers its employees health insurance and a 401(k) plan.

CONTACTS: *Note: Officers with more than one job title may be intentionally listed here more than once.*

Beth Garvey, CEO
Dan Hollenbach, CFO
L. Baker, Chairman Emeritus

FINANCIAL DATA: *Note: Data for latest year may not have been available at press time.*

In U.S. $	2021	2020	2019	2018	2017	2016
Revenue	239,027,200	207,125,500	219,764,300	286,862,900	272,600,100	253,852,200
R&D Expense						
Operating Income	12,273,570	6,278,646	15,000,540	20,484,380	18,296,040	15,535,820
Operating Margin %	.05%	.03%	.07%	.07%	.07%	.06%
SGA Expense	64,969,000	54,900,000	50,107,000	51,066,330	43,814,000	37,804,210
Net Income	14,109,480	1,441,468	13,246,990	17,549,540	5,848,434	6,882,407
Operating Cash Flow	6,663,454	22,256,950	17,953,840	18,426,480	18,063,720	9,533,840
Capital Expenditure	3,203,909	2,076,216	2,076,877	923,994	1,145,757	938,943
EBITDA	18,228,520	3,631,875	19,062,780	29,304,170	24,052,730	21,865,040
Return on Assets %						
Return on Equity %						
Debt to Equity	.50%	0.559	0.456	0.241	1.053	0.583

CONTACT INFORMATION:

Phone: 972 692-2400   Fax:
Toll-Free:
Address: 5850 Granite Pkwy, Ste. 730, Plano, TX 75024 United States

STOCK TICKER/OTHER:

Stock Ticker: BGSF   Exchange: NYS
Employees: 400   Fiscal Year Ends: 12/31
Parent Company:

SALARIES/BONUSES:

Top Exec. Salary: $425,000   Bonus: $188,388
Second Exec. Salary: $320,000   Bonus: $146,388

OTHER THOUGHTS:

Estimated Female Officers or Directors:
Hot Spot for Advancement for Women/Minorities:

Blue Apron Holdings Inc

NAIC Code: 454111

www.blueapron.com

TYPES OF BUSINESS:

Complete Meal Kits
Planned Meal Ingredients Packs
Vegetarian

GROWTH PLANS/SPECIAL FEATURES:

Blue Apron Holdings Inc is a United States-based company involved in discovering new recipes, ingredients, and cooking techniques to prepare meals that are sent along with fresh, seasonal ingredients, directly to customers. The company offers its customers two flexible plans, 2 Serving Plan and 4 Serving Plan. Its recipes are accompanied by printed and digital content, including how-to-cook instructions and the stories of its suppliers and specialty ingredients. The company also sells wine, cooking tools, utensils, and pantry items.

BRANDS/DIVISIONS/AFFILIATES:

www.blueapron.com

CONTACTS: Note: Officers with more than one job title may be intentionally listed here more than once.

Linda Kozlowski, CEO
Randy Greben, CFO
Jennifer Carr-Smith, Chairman of the Board
Danielle Simpson, Chief Marketing Officer
Irina Krechmer, Chief Technology Officer
Charlean Gmunder, COO
Meredith Deutsch, General Counsel
Terri Leitgeb, Other Executive Officer

FINANCIAL DATA: Note: Data for latest year may not have been available at press time.

In U.S. $	2021	2020	2019	2018	2017	2016
Revenue	470,377,000	460,608,000	454,868,000	667,600,000	881,191,000	795,416,000
R&D Expense						
Operating Income	-71,117,000	-38,564,000	-52,096,000	-114,378,000	-188,760,000	-54,803,000
Operating Margin %	-.15%	-.08%	-.11%	-.17%	-.21%	-.07%
SGA Expense	217,528,000	187,178,000	193,058,000	311,795,000	402,436,000	309,320,000
Net Income	-88,381,000	-46,154,000	-61,081,000	-122,149,000	-210,143,000	-54,886,000
Operating Cash Flow	-48,962,000	-5,372,000	-16,466,000	-76,900,000	-152,442,000	-23,545,000
Capital Expenditure	5,077,000	5,997,000	5,220,000	15,022,000	124,242,000	62,827,000
EBITDA	-48,914,000	-14,061,000	-20,896,000	-79,861,000	-161,922,000	-46,586,000
Return on Assets %						
Return on Equity %						
Debt to Equity	.77%	1.011	1.841	1.293	0.871	

CONTACT INFORMATION:

Phone: 347-719-4312   Fax:
Toll-Free: 888-278-4349
Address: 28 Liberty ST., New York, NY 10005 United States

STOCK TICKER/OTHER:

Stock Ticker: APRN   Exchange: NYS
Employees: 1,988   Fiscal Year Ends:
Parent Company:

SALARIES/BONUSES:

Top Exec. Salary: $460,274   Bonus: $250,000
Second Exec. Salary: $458,630   Bonus: $172,631

OTHER THOUGHTS:

Estimated Female Officers or Directors:
Hot Spot for Advancement for Women/Minorities:

Sales, profits and employees may be estimates. Financial information, benefits and other data can change quickly and may vary from those stated here.

Boatsetter Inc

www.boatsetter.com

NAIC Code: 532292

TYPES OF BUSINESS:

Recreational Goods Rental
Boat Sharing
Boat Rental
Boat Captains

BRANDS/DIVISIONS/AFFILIATES:

CONTACTS: *Note: Officers with more than one job title may be intentionally listed here more than once.*

Jaclyn Baumgarten, CEO

GROWTH PLANS/SPECIAL FEATURES:

Boatsetter, Inc. operates an online boat rental platform that connects boat owners and U.S. Coast Guard-licensed captains with people who want to go boating. The boat-sharing marketplace (Boatsetter) makes boating experiences affordable and accessible through a worldwide fleet of boats for boaters of every level of expertise and area of interest. Boatsetter provides real-time customer service support and world-class insurance, both in the U.S. and internationally, for everyone involved, including renters, boat owners and captains. Captains have the flexibility of working when they want, and boat rentals include 24/7 on-water support. Renters connect online to Boatsetter's captain network, and choose the type of boating experience desired. Renters are pre-screened and qualified through Boatsetter. The platform comprises 50,000 boat listings in more than 700 locations to choose from, with top locations including Miami, Fort Lauderdale, Tampa Bay, Seattle, Chicago, New York City, Washington DC and San Francisco in the U.S., as well as Barcelona (Spain), Cancun and Puerta Vallarta (Mexico), Cannes (France) and the Balearic Islands (Ibiza). During 2022, Boatsetter announced that it raised $38 million in Series B funding co-led by Level Equity, with participation from Suntex Marinas, Certares and others. The funding enables Boatsetter to enhance product features, boat inventory and experiential offerings, as well as to bring Boatsetter to new markets worldwide.

FINANCIAL DATA: *Note: Data for latest year may not have been available at press time.*

In U.S. $	2021	2020	2019	2018	2017	2016
Revenue		32,000,000	29,911,875	27,825,000	26,500,000	25,000,000
R&D Expense						
Operating Income						
Operating Margin %						
SGA Expense						
Net Income						
Operating Cash Flow						
Capital Expenditure						
EBITDA						
Return on Assets %						
Return on Equity %						
Debt to Equity						

CONTACT INFORMATION:

Phone: 305-600-5434   Fax:
Toll-Free:
Address: 200 SW 1st Ave., Ste. 950, Fort Lauderdale, FL 33301 United States

STOCK TICKER/OTHER:

Stock Ticker: Private
Employees: 35
Parent Company:

Exchange:
Fiscal Year Ends: 12/31

SALARIES/BONUSES:

Top Exec. Salary: $ Bonus: $
Second Exec. Salary: $ Bonus: $

OTHER THOUGHTS:

Estimated Female Officers or Directors:
Hot Spot for Advancement for Women/Minorities:

Brambles Limited

NAIC Code: 532490

www.brambles.com

TYPES OF BUSINESS:
Pallet Rental or Leasing
Pallets
Containers
Remote Procedure Call
Digital Technology
Internet of Things
Supply Chain Software
Keg Rental

BRANDS/DIVISIONS/AFFILIATES:
CHEP
BxB Digital
Kegstar

GROWTH PLANS/SPECIAL FEATURES:
Brambles is the largest pallet pooling operator globally, operating in 60 countries throughout the Americas, Europe, and Asia-Pacific under its CHEP brand. Brambles has refocused on its core pallet pooling business, having divested its global returnable crate pooling business in June 2019.

CONTACTS: Note: Officers with more than one job title may be intentionally listed here more than once.
Graham Chipchase, CEO
Nessa O'Sullivan, CFO
Patrick Bradley, Group Sr. VP-Human Resources
Rodney Hefford, CIO
Robert Gerrard, Company Sec.
James Hall, Sr. Dir.-Corp. Affairs
James Hall, Sr. Dir.-Investor Rel.
Peter Mackie, Group Pres., Pallets
Doug Pertz, Group Pres., Recall
Karl Pohler, Group Pres., RPCs
Jason Rabbino, Group Pres., Containers
John Mullen, Chmn.

FINANCIAL DATA: Note: Data for latest year may not have been available at press time.

In U.S. $	2021	2020	2019	2018	2017	2016
Revenue	5,209,800,192	4,733,599,744	4,595,299,840	5,596,599,808	4,303,129,088	5,438,124,544
R&D Expense						
Operating Income						
Operating Margin %						
SGA Expense						
Net Income	526,100,000	448,000,000	1,467,699,968	747,100,032	154,192,016	577,372,160
Operating Cash Flow						
Capital Expenditure						
EBITDA						
Return on Assets %						
Return on Equity %						
Debt to Equity						

CONTACT INFORMATION:
Phone: 61 2-9256-5222   Fax: 61-0-2-9256-5299
Toll-Free:
Address: Level 10, Angel Pl., 123 Pitt St., Sydney, NSW 2000 Australia

STOCK TICKER/OTHER:
Stock Ticker: BMBLF   Exchange: PINX
Employees: 11,569   Fiscal Year Ends: 06/30
Parent Company:

SALARIES/BONUSES:
Top Exec. Salary: $ Bonus: $
Second Exec. Salary: $ Bonus: $

OTHER THOUGHTS:
Estimated Female Officers or Directors: 3
Hot Spot for Advancement for Women/Minorities: Y

Breather Products Inc

breather.com

NAIC Code: 519130

TYPES OF BUSINESS:

Online Office Space Rental Service
Office Space Sharing
Workspace Booking
Conference and Meeting Spaces
Online and Mobile App

BRANDS/DIVISIONS/AFFILIATES:

Industrious

CONTACTS: Note: Officers with more than one job title may be intentionally listed here more than once.

Jamie Hodari, CEO-Industrious

GROWTH PLANS/SPECIAL FEATURES:

Breather Products, Inc. facilitates the rental of private workspaces and meeting rooms, with more than 500 locations across 10 cities worldwide. Launched in 2013, the firm was created to solve the problem of working while traveling. Instead of utilizing various coffee shops or other public places, Breather offers a way for people to find a quiet space to work. On-demand areas such as meeting and conference rooms or private work rooms can be reserved through the company's online website or mobile app. Admittance into the spaces themselves is unlocked through these same online channels. Booking occurs by searching, finding and reserving a Breather space nearby via iOS and Android, or on Breather.com. Rooms can be booked for 30 minutes, a few hours, an entire day or extended time periods. Spaces can include offices, conference rooms, event spaces, workshop spaces, corporate meetings, trainings, classrooms and more. They can be equipped with whiteboards, mobile chargers, WiFi and HDTVs; and floorplans can be changed by the Breather to suit meeting, presentation or workspace needs. By partnering with Breather, property owners and building managers can earn money from unused and under-performing spaces. Breather operates as a subsidiary of Industrious, which offers workspaces throughout the U.S. and in more than 65 cities internationally.

FINANCIAL DATA: Note: Data for latest year may not have been available at press time.

In U.S. $	2021	2020	2019	2018	2017	2016
Revenue						
R&D Expense						
Operating Income						
Operating Margin %						
SGA Expense						
Net Income						
Operating Cash Flow						
Capital Expenditure						
EBITDA						
Return on Assets %						
Return on Equity %						
Debt to Equity						

CONTACT INFORMATION:

Phone: 212 213-1971   Fax:
Toll-Free: 800 471-8704
Address: 36 W. 25th St., Fl. 6, New York, NY 10010 United States

STOCK TICKER/OTHER:

Stock Ticker: Subsidiary   Exchange:
Employees: 165   Fiscal Year Ends:
Parent Company: Industrious

SALARIES/BONUSES:

Top Exec. Salary: $ Bonus: $
Second Exec. Salary: $ Bonus: $

OTHER THOUGHTS:

Estimated Female Officers or Directors:
Hot Spot for Advancement for Women/Minorities:

Cabify Espana SLU

NAIC Code: 561599

cabify.com/en

TYPES OF BUSINESS:

Car Ride Dispatch Service, Mobile-App Based
Ride Sharing
Ride Hailing
Online Booking
Real-Time GPS

BRANDS/DIVISIONS/AFFILIATES:

Cabify

GROWTH PLANS/SPECIAL FEATURES:

Cabify Espana S.L.U. provides Cabify, an online application for riders to hail drivers. All journeys are geo-tracked and both riders and drivers are identified before the journey, for safety purposes. Prices for the proposed journey are clearly displayed, with options on how/when to arrive at the destination before orders are placed. Business travel for employees is offered, with costs and journeys presented in real-time. Drivers undergo a rigorous selection process, and before each driving journey, riding customers can see the name, a photograph and the vehicle number plate of the assigned driver. All vehicles must pass Cabify's requirements. Cabify is available in more than 40 cities across Argentina, Chile, Colombia, Ecuador, Spain, Mexico, Peru and Uruguay.

CONTACTS: Note: Officers with more than one job title may be intentionally listed here more than once.

Juan de Antonio Rubio, CEO
Joao Correia, Chief of Ride-Hailing Operations
Juan Barbolla, CFO
Daniel Rodrigo, VP-Mktg.
Carlos Herrera, CTO
Abel Muino, VP-Engineering

FINANCIAL DATA: Note: Data for latest year may not have been available at press time.

In U.S. $	2021	2020	2019	2018	2017	2016
Revenue	51,600,000	50,000,000	104,000,000			
R&D Expense						
Operating Income						
Operating Margin %						
SGA Expense						
Net Income						
Operating Cash Flow						
Capital Expenditure						
EBITDA						
Return on Assets %						
Return on Equity %						
Debt to Equity						

CONTACT INFORMATION:

Phone: 34 91-172-7586   Fax:
Toll-Free:
Address: 42 Pradillo St., Madrid, 28002 Spain

STOCK TICKER/OTHER:

Stock Ticker: Private   Exchange:
Employees: 1,000   Fiscal Year Ends:
Parent Company:

SALARIES/BONUSES:

Top Exec. Salary: $ Bonus: $
Second Exec. Salary: $ Bonus: $

OTHER THOUGHTS:

Estimated Female Officers or Directors:
Hot Spot for Advancement for Women/Minorities:

CanaDream Corporation

www.canadream.com

NAIC Code: 532120

TYPES OF BUSINESS:

Truck, Utility Trailer, and RV (Recreational Vehicle) Rental and Leasing
Recreational Vehicle Rental
RV Sales
Ecommerce
Online Reservations
Trip Planning Solution

BRANDS/DIVISIONS/AFFILIATES:

Apollo Tourism & Leisure Ltd
www.canadabest.com
www.canadream.com

CONTACTS: *Note: Officers with more than one job title may be intentionally listed here more than once.*

Brian Gronberg, CEO

GROWTH PLANS/SPECIAL FEATURES:

CanaDream Corporation operates a recreational vehicle (RV) rental and sales ecommerce marketplace. The firm, based in Canada, promotes the opportunity to experience Canada at one's own pace through renting an RV from its fleet of over 1,000 units. For consumers interested in purchasing an RV, the company sells them on a retail or wholesale basis. CanaDream utilizes its business-to-business (B2B), web-enabled system (www.canadabest.com) and its business-to-consumer (B2C) online reservation systems (www.canadream.com) to operate and expand its network of RV guest locations throughout the country. The corporation maintains company-owned and -operated locations, including Calgary and Edmonton, Alberta; Vancouver, British Columbia; Whitehorse/Yukon, Toronto, Ontario; Montreal, Quebec; and Halifax, Nova Scotia. CanaDream is also leveraging its proprietary technology to build a collective membership network of associate dealers that are fully connected to the ecommerce system, and currently has one associate dealer franchise in Edmonton, Alberta. Through its parent company, Apollo Tourism & Leisure Ltd., the firm offers a global RV solution in Australia, New Zealand and the U.S. CanaDream's website offers tools for trip planning, as well as information on hot deals and service and storage.

CanaDream offers employees life insurance, AD&D, dental and health coverage, educational assistance and other programs.

FINANCIAL DATA: *Note: Data for latest year may not have been available at press time.*

In U.S. $	2021	2020	2019	2018	2017	2016
Revenue	39,483,499	37,964,903	42,657,195	40,625,900	44,305,700	35,039,700
R&D Expense						
Operating Income						
Operating Margin %						
SGA Expense						
Net Income				1,152,830	3,260,480	2,604,020
Operating Cash Flow						
Capital Expenditure						
EBITDA						
Return on Assets %						
Return on Equity %						
Debt to Equity						

CONTACT INFORMATION:

Phone: 403 291-1000   Fax: 403 291-5509
Toll-Free: 888 480-9726
Address: 292154 Crosspointe Dr., Rocky View County, AB T4A 0V2 Canada

STOCK TICKER/OTHER:

Stock Ticker: Private   Exchange:
Employees: Fiscal Year Ends: 04/30
Parent Company: Apollo Tourism & Leisure Ltd

SALARIES/BONUSES:

Top Exec. Salary: $ Bonus: $
Second Exec. Salary: $ Bonus: $

OTHER THOUGHTS:

Estimated Female Officers or Directors:
Hot Spot for Advancement for Women/Minorities:

Care.com Inc

www.care.com

NAIC Code: 519130

TYPES OF BUSINESS:

Online Sitter Arrangement Service
Family Care Platform
Childcare
Senior Care
Housekeeping
Pet Care
Tutoring
Household Payroll and Tax Services

BRANDS/DIVISIONS/AFFILIATES:

IAC/InterActiveCorp
Breedlove and Associates LLC
Care.com HomePay

CONTACTS: Note: Officers with more than one job title may be intentionally listed here more than once.

Tim Allen, CEO
Michelle Arbov, CFO
Nancy Bushkin, Dir-Communications & PR
Roman Degtyur, CIO
Ryan Safarian, CTO

GROWTH PLANS/SPECIAL FEATURES:

Care.com, Inc. is an online marketplace for finding and managing family care. The firm's platform helps families address care needs such as child, senior and special needs care, as well as other non-medical family care needs including pet care, tutoring and housekeeping. More than half of the job postings needed are for part-time care services, with the remainder seeking full-time care. Examples of the types of care services families find in the marketplace include: experienced nannies to care for newborn children and help with laundry; daycare professionals seeking additional income by babysitting on occasional date nights; college students needed for watching/assisting grade-school children in relation to after-school pick-ups, driving to activities, homework and meal preparation; retired nurses who can drive an aging parent to routine medical appointments and assist with personal hygiene; and a pet lover to take family pets on walks and/or provide routine care while on vacation. Care.com's consumer matching solutions allow families to search for, connect with and hire qualified, vetted caregivers in a low-cost, reliable and convenient way. The website provides suggestions regarding personal profiles, skills and experience. The firm does not employ any caregiver and is not responsible for the conduct of site users. Care.com offers household payroll and tax services via Care.com HomePay, a service provided by Breedlove and Associates LLC, a Care.com company. Care.com itself is a subsidiary of IAC/InterActiveCorp

FINANCIAL DATA: Note: Data for latest year may not have been available at press time.

In U.S. $	2021	2020	2019	2018	2017	2016
Revenue		191,779,350	201,873,000	192,260,000	174,090,000	161,754,000
R&D Expense						
Operating Income						
Operating Margin %						
SGA Expense						
Net Income				52,890,000	10,663,000	7,046,000
Operating Cash Flow						
Capital Expenditure						
EBITDA						
Return on Assets %						
Return on Equity %						
Debt to Equity						

CONTACT INFORMATION:

Phone: 737 220-3114   Fax:
Toll-Free: 888-273-3356
Address: 1501 S. Mopac Expressway, #340, Austin, TX 78746 United States

STOCK TICKER/OTHER:

Stock Ticker: Subsidiary   Exchange:
Employees: 628   Fiscal Year Ends: 12/31
Parent Company: IAC/InterActiveCorp

SALARIES/BONUSES:

Top Exec. Salary: $ Bonus: $
Second Exec. Salary: $ Bonus: $

OTHER THOUGHTS:

Estimated Female Officers or Directors:
Hot Spot for Advancement for Women/Minorities:

Careem Networks FZ LLC

www.careem.com/en-ae

NAIC Code: 561599

TYPES OF BUSINESS:

Car Ride Dispatch Service, Mobile-App Based
Car Sharing
Delivery Services
Commute Sharing
Bike Sharing
Payments

BRANDS/DIVISIONS/AFFILIATES:

Uber Technologies Inc
Careem NOW
Careem NOW for Business
Careem for Business
Careem BUS
Careem PAY

CONTACTS: *Note: Officers with more than one job title may be intentionally listed here more than once.*

Mudassir Sheikha, CEO
Ashish Jain, Sr. VP-Finance
Ibrahim Manna, Mng. Dir.-Global Mkts.
Ruth Fletcher, VP-People
Adeeb Warsi, Mng. Dir.-Mobility of Things

GROWTH PLANS/SPECIAL FEATURES:

Careem Networks FZ, LLC provides ride-sharing and other services for the greater Middle East region. The firm enables customers to order a car online or by mobile app, track the ride in real-time, pay via credit card or cash and access receipts online. Rides can also be scheduled for particular times, and the repeat function makes it easy to schedule multiple future rides. Features within the platform include in-app support and fare estimation. Requirements for drivers include: being over 18 years of age with a valid driver's license; a smart phone; a vehicle that meets Careem standards; and a screening process of drug tests, police reports, credit checks and more. Drivers need to complete a registration form, which is located on the website, and will then be scheduled for a training session after the application has been reviewed and approved. When training is complete, drivers may begin working for Careem. The app supports Google navigation to guide where the customer is located, or the customer can guide the driver via personal contact such as a telephone call. Other apps by Careem include: Careem NOW, a food order and delivery service, including grocery and other essential products; Careem NOW for Businesses, offering delivery services from businesses to their customers; Careem for Business, a corporate travel service for pre-booking or on-demand rides; Careem BUS, an on-demand bus service for traveling within cities or for commuting; and Careem PAY, a payment program in which app users add their credit card to pay for purchases, deliveries and rides, as well as to send credit to family and friends. Careem operates in more than 100 cities across 14 countries. Careem operates as an independent subsidiary of Uber Technologies, Inc., and continues to operate independently from Uber.

FINANCIAL DATA: *Note: Data for latest year may not have been available at press time.*

In U.S. $	2021	2020	2019	2018	2017	2016
Revenue						
R&D Expense						
Operating Income						
Operating Margin %						
SGA Expense						
Net Income						
Operating Cash Flow						
Capital Expenditure						
EBITDA						
Return on Assets %						
Return on Equity %						
Debt to Equity						

CONTACT INFORMATION:

Phone: 971 44-405222   Fax:
Toll-Free:
Address: 2809, Shatha Tower, Dubai Media City, Dubai, 2668 United Arab Emirates

STOCK TICKER/OTHER:

Stock Ticker: Subsidiary
Employees:
Parent Company: Uber Technologies Inc

Exchange:
Fiscal Year Ends:

SALARIES/BONUSES:

Top Exec. Salary: $ Bonus: $
Second Exec. Salary: $ Bonus: $

OTHER THOUGHTS:

Estimated Female Officers or Directors:
Hot Spot for Advancement for Women/Minorities:

Caviar Inc

www.trycaviar.com

NAIC Code: 492210

TYPES OF BUSINESS:

Online Restaurant Meals Delivery Services
Meal Delivery Service
Catering
Online and Mobile App
Online and Mobile Ordering

BRANDS/DIVISIONS/AFFILIATES:

DoorDash Inc

CONTACTS: Note: Officers with more than one job title may be intentionally listed here more than once.

Tony Xu, CEO-DoorDash

GROWTH PLANS/SPECIAL FEATURES:

Caviar, Inc. offers an online and mobile app for ordering meals from popular local restaurants across the U.S. Caviar partners directly with restaurants to bring food to customers. Customers can order ahead of time or instantly, whether for one person or 100. Dietary options are available when ordering and checkout payment options can be automated for either immediate or at a specified time. Corporate accounts are available, enabling employees to order on their own, or enabling businesses to let employees order their own food within set spending limits, or enabling the order and billing by specific projects or departments. Catering services are available, with the capability of feeding groups of 10 or more than 200 via platter- or lunch box-style. Delivery comes through couriers who get paid by Caviar and in customer tips. Couriers are paid instantly and can work per their own schedule. Caviar partners with and delivers from restaurants located in cities such as Atlanta, Boston, Brooklyn, Chicago, Dallas, Houston, Los Angeles, Manhattan, Philadelphia, Queens, Sacramento, San Francisco Bay, Seattle, Portland and Washington, D.C. The company also offers gift cards, which are redeemable at any restaurant listed on Caviar. Caviar operates as a subsidiary of DoorDash, Inc.

Caviar, through parent DoorDash, offers its employees health and wellness benefits.

FINANCIAL DATA: Note: Data for latest year may not have been available at press time.

In U.S. $	2021	2020	2019	2018	2017	2016
Revenue						
R&D Expense						
Operating Income						
Operating Margin %						
SGA Expense						
Net Income						
Operating Cash Flow						
Capital Expenditure						
EBITDA						
Return on Assets %						
Return on Equity %						
Debt to Equity						

CONTACT INFORMATION:

Phone: Fax:
Toll-Free: 866 612-7021
Address: 1455 Market St., Ste. 600, San Francisco, CA 94103 United States

STOCK TICKER/OTHER:

Stock Ticker: Subsidiary   Exchange:
Employees: Fiscal Year Ends: 12/31
Parent Company: DoorDash Inc

SALARIES/BONUSES:

Top Exec. Salary: $ Bonus: $
Second Exec. Salary: $ Bonus: $

OTHER THOUGHTS:

Estimated Female Officers or Directors:
Hot Spot for Advancement for Women/Minorities:

CloudKitchen (City Storage Systems LLC) www.cloudkitchens.com

NAIC Code: 531120

TYPES OF BUSINESS:

Commercial Building Rental or Leasing
Ghost Kitchens
On-Demand Food Services
Food Delivery Services
Delivery-Only Kitchens
Food Order and Delivery App
Technology

BRANDS/DIVISIONS/AFFILIATES:

CONTACTS: Note: Officers with more than one job title may be intentionally listed here more than once.

Travis Kalanick, CEO

GROWTH PLANS/SPECIAL FEATURES:

City Storage Systems, LLC, doing business as CloudKitchen, provides software and logistics support for entrepreneurs, restaurant chains and local restaurants wanting to establish delivery-only kitchens, also referred to as ghost kitchens. The company's smart commercial kitchens are designed to meet the requirements of food and beverage businesses, with layouts that can be suited to specific needs. CloudKitchen equipment includes a three-compartment sink, hand wash sink, shared dry/cold/frozen storage, commercial exhaust hood, stainless steel work benches and commercial refrigeration. Infrastructure includes extraction and ventilation, natural gas and interlock system, ANSUL fire suppression system, single phase electricity, hygienic walls and skirting, and 24/7 building access. Services include fire-rated infrastructure, fire safety system, facility team, daily cleaning services, security services, Wi-Fi and phone line. CloudKitchen's software and logistics support enables clients to utilize a kitchen in days not months, and provides all the technology and support to seamlessly reach customers. The company helps facilitate demand generation via online ordering platforms (such as Uber Eats, Postmates, DoorDash, Caviar and GrubHub), cross-sell opportunities, consulting, marketing and more. The cost for a CloudKitchen is a small deposit plus the cost of equipment.

FINANCIAL DATA: Note: Data for latest year may not have been available at press time.

In U.S. $	2021	2020	2019	2018	2017	2016
Revenue						
R&D Expense						
Operating Income						
Operating Margin %						
SGA Expense						
Net Income						
Operating Cash Flow						
Capital Expenditure						
EBITDA						
Return on Assets %						
Return on Equity %						
Debt to Equity						

CONTACT INFORMATION:

Phone: 323 402-0877   Fax:
Toll-Free:
Address: 1842 W. Washington Blvd., Los Angeles, CA 90007 United States

STOCK TICKER/OTHER:

Stock Ticker: Private   Exchange:
Employees: Fiscal Year Ends:
Parent Company:

SALARIES/BONUSES:

Top Exec. Salary: $ Bonus: $
Second Exec. Salary: $ Bonus: $

OTHER THOUGHTS:

Estimated Female Officers or Directors:
Hot Spot for Advancement for Women/Minorities:

Connell Company (The)

NAIC Code: 532490

www.connellco.com

TYPES OF BUSINESS:

Mining Machinery & Equipment Leasing
Equipment Leasing Services
Industrial Equipment
Real Estate Development
Real Estate Management
Real Estate Investment
Hospitality Services
Work and Dining Spaces

BRANDS/DIVISIONS/AFFILIATES:

Connell Equipment Leasing Company
Connell Real Estate & Development Company
Park (The)
Table & Banter
Round Table Studios

GROWTH PLANS/SPECIAL FEATURES:

The Connell Company, operating through its various subsidiaries, is involved in the leasing of industry equipment, and the investment and development of real estate. The Connell Equipment Leasing Company offers lease financing for middle market equipment such as forklift trucks, cranes, tractors, automated guided vehicles and railcar movers. The firm comprises more than 12,000 pieces of equipment either on lease or in inventory. Connell Real Estate & Development Company owns interests in a diverse portfolio of Class A commercial office, retail, mixed-use and multifamily assets throughout the U.S. Connell Real Estate's hospitality division consists of The Park in northern New Jersey, an urban master-planned area that features office space, working and meeting spaces, dining and entertainment amenities, outdoor trail and parks, a game room, onsite health care and fitness spaces, as well as residential apartments and a hotel. Other brands and subsidiaries include Table & Banter, and Round Table Studios.

CONTACTS: *Note: Officers with more than one job title may be intentionally listed here more than once.*

Grover Connell, CEO

FINANCIAL DATA: *Note: Data for latest year may not have been available at press time.*

In U.S. $	2021	2020	2019	2018	2017	2016
Revenue						
R&D Expense						
Operating Income						
Operating Margin %						
SGA Expense						
Net Income						
Operating Cash Flow						
Capital Expenditure						
EBITDA						
Return on Assets %						
Return on Equity %						
Debt to Equity						

CONTACT INFORMATION:

Phone: 908 673-3700   Fax: 908-673-3800
Toll-Free:
Address: 300 Connell Dr., Berkeley Heights, NJ 07922 United States

STOCK TICKER/OTHER:

Stock Ticker: Private   Exchange:
Employees: Fiscal Year Ends: 12/31
Parent Company:

SALARIES/BONUSES:

Top Exec. Salary: $ Bonus: $
Second Exec. Salary: $ Bonus: $

OTHER THOUGHTS:

Estimated Female Officers or Directors:
Hot Spot for Advancement for Women/Minorities:

Convoy Inc

convoy.com

NAIC Code: 511210A

TYPES OF BUSINESS:

Computer Software: Supply Chain & Logistics
Freight Hauling Jobs
Trucking App
Digital Freight Technology
Machine Learning and Automation
Freight Brokering
Freight Shipping Mobile App
Brokering Services

BRANDS/DIVISIONS/AFFILIATES:

CONTACTS: *Note: Officers with more than one job title may be intentionally listed here more than once.*

Dan Lewis, CEO
Mark Okerstrom, Pres.
Melissa McCann-Tilton, Chief Revenue Officer
Brooks McMahon, Chief Bus. Dev. Officer
Maggie Brady, Dir.-People
Dorothy Li, CTO
Grant Goodale, Carrier Experience Officer

GROWTH PLANS/SPECIAL FEATURES:

Convoy, Inc. develops technology for shippers and carriers. The company's digital freight network utilizes machine learning and automation to connect shippers and carriers so that millions of truckloads can be moved. Convoy claims that its automated reloads program bundles multiple truckload shipments into one job and therefore decreases CO_2 emissions created by empty miles in freight. The Convoy app enables commercial truck owners to search and book jobs on-demand rather than wait for a broker to provide load-hauling work on their behalf. Pay is completed a day or two after the job is completed. For shippers, Convoy automates the matching, pricing and scheduling of trucks, and through its approach to carrier compliance, strives to get loads delivered safely and on time. Brokers can also utilize Convoy, which offers automated brokering technology for load matching, and features GPS load tracking, digital document management and carrier equipment. Thus, the broker remains the broker of record on shipments. All-in rates for each shipment are visible before accepting bids, and pay occurs when loads are successfully booked. Investors of Convoy include, but are not limited to, generation_, Y Combinator, T.RowePrice, greylockpartners, capitalG and Baillie Gifford.

Convoy offers its employees health benefits, 401(k), commuter benefits and flexible time off.

FINANCIAL DATA: *Note: Data for latest year may not have been available at press time.*

In U.S. $	2021	2020	2019	2018	2017	2016
Revenue	650,000,000	630,000,000	600,000,000	300,000,000		
R&D Expense						
Operating Income						
Operating Margin %						
SGA Expense						
Net Income						
Operating Cash Flow						
Capital Expenditure						
EBITDA						
Return on Assets %						
Return on Equity %						
Debt to Equity						

CONTACT INFORMATION:

Phone: 425 214-1769   Fax:
Toll-Free:
Address: 1301 2nd Ave., Ste. 1300, Seattle, WA 98101 United States

STOCK TICKER/OTHER:

Stock Ticker: Private
Employees: 1,050
Parent Company:

Exchange:
Fiscal Year Ends: 12/31

SALARIES/BONUSES:

Top Exec. Salary: $ Bonus: $
Second Exec. Salary: $ Bonus: $

OTHER THOUGHTS:

Estimated Female Officers or Directors:
Hot Spot for Advancement for Women/Minorities:

Custom Truck One Source Inc

www.customtruck.com

NAIC Code: 532412

TYPES OF BUSINESS:

Construction, Mining, and Forestry Machinery and Equipment Rental and Leasing

BRANDS/DIVISIONS/AFFILIATES:

GROWTH PLANS/SPECIAL FEATURES:

Custom Truck One Source Inc is a one-stop-shop provider of specialty equipment in the electric utility transmission and distribution, telecom, rail, and infrastructure end-markets in North America. The company's segment includes Equipment Rental Solutions (ERS), Truck and Equipment Sales (TES), and Aftermarket Parts and Services (APS). It generates maximum revenue from the TES segment. Geographically, it derives a majority of revenue from the United States.

CONTACTS: Note: Officers with more than one job title may be intentionally listed here more than once.

Fredrick Ross, CEO
Brad Meader, CFO
Marshall Heinberg, Chairman of the Board
Raymond Barrett, Chief Accounting Officer
Jim Carlsen, Chief Information Officer
Ryan McMonagle, COO
Thomas Rich, Executive VP, Divisional
Michael Turner, Executive VP, Divisional
Adam Haubenreich, General Counsel
Joseph Ross, President, Divisional
Joshua Boone, Vice President, Divisional

FINANCIAL DATA: Note: Data for latest year may not have been available at press time.

In U.S. $	2021	2020	2019	2018	2017	2016
Revenue	1,167,154,000	302,739,000	264,035,000	246,297,000		
R&D Expense						
Operating Income	9,863,000	26,786,000	46,142,000	43,604,000		
Operating Margin %	.01%	.09%	.17%	.18%		
SGA Expense	155,783,000	46,409,000	37,284,000	34,959,000		
Net Income	-181,501,000	-21,277,000	-27,052,000	-15,526,000		
Operating Cash Flow	138,926,000	42,829,000	18,792,000	41,040,000		
Capital Expenditure	188,389,000	67,546,000	106,641,000	59,235,000		
EBITDA	104,840,000	96,738,000	107,095,000	110,015,000		
Return on Assets %						
Return on Equity %						
Debt to Equity	1.57%					

CONTACT INFORMATION:

Phone: 816 241-4888   Fax:
Toll-Free: 800-252-0043
Address: 6714 Pointe Inverness Way, Ste. 220, Fort Wayne, IN 46804 United States

STOCK TICKER/OTHER:

Stock Ticker: CTOS   Exchange: NYS
Employees: 380   Fiscal Year Ends: 12/31
Parent Company:

SALARIES/BONUSES:

Top Exec. Salary: $621,154   Bonus: $66,716
Second Exec. Salary: Bonus: $49,124
$469,231

OTHER THOUGHTS:

Estimated Female Officers or Directors:
Hot Spot for Advancement for Women/Minorities:

Decorilla Inc

www.decorilla.com

NAIC Code: 541410

TYPES OF BUSINESS:

Interior Design Services
Ecommerce Interior Design Platform
Professional Designer Contact
Design Concept Proposal
Virtual Design

BRANDS/DIVISIONS/AFFILIATES:

CONTACTS: *Note: Officers with more than one job title may be intentionally listed here more than once.*

Angieska Wilk, CEO
Anna Tatsioni, Dir.-Oper.
Joshua van Aalst, Dir.-Innovation
Joshua Shammay, Dir.-Code

GROWTH PLANS/SPECIAL FEATURES:

Decorilla, Inc. operates an online platform that connects customers with professional home designers. Decorilla combines traditional in-home interior design with technology in order to make design affordable and risk-free. The company's service includes: a multiple design concept proposal, exclusive discounts of up to 45% at over 200 stores, a team of designers selected and vetted for each project, fixed prices which are approximately 80% less than traditional interior design, 100% satisfaction guarantee, 3D and VR realistic design concepts and in-home assistance in most major cities throughout the U.S. Flat rate prices are offered online for services that range from a hallway, entry space, bedroom to an entire house, patio or business office. Custom design packages range from $75 per hour to flat rate packages starting at $449. U.S. locations include Atlanta, Austin, Boston, Chicago, Dallas, Denver, Houston, Los Angeles, Miami, New Jersey, New York, Orange County, Orlando, Palo Alto, Phoenix, Pittsburgh, Richmond, Sacramento, San Diego, San Francisco, San Jose, Seattle, Tampa, Virginia and Washington, and many other cities. Decorilla offers virtual services for customers outside of its locations.

FINANCIAL DATA: *Note: Data for latest year may not have been available at press time.*

In U.S. $	2021	2020	2019	2018	2017	2016
Revenue						
R&D Expense						
Operating Income						
Operating Margin %						
SGA Expense						
Net Income						
Operating Cash Flow						
Capital Expenditure						
EBITDA						
Return on Assets %						
Return on Equity %						
Debt to Equity						

CONTACT INFORMATION:

Phone: 502 316-2968   Fax:
Toll-Free: 877 332-6760
Address: 230 Park Ave., Fl. 3, New York, NY 10169 United States

STOCK TICKER/OTHER:

Stock Ticker: Private   Exchange:
Employees: Fiscal Year Ends:
Parent Company:

SALARIES/BONUSES:

Top Exec. Salary: $ Bonus: $
Second Exec. Salary: $ Bonus: $

OTHER THOUGHTS:

Estimated Female Officers or Directors:
Hot Spot for Advancement for Women/Minorities:

Deliveroo plc

NAIC Code: 492210

deliveroo.co.uk

TYPES OF BUSINESS:

On Demand Food Delivery
Food Delivery Service
Online Ordering
Grocery Delivery
Bike Rider Delivery Service
Retail Kiosk Grocery Store
Bespoke Kitchens

BRANDS/DIVISIONS/AFFILIATES:

Deliveroo
Editions
Deliveroo HOP

CONTACTS: *Note: Officers with more than one job title may be intentionally listed here more than once.*

Will Shu, CEO
Eric French, COO
David Hancock, Interim CFO
Caleb Merkl, Chief People Officer
Devesh Mishra, CTO

GROWTH PLANS/SPECIAL FEATURES:

Deliveroo plc offers an on-demand food delivery service called Deliveroo, operating in 11 markets worldwide. The delivery platform connects local consumers, restaurants and grocers, as well as bike riders who deliver the food ordered. More than 160,000 restaurants and 13,000 grocers are partners of Deliveroo. The firm's Editions kitchen concept enables partners to prepare food for customers at delivery-only kitchens created by Deliveroo. There are more than 300 Edition kitchens worldwide, with each designed for any type of cuisine. A percentage fee covers upkeep costs, marketing support and a growth manager for building the preparer's own brand. Deliveroo has built technology to simultaneously complete hundreds of thousands of order across the globe. Delivery riders have full flexibility in when and where they work, as well as what orders to accept. Free accident insurance is provided to riders, and additional benefits are offered depending on location. In late-2022, Deliveroo launched Deliveroo HOP, a new brick-and-mortar grocery store concept in London, U.K. that enables customers to shop in-store by ordering through digital kiosks, or to order online and have the groceries delivered via riders. The Deliveroo HOP store comprised approximately 1,750 grocery items.

FINANCIAL DATA: *Note: Data for latest year may not have been available at press time.*

In U.S. $	2021	2020	2019	2018	2017	2016
Revenue	221,778,000	1,616,772,976	1,012,292,880	604,269,000	373,899,000	158,154,000
R&D Expense						
Operating Income						
Operating Margin %						
SGA Expense						
Net Income	-369,631,000	-302,907,332	-417,219,960	-294,428,000	-247,601,000	-158,785,000
Operating Cash Flow						
Capital Expenditure						
EBITDA						
Return on Assets %						
Return on Equity %						
Debt to Equity						

CONTACT INFORMATION:

Phone: 44 20 3699 9977   Fax:
Toll-Free:
Address: 1 Cousin Ln., The River Bldg., Level 1, London, EC4R 3TE United Kingdom

STOCK TICKER/OTHER:

Stock Ticker: ROO   Exchange: London
Employees: 2,060   Fiscal Year Ends: 12/31
Parent Company:

SALARIES/BONUSES:

Top Exec. Salary: $ Bonus: $
Second Exec. Salary: $ Bonus: $

OTHER THOUGHTS:

Estimated Female Officers or Directors:
Hot Spot for Advancement for Women/Minorities:

Sales, profits and employees may be estimates. Financial information, benefits and other data can change quickly and may vary from those stated here.

DiDi Global Inc

www.didiglobal.com

NAIC Code: 561599

TYPES OF BUSINESS:

Car Ride Dispatch Service, Mobile App-Based
Mobility Technology
Mobile Apps
Ride Hailing
Taxi Hailing
Shared Mobility
Automotive Solutions
Artificial Intelligence

BRANDS/DIVISIONS/AFFILIATES:

DiDi
DiDi Finance
DiDi Consumer Loans
DiDi Driver Insurance

GROWTH PLANS/SPECIAL FEATURES:

DiDi Global Inc is a mobility technology platform. It is building four key components of its platform that work together to improve the consumer experience: shared mobility, auto solutions, electric mobility, and autonomous driving. It is a go-to brand in China for shared mobility, providing consumers with a range of safe, affordable, and convenient mobility services, including ride-hailing, taxi-hailing, chauffeur, hitch, and other forms of shared mobility. The company operates in three segments: China Mobility, which mainly includes ride-hailing services to riders, and also acts as an agent by connecting end-users to service providers who provide taxi hailing, chauffeur, hitch, and other services; International; and Other Initiatives.

CONTACTS: Note: Officers with more than one job title may be intentionally listed here more than once.

Will Wei Cheng, CEO
Jean Qing Liu, Pres.

FINANCIAL DATA: Note: Data for latest year may not have been available at press time.

In U.S. $	2021	2020	2019	2018	2017	2016
Revenue	25,141,000,000	20,499,580,000	22,387,030,000	19,566,970,000		
R&D Expense	1,361,659,000	913,611,600	773,408,000	633,119,600		
Operating Income	-6,602,801,000	-1,994,177,000	-1,158,991,000	-1,799,588,000		
Operating Margin %	-.26%	-.10%	-.05%	-.09%		
SGA Expense	6,606,288,000	2,702,806,000	1,982,820,000	1,713,268,000		
Net Income	-7,136,672,000	-1,520,733,000	-1,407,046,000	-2,166,266,000		
Operating Cash Flow	-1,940,073,000	164,536,500	208,942,600	-1,334,729,000		
Capital Expenditure	957,491,400	838,734,800	325,781,800	793,117,600		
EBITDA	-6,196,812,000	-796,243,000	-867,653,600	-1,831,586,000		
Return on Assets %						
Return on Equity %						
Debt to Equity	.02%					

CONTACT INFORMATION:

Phone: 86 40 0766 6998   Fax:
Toll-Free:
Address: No. 1 Blk B, No. 8 Dongbeiwang W. Rd., Haidian Dist., Beijing, Beijing 100000 China

STOCK TICKER/OTHER:

Stock Ticker: DIDIY
Employees: 15,914
Parent Company:

Exchange: PINX
Fiscal Year Ends: 12/31

SALARIES/BONUSES:

Top Exec. Salary: $ Bonus: $
Second Exec. Salary: $ Bonus: $

OTHER THOUGHTS:

Estimated Female Officers or Directors:
Hot Spot for Advancement for Women/Minorities:

Doctor On Demand Inc

NAIC Code: 621111

www.doctorondemand.com

TYPES OF BUSINESS:

Online Medical Services
TeleHealth Platform
Online and Mobile Health Care
Mental Health Care
Employer/Employee Care
Healthcare Matching Technology

BRANDS/DIVISIONS/AFFILIATES:

Included Health Inc

CONTACTS: *Note: Officers with more than one job title may be intentionally listed here more than once.*

Owen Tripp, CEO

GROWTH PLANS/SPECIAL FEATURES:

Doctor On Demand, Inc. operates an online platform that connects patients (with or without insurance) with physicians throughout the U.S. The platform enables video chat concerning medical advice, preventive care and various medical conditions, including cold, flu, sore throat, urinary tract infections, travel problems, sports injuries, skin issues, pediatrics, lactation issues, psychological problems, diarrhea, vomiting and eye problems. More serious or life-threatening conditions require a visit to a doctor or hospital and cannot be addressed via video chat. Therefore, Doctor On Demand's website offers connections to physicians in relation to urgent care, chronic conditions, lab and screening results, preventive care and more. Mental health connections include physicians who specialize in addition, depression, mood issues, therapy to help with life issues, trauma and loss, stress and anxiety, and medication management. Doctor On Demand also partners with employers to deliver care when and where employees need it, 24/7. For health plans, the firm provides nationwide access to care, anywhere, anytime; and for partners, it works closely in the enterprise ecosystem, aligning objectives and maximizing value for clients and patients. Doctor On Demand operates within Included Health, Inc.

FINANCIAL DATA: *Note: Data for latest year may not have been available at press time.*

In U.S. $	2021	2020	2019	2018	2017	2016
Revenue		19,500,000	10,552,500	10,050,000	10,000,000	6,800,000
R&D Expense						
Operating Income						
Operating Margin %						
SGA Expense						
Net Income						
Operating Cash Flow						
Capital Expenditure						
EBITDA						
Return on Assets %						
Return on Equity %						
Debt to Equity						

CONTACT INFORMATION:

Phone: 415 504-3838   Fax:
Toll-Free: 800 997-6196
Address: 600 California St., Ste. 15-019, San Francisco, CA 94109
United States

STOCK TICKER/OTHER:

Stock Ticker: Private
Employees: 350
Parent Company: Included Health Inc

Exchange:
Fiscal Year Ends: 12/31

SALARIES/BONUSES:

Top Exec. Salary: $ Bonus: $
Second Exec. Salary: $ Bonus: $

OTHER THOUGHTS:

Estimated Female Officers or Directors:
Hot Spot for Advancement for Women/Minorities:

Dolly Inc

NAIC Code: 484210

dolly.com

TYPES OF BUSINESS:
On-Demand Moving Services
On-Demand Local Moving Services
Delivery Marketplace
Online Booking
Mobile App
Moving Help
Delivery Management

BRANDS/DIVISIONS/AFFILIATES:
Updater Inc
Lighthouse

CONTACTS: *Note: Officers with more than one job title may be intentionally listed here more than once.*
Michael Howell, CEO
Jay Sackos, VP

GROWTH PLANS/SPECIAL FEATURES:
Dolly, Inc. has developed and operates an on-demand local moving and delivery marketplace that connects Dolly users with truck owners who are ready to help. The service includes loading, hauling and/or delivering items that need to be moved. For those not needing a truck, but muscle strength, Dolly helpers can assist with many home projects, including furniture or appliance relocation/removal, or loading/unloading a box truck. Dolly helpers are independent contractors who are background checked, reviewed and backed by a commercial insurance policy. Helpers do not have 4-hour delivery windows but set agreed-upon schedules between themselves and Dolly customers. Guaranteed pricing is provided upfront before booking, with pay, tip and review available on the Dolly app or online website. There are more than 2,000 Dolly helpers willing to help with an apartment move, retail store delivery, furniture donation, storage unit move, mattress removal, office move and more. Dolly's services are available in 45 cities nationwide, to individuals and retailers. Lighthouse is Dolly's delivery platform, and is secure, customizable and web-accessible, creating a one-stop-shop for managing and analyzing Dolly deliveries. Dolly operates as a subsidiary of Updater, Inc.

FINANCIAL DATA: *Note: Data for latest year may not have been available at press time.*

In U.S. $	2021	2020	2019	2018	2017	2016
Revenue						
R&D Expense						
Operating Income						
Operating Margin %						
SGA Expense						
Net Income						
Operating Cash Flow						
Capital Expenditure						
EBITDA						
Return on Assets %						
Return on Equity %						
Debt to Equity						

CONTACT INFORMATION:
Phone: 312625-5355   Fax:
Toll-Free:
Address: 901 5th Ave., Ste. 600, Seattle, WA 98104 United States

STOCK TICKER/OTHER:
Stock Ticker: Subsidiary   Exchange:
Employees: 27   Fiscal Year Ends: 12/31
Parent Company: Updater Inc

SALARIES/BONUSES:
Top Exec. Salary: $ Bonus: $
Second Exec. Salary: $ Bonus: $

OTHER THOUGHTS:
Estimated Female Officers or Directors:
Hot Spot for Advancement for Women/Minorities:

DoorDash Inc

www.doordash.com

NAIC Code: 492210

TYPES OF BUSINESS:

Online Restaurant Meals Delivery Services

BRANDS/DIVISIONS/AFFILIATES:

Caviar Inc

GROWTH PLANS/SPECIAL FEATURES:

Founded in 2013 and headquartered in San Francisco, DoorDash is an online food order demand aggregator. Consumers can use its app to order food on-demand for pickup or delivery from merchants mainly in the U.S. The firm provides a marketplace for the merchants to create a presence online, market their offerings, and meet demand by making the offerings available for pickup or delivery. The firm provides similar service to businesses in addition to restaurants, such as grocery, retail, pet supplies, and flowers. At the end of 2020, DoorDash had over 450,000 merchants, 20 million consumers, and over 1 million dashers on its platform. In 2020, the firm generated $24.7 billion in gross order volume (up 207% year over year) and $2.9 billion in revenue (up 226%).

The company offers its employees health, dental and vision coverage; unlimited PTO; flexible hours; meal and delivery perks; and gym membership stipends.

CONTACTS: Note: Officers with more than one job title may be intentionally listed here more than once.

Tony Xu, CEO
Prabir Adarkar, CFO
Gordon Lee, Chief Accounting Officer
Keith Yandell, Chief Legal Officer
Stanley Tang, Co-Founder
Andy Fang, Co-Founder
Christopher Payne, COO

FINANCIAL DATA: Note: Data for latest year may not have been available at press time.

In U.S. $	2021	2020	2019	2018	2017	2016
Revenue	4,888,000,000	2,886,000,000	885,000,000	291,000,000		
R&D Expense	430,000,000	321,000,000	107,000,000	51,000,000		
Operating Income	-452,000,000	-436,000,000	-616,000,000	-210,000,000		
Operating Margin %	- .09%	- .15%	- .70%	- .72%		
SGA Expense	2,416,000,000	1,513,000,000	839,000,000	213,000,000		
Net Income	-468,000,000	-461,000,000	-667,000,000	-204,000,000		
Operating Cash Flow	692,000,000	252,000,000	-467,000,000	-159,000,000		
Capital Expenditure	237,000,000	159,000,000	92,000,000	16,000,000		
EBITDA	-293,000,000	-306,000,000	-634,000,000	-194,000,000		
Return on Assets %						
Return on Equity %						
Debt to Equity	.08%	0.051				

CONTACT INFORMATION:

Phone: 650 487-3970   Fax:
Toll-Free: 844-285-0248
Address: 303 2nd St., S. Tower, Fl. 8, San Francisco, CA 94107 United States

STOCK TICKER/OTHER:

Stock Ticker: DASH   Exchange: NYS
Employees: 8,600   Fiscal Year Ends:
Parent Company:

SALARIES/BONUSES:

Top Exec. Salary: $350,000   Bonus: $
Second Exec. Salary: $350,000   Bonus: $

OTHER THOUGHTS:

Estimated Female Officers or Directors:
Hot Spot for Advancement for Women/Minorities:

EatWith Media Ltd

www.eatwith.com

NAIC Code: 519130

TYPES OF BUSINESS:

Online Private Dining Experience Arrangement
Meal-Sharing
Culture Experiences
Online Booking
Immersive Travel

BRANDS/DIVISIONS/AFFILIATES:

VizEat SARLU

CONTACTS: *Note: Officers with more than one job title may be intentionally listed here more than once.*

Jean-Michel Petit, CEO
Camille Rumani, COO
Fernando Beck, CTO

GROWTH PLANS/SPECIAL FEATURES:

EatWith Media Ltd., owned by VizEat SARLU, is a global marketplace for communal dining, connecting chefs and people for unique dining experiences. The firm's strategy creates economic opportunity for culinary entrepreneurs who want to share their passion and monetize their craft. EatWith hosts are chefs who set their own menu and dining schedules, having the capability to earn up to $700 for each hosted event. EatWith enables users to connect with 25,000 hosts located across 130 countries worldwide. Each chef listed on the dining platform filled out an online application, and once reviewed and considered by EatWith, threw a demo event and was approved. Guests are able to check out the entrepreneur's cooking skills and his/her ability to wine and dine as a host. Selected and approved hosts have access to EatWith incentive programs, chef mentors and more, all for the purpose of developing and growing as an entrepreneur.

FINANCIAL DATA: *Note: Data for latest year may not have been available at press time.*

In U.S. $	2021	2020	2019	2018	2017	2016
Revenue						
R&D Expense						
Operating Income						
Operating Margin %						
SGA Expense						
Net Income						
Operating Cash Flow						
Capital Expenditure						
EBITDA						
Return on Assets %						
Return on Equity %						
Debt to Equity						

CONTACT INFORMATION:

Phone: 972 3-540-7239   Fax:
Toll-Free:
Address: 40 Hanamal St., Tel Aviv, 68034 Israel

STOCK TICKER/OTHER:

Stock Ticker: Private   Exchange:
Employees: 34   Fiscal Year Ends:
Parent Company: VizEat SARLU

SALARIES/BONUSES:

Top Exec. Salary: $ Bonus: $
Second Exec. Salary: $ Bonus: $

OTHER THOUGHTS:

Estimated Female Officers or Directors:
Hot Spot for Advancement for Women/Minorities:

Sales, profits and employees may be estimates. Financial information, benefits and other data can change quickly and may vary from those stated here.

eHi Car Services Limited

www.1hai.cn

NAIC Code: 532111

TYPES OF BUSINESS:

Car Rental
Automobile Rental
Chauffeuring Services
Temporary Chinese Driving Permits
Business Transport Services
Event Transport Services
Rental Car Partnerships

BRANDS/DIVISIONS/AFFILIATES:

CONTACTS: *Note: Officers with more than one job title may be intentionally listed here more than once.*

Ray Ruiping Zhang, CEO
Leo Cai, Chief Strategy Officer
Nina Wu, VP-Human Resources
Chun Xie, CTO

GROWTH PLANS/SPECIAL FEATURES:

eHi Car Services Limited is an auto rental and chauffeuring company. eHi provides car rentals from more than 10,000 locations in over 500 cities, with a vehicle fleet of more than 200 models. The firm offers self-drive car rental services to individual customers and corporate clients. The company has a short-term program (less than one year) designed to match customers' short-term needs including weekend travels, business trips and replacement rentals. Its long-term program (one year or longer) is designed to benefit customers who need to rent a car on a daily basis, such as large organizations or government agencies. Applications for a temporary Chinese driving permit can be obtained through eHi. Additional services by eHi include airport pickup and drop-off, inter-office transfers and other types of business transportation, as well as chauffer services. Transportation can be scheduled for events such as conventions, promotional tours or special events to corporate clients. Through Enterprise Rent-A-Car, Alamo Rent-A-Car and National Car Rental, eHi offers international services for customers traveling abroad.

FINANCIAL DATA: *Note: Data for latest year may not have been available at press time.*

In U.S. $	2021	2020	2019	2018	2017	2016
Revenue	300,000,000	300,000,000	449,319,165	427,923,014	407,545,728	313,737,632
R&D Expense						
Operating Income						
Operating Margin %						
SGA Expense						
Net Income			19,665,142	18,908,791	18,181,530	4,929,354
Operating Cash Flow						
Capital Expenditure						
EBITDA						
Return on Assets %						
Return on Equity %						
Debt to Equity						

CONTACT INFORMATION:

Phone: 86 2164687000　　　Fax: 86 2154891121
Toll-Free:
Address: 388 Daduhe Road, Fl. 17, Bldg. 5, Shanghai, Shanghai 200062 China

STOCK TICKER/OTHER:

Stock Ticker: Private　　　　　　Exchange:
Employees: 7,000　　　　　　　　Fiscal Year Ends: 12/31
Parent Company:

SALARIES/BONUSES:

Top Exec. Salary: $　　　　Bonus: $
Second Exec. Salary: $　　　Bonus: $

OTHER THOUGHTS:

Estimated Female Officers or Directors:
Hot Spot for Advancement for Women/Minorities:

Enterprise Holdings Inc

www.enterpriseholdings.com

NAIC Code: 532111

TYPES OF BUSINESS:

Car & Truck Rental
Vanpool Services
Rental Car Services
Commercial Vehicle Rental
Ride-Sharing
Car-Sharing
Collection Car Rental

BRANDS/DIVISIONS/AFFILIATES:

Alamo Rent A Car
National Car Rental
Enterprise Rent-A-Car
Enterprise Car Sales
Enterprise Truck Rental
Exotic Car Collection by Enterprise
Enterprise CarShare

CONTACTS: Note: Officers with more than one job title may be intentionally listed here more than once.

Christine Taylor, CEO
David Nestor, COO
Rick Short, CFO
Randal Narike, Chief Strategy Officer
Shelley Roither, Sr. VP-Human Resources
Russ Willey, CIO
Lee Kaplan, Chief Admin. Officer
Matthew G. Darrah, Exec. VP-North American Oper.
Greg Stubblefield, Chief Strategy Officer
Patrick T. Farrell, Chief Comm. Officer
Rose Langhorst, Treas.
Steve Bloom, Pres., Enterprise Fleet Mgmt.
Jo Ann Taylor Kindle, Pres., Enterprise Holdings Foundation
Andrew C. Taylor, Chmn.
Greg Stubblefield, Exec. VP-Global Sales & Mktg.

GROWTH PLANS/SPECIAL FEATURES:

Enterprise Holdings, Inc. is the parent company of Alamo Rent A Car, National Car Rental and Enterprise Rent-A-Car car rental agencies. The company also owns Enterprise Car Sales, Enterprise Truck Rental and Exotic Car Collection by Enterprise, as well as the car/ride sharing Enterprise CarShare. The firm's combined rental fleet is the largest in the world, with approximately 2.1 million vehicles. Enterprise Holdings serves 10,000 fully-staffed neighborhood and airport locations in more than 90 countries and territories worldwide. Alamo Rent A Car is a budget rental car company catering to leisure and vacation customers, particularly international travelers visiting North America. Enterprise Holdings operates self-service kiosks throughout the U.S. National Car Rental is a premium rental brand that serves frequent business travelers and offers the Emerald Club frequent-renter benefits program. Enterprise Rent-A-Car offers vehicles for rent internationally. Enterprise Car Sales is a used-car reseller that provides non-negotiable pricing and after-market warranties on used cars acquired through trade-in or extracted from the rental fleet. Enterprise Truck Rental provides commercial-grade trucks such as ¾- to 1-ton pickups, cargo vans, straight trucks, as well as stake bed trucks (from 16 to 26 feet long), all equipped for commercial use. Exotic Car Collection enables customers to rent vehicles such as exotic sports cars and luxury sedans, including Ferrari, Maserati, Porsche, Bentley, Range Rover and more. Enterprise CarShare is a car sharing program that allows customers to rent a car for flexible periods of time through an online membership portal.

Enterprise Holdings offers its employees medical, dental and vision insurance; prescription drug coverage; flexible spending accounts; life insurance; and long-term disability plans.

FINANCIAL DATA: Note: Data for latest year may not have been available at press time.

In U.S. $	2021	2020	2019	2018	2017	2016
Revenue	23,900,000,000	22,500,000,000	25,900,000,000	24,100,000,000	22,300,000,000	20,900,000,000
R&D Expense						
Operating Income						
Operating Margin %						
SGA Expense						
Net Income						
Operating Cash Flow						
Capital Expenditure						
EBITDA						
Return on Assets %						
Return on Equity %						
Debt to Equity						

CONTACT INFORMATION:

Phone: 314-512-2880   Fax: 314-512-4706
Toll-Free:
Address: 600 Corporate Park Dr., St. Louis, MO 63105 United States

STOCK TICKER/OTHER:

Stock Ticker: Private   Exchange:
Employees: 96,000   Fiscal Year Ends: 03/31
Parent Company:

SALARIES/BONUSES:

Top Exec. Salary: $ Bonus: $
Second Exec. Salary: $ Bonus: $

OTHER THOUGHTS:

Estimated Female Officers or Directors: 5
Hot Spot for Advancement for Women/Minorities: Y

Fancy Hands Inc

www.fancyhands.com

NAIC Code: 519130

TYPES OF BUSINESS:

Internet Publishing and Broadcasting and Web Search Portals
Online Virtual Assistance Services
Assistance Matching Technology
Live Assistance
Developer Tools

BRANDS/DIVISIONS/AFFILIATES:

CONTACTS: *Note: Officers with more than one job title may be intentionally listed here more than once.*

Ted Roden, CEO

GROWTH PLANS/SPECIAL FEATURES:

Fancy Hands, Inc. operates a virtual assistance platform for those who need a dedicated assistant or want to delegate a task. The assistants are U.S.-based and perform assignments such as calling a cable/phone company to resolve a billing issue, researching and booking the best places to hold a work dinner, or locating a qualified SAT tutor for a student. For businesses, Fancy Hands' virtual assistants can perform personal tasks so that employers and employees can focus on productivity. Developers can build apps with the help of Fancy Hands' assistants and online tools. The company's application programming interface (API) enables developers to quickly build some of the most complex apps in the world just by providing plain text instructions to Fancy Hands, saying what type of structured data is preferred and how much they are willing to pay for the tasks. Examples of what can be built include: on-demand car service, food delivery service, an outbound call center, a sales lead generation service or an appointment scheduling service. Developers can generate their API credentials and have immediate access to Fancy Hands' interactive API Explorer; or have access to its official API documentation. Recurring requests can be scheduled, and all requests can be made via phone, web, text, email or mobile app. Price plans are offered on a monthly or annual basis, and depend on how often assistance would be needed.

FINANCIAL DATA: *Note: Data for latest year may not have been available at press time.*

In U.S. $	2021	2020	2019	2018	2017	2016
Revenue		80,000,000	12,600,000	12,000,000	11,000,000	10,000,000
R&D Expense						
Operating Income						
Operating Margin %						
SGA Expense						
Net Income						
Operating Cash Flow						
Capital Expenditure						
EBITDA						
Return on Assets %						
Return on Equity %						
Debt to Equity						

CONTACT INFORMATION:

Phone: 374 836-9566   Fax:
Toll-Free:
Address: 200 E 10th St., Ste. 718, New York, NY 10003 United States

STOCK TICKER/OTHER:

Stock Ticker: Private   Exchange:
Employees: 140   Fiscal Year Ends: 12/31
Parent Company:

SALARIES/BONUSES:

Top Exec. Salary: $ Bonus: $
Second Exec. Salary: $ Bonus: $

OTHER THOUGHTS:

Estimated Female Officers or Directors:
Hot Spot for Advancement for Women/Minorities:

First Ship Lease Trust (FSL Trust)   www.firstshipleasetrust.com

NAIC Code: 532411

TYPES OF BUSINESS:
Commercial Air, Rail, and Water Transportation Equipment Rental and Leasing

BRANDS/DIVISIONS/AFFILIATES:
FSL Trust Management Pte Ltd

GROWTH PLANS/SPECIAL FEATURES:
First Ship Lease Trust or FSL is a Singapore-based firm engaged in the shipping business. The company operates a portfolio of approximately 20 ocean-going vessels comprising container ships and a variety of tankers. It holds vessels acquired through special purpose companies, on trust for unitholders of FSL Trust. Bareboat charter lease income relates to lease income derived from operating leases which accounts for the majority of its revenues through its operations in Europe and Asia.

CONTACTS: Note: Officers with more than one job title may be intentionally listed here more than once.
Roger Woods, CEO
Markus Wender, CFO
Stathis Topouzoglou, Chmn.

FINANCIAL DATA: Note: Data for latest year may not have been available at press time.

In U.S. $	2021	2020	2019	2018	2017	2016
Revenue	24,975,000	48,332,000	73,107,000	67,046,000	81,499,000	98,144,000
R&D Expense						
Operating Income	977,000	14,350,000	21,862,000	9,273,000	15,123,000	26,477,000
Operating Margin %	.04%	.30%	.30%	.14%	.19%	.27%
SGA Expense	2,447,000	3,400,000	4,460,000	4,305,000	4,515,000	3,029,000
Net Income	-1,522,000	6,246,000	10,131,000	-18,986,000	-73,888,000	-30,995,000
Operating Cash Flow	5,683,000	37,971,000	44,433,000	37,468,000	47,540,000	66,971,000
Capital Expenditure	69,080,000	24,240,000	23,829,000	46,000	3,451,000	2,220,000
EBITDA	4,870,000	23,293,000	41,228,000	20,799,000	-28,309,000	21,435,000
Return on Assets %						
Return on Equity %						
Debt to Equity	.20%	0.103	0.17	0.516		

CONTACT INFORMATION:
Phone: 65 6836-3000   Fax: 65 6836-6001
Toll-Free:
Address: 9 Temasek Blvd., #19-03 Suntec Tower Two, Singapore, 038989 Singapore

STOCK TICKER/OTHER:
Stock Ticker: FSLUF
Employees:
Parent Company:

Exchange: PINX
Fiscal Year Ends: 12/31

SALARIES/BONUSES:
Top Exec. Salary: $ Bonus: $
Second Exec. Salary: $ Bonus: $

OTHER THOUGHTS:
Estimated Female Officers or Directors:
Hot Spot for Advancement for Women/Minorities:

Sales, profits and employees may be estimates. Financial information, benefits and other data can change quickly and may vary from those stated here.

Fiverr International Limited

NAIC Code: 519130

www.fiverr.com

TYPES OF BUSINESS:

Online Freelance Work Arrangement Services
Outsourcing
eCommerce

GROWTH PLANS/SPECIAL FEATURES:

Fiverr International Ltd is involved in buying and selling digital services in the same fashion as physical goods on an e-commerce platform. It is set out to design a digital marketplace that is built with a comprehensive SKU-like services catalog and a search, finds, and order process that mirrors a typical e-commerce transaction. The service offerings of the company include Graphics and Design, Digital Marketing, Wiring and Translation, and Video and Animation among others.

BRANDS/DIVISIONS/AFFILIATES:

www.fiverr.com
Fiverr Pro
AND CO
Learn
ClearVoice

CONTACTS: Note: Officers with more than one job title may be intentionally listed here more than once.

Micha Kaufman, CEO

FINANCIAL DATA: Note: Data for latest year may not have been available at press time.

In U.S. $	2021	2020	2019	2018	2017	2016
Revenue	297,662,000	189,510,000	107,073,000	75,503,000	52,112,000	
R&D Expense	79,298,000	45,719,000	34,483,000	26,035,000	16,074,000	
Operating Income	-45,340,000	-11,810,000	-34,750,000	-36,469,000	-19,523,000	
Operating Margin %	- .15%	- .06%	- .32%	- .48%	- .37%	
SGA Expense	211,981,000	122,413,000	85,116,000	70,316,000	42,199,000	
Net Income	-65,012,000	-14,810,000	-33,539,000	-36,061,000	-19,324,000	
Operating Cash Flow	38,037,000	17,135,000	-13,944,000	-51,676,000	-5,263,000	
Capital Expenditure	2,578,000	4,035,000	1,755,000	1,597,000	3,397,000	
EBITDA	-38,464,000	-7,472,000	-31,179,000	-34,219,000	-18,433,000	
Return on Assets %						
Return on Equity %						
Debt to Equity	1.10%	1.066	0.017	0.052	0.15	

CONTACT INFORMATION:

Phone: 972-72-2280910   Fax:
Toll-Free:
Address: 8 Eliezer Kaplan St., Tel Aviv, 6473409 Israel

STOCK TICKER/OTHER:

Stock Ticker: FVRR   Exchange: NYS
Employees: 787   Fiscal Year Ends:
Parent Company:

SALARIES/BONUSES:

Top Exec. Salary: $ Bonus: $
Second Exec. Salary: $ Bonus: $

OTHER THOUGHTS:

Estimated Female Officers or Directors:
Hot Spot for Advancement for Women/Minorities:

FlipKey LLC

www.flipkey.com

NAIC Code: 561510

TYPES OF BUSINESS:

Travel Agencies
Online Vacation Rental Service
Online Booking
Online Property Listing
Rental Photos
Rental Reviews

BRANDS/DIVISIONS/AFFILIATES:

TripAdvisor Inc
TripAdvisor Rentals
www.flipkey.com

GROWTH PLANS/SPECIAL FEATURES:

FlipKey, Inc. provides a vacation rental marketplace with more than 300,000 properties to choose from throughout the world. FlipKey's website and mobile app features rentals such as a city-center studio, apartment, private island, ski chalet, beach house or other. Users search for rental options and submit a booking preference directly to the property manager or owner. Rental managers and owners are verified by the company's staff before being added to the FlipKey platform. Photos, travel reviews and ratings for listed properties are digitally presented. FlipKey also publishes ratings for travel-related items such as food blogs and national historic sites (in the U.S.). FlipKey is part of TripAdvisor Rentals, itself a subsidiary of TripAdvisor, Inc.

Parent TripAdvisor offers employees differentiated benefits depending on location.

CONTACTS: Note: Officers with more than one job title may be intentionally listed here more than once.

T.J. Mahony, CEO

FINANCIAL DATA: Note: Data for latest year may not have been available at press time.

In U.S. $	2021	2020	2019	2018	2017	2016
Revenue						
R&D Expense						
Operating Income						
Operating Margin %						
SGA Expense						
Net Income						
Operating Cash Flow						
Capital Expenditure						
EBITDA						
Return on Assets %						
Return on Equity %						
Debt to Equity						

CONTACT INFORMATION:

Phone: Fax:
Toll-Free: 877 354-7539
Address: 226 Causeway St., Fl. 2, Boston, MA 02114 United States

STOCK TICKER/OTHER:

Stock Ticker: Subsidiary   Exchange:
Employees: Fiscal Year Ends: 12/31
Parent Company: TripAdvisor Inc

SALARIES/BONUSES:

Top Exec. Salary: $ Bonus: $
Second Exec. Salary: $ Bonus: $

OTHER THOUGHTS:

Estimated Female Officers or Directors:
Hot Spot for Advancement for Women/Minorities:

Sales, profits and employees may be estimates. Financial information, benefits and other data can change quickly and may vary from those stated here.

Freelancer Limited

NAIC Code: 519130

www.freelancer.com

TYPES OF BUSINESS:

Online Freelance Work Arrangement Services

BRANDS/DIVISIONS/AFFILIATES:

Freelancer Limited
Freelancer.com
GetAFreelancer.com
LimeExchange
Scriptlance.com
Freelancer.de
Freelancer.co.uk
Rent-A-Coder

CONTACTS: *Note: Officers with more than one job title may be intentionally listed here more than once.*

Matt Barrie, CEO

GROWTH PLANS/SPECIAL FEATURES:

Freelancer Technology Pty Limited provides an online crowdsourcing marketplace from which freelancers can be hired. The Freelancer.com website enables people to hire or be hired for help with various tasks primarily in relation to technology, including websites, apps, designs, writing, product development, sales and more. Those who need to hire enter what needs to be done, and the site presents freelancers skilled in that area via profiles, ratings and portfolios. Examples of pricing include: logo design for $30 in one day, developing a website for $200 in nine days, 3D modeling for $110 in 28 days and graphic design for 460 in 10 days. Free quotes are presented by the freelancers. In addition, people can choose a design or product via contest on the Freelancer website. This is done by setting up a prize, launching a contest and having Freelancer members compete for the win. Registered users have posted millions of projects and contests in over 1,000 areas as diverse as those mentioned above, as well as marketing, copywriting, astrophysics, aerospace engineering and manufacturing. Freelancer.com owns several outsourcing marketplaces, including GetAFreelancer.com and EUFreelance.com, LimeExchange, Scriptlance.com, Freelancer.de, Freelancer.co.uk, Webmaster-talk.com, Rent-A-Coder and vWorker. Freelancer Technology operates as a subsidiary of Freelancer Limited. As of January 2022, Freelancer.com was connecting more than 57.8 million employers and freelancers in over 247 countries.

FINANCIAL DATA: *Note: Data for latest year may not have been available at press time.*

In U.S. $	2021	2020	2019	2018	2017	2016
Revenue			40,857,368	36,457,744	32,277,416	38,307,212
R&D Expense						
Operating Income						
Operating Margin %						
SGA Expense						
Net Income			-1,122,482	-1,046,992	-3,095,130	-855,762
Operating Cash Flow						
Capital Expenditure						
EBITDA						
Return on Assets %						
Return on Equity %						
Debt to Equity						

CONTACT INFORMATION:

Phone: 61-2969-29980   Fax:
Toll-Free:
Address: Level 20, World Square, 680 George St., Sydney, NSW 2000 Australia

STOCK TICKER/OTHER:

Stock Ticker: FLNCF   Exchange: OTC
Employees: 478   Fiscal Year Ends:
Parent Company: Freelancer Limited

SALARIES/BONUSES:

Top Exec. Salary: $ Bonus: $
Second Exec. Salary: $ Bonus: $

OTHER THOUGHTS:

Estimated Female Officers or Directors:
Hot Spot for Advancement for Women/Minorities:

FreshDirect LLC

www.freshdirect.com

NAIC Code: 454111

TYPES OF BUSINESS:

Online Grocery Sales
Home Grocery Delivery
Catering
Online Ordering
Business Grocery Delivery
Processing Facility

BRANDS/DIVISIONS/AFFILIATES:

CONTACTS: *Note: Officers with more than one job title may be intentionally listed here more than once.*

David McInerney, CEO
Tina Bourbeau, Exec. Chef
Amaury Garcia, Mgr.-Sortation

GROWTH PLANS/SPECIAL FEATURES:

FreshDirect, LLC is an online retail grocery business serving customers in New York City metropolitan area, with seasonal service to eastern Long Island and the New Jersey shore. FreshDirect offers fresh food and grocery items, including fruits and vegetables, meat, seafood, deli items, cheese, dairy, coffee, tea, bakery goods, pasta and frozen food as well as kosher and gluten free foods, local and organic produce, health and beauty items and wine. It also provides catering services and a full line of ready-to-heat meals prepared by its on-staff chefs. FreshDirect owns and operates a 500,000-square-foot processing facility, which enables the firm to process and ship fresh meats, produce and dairy products quickly and efficiently. The company is also able to offer lower prices, on average 25% lower than traditional retail grocers, due to the lack of intermediary distribution channels. There is a minimum order amount for home deliveries, and each order is charged a delivery fee depending on location. For offices, there is a minimum order amount and a delivery fee, Monday through Friday from 8 a.m. to 4p.m. Customers can also pick up their orders at the facility. FreshDirect offers gift cards. FreshDirect is 80%-owned by international supermarket operator Koninklijke Ahold Delhaize NV (Ahold Delhaize) and 20%-owned by Centerbridge Partners.

FreshDirect offers its employees health coverage, learning and development opportunities and company perks.

FINANCIAL DATA: *Note: Data for latest year may not have been available at press time.*

In U.S. $	2021	2020	2019	2018	2017	2016
Revenue	1,100,000,000	1,100,000,000	678,037,500	645,750,000	615,000,000	555,000,000
R&D Expense						
Operating Income						
Operating Margin %						
SGA Expense						
Net Income						
Operating Cash Flow						
Capital Expenditure						
EBITDA						
Return on Assets %						
Return on Equity %						
Debt to Equity						

CONTACT INFORMATION:

Phone: 718-928-1000   Fax: 718-433-0648
Toll-Free: 866-283-7374
Address: 2 Saint Anns Ave., Bronx, NY 10454 United States

STOCK TICKER/OTHER:

Stock Ticker: Subsidiary   Exchange:
Employees: 3,400   Fiscal Year Ends: 12/31
Parent Company: Ahold Delhaize

SALARIES/BONUSES:

Top Exec. Salary: $ Bonus: $
Second Exec. Salary: $ Bonus: $

OTHER THOUGHTS:

Estimated Female Officers or Directors: 1
Hot Spot for Advancement for Women/Minorities:

Sales, profits and employees may be estimates. Financial information, benefits and other data can change quickly and may vary from those stated here.

Freshly Inc

NAIC Code: 454111

www.freshly.com

TYPES OF BUSINESS:

Meal Delivery Service
Prepared Meals
Delivered Meals
Fresh Food
Online Ordering
Mobile App Ordering
Business and Partnership Meals

BRANDS/DIVISIONS/AFFILIATES:

Nestle SA
FreshlyFit
FreshlyWell

CONTACTS: *Note: Officers with more than one job title may be intentionally listed here more than once.*

Anna Fabrega, CEO

GROWTH PLANS/SPECIAL FEATURES:

Freshly, Inc. offers an online platform from which customers can order healthy meals prepared by local chefs and delivered to their home or business. The firm's plans range from four to 12 per week. The more meals ordered, the less they are per meal. Plans can be paused, canceled or changed at any time. Menus are updated weekly, and Freshly offers dozens of lunch and dinner options to choose from. Meals are delivered ready-to-eat and are never frozen, and come with nutritional information, a full ingredient list and heating instructions. They are packaged in a refrigerated recycled-materials box and shipped with ice packs to be kept cold. Shipments are delivered directly to the premises and left at the door if unanswered. Freshly accommodates a variety of dietary preferences, and its entire menu is free of gluten and peanuts. FreshlyFit specifically caters to active lifestyles, offering low-carb, high-protein meals. FreshlyWell provides tailored, freshly-prepared meals for making life easier, including on-site grab-and-go options or flexible meal delivery solutions. FreshlyWell offers its custom solutions to employers, healthcare systems, colleges and universities, health plans, senior living and other similar partnerships. Examples of meals include: Homestyle Chicken with Butternut Mac & Cheese, Penne Bolognese, Sausage Baked Penne with Sauteed Zucchini and Spinach, Chicken Tikka Masala, Slow-cooked Beef Chili, Turkey Shepherd's Pie and Southwest Veggie Bowl. Meals are made with all-natural ingredients, are high in protein and nutrient-dense vegetables. eGifts are available. Freshly is a subsidiary of Nestle SA.

FINANCIAL DATA: *Note: Data for latest year may not have been available at press time.*

In U.S. $	2021	2020	2019	2018	2017	2016
Revenue						
R&D Expense						
Operating Income						
Operating Margin %						
SGA Expense						
Net Income						
Operating Cash Flow						
Capital Expenditure						
EBITDA						
Return on Assets %						
Return on Equity %						
Debt to Equity						

CONTACT INFORMATION:

Phone: 212 702-8791   Fax:
Toll-Free: 844 373-7459
Address: 115 E. 23rd St., New York, NY 10010-4508 United States

STOCK TICKER/OTHER:

Stock Ticker: Subsidiary   Exchange:
Employees: 1,100   Fiscal Year Ends:
Parent Company: Nestle SA

SALARIES/BONUSES:

Top Exec. Salary: $ Bonus: $
Second Exec. Salary: $ Bonus: $

OTHER THOUGHTS:

Estimated Female Officers or Directors:
Hot Spot for Advancement for Women/Minorities:

Full Truck Alliance Co Ltd (Manbang Group)   www.ymm56.com

NAIC Code: 561599

TYPES OF BUSINESS:

General Freight Trucking Dispatch Service, Mobile App-Based
Shipping
Truck Fleets
Software Platform
Dispatch

GROWTH PLANS/SPECIAL FEATURES:

Full Truck Alliance Co Ltd, through its subsidiaries, provides comprehensive services for shippers and truckers through its mobile and website platforms. Its principal operations are in the People's Republic of China. The group derives its revenues principally from shippers' and truckers' use of its platforms in connection with freight matching services and value-added services.

BRANDS/DIVISIONS/AFFILIATES:

Full Truck Alliance

CONTACTS: Note: Officers with more than one job title may be intentionally listed here more than once.

Hui Zhang, CEO

FINANCIAL DATA: Note: Data for latest year may not have been available at press time.

In U.S. $	2021	2020	2019	2018	2017	2016
Revenue	673,553,900	373,269,100	357,683,700			
R&D Expense	105,533,300	59,786,380	57,374,350			
Operating Income	-549,014,700	-522,787,200	-147,611,700			
Operating Margin %	- .82%	-1.40%	- .41%			
SGA Expense	738,845,600	635,354,900	230,332,200			
Net Income	-528,550,100	-501,941,200	-220,368,500			
Operating Cash Flow	-30,577,950	83,126,080	-133,634,900			
Capital Expenditure	6,250,995	7,674,752	1,506,776			
EBITDA	-516,752,000	-488,792,400	-209,085,600			
Return on Assets %						
Return on Equity %						
Debt to Equity						

CONTACT INFORMATION:

Phone: 400-862-5656   Fax:
Toll-Free:
Address: Bldg. A, No. 20 Fengxin Rd., Yuhuatai Dist., Nanjing, Jiangsu 210012 China

STOCK TICKER/OTHER:

Stock Ticker: YMM   Exchange: NYS
Employees: 7,103   Fiscal Year Ends:
Parent Company:

SALARIES/BONUSES:

Top Exec. Salary: $ Bonus: $
Second Exec. Salary: $ Bonus: $

OTHER THOUGHTS:

Estimated Female Officers or Directors:
Hot Spot for Advancement for Women/Minorities:

Sales, profits and employees may be estimates. Financial information, benefits and other data can change quickly and may vary from those stated here.

GEE Group Inc

NAIC Code: 561320

www.geegroup.com

TYPES OF BUSINESS:

Temporary Staffing Services

GROWTH PLANS/SPECIAL FEATURES:

GEE Group Inc is a provider of specialized staffing solutions across the United States. The company's operating segment includes Industrial Staffing Services and Professional Staffing Services. It generates maximum revenue from the Professional Staffing Services segment. The company provides the following services, direct hire placement services, temporary professional services staffing in the fields of information technology, accounting, finance and office, engineering, and medical, and temporary light industrial staffing.

BRANDS/DIVISIONS/AFFILIATES:

Ashley Ellis
Certes Financial Professionals
General Employment Enterprises
Omni One
Access Data Consulting Corporation
Agile Resources Inc
BMCH Inc
Paladin Consulting Inc

CONTACTS: *Note: Officers with more than one job title may be intentionally listed here more than once.*

Derek Dewan, CEO
Kim Thorpe, CFO
Alex Stuckey, Chief Administrative Officer

FINANCIAL DATA: *Note: Data for latest year may not have been available at press time.*

In U.S. $	2021	2020	2019	2018	2017	2016
Revenue	148,880,000	129,835,000	151,674,000	165,284,000	134,978,000	
R&D Expense						
Operating Income	6,490,000	-4,983,000	-653,000	5,554,000	1,524,000	
Operating Margin %	.04%	-.04%	.00%	.03%	.01%	
SGA Expense	41,651,000	44,401,000	46,739,000	47,406,000	39,498,000	
Net Income	6,000	-14,347,000	-17,763,000	-7,564,000	-2,372,000	
Operating Cash Flow	370,000	-2,247,000	-394,000	1,507,000	222,000	
Capital Expenditure	126,000	119,000	209,000	324,000	250,000	
EBITDA	10,342,000	3,769,000	982,000	9,051,000	1,558,000	
Return on Assets %						
Return on Equity %						
Debt to Equity	.04%	2.604	7.406	3.311	2.81	

CONTACT INFORMATION:

Phone: 630 954-0400   Fax: 630 954-0447
Toll-Free:
Address: 7751 Belfort Pkwy., Ste. 150, Jacksonville, FL 32256 United States

STOCK TICKER/OTHER:

Stock Ticker: JOB   Exchange: ASE
Employees: 271   Fiscal Year Ends: 09/30
Parent Company:

SALARIES/BONUSES:

Top Exec. Salary: $300,000   Bonus: $
Second Exec. Salary: $270,000   Bonus: $

OTHER THOUGHTS:

Estimated Female Officers or Directors:
Hot Spot for Advancement for Women/Minorities:

Getaround Inc

www.getaround.com

NAIC Code: 532111

TYPES OF BUSINESS:

Passenger Car Rental
Vehicle Sharing
Mobile App Booking
Online Booking
Peer-to-Peer Car Sharing
Insurance Coverage
Digital Technology

BRANDS/DIVISIONS/AFFILIATES:

CONTACTS: Note: Officers with more than one job title may be intentionally listed here more than once.

Sam Zaid, CEO
Tim Alderman, CFO

GROWTH PLANS/SPECIAL FEATURES:

Getaround, Inc. provides an online car-sharing or peer-to-peer car-sharing service that allows drivers to rent automobiles from the vehicle's owner in return for payment. Getaround offers a 100% digital experience. Owners set their rental prices and earn a commission from the rental revenue. Vehicles include convertibles, exotic and luxury cars, snow vehicles, sport utility vehicles, trucks and vans. Renting rates are provided in hourly or daily increments, and insurance as well as 24/7 roadside assistance are included in the stated price. Thousands of cars are featured on the site. Photos of the vehicles are displayed, along with miles per gallon, how many seats and other descriptions. Drivers search for cars nearby, enter their license number and credit card, and book and unlock the vehicle via mobile phone. Getaround screens all renters and provides third-party liability insurance in supplement to their personal automobile liability coverage during active trips. Hosts receive liability, collision and comprehensive coverage during active trips. There is no signup fee and no monthly or annual fee for drivers to utilize Getaround. Vehicles are available in more than 950 cities across the U.S. and the world. In late-2022, Getaround and InterPrivate II Acquisition Corp. (NYSE: IPVA) agreed to merge, with the combined entity to be listed on the New York Stock Exchange under ticker symbols GETR and GETR.WS, respectively. The transaction was expected to close by year's end.

FINANCIAL DATA: *Note: Data for latest year may not have been available at press time.*

In U.S. $	2021	2020	2019	2018	2017	2016
Revenue						
R&D Expense						
Operating Income						
Operating Margin %						
SGA Expense						
Net Income						
Operating Cash Flow						
Capital Expenditure						
EBITDA						
Return on Assets %						
Return on Equity %						
Debt to Equity						

CONTACT INFORMATION:

Phone: 415 551-7370   Fax:
Toll-Free: 866 438-2768
Address: 1177 Harrison St., San Franscisco, CA 94103 United States

STOCK TICKER/OTHER:

Stock Ticker: Private
Employees: 400
Parent Company:

Exchange:
Fiscal Year Ends: 12/31

SALARIES/BONUSES:

Top Exec. Salary: $ Bonus: $
Second Exec. Salary: $ Bonus: $

OTHER THOUGHTS:

Estimated Female Officers or Directors:
Hot Spot for Advancement for Women/Minorities:

Gigwalk

www.gigwalk.com

NAIC Code: 519130

TYPES OF BUSINESS:
Online Labor Arrangement Services
Outsourcing
Business Projects
Marketing Products
Team Collaboration
Technology
Software
Mobile Platform

BRANDS/DIVISIONS/AFFILIATES:
Gigwalkers
Gigwalk Enterprise

CONTACTS: *Note: Officers with more than one job title may be intentionally listed here more than once.*
Sriram Yadavalli, CEO

GROWTH PLANS/SPECIAL FEATURES:
Gigwalk provides a cloud-based mobile intermediation platform that connects people with work. It operates like this: a business or business person creates a project and pushes it to Gigwalk's 1.7 million on-demand workers known as Gigwalkers, the platform matches potential Gigwalkers based on global positioning system (GPS) locations; the business or business person chooses a Gigwalker to execute the work, and the platform then provides real-time analytics for decision-making advantages. This solution instantly connects businesses to a network of Gigwalkers in North America (U.S. and Canada) who can provide immediate, actionable insights that help Gigwalk customers improve their sales and operations. For example, Gigwalkers can confirm whether products are stocked and appropriately displayed, can validate in-store execution when promoting a product, and can research/collect data in real-time for business-decision purposes. Gigwalk Enterprise is a software-as-a-service workforce management application that enables firms to communicate with teams, such as: creating a project and pushing it to a specific division or team; executives collaborating with a team to derive a project consensus; various teams engaged in executing a single project; and collaboratives meeting in order to analyze a project's process, all in real-time, from start to finish. The Gigwalk mobile platform comes with an app, featuring work assignments, scheduling, messaging/communication, real-time data and tracking, work validation and compliance, and the list of on-demand Gigwalkers. Industries served by Gigwalk include consumer brands, website and mobile app testing, consulting, market research, restaurants, software, artificial intelligence, insurance and real estate.

FINANCIAL DATA: *Note: Data for latest year may not have been available at press time.*

In U.S. $	2021	2020	2019	2018	2017	2016
Revenue		75,000,000	10,032,750	9,555,000	9,100,000	8,400,000
R&D Expense						
Operating Income						
Operating Margin %						
SGA Expense						
Net Income						
Operating Cash Flow						
Capital Expenditure						
EBITDA						
Return on Assets %						
Return on Equity %						
Debt to Equity						

CONTACT INFORMATION:
Phone: 650 387-4567   Fax:
Toll-Free: 888 237-5896
Address: 539 Bryant St., Ste. 404, San Francisco, CA 94107 United States

STOCK TICKER/OTHER:
Stock Ticker: Private   Exchange:
Employees: 30   Fiscal Year Ends: 12/31
Parent Company:

SALARIES/BONUSES:
Top Exec. Salary: $ Bonus: $
Second Exec. Salary: $ Bonus: $

OTHER THOUGHTS:
Estimated Female Officers or Directors:
Hot Spot for Advancement for Women/Minorities:

Sales, profits and employees may be estimates. Financial information, benefits and other data can change quickly and may vary from those stated here.

GLAMSQUAD Inc

NAIC Code: 812112

TYPES OF BUSINESS:

On-Demand In-Home Beauty Services
Cosmetology
Home Service
Business Service
Hair Service
Makeup Service
Nails Service
Online Booking and Technology

BRANDS/DIVISIONS/AFFILIATES:

CONTACTS: *Note: Officers with more than one job title may be intentionally listed here more than once.*

Amy Schecter, CEO

GROWTH PLANS/SPECIAL FEATURES:

GLAMSQUAD, Inc. provides an on-demand mobile marketplace that connects a hair, makeup and/or nail professional directly with a client. The hired professional goes to the client's home, office or hotel, with services provided daily between 6AM to 10PM for customers in the following locations: New York City, southern California, southern Florida, Boston, the Hamptons/Long Island, San Francisco Bay area and metro Washington DC. Hair services include any type of styling, including waves, braids and up-dos for every hair type, texture and occasion. Makeup services range from a natural look to a glamorous one. Nail services include manicures, pedicures, nail designs, Shellac and spa services. GLAMSQUAD provides wedding styling services, and can comprise any and all events that lead up to the wedding itself, for the bride, the bridal party, as well as family and friends. Wedding styling prices are negotiated beforehand. GLAMSQUAD comprises more than 1,000 beauty professionals who average more than eight years of experience in their styling trade, and are background checked. Bookings can be made online or through the GLAMSQUAD mobile app. Hair and makeup products are available for purchase online. eGift cards are also available.

FINANCIAL DATA: *Note: Data for latest year may not have been available at press time.*

In U.S. $	2021	2020	2019	2018	2017	2016
Revenue	20,000,000	20,000,000	31,500,000	30,000,000	20,000,000	16,500,000
R&D Expense						
Operating Income						
Operating Margin %						
SGA Expense						
Net Income						
Operating Cash Flow						
Capital Expenditure						
EBITDA						
Return on Assets %						
Return on Equity %						
Debt to Equity						

CONTACT INFORMATION:

Phone: 212 202-2938   Fax:
Toll-Free: 844 695-4526
Address: 54 W. 21st St., Ste. 301, New York, NY 10010 United States

STOCK TICKER/OTHER:

Stock Ticker: Private   Exchange:
Employees: 10   Fiscal Year Ends: 12/31
Parent Company:

SALARIES/BONUSES:

Top Exec. Salary: $ Bonus: $
Second Exec. Salary: $ Bonus: $

OTHER THOUGHTS:

Estimated Female Officers or Directors: 1
Hot Spot for Advancement for Women/Minorities:

Gojek

NAIC Code: 561599

TYPES OF BUSINESS:

Motorcycle Ride Dispatch Service, Mobile App Based
Online and Mobile Services Platform
Transport Services and Logistics Technology
Digital Payments
Food and Shopping Services
Entertainment Booking Services
Business Ecommerce Solutions
Marketing Solutions

BRANDS/DIVISIONS/AFFILIATES:

PT GoTo Gojek Tokopedia
goride
gocar
gopay
goinvest
gofood
goshop
gobiz

CONTACTS: *Note: Officers with more than one job title may be intentionally listed here more than once.*

Andre Soelistyo, CEO

GROWTH PLANS/SPECIAL FEATURES:

Gojek is an Indonesia-based online/mobile platform owned and operated by PT GoTo Gojek Tokopedia Tbk. The multi-services platform serves millions of users in southeast Asia, primarily in Indonesia, Singapore, Vietnam and India. Official categories for Gojek services include transport and logistics, payments, food and shopping, entertainment and business. The transport and logistics division has more than 2 million partner drivers, and include brands such as goride, gocar, gosend, gobox and gobluebird. The payments division is a FinTech entity that makes transactions reliable and cashless, with brands including gopay, gotagihan, gopaylater, gogive, gosure, goinvest and gocorp. The food and shopping division enables shoppers to purchase food, groceries, medicines, electronics and more on behalf of users, with brands including gofood, gomart, gomed and goshop. The entertainment division enables users to book tickets for movies, events, watching television series and more, with brands including goplay and gotix. Last, the business division enables businesses to manage their restaurants, run advertisements, create promotions and more, with brands including gobiz, midtrans, moka and selly. Gojek offers a loyalty program that rewards users for their transactions - the more transactions, the more rewards.

FINANCIAL DATA: *Note: Data for latest year may not have been available at press time.*

In U.S. $	2021	2020	2019	2018	2017	2016
Revenue						
R&D Expense						
Operating Income						
Operating Margin %						
SGA Expense						
Net Income						
Operating Cash Flow						
Capital Expenditure						
EBITDA						
Return on Assets %						
Return on Equity %						
Debt to Equity						

CONTACT INFORMATION:

Phone: 62 21 502 51110   Fax:
Toll-Free:
Address: Pasaraya Block M, Gedung B Lt. 6, Melawai, Jakarta, 12160 Indonesia

STOCK TICKER/OTHER:

Stock Ticker: Subsidiary   Exchange:
Employees: 4,000   Fiscal Year Ends:
Parent Company: PT GoTo Gojek Tokopedia

SALARIES/BONUSES:

Top Exec. Salary: $ Bonus: $
Second Exec. Salary: $ Bonus: $

OTHER THOUGHTS:

Estimated Female Officers or Directors:
Hot Spot for Advancement for Women/Minorities:

Gopuff (GoBrands Inc)

gopuff.com

NAIC Code: 492210

TYPES OF BUSINESS:

Local Messengers and Local Delivery
Delivery Platform
Micro-Fulfillment Centers

BRANDS/DIVISIONS/AFFILIATES:

Gopuff
Gopuff Fam
Gopuff Points
BevMo!
Liquor Barn
Fancy
RideOS

CONTACTS: *Note: Officers with more than one job title may be intentionally listed here more than once.*

Rafael Ilishayev, Co-CEO
Yakir Gola, Co-CEO

GROWTH PLANS/SPECIAL FEATURES:

GoBrands, Inc. offers a delivery platform called Gopuff, which delivers food and drinks, cleaning supplies, home needs, over-the-counter medication and more within a few minutes' time. The firm stores about 4,000 products at its micro-fulfillment centers, packages and delivers them directly for a $3.95 flat service fee. An additional $3.95 fee is added to all orders containing regulated products (including alcohol, tobacco and vaping products). Those with a Gopuff Fam membership receive a variety of perks and free delivery on all orders for $7.99 per month. Gopuff's rewards program, Puff Points, lets customers earn points with each purchase, which can be redeemed on orders. Gopuff is open 24/7 in many areas and late night everywhere else. Gopuff offers its services in more than 1,000 cities throughout the U.S., the U.K. and France. Subsidiaries of GoBrands include U.S. liquor chains BevMo! And Liquor Barn, U.K. food delivery service Fancy, and the RideOS marketplaces/mapping service for ride-hailing fleets.

FINANCIAL DATA: *Note: Data for latest year may not have been available at press time.*

In U.S. $	2021	2020	2019	2018	2017	2016
Revenue						
R&D Expense						
Operating Income						
Operating Margin %						
SGA Expense						
Net Income						
Operating Cash Flow						
Capital Expenditure						
EBITDA						
Return on Assets %						
Return on Equity %						
Debt to Equity						

CONTACT INFORMATION:

Phone: 215 278-7982   Fax:
Toll-Free: 855 400-7833
Address: 454 N. 12th St., Philadelphia, PA 19123 United States

STOCK TICKER/OTHER:

Stock Ticker: Private
Employees:
Parent Company:

Exchange:
Fiscal Year Ends:

SALARIES/BONUSES:

Top Exec. Salary: $ Bonus: $
Second Exec. Salary: $ Bonus: $

OTHER THOUGHTS:

Estimated Female Officers or Directors:
Hot Spot for Advancement for Women/Minorities:

Sales, profits and employees may be estimates. Financial information, benefits and other data can change quickly and may vary from those stated here.

Grab Holdings Inc

NAIC Code: 561599

TYPES OF BUSINESS:

Car Ride Dispatch Service, Mobile App-Based
Ridesharing App
Food Deliveries

GROWTH PLANS/SPECIAL FEATURES:

Grab Holdings Inc is an investment holding company. The Group enables access to transportation, delivery, mobile payment, financial services and enterprise offerings in Southeast Asia through its mobile application (the Grab Platform).

BRANDS/DIVISIONS/AFFILIATES:

Grab
GrabFamily
JustGrab
GrabTaxi
GrabFood
GrabExpress
Grab Assist Plus
GrabPay

CONTACTS: *Note: Officers with more than one job title may be intentionally listed here more than once.*

Anthony Tan, CEO
Ming Maa, Pres.
Peter Oey, CFO

FINANCIAL DATA: *Note: Data for latest year may not have been available at press time.*

In U.S. $	2021	2020	2019	2018	2017	2016
Revenue	675,000,000	469,000,000	-845,000,000			
R&D Expense	356,000,000	257,000,000	231,000,000			
Operating Income	-1,529,000,000	-1,210,000,000	-2,938,000,000			
Operating Margin %	-2.27%	-2.58%				
SGA Expense	786,000,000	477,000,000	542,000,000			
Net Income	-3,449,000,000	-2,608,000,000	-3,747,000,000			
Operating Cash Flow	-938,000,000	-643,000,000	-2,112,000,000			
Capital Expenditure	85,000,000	40,000,000	140,000,000			
EBITDA	-1,506,000,000	-923,000,000	-2,281,000,000			
Return on Assets %						
Return on Equity %						
Debt to Equity	.26%					

CONTACT INFORMATION:

Phone: 65-6655-0005   Fax:
Toll-Free:
Address: 28 Sin Ming Lane, #01-143, Midview City, Singapore, 573972
Singapore

STOCK TICKER/OTHER:

Stock Ticker: GRAB   Exchange: NAS
Employees: Fiscal Year Ends: 03/31
Parent Company:

SALARIES/BONUSES:

Top Exec. Salary: $ Bonus: $
Second Exec. Salary: $ Bonus: $

OTHER THOUGHTS:

Estimated Female Officers or Directors:
Hot Spot for Advancement for Women/Minorities:

Graphite Solutions Inc

www.graphite.com

NAIC Code: 519130

TYPES OF BUSINESS:

Internet Publishing and Broadcasting and Web Search Portals
Online Executive Search Service
Outsourcing
Online Work Marketplace

BRANDS/DIVISIONS/AFFILIATES:

GROWTH PLANS/SPECIAL FEATURES:

Graphite Solutions, Inc. has designed a proprietary work vetting process powered by people and technology for identifying available work talent. Graphite experts perform at a very high level and have been rated 4.8 out of 5 stars by clients across thousands of work engagements. The individuals choose to work independently and typically perform consulting work for a living. Functional skills by Graphite experts include corporate strategy, finance and accounting, human resources, marketing and sales, market research, operations and supply chain, and technology and information technology (IT). Industry skills of the experts span automotive, consumer goods, energy, financial services, healthcare, life sciences, manufacturing, media and entertainment, retail and technology. Graphite serves enterprise companies, professional services firms and investment firms. The average years of work experience of the experts range between 12 and 15 years. Investors of Graphite Solutions include Alumni Ventures, Correlation Ventures, Communitas Capital, Valor Equity Partners, and Accomplice.

CONTACTS: Note: Officers with more than one job title may be intentionally listed here more than once.

Vikram Ashok, CEO
Abhi Bhattacharya, VP-Product
John Reed, VP-Finance
Jeff Troxclair, VP-Sales
Audrianna Hart, Sr. Dir.-People
Jason Gordon, CTO
Lesley Croll Henry, VP-Network

FINANCIAL DATA: Note: Data for latest year may not have been available at press time.

In U.S. $	2021	2020	2019	2018	2017	2016
Revenue						
R&D Expense						
Operating Income						
Operating Margin %						
SGA Expense						
Net Income						
Operating Cash Flow						
Capital Expenditure						
EBITDA						
Return on Assets %						
Return on Equity %						
Debt to Equity						

CONTACT INFORMATION:

Phone: 415 805-7047   Fax:
Toll-Free:
Address: 95 3rd St., Fl. 2, San Francisco, CA 94103 United States

STOCK TICKER/OTHER:

Stock Ticker: Private   Exchange:
Employees: Fiscal Year Ends:
Parent Company:

SALARIES/BONUSES:

Top Exec. Salary: $ Bonus: $
Second Exec. Salary: $ Bonus: $

OTHER THOUGHTS:

Estimated Female Officers or Directors:
Hot Spot for Advancement for Women/Minorities:

Grubhub Inc

NAIC Code: 492210

www.grubhub.com

TYPES OF BUSINESS:

Online Restaurant Pick-Up and Delivery
Online Food Ordering Services
Food Delivery Services
Catering Delivery Services
Ecommerce Payment Solutions
Corporate Credit Cards

BRANDS/DIVISIONS/AFFILIATES:

Just Eat Takeaway.com NV
Grubhub+
Grubhub Pay Card

CONTACTS: Note: Officers with more than one job title may be intentionally listed here more than once.

Adam DeWitt, CEO
Eric Ferguson, COO
Adam Patnaude, CFO
Maggie Drucker, Chief Legal Officer
Kelley Berlin, Chief Human Resources Officer
Greg Russell, CTO
Margo Drucker, General Counsel
Samuel Hall, Other Executive Officer

GROWTH PLANS/SPECIAL FEATURES:

Grubhub, Inc. is an online and mobile food ordering company that connects diners with local takeout restaurants. Its online and mobile ordering platforms allow 32 million active diners to order directly from more than 320,000 takeout restaurants in over 4,000 U.S. cities. Every order is supported by the company's 24/7 customer service teams. Grubhub also provides catering delivery services, in which users can schedule an order for ten or more than 200 people from a local restaurant and have it delivered. Grubhub offers gift cards. Grubhub+ is a membership program that costs about $10 per month and offers unlimited delivery fees on eligible orders, as well as exclusive rewards and other perks. GrubHub operates as a subsidiary of Just Eat Takeaway.com N.V., an Amsterdam-based food delivery service. During 2022, Grubhub announced the offering of a corporate pay card to help drive orders to local restaurants and increase order flexibility for in-office and at-home employees. The Grubhub Pay Card allows employees working for companies that have a Grubhub Corporate Account to order on and off the Grubhub marketplace with their allocated line of credit, and use it at any restaurant that takes debit or credit card payment.

FINANCIAL DATA: Note: Data for latest year may not have been available at press time.

In U.S. $	2021	2020	2019	2018	2017	2016
Revenue	1,910,981,049	1,819,981,952	1,312,151,040	1,007,257,024	683,067,008	493,331,008
R&D Expense						
Operating Income						
Operating Margin %						
SGA Expense						
Net Income		-155,860,992	-18,566,000	78,481,000	98,983,000	49,557,000
Operating Cash Flow						
Capital Expenditure						
EBITDA						
Return on Assets %						
Return on Equity %						
Debt to Equity						

CONTACT INFORMATION:

Phone: 877-585-7878   Fax:
Toll-Free:
Address: 111 W. Washington St., Ste. 2100, Chicago, IL 60602 United States

STOCK TICKER/OTHER:

Stock Ticker: Subsidiary   Exchange:
Employees: 2,841   Fiscal Year Ends: 12/31
Parent Company: Just Eat Takeaway.com NV

SALARIES/BONUSES:

Top Exec. Salary: $ Bonus: $
Second Exec. Salary: $ Bonus: $

OTHER THOUGHTS:

Estimated Female Officers or Directors:
Hot Spot for Advancement for Women/Minorities:

Gwynnie Bee (CaaStle Inc)

closet.gwynniebee.com

NAIC Code: 454111

TYPES OF BUSINESS:

Online Rental of Luxury Apparel and Accessories
Apparel Sharing
Clothing Rental
Online Ordering
Mobile App Ordering
Payment Solution
Analytics
Algorithms

BRANDS/DIVISIONS/AFFILIATES:

Gwynnie Bee
Pepperjam

CONTACTS: Note: Officers with more than one job title may be intentionally listed here more than once.

Christine Hunsicker, CEO
George Goldenberg, COO
Chirag Jain, Sr. VP-Finance
David Sabel, Sr. VP-Product
Gail Fierstein, Sr. VP-People
Xiang Yu, Dir.-Technology
Tait Morrison, VP-Platform Solutions

GROWTH PLANS/SPECIAL FEATURES:

CaaStle, Inc. offers an online/mobile service that provides unlimited fashion styles for women for rent or for sale. The online/mobile service is called Gwynnie Bee. CaaStle's customer-as-a-service (hence, CaaS-tle) platform builds and manages all aspects of the subscription model, including the website, databases, algorithms and analytics. Gwynnie Bee's apparel categories include shirts, blouses, dresses, denim, pants, cardigans, sweaters, jackets, outerwear, skirts and more. Prices for each item are displayed on the app or website, and other features include size advisory and fit guide. Suggestions for weekend and work wear are offered on the site, as well as styles to consider. The company's distribution centers comprise state-of-the-art inventory and garment care systems that manage the cleaning, shipping and receiving processes for its customers. Subscribers choose apparel as often as they'd like, anytime, anywhere, complimented with free shipping and unlimited returns. Subscribers can explore top brands and curated collections and wear them as often as they'd like. Those who wish to purchase an item can do so for less than retail price. CaaStle's affiliate program is built on rewarding subscribers for being an advocate to its attire-sharing marketplace via Pepperjam. Affiliates get paid for: displaying related ads, banners and links; reviewing the service and collections; and advertising CaaStle/Gwynnie Bee promotions.

FINANCIAL DATA: Note: Data for latest year may not have been available at press time.

In U.S. $	2021	2020	2019	2018	2017	2016
Revenue						
R&D Expense						
Operating Income						
Operating Margin %						
SGA Expense						
Net Income						
Operating Cash Flow						
Capital Expenditure						
EBITDA						
Return on Assets %						
Return on Equity %						
Debt to Equity						

CONTACT INFORMATION:

Phone: 718 752-1470   Fax:
Toll-Free: 855 499-6643
Address: 5 Penn Plaza, Fl. 4, New York, NY 10001 United States

STOCK TICKER/OTHER:

Stock Ticker: Private   Exchange:
Employees: Fiscal Year Ends:
Parent Company:

SALARIES/BONUSES:

Top Exec. Salary: $ Bonus: $
Second Exec. Salary: $ Bonus: $

OTHER THOUGHTS:

Estimated Female Officers or Directors:
Hot Spot for Advancement for Women/Minorities:

Handy Technologies Inc

www.handy.com

NAIC Code: 519130

TYPES OF BUSINESS:

Online Labor Arrangement Services
Handyman Services
Professional Help Services
Handyperson Search Platform
Handyperson Booking
Handyman Service Technology

BRANDS/DIVISIONS/AFFILIATES:

Angi Inc

CONTACTS: *Note: Officers with more than one job title may be intentionally listed here more than once.*

Oisin Hanrahan, CEO

GROWTH PLANS/SPECIAL FEATURES:

Handy Technologies, Inc. has developed and operates an online/mobile platform called Handy, which offers pre-priced booking home services. Handy's services are grouped into five categories, including: cleaning, offering home, move-out, office and deep cleaning services; installation, offering TV mounting, picture or shelf hanging, light fixture and ceiling fan installation; handyman, offering furniture assembly, general handyman, general plumbing, faucets, toilets, general electric, outlets/switches and moving help services; outdoor projects, such as lawn care, gutters/downspouts, tree removal, tree trimming, wood fence installation, deck and porch repair, deck installation, exterior painting and exterior surfaces services; and home renovation, such as bathroom or kitchen remodel, major home renovations, refinishing wood flooring, roofing installation or repair, new window installation, interior painting and more. Handy's platform enables users to shop for home products, and installation is included in the price provided. Shopping categories span air conditioners, bedroom, living room, dining room, kitchen, office, wall decor, lighting, outdoor and smart home, among other categories. Handy operates throughout the U.S., Canada and the U.K. Handy Technologies is owned by Angi Inc., which itself operates the Angi platform that connects home service professionals with consumers across 500+ categories, from repairing and remodeling homes to cleaning and landscaping. All handy persons are hired through parent company, Angi Inc.

FINANCIAL DATA: *Note: Data for latest year may not have been available at press time.*

In U.S. $	2021	2020	2019	2018	2017	2016
Revenue	357,976,000	368,550,000	378,000,000	360,000,000	355,500,000	350,000,000
R&D Expense						
Operating Income						
Operating Margin %						
SGA Expense						
Net Income						
Operating Cash Flow						
Capital Expenditure						
EBITDA						
Return on Assets %						
Return on Equity %						
Debt to Equity						

CONTACT INFORMATION:

Phone: 617 970-4813   Fax:
Toll-Free: 888 847-6036
Address: P.O. Box 1122, New York, NY 10159 United States

STOCK TICKER/OTHER:

Stock Ticker: Subsidiary   Exchange:
Employees: 200   Fiscal Year Ends: 12/31
Parent Company: Angi Inc

SALARIES/BONUSES:

Top Exec. Salary: $ Bonus: $
Second Exec. Salary: $ Bonus: $

OTHER THOUGHTS:

Estimated Female Officers or Directors:
Hot Spot for Advancement for Women/Minorities:

Sales, profits and employees may be estimates. Financial information, benefits and other data can change quickly and may vary from those stated here.

Healthcare Locum Limited

www.hclworkforce.com

NAIC Code: 561320

TYPES OF BUSINESS:

Temporary Help Services
Medical Staffing
Social Work Staffing
Recruitment Agency Services
Online Platform Technology

BRANDS/DIVISIONS/AFFILIATES:

Castlerock Recruitment Group Ltd
HCL Workforce Solutions
Clarity Workforce Technology

CONTACTS: *Note: Officers with more than one job title may be intentionally listed here more than once.*

Naeem Aslam, CEO

GROWTH PLANS/SPECIAL FEATURES:

Healthcare Locum Limited, doing business as HCL Workforce Solutions, is a recruitment agency that provides temporary and permanent staff to healthcare and social care sectors. These sectors and recruitment positions include administration, clerical, allied health, doctors, health sciences, mental health, nursing and social work. HCL's solutions also include managed services, through its partnership with Clarity, which manages all the recruitment needs of the client as needed. Through the Clarity Workforce Technology platform, HCL can find, deploy and manage all the temporary (locum) staff needed at every level, across every medical discipline. The software platform also makes rostering, planning, managing and monitoring agency and bank staff more efficient. It supports master vendor, neutral vendor and direct engagement solutions in order to make complex tasks simple and to save time. To ensure that compliance and legislation are adhered to, HCL checks full employment history, performance history, training verification, qualification verification, identity verification, immigration status, police checks, occupational health screening for role/occupational health review for all clinical staff, agency induction and engages in face-to-face interviewing. Healthcare Locum is owned by Castlerock Recruitment Group Ltd., a healthcare recruitment agency based in Merseyside, U.K.

HCL offers its employees a pension scheme, commission/bonus schemes, individual employee development, childcare vouchers, an annual holiday/leave scheme and more.

FINANCIAL DATA: *Note: Data for latest year may not have been available at press time.*

In U.S. $	2021	2020	2019	2018	2017	2016
Revenue						
R&D Expense						
Operating Income						
Operating Margin %						
SGA Expense						
Net Income						
Operating Cash Flow						
Capital Expenditure						
EBITDA						
Return on Assets %						
Return on Equity %						
Debt to Equity						

CONTACT INFORMATION:

Phone: 44 20-7451-1451   Fax:
Toll-Free:
Address: 33 Soho Square, London, W1D 3QU United Kingdom

STOCK TICKER/OTHER:

Stock Ticker: Private   Exchange:
Employees: 300   Fiscal Year Ends: 12/31
Parent Company: Castlerock Recruitment Group

SALARIES/BONUSES:

Top Exec. Salary: $ Bonus: $
Second Exec. Salary: $ Bonus: $

OTHER THOUGHTS:

Estimated Female Officers or Directors: 1
Hot Spot for Advancement for Women/Minorities:

HelloFresh SE

www.hellofreshgroup.com

NAIC Code: 454111

TYPES OF BUSINESS:

Complete Meal Kits
Fresh Food
Delivery

GROWTH PLANS/SPECIAL FEATURES:

HelloFresh SE provides fresh, healthy, and personalized meal solutions. The company operates an internet platform that provides customers the choice between various kinds of meals and recipes to be delivered on selected weekdays. It operates in two geographical regions: International and USA. International companies comprise operations in the United Kingdom, The Netherlands, Belgium, Luxembourg, Australia, Germany, Austria, Canada, and Switzerland. The company generates a majority of its revenue from the United States of America.

BRANDS/DIVISIONS/AFFILIATES:

Green Chef
EveryPlate
Chefs Plate
Factor75 Inc

CONTACTS: Note: Officers with more than one job title may be intentionally listed here more than once.

Dominik Richter, Co-CEO
Thomas Griesel, Co-CEO
Christian Gaertner, CFO
Edward Boyes, CCO
Jeffrey Lieberman, Chmn.

FINANCIAL DATA: Note: Data for latest year may not have been available at press time.

In U.S. $	2021	2020	2019	2018	2017	2016
Revenue	6,321,151,488	3,824,009,216	1,907,926,016	1,444,656,512	1,083,950,000	629,068,000
R&D Expense						
Operating Income						
Operating Margin %						
SGA Expense						
Net Income	270,104,960	376,292,544	-10,757,792	-93,170,856	-110,203,000	-98,898,900
Operating Cash Flow						
Capital Expenditure						
EBITDA						
Return on Assets %						
Return on Equity %						
Debt to Equity						

CONTACT INFORMATION:

Phone: 49-30-2084831-60   Fax:
Toll-Free:
Address: Saarbrucker Strasse 37a, Berlin, 10405 Germany

STOCK TICKER/OTHER:

Stock Ticker: HLFFF   Exchange: PINX
Employees: 14,635   Fiscal Year Ends: 12/31
Parent Company:

SALARIES/BONUSES:

Top Exec. Salary: $ Bonus: $
Second Exec. Salary: $ Bonus: $

OTHER THOUGHTS:

Estimated Female Officers or Directors:
Hot Spot for Advancement for Women/Minorities:

HelloTech Inc

www.hellotech.com

NAIC Code: 541511

TYPES OF BUSINESS:

At-Home IT Services
On-Demand Tech Support
In-Home Support Services
Remote Support Services
Technical Troubleshooting
Product Purchasing

BRANDS/DIVISIONS/AFFILIATES:

CONTACTS: *Note: Officers with more than one job title may be intentionally listed here more than once.*

Greg Steiner, CEO

GROWTH PLANS/SPECIAL FEATURES:

HelloTech, Inc. provides in-home business and remote tech support services on-demand. The firm's technical solutions include troubleshooting, installation and repairs. Its support and services are primarily in relation to computers, smart home networking, television mounting, audio/visual equipment and connections, Wi-Fi, mobile phones and tablets. HelloTech membership plans include: HelloTech Online, billed monthly of annually, and offers a home tech specialist and unlimited 24/7 online support; and HelloTech Home, billed monthly or annually, and offers a home tech specialist, unlimited 24/7 online support, in-home services, savings on products, a home technology checkup, antivirus software and password management. HelloTech operates throughout the U.S. Each expert is hand-selected, background checked and insured. HelloTech also has an ecommerce link on its website, where consumers can purchase products such as video doorbells, smart thermostats, smart garage door openers, smart home security cameras, WiFi networking items, TV mounts, smoke alarms and more.

FINANCIAL DATA: *Note: Data for latest year may not have been available at press time.*

In U.S. $	2021	2020	2019	2018	2017	2016
Revenue						
R&D Expense						
Operating Income						
Operating Margin %						
SGA Expense						
Net Income						
Operating Cash Flow						
Capital Expenditure						
EBITDA						
Return on Assets %						
Return on Equity %						
Debt to Equity						

CONTACT INFORMATION:

Phone: Fax:
Toll-Free: 800 640-9005
Address: 900 Hilgard Ave., Los Angeles, CA 90024 United States

STOCK TICKER/OTHER:

Stock Ticker: Private
Employees: 25
Parent Company:

Exchange:
Fiscal Year Ends: 12/31

SALARIES/BONUSES:

Top Exec. Salary: $ Bonus: $
Second Exec. Salary: $ Bonus: $

OTHER THOUGHTS:

Estimated Female Officers or Directors:
Hot Spot for Advancement for Women/Minorities:

Herc Holdings Inc

www.hercrentals.com

NAIC Code: 532490

TYPES OF BUSINESS:

Equipment Rental and Leasing, Commercial and Industrial Machinery

BRANDS/DIVISIONS/AFFILIATES:

GROWTH PLANS/SPECIAL FEATURES:

Herc Holdings is an equipment rental company that was spun out of Hertz Global in 2016. It is currently the third-largest equipment rental company (3% market share) in North America, after United Rentals and Sunbelt Rentals, with a fleet size of $5.1 billion. It serves commercial and residential construction customers, the environmental sector, industrial entities, and entertainment production companies. During much of its 50-year-plus history, the company has rented equipment such as aerial lifts to its customers for intermittent use. More recently, it has broadened its catalog to include a host of specialty items. Separately, Herc Holdings' strategy now incorporates long-term rentals to industrial customers where Herc maintains its own staff at the customer site.

CONTACTS:
Note: Officers with more than one job title may be intentionally listed here more than once.

Lawrence Silber, CEO
Mark Irion, CFO
Patrick Campbell, Chairman of the Board
W. Humphrey, Chief Accounting Officer
Tamir Peres, Chief Information Officer
S. Sheek, Chief Legal Officer
Aaron Birnbaum, COO
Christian Cunningham, Other Executive Officer

FINANCIAL DATA:
Note: Data for latest year may not have been available at press time.

In U.S. $	2021	2020	2019	2018	2017	2016
Revenue	2,073,100,000	1,781,300,000	1,999,000,000	1,976,700,000	1,754,500,000	1,554,800,000
R&D Expense						
Operating Income	377,700,000	206,700,000	247,500,000	210,700,000	106,100,000	76,100,000
Operating Margin %	.18%	.12%	.12%	.11%	.06%	.05%
SGA Expense	310,800,000	257,400,000	294,800,000	311,300,000	319,100,000	275,300,000
Net Income	224,100,000	73,700,000	47,500,000	69,100,000	160,300,000	-19,700,000
Operating Cash Flow	744,000,000	610,900,000	635,600,000	559,100,000	349,100,000	433,400,000
Capital Expenditure	641,800,000	385,500,000	695,300,000	849,000,000	576,000,000	516,100,000
EBITDA	865,400,000	653,100,000	707,200,000	650,600,000	506,000,000	474,600,000
Return on Assets %						
Return on Equity %						
Debt to Equity	2.47%	2.696	3.649	3.922	4.408	6.857

CONTACT INFORMATION:

Phone: 239 301-1000   Fax:
Toll-Free:
Address: 27500 Riverview Center Boulevard, Bonita Springs, FL 34134 United States

STOCK TICKER/OTHER:

Stock Ticker: HRI   Exchange: NYS
Employees: 5,600   Fiscal Year Ends: 12/31
Parent Company:

SALARIES/BONUSES:

Top Exec. Salary: $946,635   Bonus: $
Second Exec. Salary: $496,635   Bonus: $

OTHER THOUGHTS:

Estimated Female Officers or Directors:
Hot Spot for Advancement for Women/Minorities:

Hertz Global Holdings Inc

www.hertz.com

NAIC Code: 532111

TYPES OF BUSINESS:

Automobile Rental
Truck Rental
Claims Management
Heavy Equipment Rental
Used Automobile Sales
Leasing
Actuarial Services
Franchising

BRANDS/DIVISIONS/AFFILIATES:

Hertz
Dollar
Thrifty
Firefly
Certares Management LLC
Knighthead Capital Management LLC

GROWTH PLANS/SPECIAL FEATURES:

Hertz Global Holdings Inc operates an automotive vehicle rental service through the Hertz, Dollar, Thrifty, and Firefly brands. The company offers cars, crossovers, and light trucks for rent; ancillary products and services; rental of industrial, construction, and material handling equipment; and fleet-leasing and fleet-management services. The company operates a network of car rental locations and licenses its brands to associates and franchisees.

CONTACTS: Note: Officers with more than one job title may be intentionally listed here more than once.

Mark Fields, CEO
Kenny Cheung, CFO
M. O'Hara, Chairman of the Board
Alexandra Brooks, Chief Accounting Officer
Paul Stone, COO
Thomas Wagner, Director
Laura Smith, Executive VP, Divisional
Darren Arrington, Executive VP, Divisional
Joseph McPherson, Executive VP, Geographical
M. Galainena, Executive VP
Angela Brav, President, Divisional

FINANCIAL DATA: Note: Data for latest year may not have been available at press time.

In U.S. $	2021	2020	2019	2018	2017	2016
Revenue	7,336,000,000	5,258,000,000	9,779,000,000	9,504,000,000	8,803,000,000	8,803,000,000
R&D Expense						
Operating Income	2,035,000,000	-1,065,000,000	759,000,000	442,000,000	167,000,000	371,000,000
Operating Margin %	.28%	-.20%	.08%	.05%	.02%	.04%
SGA Expense	688,000,000	645,000,000	949,000,000	1,017,000,000	880,000,000	899,000,000
Net Income	366,000,000	-1,714,000,000	-58,000,000	-225,000,000	327,000,000	-491,000,000
Operating Cash Flow	1,806,000,000	953,000,000	2,900,000,000	2,556,000,000	2,394,000,000	2,529,000,000
Capital Expenditure	7,225,000,000	5,640,000,000	13,938,000,000	12,670,000,000	10,769,000,000	11,006,000,000
EBITDA	1,948,000,000	1,040,000,000	3,812,000,000	3,246,000,000	3,024,000,000	2,950,000,000
Return on Assets %						
Return on Equity %						
Debt to Equity	4.17%	136.661	10.622	15.248	9.536	12.28

CONTACT INFORMATION:

Phone: 239-301-7000   Fax:
Toll-Free: 800-654-3131
Address: 8501 Williams Rd., Estero, FL 33928 United States

STOCK TICKER/OTHER:

Stock Ticker: HTZ   Exchange: NAS
Employees: 23,000   Fiscal Year Ends: 12/31
Parent Company: Certares Management LLC

SALARIES/BONUSES:

Top Exec. Salary: $1,000,000   Bonus: $1,400,000
Second Exec. Salary: Bonus: $660,000
$600,000

OTHER THOUGHTS:

Estimated Female Officers or Directors: 6
Hot Spot for Advancement for Women/Minorities: Y

Sales, profits and employees may be estimates. Financial information, benefits and other data can change quickly and may vary from those stated here.

HireQuest Inc

www.hirequest.com

NAIC Code: 561320

TYPES OF BUSINESS:

Temporary employment services
On-Demand Outsourcing
Staffing Services

GROWTH PLANS/SPECIAL FEATURES:

HireQuest Inc operates as a staffing company in the United State. The company is engaged in the provision of on-demand and temporary staffing solutions. It serves small to mid-sized businesses in the retail, construction, warehousing, industrial/manufacturing, transportation, and hospitality industries.

BRANDS/DIVISIONS/AFFILIATES:

HireQuest Direct
HireQuest

CONTACTS: Note: Officers with more than one job title may be intentionally listed here more than once.

Richard Hermanns, CEO
Cory Smith, CFO
John McAnnar, Chief Legal Officer
R. Malhotra, Director

FINANCIAL DATA: Note: Data for latest year may not have been available at press time.

In U.S. $	2021	2020	2019	2018	2017	2016
Revenue	22,759,790	13,809,130	15,876,460	97,388,820	98,072,200	93,259,500
R&D Expense						
Operating Income	7,662,200	4,979,497	2,784,031	1,181,475	3,696,495	1,104,322
Operating Margin %	.34%	.36%	.18%	.01%	.04%	.01%
SGA Expense	13,363,960	8,700,446	12,692,300	23,433,200	21,347,680	22,276,480
Net Income	11,849,930	5,359,414	-289,979	974,287	1,679,348	556,553
Operating Cash Flow	17,381,560	10,880,330	4,957,813	2,622,950	4,747,668	-464,207
Capital Expenditure	1,975,203	1,764,572	507,602	158,578	103,665	100,609
EBITDA	14,208,320	6,279,298	3,935,240	1,505,327	4,082,908	1,402,622
Return on Assets %						
Return on Equity %						
Debt to Equity	.06%					

CONTACT INFORMATION:

Phone: 843-723-7400   Fax:
Toll-Free: 800-835-6755
Address: 111 Springhall Dr., Goose Creek, SC 29445 United States

STOCK TICKER/OTHER:

Stock Ticker: HQI   Exchange: NAS
Employees: 73,000   Fiscal Year Ends: 12/29
Parent Company:

SALARIES/BONUSES:

Top Exec. Salary: $375,000   Bonus: $650,000
Second Exec. Salary: Bonus: $130,000
$196,667

OTHER THOUGHTS:

Estimated Female Officers or Directors:
Hot Spot for Advancement for Women/Minorities:

Homestay Technologies Limited

www.homestay.com

NAIC Code: 561510

TYPES OF BUSINESS:

Travel Agencies
Online Vacation Rental Services
Room Rental
Online Booking Technology

BRANDS/DIVISIONS/AFFILIATES:

Homestay.com

GROWTH PLANS/SPECIAL FEATURES:

Homestay Technologies Limited has developed and operates an online platform, Homestay.com, which offers guests culturally-immersive travel experiences at affordable prices. The average price per night, globally, is about $38 per room, with hosts averaging approximately $1,200 in earnings per year. How it works is that hosts rent out rooms from their homes while simultaneously remaining present in the home, much like a bed and breakfast. Hosts educate traveling guests about the local culture and provide rooms with beds and access to a bathroom along with fresh linens in each. Currently, there are approximately 33,000 Homestay listings in 175 countries. Homestay also offers long-term accommodation, including student accommodation for students studying abroad or doing an internship.

CONTACTS: Note: Officers with more than one job title may be intentionally listed here more than once.

Tom Kennedy, CEO

FINANCIAL DATA: Note: Data for latest year may not have been available at press time.

In U.S. $	2021	2020	2019	2018	2017	2016
Revenue						
R&D Expense						
Operating Income						
Operating Margin %						
SGA Expense						
Net Income						
Operating Cash Flow						
Capital Expenditure						
EBITDA						
Return on Assets %						
Return on Equity %						
Debt to Equity						

CONTACT INFORMATION:

Phone: 353 1-6753010   Fax:
Toll-Free:
Address: 77 Camden St. Lower, Dublin 2, D02 XE80 Ireland

STOCK TICKER/OTHER:

Stock Ticker: Private
Employees:
Parent Company:

Exchange:
Fiscal Year Ends:

SALARIES/BONUSES:

Top Exec. Salary: $ Bonus: $
Second Exec. Salary: $ Bonus: $

OTHER THOUGHTS:

Estimated Female Officers or Directors:
Hot Spot for Advancement for Women/Minorities:

Honor Technology Inc

www.joinhonor.com

NAIC Code: 519130

TYPES OF BUSINESS:

Online In-Home Care Giver Service Arrangement
In-Home Senior Care
Caregiving Communication
Technology Platform
Care Management Platform
Franchising

BRANDS/DIVISIONS/AFFILIATES:

Home Instead Inc

CONTACTS: *Note: Officers with more than one job title may be intentionally listed here more than once.*

Ian Clarkson, Pres.

GROWTH PLANS/SPECIAL FEATURES:

Honor Technology, Inc. has developed and operates an online and mobile platform that connects home care agency owners, in-home caregivers, seniors and their families. Honor provides in-home senior care, helping older adults continue to live well and independently at home. Families are encouraged to call Honor to schedule a free consultation. The company's easy-to-use applications enable family members to schedule and monitor care from anywhere. Care can be scheduled by the hour, and pay is paid by the hour as well; there are no long-term contracts. Honor Care professionals help 24/7 and are hand-selected and skilled in their trade. Families can stay in touch with the Honor Care professional and be informed in real-time. They are informed of who would be going to the senior's home and when. Changing the location of care can be made through the app, and the company offers 24/7 phone support in relation to questions or concerns. Honor care professionals can help with medication reminders, staying active, meal preparation, groceries, transportation, light housekeeping, personal care and hygiene, companionship and check-in visits. In addition, Honor Technology is the parent company of Home Instead, Inc., a franchisor of independently-owned and -operated franchise businesses.

FINANCIAL DATA: *Note: Data for latest year may not have been available at press time.*

In U.S. $	2021	2020	2019	2018	2017	2016
Revenue						
R&D Expense						
Operating Income						
Operating Margin %						
SGA Expense						
Net Income						
Operating Cash Flow						
Capital Expenditure						
EBITDA						
Return on Assets %						
Return on Equity %						
Debt to Equity						

CONTACT INFORMATION:

Phone: 415 300-2515   Fax:
Toll-Free: 877 777-5116
Address: 201 3rd St., Fl. 10, San Francisco, CA 94103 United States

STOCK TICKER/OTHER:

Stock Ticker: Private   Exchange:
Employees: 23   Fiscal Year Ends:
Parent Company:

SALARIES/BONUSES:

Top Exec. Salary: $ Bonus: $
Second Exec. Salary: $ Bonus: $

OTHER THOUGHTS:

Estimated Female Officers or Directors:
Hot Spot for Advancement for Women/Minorities:

HopSkipDrive Inc

www.hopskipdrive.com

NAIC Code: 561599

TYPES OF BUSINESS:
Car Ride Dispatch Service, Mobile App-Based
Transportation Services
School Transportation
Platform Analytics
Real-Time Technology

BRANDS/DIVISIONS/AFFILIATES:
www.hopskipdrive.com
CareDriver
Safe Ride Support Team

CONTACTS: Note: Officers with more than one job title may be intentionally listed here more than once.
Joanna McFarland, CEO
Joseph Brumfield, Dir.-Bus. Dev.
Carol Koh Evans, Dir-Finance
Toby McGraw, Dir.-Sales
Katrina Kardassakis, Dir.-Strategy
Miriam Ravkin, Dir.-Mktg.
Corey McMahon, Dir.-Product & Technology

GROWTH PLANS/SPECIAL FEATURES:
HopSkipDrive, Inc. has developed and operates an online platform, www.hopskipdrive.com, which offers a ride service primarily for transporting kids. The ride-sharing service is designed to help with a family's busy schedule by providing a solution that makes scheduling rides with experienced caregivers easy and convenient. With built-in safety features, the company's platform and strategy helps bring peace of mind to parents. For example, HopSkipDrive fingerprints and screens every CareDriver, and every ride can be monitored in real-time. All drivers must pass the firm's 15-point certification process, which includes extensive background checks, ongoing Department of Motor Vehicles checks, ride-alongs, reference checks, driver training and meeting each one in person. The HopSkipDrive app and/or website enables parents to: schedule a ride, as well as weekday rides; see the CareDriver's profile, picture and car information (users are matched with a driver via the company's technology), and this information can be shared with the child so they know who to expect; and track the ride through the HopSkipDrive app. In addition, HopSkipDrive is expanding its services and will also transport a parent or relative who does not drive, whether it is to an appointment or to lunch with friends. The more families that sign up to drive, the more the ride service will grow. HopSkipDrive has insurance specifically designed for transporting children; and monitors every ride in real time with its Safe Ride Support Team. The firm's website offers gift cards.

FINANCIAL DATA: Note: Data for latest year may not have been available at press time.

In U.S. $	2021	2020	2019	2018	2017	2016
Revenue						
R&D Expense						
Operating Income						
Operating Margin %						
SGA Expense						
Net Income						
Operating Cash Flow						
Capital Expenditure						
EBITDA						
Return on Assets %						
Return on Equity %						
Debt to Equity						

CONTACT INFORMATION:
Phone: 213 275-1230   Fax:
Toll-Free: 844 467-7547
Address: 1933 S. Broadway, Ste. 1144, Los Angeles, CA 90007 United States

STOCK TICKER/OTHER:
Stock Ticker: Private   Exchange:
Employees: 100   Fiscal Year Ends:
Parent Company:

SALARIES/BONUSES:
Top Exec. Salary: $ Bonus: $
Second Exec. Salary: $ Bonus: $

OTHER THOUGHTS:
Estimated Female Officers or Directors:
Hot Spot for Advancement for Women/Minorities:

Sales, profits and employees may be estimates. Financial information, benefits and other data can change quickly and may vary from those stated here.

Hubstaff Talent (Netsoft Holdings LLC)   talent.hubstaff.com
NAIC Code: 519130

TYPES OF BUSINESS:
Online Freelance Work Arrangement Services
Workplace Tracking Software
Workplace Management
Time Tracking
Work Tracing
Project Budgeting Management
Reporting and Online Timesheets
Payroll Software

BRANDS/DIVISIONS/AFFILIATES:
HubstaffTasks
HubstaffTalent

CONTACTS: Note: Officers with more than one job title may be intentionally listed here more than once.
Jared Brown, CEO

GROWTH PLANS/SPECIAL FEATURES:
Netsoft Holdings, LLC, doing business as Hubstaff Talent, has developed and operates a single platform for tracking employee time and team management, as well as for locating talent all over the world via desktop or mobile app. The software is suitable for Windows, Mac, iOS and Android, among others. The Hubstaff platform integrates with more than 30 systems, with features including time tracking (including mobile time tracking), automated work tracing (GeoFencing), employee monitoring, GPS tracking, project budgeting, detailed reporting, online timesheets, payroll software, productivity measurement, online invoicing and employee scheduling. HubstaffTasks is an agile project management software that helps teams collaborate and communicate on projects. HubstaffTalent is a free resource that enables business owners to browse top agencies and freelancers who are listed for hire. Searches can be based on skill, location or category, and agencies and freelancers can then be contacted directly. Likewise, agencies and contractors can add employees for hire on the platform, and freelancers can upload themselves for hire. Hubstaff is used across a range of industries, including cleaning, landscaping, consulting, manufacturing, accounting, software development, real estate, design, construction, healthcare, agency, architecture, engineering, attorney, ecommerce and non-profit.

FINANCIAL DATA: Note: Data for latest year may not have been available at press time.

In U.S. $	2021	2020	2019	2018	2017	2016
Revenue						
R&D Expense						
Operating Income						
Operating Margin %						
SGA Expense						
Net Income						
Operating Cash Flow						
Capital Expenditure						
EBITDA						
Return on Assets %						
Return on Equity %						
Debt to Equity						

CONTACT INFORMATION:
Phone: 773 860-4653   Fax:
Toll-Free:
Address: 11650 Olio Rd., Indianapolis, IN 46037 United States

STOCK TICKER/OTHER:
Stock Ticker: Private   Exchange:
Employees: Fiscal Year Ends:
Parent Company:

SALARIES/BONUSES:
Top Exec. Salary: $ Bonus: $
Second Exec. Salary: $ Bonus: $

OTHER THOUGHTS:
Estimated Female Officers or Directors:
Hot Spot for Advancement for Women/Minorities:

Imperial Logistics Limited

www.imperiallogistics.com

NAIC Code: 532111

TYPES OF BUSINESS:

Car Rental
Logistics Services
Market Access Services
Supply Chain Management
Ecommerce
Multi-Modal Transport
Consumer Goods Transportation Services
Digital and Automated Logistics Technology

BRANDS/DIVISIONS/AFFILIATES:

DP World Company

CONTACTS: *Note: Officers with more than one job title may be intentionally listed here more than once.*

Yuvraj Narayan, CEO
Ahmed Bin Sulayem, Chmn.

GROWTH PLANS/SPECIAL FEATURES:

Imperial Logistics Limited is based in South Africa and a provider of integrated market access and logistics solutions, with a focus on serving the healthcare, consumer, automotive, chemicals, industrial and commodities industries. The firm seeks and leverages innovative technology to deliver its logistics solutions, enabling a seamless experience for clients throughout Africa and Europe. Imperial's market access division provides route-to-market solutions, including sourcing, sales, distribution and marketing. Its operations are mainly located in eastern, western and southern Africa, which offers services to more than 20 countries. This division takes ownership of inventory, from order to payment to picking and packaging to delivery. It also provides marketing and promotional services, as well as contract manufacturing services. The logistics division manages the movement of goods on behalf of Imperial's clients, combining various types of transportation including over-the-road, river, rail, air and ocean. It will also work in partnership with clients to integrate logistics functions across their end-to-end supply chain. Transport solutions are also provided for Asia-Europe trade, including long-haul transport, intercontinental rail freight forwarding and door-to-door services. Imperial's investment in digitization, data, new technologies and automation enhances its global ecommerce capabilities, including online consumer engagement, telemedicine and more. Imperial Logistics operates as a subsidiary of DP World Company.

FINANCIAL DATA: *Note: Data for latest year may not have been available at press time.*

In U.S. $	2021	2020	2019	2018	2017	2016
Revenue	3,242,104,576	2,880,186,880	3,087,600,128	3,185,903,872	6,349,324,288	7,115,901,440
R&D Expense						
Operating Income						
Operating Margin %						
SGA Expense						
Net Income	59,056,872	-18,816,228	213,685,280	203,252,512	141,344,864	187,461,184
Operating Cash Flow						
Capital Expenditure						
EBITDA						
Return on Assets %						
Return on Equity %						
Debt to Equity						

CONTACT INFORMATION:

Phone: 27 113726500   Fax:
Toll-Free:
Address: Imperial Place, 79 Boeing Rd. East, Bedfordview, 2008 South Africa

STOCK TICKER/OTHER:

Stock Ticker: Subsidiary   Exchange:
Employees: 25,232   Fiscal Year Ends: 06/30
Parent Company: DP World Company

SALARIES/BONUSES:

Top Exec. Salary: $ Bonus: $
Second Exec. Salary: $ Bonus: $

OTHER THOUGHTS:

Estimated Female Officers or Directors:
Hot Spot for Advancement for Women/Minorities:

Innova Solutions Inc

www.innovasolutions.com

NAIC Code: 561320

TYPES OF BUSINESS:

Technology Staffing
Business Transformation Solutions
Technology Innovation
Digital Innovation
Cloud Services
Data Analytics
Internet of Things, Artificial Intelligence
Machine Learning

BRANDS/DIVISIONS/AFFILIATES:

Analysts International Corporation

CONTACTS: Note: Officers with more than one job title may be intentionally listed here more than once.

Raj Sardana, CEO
Sanjeev Sardana, COO
P. Nick Goel, CFO
Richard McCormack, Sr. VP-Mktg.
Brenda Neihaus, Global VP-Human Resources
Mike Dietrich, CIO
Sanjeev Sardana, Sr. VP-Corp. Dev.
Joe Thiel, Regional VP-Western Region
Mike Brown, Regional VP-Eastern Region
Allison Gross, Regional VP-Central Region
Sreedhar Kajeepeta, CTO

GROWTH PLANS/SPECIAL FEATURES:

Innova Solutions, Inc. (formerly Analysts International Corporation) designs and produces strategic technology and business transformation solutions for business clients, enabling them to operate more successfully via digital innovation. Innova's services are grouped into several categories, including digital product engineering, cloud services, data and analytics, intelligent automation, cybersecurity, build/operate/transfer, and talent solutions. Solutions within these services span digital application, user interface and experience management, quality engineering, enterprise content management, cloud strategy, managed cloud, cloud migration, Internet of Things (IoT), native applications, data modernization, data engineering, data visualization, data science, cognitive artificial intelligence (AI), machine learning, hyper-automation, threat detection and response, DevSecOps, compliance assessments, managed security services and more. Industries served by Innova Solutions include banking, financial services, communications, media, technology, energy and utilities, healthcare, life sciences, manufacturing, retail, transportation and logistics, travel and hospitality. Headquartered in the U.S., Innova Solutions has global offices across North America, Europe and Asia-Pacific.

Innova offers its employees medical and dental benefits, a 401(k), employee learning and development programs.

FINANCIAL DATA: Note: Data for latest year may not have been available at press time.

In U.S. $	2021	2020	2019	2018	2017	2016
Revenue	112,200,000	110,000,000	165,375,000	157,500,000	150,000,000	140,000,000
R&D Expense						
Operating Income						
Operating Margin %						
SGA Expense						
Net Income						
Operating Cash Flow						
Capital Expenditure						
EBITDA						
Return on Assets %						
Return on Equity %						
Debt to Equity						

CONTACT INFORMATION:

Phone: 770-493-5588   Fax: 770-623-4314
Toll-Free:
Address: 2400 Meadowbrook Pkwy., Duluth, GA 30096 United States

SALARIES/BONUSES:

Top Exec. Salary: $ Bonus: $
Second Exec. Salary: $ Bonus: $

STOCK TICKER/OTHER:

Stock Ticker: Private   Exchange:
Employees: 21,000   Fiscal Year Ends: 12/31
Parent Company:

OTHER THOUGHTS:

Estimated Female Officers or Directors: 2
Hot Spot for Advancement for Women/Minorities: Y

Instacart

www.instacart.com

NAIC Code: 492210

TYPES OF BUSINESS:

Grocery Delivery Services
Online Food Order
Food Delivery
Curbside Service
Food Delivery Membership Service
API Technology Solutions
Nano-Fulfillment Centers
Data and Insights

BRANDS/DIVISIONS/AFFILIATES:

Maplebear Inc
Instacart+
Instacart Connect
Instacart Platform

CONTACTS: *Note: Officers with more than one job title may be intentionally listed here more than once.*

Fidji Simo, CEO

GROWTH PLANS/SPECIAL FEATURES:

Instacart, an operating unit of Maplebear, Inc., offers an online and mobile delivery service. The firm lets customers purchase items online from various stores in the area and have them delivered to their house in as little as one hour. Instacart also offers a curbside ecommerce service in which customers order online and then swing by the store of their choice to pick up the groceries without leaving their vehicle. Curbside service can also be ready in an hour's time. Instacart hires personal shoppers to hand-pick items, even grocery items, from actual stores that have a partnership agreement with Instacart. Food delivery service is offered throughout the U.S. as well as across parts of Canada. Instacart+ is a membership program offering unlimited free delivery on orders over $35, 5% credit back on pickup orders (excluding alcohol), lower service fees, exclusive offers and more. Instacart Connect offers application programming interfaces (APIs), which enables branded ecommerce sites to add Instacart capabilities so their customers can benefit from Instacart's scheduling/order services. Developers can integrate selected capabilities through the API using any language, including Java and Python. During 2022, Instacart announced the launch of its Instacart Platform, a suite of technologies and services for retailers that includes 15-minute delivery via nano-fulfillment centers, as well as tools such as advertising solutions and data insights.

FINANCIAL DATA: *Note: Data for latest year may not have been available at press time.*

In U.S. $	2021	2020	2019	2018	2017	2016
Revenue	1,825,000,000	1,500,000,000	775,000,000	680,000,000	500,000,000	300,000,000
R&D Expense						
Operating Income						
Operating Margin %						
SGA Expense						
Net Income						
Operating Cash Flow						
Capital Expenditure						
EBITDA						
Return on Assets %						
Return on Equity %						
Debt to Equity						

CONTACT INFORMATION:

Phone: Fax:
Toll-Free: 888 246-7822
Address: 50 Beale, Ste. 600, San Francisco, CA 94107 United States

STOCK TICKER/OTHER:

Stock Ticker: Private   Exchange:
Employees: 8,000   Fiscal Year Ends:
Parent Company: Maplebear Inc

SALARIES/BONUSES:

Top Exec. Salary: $ Bonus: $
Second Exec. Salary: $ Bonus: $

OTHER THOUGHTS:

Estimated Female Officers or Directors:
Hot Spot for Advancement for Women/Minorities: Y

IWG plc

NAIC Code: 531120

TYPES OF BUSINESS:

Shared Office Space
Workspace Rental

GROWTH PLANS/SPECIAL FEATURES:

IWG PLC owns a network of business centers that are leased to a variety of business customers and offer flexible workspace options. It owns and operates brands like Regus, Spaces, Signature, HQ, and No 18. The company operates in four principal geographical segments: the Americas; Europe, Middle East, and Africa; Asia-Pacific; and the United Kingdom. The Americas segment generates the largest proportion of revenue.

BRANDS/DIVISIONS/AFFILIATES:

International Workplace Group
Regus
Spaces
No18
HQ
Basepoint Business Centres
OpenOffice
bizDojo

CONTACTS: *Note: Officers with more than one job title may be intentionally listed here more than once.*

Mark Dixon, CEO
Eric Hageman, CFO
Douglas Sutherland, Chmn.

FINANCIAL DATA: *Note: Data for latest year may not have been available at press time.*

In U.S. $	2021	2020	2019	2018	2017	2016
Revenue	2,666,738,432	2,938,887,424	3,170,664,704	3,375,896,832	2,901,208,832	2,930,202,112
R&D Expense						
Operating Income						
Operating Margin %						
SGA Expense						
Net Income	-245,140,288	-781,640,832	539,356,480	140,740,048	140,601,872	182,104,432
Operating Cash Flow						
Capital Expenditure						
EBITDA						
Return on Assets %						
Return on Equity %						
Debt to Equity						

CONTACT INFORMATION:

Phone: 41 7584376533   Fax:
Toll-Free:
Address: Dammstrasse 19, Zug, CH-6300 Switzerland

STOCK TICKER/OTHER:

Stock Ticker: IWGFF   Exchange: PINX
Employees: 8,239   Fiscal Year Ends: 12/31
Parent Company:

SALARIES/BONUSES:

Top Exec. Salary: $ Bonus: $
Second Exec. Salary: $ Bonus: $

OTHER THOUGHTS:

Estimated Female Officers or Directors:
Hot Spot for Advancement for Women/Minorities:

Just Eat Takeaway.com NV

corporate.takeaway.com

NAIC Code: 492210

TYPES OF BUSINESS:

Online Restaurant Meals Delivery Services
Online Food Ordering
Food Delivery Service
Online Marketplace

BRANDS/DIVISIONS/AFFILIATES:

Takeaway.com
Just Eat
Menulog
SkipTheDishes
iFood
CityPantry

GROWTH PLANS/SPECIAL FEATURES:

Just Eat Takeaway operates an online marketplace that connects restaurants with users in Europe and North America. The company operates mainly as an order-only marketplace, although it also offers last-mile delivery services. The company is the result of the merger of Just Eat Plc and Takeaway.com NV in early 2020. The company had close to 99 million active users on its platform generating revenue of more than EUR 5 billion and a gross transaction value of EUR 28 billion in fiscal 2021. Excluding the U.S. after its recent acquisition of Grubhub, the company's largest geographical presence by revenue is in the U.K., Germany, Canada, and the Netherlands.

CONTACTS: Note: Officers with more than one job title may be intentionally listed here more than once.

Jitse Groen, CEO
Jorg Gerbig, COO
Brent Wissink, CFO
Adriaan Nuhn, Chmn.

FINANCIAL DATA: Note: Data for latest year may not have been available at press time.

In U.S. $	2021	2020	2019	2018	2017	2016
Revenue	4,740,811,264	2,082,355,968	438,749,152	262,362,368	179,952,864	131,774,888
R&D Expense						
Operating Income						
Operating Margin %						
SGA Expense						
Net Income	-1,071,560,448	-173,359,712	-127,616,944	-15,830,011	-45,425,456	-36,457,316
Operating Cash Flow						
Capital Expenditure						
EBITDA						
Return on Assets %						
Return on Equity %						
Debt to Equity						

CONTACT INFORMATION:

Phone: 31 6 14 315 479   Fax:
Toll-Free:
Address: Oosterdoksstraat 80, Amsterdam, 1011 DK Netherlands

STOCK TICKER/OTHER:

Stock Ticker: TKAYF   Exchange: PINX
Employees: 5,423   Fiscal Year Ends: 12/31
Parent Company:

SALARIES/BONUSES:

Top Exec. Salary: $ Bonus: $
Second Exec. Salary: $ Bonus: $

OTHER THOUGHTS:

Estimated Female Officers or Directors:
Hot Spot for Advancement for Women/Minorities:

Sales, profits and employees may be estimates. Financial information, benefits and other data can change quickly and may vary from those stated here.

Kakao Corporation

www.kakaocorp.com

NAIC Code: 519130

TYPES OF BUSINESS:

Internet Portal Service
Mobile Platforms
Online Platforms
Communications
Artificial Intelligence
Development Software
Payment Solutions
Blockchain Technology

BRANDS/DIVISIONS/AFFILIATES:

GROWTH PLANS/SPECIAL FEATURES:

Kakao Corporation is a Korea-based global mobile platform company, with services that connect people via technology. The firm's offerings are divided into two segments: technology and service. The technology segment consists of artificial intelligence (AI) services, opensource services, people and technology connection software, development software, machine learning services, teaching software, blockchain technology, mobility solutions and more. The service segment consists of online/mobile calendars, communication platforms, ecommerce platforms, business platforms, social platforms, lifestyle platforms, AI-based business-to-business (B2B) connections, daily routine platforms, banking platforms, emoticon platform, payment solutions, story reading sharing, self-care platforms, television and content viewing, food ordering platform, and writing platform, among many others.

CONTACTS: Note: Officers with more than one job title may be intentionally listed here more than once.

Whon Namkoong, CEO
Jaehyuk Lee, Head-Strategy
Hyunyoung Kim, Head-Global Mgmt.
Sung-su Kim, Chmn.

FINANCIAL DATA: Note: Data for latest year may not have been available at press time.

In U.S. $	2021	2020	2019	2018	2017	2016
Revenue	4,933,370,000	3,818,970,780	2,668,300,000	2,163,380,000	1,846,900,000	1,365,848,000
R&D Expense						
Operating Income						
Operating Margin %						
SGA Expense						
Net Income	132,337,000	153,498,000	-293,466,000	14,262,900	119,449,000	56,127,300
Operating Cash Flow						
Capital Expenditure						
EBITDA						
Return on Assets %						
Return on Equity %						
Debt to Equity						

CONTACT INFORMATION:

Phone: 82-064-795-1500   Fax: 82-2-60035401
Toll-Free:
Address: 242, Cheomdan-ro, Jeju-si Jeju-do, 63309 South Korea

STOCK TICKER/OTHER:

Stock Ticker: 35720   Exchange: Seoul
Employees: 2,450   Fiscal Year Ends: 12/31
Parent Company:

SALARIES/BONUSES:

Top Exec. Salary: $ Bonus: $
Second Exec. Salary: $ Bonus: $

OTHER THOUGHTS:

Estimated Female Officers or Directors: 1
Hot Spot for Advancement for Women/Minorities:

Kelly Services Inc

www.kellyservices.com

NAIC Code: 561320

TYPES OF BUSINESS:

Staffing & Temporary Help
Human Resources Consulting
Outsourcing Solutions
Permanent Hiring Programs
Call Center Services
Benefits & Payroll Outsourcing

BRANDS/DIVISIONS/AFFILIATES:

Kelly Education

GROWTH PLANS/SPECIAL FEATURES:

Kelly Services Inc is a provider of workforce solutions and consulting and staffing services. The company's operations are divided into five business segments namely Professional & Industrial, Science, Engineering & Technology, Education, Outsourcing & Consulting, and International.Â It provides staffing solutions through its branch networks in Americas and International operations and also provides a suite of innovative talent fulfilment and outcome-based solutions.Â Professional & Industrial generates maximum revenue from its operations.

CONTACTS: *Note: Officers with more than one job title may be intentionally listed here more than once.*

Vanessa Williams, Assistant Secretary
Peter Quigley, CEO
Olivier Thirot, CFO
Donald Parfet, Chairman of the Board
Laura Lockhart, Chief Accounting Officer
James Bradley, Chief Administrative Officer
Peter Boland, Chief Marketing Officer
Nicola Soares, President, Divisional
Tammy Browning, President, Divisional
Dinette Koolhaas, President, Divisional
Daniel Malan, President, Divisional
Timothy Dupree, President, Divisional

FINANCIAL DATA: *Note: Data for latest year may not have been available at press time.*

In U.S. $	2021	2020	2019	2018	2017	2016
Revenue	4,909,700,000	4,516,000,000	5,355,600,000	5,513,900,000	5,374,400,000	5,276,800,000
R&D Expense						
Operating Income	48,600,000	22,000,000	85,300,000	87,400,000	83,300,000	63,200,000
Operating Margin %	.01%	.00%	.02%	.02%	.02%	.01%
SGA Expense	870,600,000	805,600,000	883,100,000	884,800,000	870,800,000	843,100,000
Net Income	156,100,000	-72,000,000	112,400,000	22,900,000	71,600,000	120,800,000
Operating Cash Flow	85,000,000	186,000,000	102,200,000	61,400,000	70,800,000	40,100,000
Capital Expenditure	11,200,000	15,500,000	20,000,000	25,600,000	24,600,000	12,700,000
EBITDA	239,300,000	-58,500,000	174,500,000	19,900,000	107,100,000	174,800,000
Return on Assets %						
Return on Equity %						
Debt to Equity	.05%	0.056	0.034			

CONTACT INFORMATION:

Phone: 248 362-4444   Fax: 248 362-2258
Toll-Free:
Address: 999 W. Big Beaver Rd., Troy, MI 48084 United States

SALARIES/BONUSES:

Top Exec. Salary: $840,000   Bonus: $
Second Exec. Salary: $588,000   Bonus: $

STOCK TICKER/OTHER:

Stock Ticker: KELYA   Exchange: NAS
Employees: 7,400   Fiscal Year Ends: 12/31
Parent Company:

OTHER THOUGHTS:

Estimated Female Officers or Directors: 11
Hot Spot for Advancement for Women/Minorities: Y

Kforce Inc

NAIC Code: 561320

www.kforce.com

TYPES OF BUSINESS:
Professional Staffing Services
Temporary Staffing
Permanent Staffing

BRANDS/DIVISIONS/AFFILIATES:

GROWTH PLANS/SPECIAL FEATURES:
Kforce Inc provides professional and technical specialty staffing services and solutions. The company operates three business segments: technology, finance and accounting, and government solutions. Its largest segment by revenue, technology, offers temporary staffing and permanent placement services focusing on system architecture and development, project management, enterprise data management, e-commerce, and security. The remaining operating units provide staffing for general accounting, financial analysis, and technology. Its primary revenue driver for the company is temporary placements. The largest end market is the United States.

CONTACTS: Note: Officers with more than one job title may be intentionally listed here more than once.
David Dunkel, CEO
David Kelly, CFO
Jeffrey Hackman, Chief Accounting Officer
Andrew Thomas, Chief Marketing Officer
Kye Mitchell, COO
Michael Blackman, Other Executive Officer
Joseph Liberatore, President

FINANCIAL DATA: Note: Data for latest year may not have been available at press time.

In U.S. $	2021	2020	2019	2018	2017	2016
Revenue	1,579,922,000	1,397,700,000	1,347,387,000	1,303,937,000	1,253,646,000	1,319,706,000
R&D Expense						
Operating Income	106,643,000	80,256,000	74,821,000	72,401,000	60,018,000	59,056,000
Operating Margin %	.07%	.06%	.06%	.06%	.05%	.04%
SGA Expense	345,721,000	310,713,000	314,167,000	307,250,000	308,313,000	340,742,000
Net Income	75,177,000	56,039,000	130,862,000	57,980,000	33,285,000	32,773,000
Operating Cash Flow	72,898,000	109,159,000	66,617,000	87,723,000	29,339,000	39,823,000
Capital Expenditure	6,441,000	6,475,000	10,359,000	5,170,000	5,846,000	12,420,000
EBITDA	111,143,000	85,511,000	81,302,000	80,666,000	68,526,000	67,852,000
Return on Assets %						
Return on Equity %						
Debt to Equity	.59%	0.637	0.476	0.427	0.887	0.949

CONTACT INFORMATION:
Phone: 813 552-5000   Fax: 813 552-2493
Toll-Free: 877-395-5575
Address: 1001 E. Palm Ave., Tampa, FL 33605 United States

STOCK TICKER/OTHER:
Stock Ticker: KFRC   Exchange: NAS
Employees: 13,900   Fiscal Year Ends: 12/31
Parent Company:

SALARIES/BONUSES:
Top Exec. Salary: $875,000   Bonus: $175,000
Second Exec. Salary: Bonus: $118,800
$660,000

OTHER THOUGHTS:
Estimated Female Officers or Directors: 3
Hot Spot for Advancement for Women/Minorities: Y

Knotel Inc

knotel.com

NAIC Code: 531120

TYPES OF BUSINESS:

Shared Office Space Services
Office and Workspace Rental
Online Booking
Client Meeting Space Rental
Workspace Buildout Services
Flexible Work Spaces

BRANDS/DIVISIONS/AFFILIATES:

Newmark Group Inc

GROWTH PLANS/SPECIAL FEATURES:

Knotel, Inc. offers a flexible office platform for established businesses that require turnkey, customizable solutions to alleviate the burden of long-term lease commitments, costly build-outs and facilities management. Knotel works with companies that have 20 or more employees, and finds, builds, designs and operates office spaces for them. Available spaces can be searched online or via mobile app. Property owners and managers that have spaces to let can request a consultation with Knotel. For brokers interested in partnering with Knotel, the firm will provide the office space and flexible terms while the brokers continue to manage the relationship between themselves and their clients. Knotel operates in leading cities such as New York, Miami, London, Los Angeles, Paris and San Francisco. Knotel operates as a subsidiary of Newmark Group, Inc., a full-service commercial real estate services business.

CONTACTS: Note: Officers with more than one job title may be intentionally listed here more than once.

Barry Gosin, CEO-Newmark

FINANCIAL DATA: Note: Data for latest year may not have been available at press time.

In U.S. $	2021	2020	2019	2018	2017	2016
Revenue	78,000,000	60,000,000	150,000,000	100,000,000	95,000,000	
R&D Expense						
Operating Income						
Operating Margin %						
SGA Expense						
Net Income						
Operating Cash Flow						
Capital Expenditure						
EBITDA						
Return on Assets %						
Return on Equity %						
Debt to Equity						

CONTACT INFORMATION:

Phone: 646 883-6300   Fax:
Toll-Free:
Address: 228 Park Ave., #90047, New York, NY 10003 United States

STOCK TICKER/OTHER:

Stock Ticker: Subsidiiary   Exchange:
Employees: 200   Fiscal Year Ends:
Parent Company: Newmark Group Inc

SALARIES/BONUSES:

Top Exec. Salary: $ Bonus: $
Second Exec. Salary: $ Bonus: $

OTHER THOUGHTS:

Estimated Female Officers or Directors:
Hot Spot for Advancement for Women/Minorities:

Lawn Love Inc

lawnlove.com

NAIC Code: 561730

TYPES OF BUSINESS:

Online Lawn Care Services Arrangement
Lawn Care Services
Gardening
Online Quotes
Online Booking
Tree Trimming Services
Gutter Cleaning Services
Fertilization and Snow Removal

BRANDS/DIVISIONS/AFFILIATES:

GROWTH PLANS/SPECIAL FEATURES:

Lawn Love, Inc. operates a proprietary online lawn service and lawn care marketplace. The firm has combined advanced technology with lawn care and customer service for the purpose of wanting to provide the best lawn service possible. Lawn Love is bonded and carries a multi-million-dollar liability insurance policy. The company guarantees that if a customer is not completely satisfied, they'll return and fix the problem for free. Lawn Love's services include lawn mowing, gardening, lawn fertilization, lawn aeration, weed control, lawn seeding, yard cleanup, leaf removal, gutter cleaning and snow removal. Through the firm's online platform and mobile app, bookings, service and payments are convenient for customers to manage remotely and on-the-go. Reviews are also displayed, as well as a blog for information purposes. Quotes are offered swiftly by the company online or by telephone, and are based on the size of the lawn, location and requested service. Lawn Love's lawn care services are available throughout the U.S.

CONTACTS:
Note: Officers with more than one job title may be intentionally listed here more than once.

Jeremy Yamaguchi, CEO

FINANCIAL DATA:
Note: Data for latest year may not have been available at press time.

In U.S. $	2021	2020	2019	2018	2017	2016
Revenue						
R&D Expense						
Operating Income						
Operating Margin %						
SGA Expense						
Net Income						
Operating Cash Flow						
Capital Expenditure						
EBITDA						
Return on Assets %						
Return on Equity %						
Debt to Equity						

CONTACT INFORMATION:

Phone: 619 320-1006   Fax:
Toll-Free: 800 706-4117
Address: 402 W. Broadway, Ste. 442, San Diego, CA 92101 United States

STOCK TICKER/OTHER:

Stock Ticker: Subsidiary   Exchange:
Employees: Fiscal Year Ends:
Parent Company: LawnStarter Inc

SALARIES/BONUSES:

Top Exec. Salary: $ Bonus: $
Second Exec. Salary: $ Bonus: $

OTHER THOUGHTS:

Estimated Female Officers or Directors:
Hot Spot for Advancement for Women/Minorities:

Lawtrades Inc

www.lawtrades.com

NAIC Code: 541110

TYPES OF BUSINESS:

Online Legal Services
Legal Services
Online Platform
Outsourcing

BRANDS/DIVISIONS/AFFILIATES:

GROWTH PLANS/SPECIAL FEATURES:

Lawtrades, Inc. has developed and operates an online message-based platform that enables users to find, hire and work with lawyers and paralegals at affordable prices. Each lawyer engages with the customer directly, as well as through online and mobile channels, instead of at costly office locations. Services offered by Lawtrades include business formation, intellectual property, web agreements, employment, fundraising, immigration, contracts and more. In addition, Lawtrades provides tech-enabled talent solutions for in-house legal departments, with a focus on overflow, part-time and full-time engagements. The firm's website (www.lawtrades.com) offers free resources such as contract templates, answers to common questions, forming a new business, a dictionary on common business terms and more. Primary investors of Lawtrades include C Four Cities, AngelList, Draper Associates, 500 and Social Capital_.

CONTACTS: Note: Officers with more than one job title may be intentionally listed here more than once.

Raad Ahmed, CEO

FINANCIAL DATA: Note: Data for latest year may not have been available at press time.

In U.S. $	2021	2020	2019	2018	2017	2016
Revenue						
R&D Expense						
Operating Income						
Operating Margin %						
SGA Expense						
Net Income						
Operating Cash Flow						
Capital Expenditure						
EBITDA						
Return on Assets %						
Return on Equity %						
Debt to Equity						

CONTACT INFORMATION:

Phone: 646 781-7197   Fax:
Toll-Free:
Address: 43-01 22nd St., #514, Long Island City, NY 11101 United States

STOCK TICKER/OTHER:

Stock Ticker: Private   Exchange:
Employees: Fiscal Year Ends:
Parent Company:

SALARIES/BONUSES:

Top Exec. Salary: $ Bonus: $
Second Exec. Salary: $ Bonus: $

OTHER THOUGHTS:

Estimated Female Officers or Directors:
Hot Spot for Advancement for Women/Minorities:

Le Tote Inc

NAIC Code: 454111

letote.com

TYPES OF BUSINESS:

Online Rental of Luxury Apparel and Accessories
Online Clothing Rental
Clothes Sharing
Ecommerce

BRANDS/DIVISIONS/AFFILIATES:

Saadia Group LLC

CONTACTS: *Note: Officers with more than one job title may be intentionally listed here more than once.*

Rakesh Tondon, CEO

GROWTH PLANS/SPECIAL FEATURES:

Le Tote, Inc. operates an ecommerce clothing and accessories rental business. The firm's online platform provides customers access to women's clothing and accessories for a monthly membership fee. Featured brands include Splendid, Vince Camuto, BCBGeneration, French Connection, Rebecca Minkoff, Rachel Rachel Roy, Adrianna Papell and KUT from the Kloth, among others. Le Tote utilizes an analytical, data-driven and customer-first approach, serving consumers in 48 U.S. states. How it works: members browse styles and pick items they want to rent; once received by mail, wear them as often as preferred; and then either return items in a provided, pre-paid USPS envelope or keep items and pay up to 50% off retail price. Payment capabilities are offered online or through the app. Fashion styles include casual, athletic leisure, going to an event, business casual, professional or going out. Monthly rental plans start at $59. There is no commitment with Le Tote, memberships can be changed, paused or canceled at any time. Gift cards are available online. Le Tote owns the Lord + Taylor brand. Le Tote operates as a subsidiary of Saadia Group LLC.

FINANCIAL DATA: *Note: Data for latest year may not have been available at press time.*

In U.S. $	2021	2020	2019	2018	2017	2016
Revenue						
R&D Expense						
Operating Income						
Operating Margin %						
SGA Expense						
Net Income						
Operating Cash Flow						
Capital Expenditure						
EBITDA						
Return on Assets %						
Return on Equity %						
Debt to Equity						

CONTACT INFORMATION:

Phone: 415 260-1809   Fax:
Toll-Free: 844 899-8683
Address: 3130 20th St., Ste. 225, San Francisco, CA 94110 United States

STOCK TICKER/OTHER:

Stock Ticker: Subsidiary
Employees:
Parent Company: Saadia Group LLC

Exchange:
Fiscal Year Ends: 12/31

SALARIES/BONUSES:

Top Exec. Salary: $ Bonus: $
Second Exec. Salary: $ Bonus: $

OTHER THOUGHTS:

Estimated Female Officers or Directors:
Hot Spot for Advancement for Women/Minorities:

LegalShield (Pre-Paid Legal Services Inc)   www.legalshield.com

NAIC Code: 541110

TYPES OF BUSINESS:

Pre-Paid Legal Services
Online Legal Services
Online Legal Membership Platform
Individual and Family Legal Services
Small Business Legal Services
Business Startup Legal Services

BRANDS/DIVISIONS/AFFILIATES:

MidOcean Partners
Stone Point Capital LLC
Further Global Capital Management
LegalShield

CONTACTS: Note: Officers with more than one job title may be intentionally listed here more than once.

Kathy Pinson, COO
Steve Williamson, CFO
Cara Whitley, CMO
Arnold Blinn, CTO

GROWTH PLANS/SPECIAL FEATURES:

Pre-Paid Legal Services, Inc. has developed and operates an online, membership-based, legal platform called LegalShield. The platform provides legal services through a network of law firms to LegalShield members and their covered family members. Services for individuals and families include areas such as estate planning, renters, landlords, family law, real estate, commercial drivers, home business, trial defense, gun owners, ride-share and delivery, consumer finance, employment, and traffic and accident. Services for small businesses span intellectual property, debt collection, contracts and agreements, employment, business licenses, civil litigation, trial defense and more. Legal advisory and related services for business startups include business permits, choosing a business structure, business name check, business type (comparisons) and forming a limited liability company (LLC). Monthly and annual membership plans are listed on the LegalShield website. Members have 24/7 emergency access to a dedicated law firm. Pre-Paid Legal Services is privately owned by MidOcean Partners, Stone Point Capital LLC and Further Global Capital Management.

FINANCIAL DATA: Note: Data for latest year may not have been available at press time.

In U.S. $	2021	2020	2019	2018	2017	2016
Revenue						
R&D Expense						
Operating Income						
Operating Margin %						
SGA Expense						
Net Income						
Operating Cash Flow						
Capital Expenditure						
EBITDA						
Return on Assets %						
Return on Equity %						
Debt to Equity						

CONTACT INFORMATION:

Phone: 580 436-1234   Fax:
Toll-Free: 800 654-7757
Address: One Pre-Paid Way, Ada, OK 74820 United States

STOCK TICKER/OTHER:

Stock Ticker: Private   Exchange:
Employees: Fiscal Year Ends:
Parent Company:

SALARIES/BONUSES:

Top Exec. Salary: $ Bonus: $
Second Exec. Salary: $ Bonus: $

OTHER THOUGHTS:

Estimated Female Officers or Directors:
Hot Spot for Advancement for Women/Minorities:

LegalZoom.com Inc

NAIC Code: 541110

www.legalzoom.com

TYPES OF BUSINESS:
Offices of Lawyers
Online Subscription Legal Advisory
Business Compliance Solutions
Business Formation Advisory
Tax and Filing Advisory
Trademark Filing Advisory
Estate Planning Services

BRANDS/DIVISIONS/AFFILIATES:
Revv

GROWTH PLANS/SPECIAL FEATURES:
LegalZoom.com, Inc. has developed and operates an online subscription platform that offers legal and compliance solutions to businesses. The firm offers advisory services, supporting the changing needs of a new business across its lifecycle. These services span formation, ongoing compliance, tax advice and filings, trademark filings and estate planning. LegalZoom.com operates in all 50 U.S. states, and specializes in multiple third-party interactions and regulatory compliance. In late-2022, Legalzoom.com acquired Revv, a global software-as-a-service (SaaS) document automation and forms template company based in Bangalore, India. The transaction gives LegalZoom.com access into the Bangalore market.

CONTACTS: Note: Officers with more than one job title may be intentionally listed here more than once.
Dan Wernikoff, CEO
Noel Watson, CFO

FINANCIAL DATA: Note: Data for latest year may not have been available at press time.

In U.S. $	2021	2020	2019	2018	2017	2016
Revenue						
R&D Expense						
Operating Income						
Operating Margin %						
SGA Expense						
Net Income						
Operating Cash Flow						
Capital Expenditure						
EBITDA						
Return on Assets %						
Return on Equity %						
Debt to Equity						

CONTACT INFORMATION:
Phone: 323 962-8600   Fax:
Toll-Free:
Address: 101 N. Brand Blvd., Fl. 11, Glendale, CA 91203 United States

STOCK TICKER/OTHER:
Stock Ticker: LZ   Exchange: NAS
Employees: 457   Fiscal Year Ends: 12/31
Parent Company:

SALARIES/BONUSES:
Top Exec. Salary: $ Bonus: $
Second Exec. Salary: $ Bonus: $

OTHER THOUGHTS:
Estimated Female Officers or Directors:
Hot Spot for Advancement for Women/Minorities:

Lifealike Limited (onefinestay)

www.onefinestay.com

NAIC Code: 519130

TYPES OF BUSINESS:

Online Vacation Rental Services
Home Vacation Rental
Home Sharing
Online Booking
Hospitality Services

BRANDS/DIVISIONS/AFFILIATES:

Accor SA
onefinestay

CONTACTS: *Note: Officers with more than one job title may be intentionally listed here more than once.*

David Whiteside, COO
Dorothee Guiol, CFO
Amanda Dyjecinski, CMO
Helen Gribble, Chief People Officer
Guillaume Fontana, Sr. Dir.-IT

GROWTH PLANS/SPECIAL FEATURES:

Lifealike Limited operates as onefinestay, which provides hospitality services for stays in homes while the owners are away. The online marketplace offers a range of distinctive private homes and villas throughout Europe, North America, Caribbean, Central America, Asia and Oceania. Pictures are provided of the homes, as well as information such as how many guests each residence accommodates, the number of beds and bathrooms, whether there is a view or a pool and more. Services can be tailored into the bookings, including airport transfers, housekeeping, childcare and grocery service. Onefinestay visits and vets each home in person, and every home is prepared to the exact hospitality standards of its guests. The company's customer service team is available 24/7 for anything needed. The onefinestay marketplace comprises homes within worldwide cities, including countryside homes, beach homes, mountain homes and more. Top destinations include London, Paris, New York, Los Angeles, San Francisco, Rome, Florence and Sydney. Lifealike operates as a subsidiary of Accor SA, a French multi-national hotel group.

FINANCIAL DATA: *Note: Data for latest year may not have been available at press time.*

In U.S. $	2021	2020	2019	2018	2017	2016
Revenue		3,343,019	6,822,489	10,852,719	11,620,200	10,708,700
R&D Expense						
Operating Income						
Operating Margin %						
SGA Expense						
Net Income			72,781,332	-29,359,908	-14,214,900	-32,056,000
Operating Cash Flow						
Capital Expenditure						
EBITDA						
Return on Assets %						
Return on Equity %						
Debt to Equity						

CONTACT INFORMATION:

Phone: 44 20-3588-0600   Fax:
Toll-Free:
Address: 34-43 Russell St., Drury House, London, WC2B 5HA United Kingdom

STOCK TICKER/OTHER:

Stock Ticker: Subsidiary
Employees:
Parent Company: Accor SA

Exchange:
Fiscal Year Ends: 12/31

SALARIES/BONUSES:

Top Exec. Salary: $ Bonus: $
Second Exec. Salary: $ Bonus: $

OTHER THOUGHTS:

Estimated Female Officers or Directors:
Hot Spot for Advancement for Women/Minorities:

LiquidSpace Inc

NAIC Code: 519130

liquidspace.com

TYPES OF BUSINESS:

Online Office Space Rental Service
Office Rental
Space Sharing
Online Team Collaboration
Hybrid Workplace

BRANDS/DIVISIONS/AFFILIATES:

Workplace Manager

CONTACTS: *Note: Officers with more than one job title may be intentionally listed here more than once.*

Mark Gilbreath, CEO

GROWTH PLANS/SPECIAL FEATURES:

LiquidSpace, Inc. has developed and operates an office-sharing network from which office space can be booked via online or mobile app. This platform enables individuals, startups and/or business teams to connect directly with real estate owners, operators and companies that have space to share. LiquidSpace's proprietary tools simplify this process, as well as the legal framework that comes with traditional office lease agreements, and therefore significantly reduces costs and contract complexities. Available office spaces can be obtained by users with a simple click. There is no lease agreement; spaces are simply paid for by the hour or month. Tailored flexible office solutions can also be arranged for enterprises at agreed-upon prices. Liquidspace.com offers spaces to accommodate practically any rent budget. Types of workspaces include: conference room, remote office, presentation room, shared office space, co-working, cubicle, deposition room, document review, meeting room, board room, personal workspace, private office, training room and desk space. Office spaces are available in the U.S. Australia and Canada, with top cities including San Francisco, Chicago, Sydney, New York, Washington DC, Melbourne, Boston, Austin, Los Angeles and Atlanta. For enterprises, LiquidSpace also offers a hybrid workplace solution, which enables employees to work anywhere they want or need to be. The Workplace Manager enables teams to collaborate no matter if dispersed, curates work spaces to meet each employee's needs, assigns budget limits/payment methods through the platform, ensures secure online access and many other capabilities.

FINANCIAL DATA: *Note: Data for latest year may not have been available at press time.*

In U.S. $	2021	2020	2019	2018	2017	2016
Revenue						
R&D Expense						
Operating Income						
Operating Margin %						
SGA Expense						
Net Income						
Operating Cash Flow						
Capital Expenditure						
EBITDA						
Return on Assets %						
Return on Equity %						
Debt to Equity						

CONTACT INFORMATION:

Phone: 208 720-8107   Fax:
Toll-Free: 855 254-7843
Address: 1900 S. Norfolk St., Ste. 350, San Mateo, CA 94403 United States

STOCK TICKER/OTHER:

Stock Ticker: Private   Exchange:
Employees: Fiscal Year Ends:
Parent Company:

SALARIES/BONUSES:

Top Exec. Salary: $ Bonus: $
Second Exec. Salary: $ Bonus: $

OTHER THOUGHTS:

Estimated Female Officers or Directors:
Hot Spot for Advancement for Women/Minorities:

Localiza Rent A Car S/A

www.localiza.com

NAIC Code: 532111

TYPES OF BUSINESS:

Car Rental
Car Rental
Vehicle Franchises
Used Vehicle Sales

BRANDS/DIVISIONS/AFFILIATES:

Localiza Seminovos

GROWTH PLANS/SPECIAL FEATURES:

Localiza Rent A Car SA is a car rental service provider with the majority of its operations in Brazil. Through its subsidiaries, the company rents cars to individuals, manages corporate car fleets, sells its fleet to the general public, and offers a franchise model. Franchisees account for roughly half of Localize's car rental locations, while the majority of cars accessible with Localize are owned by the company. The fleet rental division has long-term agreements with companies that come up for renewal roughly every two to three years. The car rental segment delivers three-quarters of yearly revenue, and fleet rental makes up the rest, with an insignificant share contributed by the franchise management division.

CONTACTS: Note: Officers with more than one job title may be intentionally listed here more than once.

Eugenio Pacelli Mattar, CEO

FINANCIAL DATA: Note: Data for latest year may not have been available at press time.

In U.S. $	2021	2020	2019	2018	2017	2016
Revenue	1,989,839,616	2,017,106,432	1,861,027,200	1,409,788,800	1,041,460,352	847,836,672
R&D Expense						
Operating Income						
Operating Margin %						
SGA Expense						
Net Income	373,035,872	205,119,280	152,220,128	117,701,000	86,929,224	78,173,224
Operating Cash Flow						
Capital Expenditure						
EBITDA						
Return on Assets %						
Return on Equity %						
Debt to Equity						

CONTACT INFORMATION:

Phone: 55 3132477753   Fax: 55 3132477755
Toll-Free: 800-979-2000
Address: Avenida Bernardo Vasconcelos, N-377 Cachoeirinha, Belo Horizonte, MG 31150 000 Brazil

STOCK TICKER/OTHER:

Stock Ticker: LZRFY
Employees: 12,223
Parent Company:

Exchange: PINX
Fiscal Year Ends: 12/31

SALARIES/BONUSES:

Top Exec. Salary: $ Bonus: $
Second Exec. Salary: $ Bonus: $

OTHER THOUGHTS:

Estimated Female Officers or Directors:
Hot Spot for Advancement for Women/Minorities:

Lyft Inc

NAIC Code: 561599

TYPES OF BUSINESS:

Car Ride Dispatch Service, Mobile App-Based
Bicycle Rental & Sharing Systems
Augmented Reality Technology
Rental Cars
Vehicle Sharing

BRANDS/DIVISIONS/AFFILIATES:

Lyft
Lyft Rental

GROWTH PLANS/SPECIAL FEATURES:

Lyft is the second-largest ride-sharing service provider in the U.S., connecting riders and drivers over the Lyft app. Lyft recently entered the Canadian market in an effort to expand its market outside the U.S. Incorporated in 2013, Lyft offers a variety of rides via private vehicles, including traditional private rides, shared rides, and luxury ones. Besides ride-share, Lyft also has entered the bike- and scooter-share market to bring multimodal transportation options to users.

CONTACTS: Note: Officers with more than one job title may be intentionally listed here more than once.

Logan Green, CEO
Brian Roberts, CFO
Prashant Aggarwal, Chairman of the Board
Lisa Blackwood-Kapral, Chief Accounting Officer
John Zimmer, Co-Founder
Eisar Lipkovitz, Executive VP, Divisional
Lindsay Llewellyn, General Counsel
Ashwin Raj, Other Corporate Officer
Kristin Sverchek, President, Divisional

FINANCIAL DATA: Note: Data for latest year may not have been available at press time.

In U.S. $	2021	2020	2019	2018	2017	2016
Revenue	3,208,323,000	2,364,681,000	3,615,960,000	2,156,616,000	1,059,881,000	343,298,000
R&D Expense	911,946,000	909,126,000	1,505,640,000	300,836,000	136,646,000	64,704,000
Operating Income	-1,135,217,000	-1,808,382,000	-2,702,480,000	-977,711,000	-708,272,000	-692,603,000
Operating Margin %	-.35%	-.76%	-.75%	-.45%	-.67%	-2.02%
SGA Expense	1,327,044,000	1,362,458,000	2,000,215,000	1,251,689,000	788,461,000	594,306,000
Net Income	-1,062,144,000	-1,752,857,000	-2,602,241,000	-911,335,000	-688,301,000	-682,794,000
Operating Cash Flow	-101,721,000	-1,378,899,000	-105,702,000	-280,673,000	-393,526,000	-487,163,000
Capital Expenditure	79,176,000	93,639,000	178,088,000	70,868,000	12,023,000	8,819,000
EBITDA	-859,937,000	-1,607,360,000	-2,491,456,000	-891,845,000	-705,661,000	-692,076,000
Return on Assets %						
Return on Equity %						
Debt to Equity	.65%	0.543	0.134			

CONTACT INFORMATION:

Phone: 412 620-6133   Fax:
Toll-Free: 844-250-2773
Address: 185 Berry St., Ste. 5000, San Francisco, CA 94107 United States

STOCK TICKER/OTHER:

Stock Ticker: LYFT
Employees: 4,453
Parent Company:

Exchange: NAS
Fiscal Year Ends:

SALARIES/BONUSES:

Top Exec. Salary: $450,000   Bonus: $32,712
Second Exec. Salary: $450,000   Bonus: $32,712

OTHER THOUGHTS:

Estimated Female Officers or Directors: 2
Hot Spot for Advancement for Women/Minorities:

ManpowerGroup Inc

www.manpowergroup.com

NAIC Code: 561320

TYPES OF BUSINESS:

Staffing & Temporary Help
Employee Testing, Training & Development
Internal Audit, Accounting & Tax Services
Organizational Performance Consulting
IT Recruitment & Managed Services
Business Function Outsourcing
Market Research

BRANDS/DIVISIONS/AFFILIATES:

Experis
Manpower
ManpowerGroup Solutions
Right Management
Manpower Switzerland

GROWTH PLANS/SPECIAL FEATURES:

ManpowerGroup is one of the largest firms in the fragmented global staffing industry. It serves each main staffing category-- temporary, permanent, and project-based--and offers a suite of human resources outsourcing and outplacement services. Manpower generates annual revenue and operating income of more than $20 billion and nearly $600 million, respectively. A vast majority of sales are generated outside the U.S. from operations in 80 countries. Its 30,000 employees serve an estimated 600,000 clients and place millions of job candidates.

CONTACTS: Note: Officers with more than one job title may be intentionally listed here more than once.

Jonas Prising, CEO
John McGinnis, CFO
Donald Mondano, Chief Accounting Officer
Richard Buchband, General Counsel
Michelle Nettles, Other Executive Officer

FINANCIAL DATA: Note: Data for latest year may not have been available at press time.

In U.S. $	2021	2020	2019	2018	2017	2016
Revenue	20,724,400,000	18,001,000,000	20,863,500,000	21,991,200,000	21,034,300,000	19,654,100,000
R&D Expense						
Operating Income	585,400,000	254,400,000	708,900,000	796,700,000	789,200,000	745,500,000
Operating Margin %	.03%	.01%	.03%	.04%	.04%	.04%
SGA Expense	2,822,100,000	2,570,300,000	2,666,200,000	2,782,300,000	2,695,400,000	2,588,300,000
Net Income	382,400,000	23,800,000	465,700,000	556,700,000	545,400,000	443,700,000
Operating Cash Flow	644,800,000	936,400,000	814,400,000	483,100,000	400,900,000	600,000,000
Capital Expenditure	64,200,000	50,700,000	52,900,000	64,700,000	54,700,000	56,900,000
EBITDA	680,300,000	267,300,000	807,100,000	887,500,000	871,100,000	836,100,000
Return on Assets %						
Return on Equity %						
Debt to Equity	.33%	0.577	0.492	0.391	0.172	0.333

CONTACT INFORMATION:

Phone: 414 961-1000   Fax: 414 332-0796
Toll-Free:
Address: 100 Manpower Pl., Milwaukee, WI 53212 United States

STOCK TICKER/OTHER:

Stock Ticker: MAN
Employees: 30,000
Parent Company:

Exchange: NYS
Fiscal Year Ends: 12/31

SALARIES/BONUSES:

Top Exec. Salary: $1,250,000   Bonus: $
Second Exec. Salary: $746,750   Bonus: $

OTHER THOUGHTS:

Estimated Female Officers or Directors: 5
Hot Spot for Advancement for Women/Minorities: Y

Mastech Digital Inc

www.mastechdigital.com

NAIC Code: 561320

TYPES OF BUSINESS:

IT Staffing
Digital Transformation
Information Technology
IT Consultancy

BRANDS/DIVISIONS/AFFILIATES:

InfoTrellis Inc
Mas-Remote
AmberLeaf Partners Inc

GROWTH PLANS/SPECIAL FEATURES:

Mastech Digital Inc is a provider of Digital Transformation IT Services. The Company offers data and analytics solutions; digital learning; and IT staffing services for both digital and mainstream technologies. Its Data and Analytics Services segment delivers specialized data management, data engineering, customer experience consulting, data analytics, and cloud services to customers globally. IT Staffing Services segment combines technical expertise with business process experience to deliver a broad range of services in digital and mainstream technologies. Its digital transformation services also include staffing and project-based services around digital learning. The company earns the majority of the revenue from IT staffing services.

CONTACTS: Note: Officers with more than one job title may be intentionally listed here more than once.

Paul Burton, CEO, Subsidiary
Vivek Gupta, CEO
John Cronin, CFO
Sunil Wadhwani, Co-Chairman of the Board
Ashok Trivedi, Co-Chairman of the Board

FINANCIAL DATA: Note: Data for latest year may not have been available at press time.

In U.S. $	2021	2020	2019	2018	2017	2016
Revenue	222,012,000	194,101,000	193,574,000	177,164,000	147,882,000	132,008,000
R&D Expense						
Operating Income	14,728,000	13,403,000	10,918,000	10,307,000	4,081,000	4,507,000
Operating Margin %	.07%	.07%	.06%	.06%	.03%	.03%
SGA Expense						21,790,000
Net Income	12,221,000	9,861,000	11,145,000	6,691,000	1,626,000	2,520,000
Operating Cash Flow	5,216,000	21,231,000	16,084,000	-471,000	3,347,000	2,292,000
Capital Expenditure	1,895,000	298,000	1,014,000	771,000	1,127,000	105,000
EBITDA	18,707,000	16,992,000	14,352,000	13,489,000	6,023,000	5,523,000
Return on Assets %						
Return on Equity %						
Debt to Equity	.16%	0.255	0.519	0.996	1.258	0.424

CONTACT INFORMATION:

Phone: 412 787-2100   Fax:
Toll-Free:
Address: 1305 Cherrington Pkwy, Bldg. 210, Ste 400, Moon Township, PA 15108 United States

STOCK TICKER/OTHER:

Stock Ticker: MHH   Exchange: ASE
Employees: 2,014   Fiscal Year Ends: 12/31
Parent Company:

SALARIES/BONUSES:

Top Exec. Salary: $548,627   Bonus: $
Second Exec. Salary: $427,788   Bonus: $

OTHER THOUGHTS:

Estimated Female Officers or Directors:
Hot Spot for Advancement for Women/Minorities:

Sales, profits and employees may be estimates. Financial information, benefits and other data can change quickly and may vary from those stated here.

Meituan Dianping

about.meituan.com/en

NAIC Code: 519130

TYPES OF BUSINESS:

Online Reviews
Food Delivery
Attraction Tickets
Hotel Booking
Bike Sharing
Websites
Mobile Apps

BRANDS/DIVISIONS/AFFILIATES:

Dianping.com
Meituan.com

GROWTH PLANS/SPECIAL FEATURES:

Meituan is the largest food delivery service in China, with a 70.7% share of the market in 2020 per the Chinese government. For the quarter ended Sept. 30, 2021, the firm generated 54.2% of revenue from food delivery services, 17.7% from hotel booking, coupon sales, advertising, and 28.1% from new initiatives. In the long term, its new initiatives business may transform the company into an all-encompassing grocer and logistics business involving community group buying, nonfood delivery, and online grocery, overtaking food delivery as its main business.

CONTACTS: *Note: Officers with more than one job title may be intentionally listed here more than once.*

Wang Xing, CEO
Zhang Tao, CEO-Shanghai Han Tao

FINANCIAL DATA: *Note: Data for latest year may not have been available at press time.*

In U.S. $	2021	2020	2019	2018	2017	2016
Revenue	25,907,640,000	16,602,960,000	14,105,740,000	9,433,950,000	4,907,072,000	1,878,491,000
R&D Expense	2,411,824,000	1,575,406,000	1,221,513,000	1,022,823,000	527,419,900	342,296,700
Operating Income	-3,181,087,000	-279,224,600	188,978,300	-1,907,875,000	-645,296,000	-927,160,400
Operating Margin %	-.12%	-.02%	.01%	-.20%	-.13%	-.49%
SGA Expense	7,129,748,000	3,829,360,000	3,349,390,000	3,097,719,000	1,891,800,000	762,001,700
Net Income	-3,404,402,000	680,972,700	323,797,600	-16,701,690,000	-2,735,948,000	-837,404,700
Operating Cash Flow	-580,185,000	1,225,758,000	806,210,400	-1,327,695,000	-44,864,840	-277,407,600
Capital Expenditure	1,303,200,000	2,288,720,000	434,147,000	329,755,300	107,885,500	51,434,750
EBITDA	-1,960,886,000	1,443,061,000	1,125,875,000	-15,923,900,000	-2,616,020,000	-842,435,100
Return on Assets %						
Return on Equity %						
Debt to Equity						

CONTACT INFORMATION:

Phone: 86 215-355-9777   Fax:
Toll-Free:
Address: No. 4 Wang Jing East Rd., Beijing, Beijing 100102 China

STOCK TICKER/OTHER:

Stock Ticker: MPNGF
Employees: 100,033
Parent Company:

Exchange: PINX
Fiscal Year Ends: 12/31

SALARIES/BONUSES:

Top Exec. Salary: $ Bonus: $
Second Exec. Salary: $ Bonus: $

OTHER THOUGHTS:

Estimated Female Officers or Directors:
Hot Spot for Advancement for Women/Minorities:

Motivate LLC

NAIC Code: 532292

www.motivateco.com

TYPES OF BUSINESS:

Bike Sharing Services
Bike-Sharing
Technology
Mobile App Booking
Online Management

BRANDS/DIVISIONS/AFFILIATES:

Lyft Inc
Bikeshare Holdings LLC
Capital Bikeshare

CONTACTS: *Note: Officers with more than one job title may be intentionally listed here more than once.*

Matthew Parker, CEO
Grant Barkey, Chief Admin. Officer
Kenneth Ezeadichie, CFO
Troy Poe, Chief People Officer
Matthew Baker, VP-Global Development
Albert Grice, Chief of Staff

GROWTH PLANS/SPECIAL FEATURES:

Motivate, LLC is a global full-service bikeshare operator and technology innovator. The firm offers a full suite of services that help plan, launch, operate and grow bikeshare systems (micromobility). Each Motivate system is run by a local general manager responsible for day-to-day operations; and each general manager is supported by corporate resources such as business intelligence, and a peer-network experienced in bike share. Regional bike share programs serve as a transportation option, and Motivate contracts and operates multi-jurisdiction systems. Many of its systems operate in multiple U.S. cities and some span state lines. Capital Bikeshare is the company's multi-jurisdiction system that operates multiple municipalities. Currently, Motivate operates in the metro areas of Chicago, New York, Washington DC, Boston, San Francisco Bay area, Minneapolis, Columbus and Portland. Motivate takes a data-driven approach to maintenance and repair, keeping bikes and docks in good repair, safe and available for riders. Customer service support teams work 24/7 by phone, email and social media to troubleshoot problems. Motivate's bike valets and corrals help increase capacity at high-demand locations during peak hours by providing staff to receive or supply bikes from strategically-located bike corrals. Motivate operates as a subsidiary of Bikeshare Holdings, LLC, itself a subsidiary of Lyft, Inc.

Motivate offers full-time employees health benefits, 401(k) and paid time off.

FINANCIAL DATA: *Note: Data for latest year may not have been available at press time.*

In U.S. $	2021	2020	2019	2018	2017	2016
Revenue	60,000,000	44,100,000	110,250,000	105,000,000	100,000,000	
R&D Expense						
Operating Income						
Operating Margin %						
SGA Expense						
Net Income						
Operating Cash Flow						
Capital Expenditure						
EBITDA						
Return on Assets %						
Return on Equity %						
Debt to Equity						

CONTACT INFORMATION:

Phone: 503-482-7042   Fax:
Toll-Free:
Address: 353 West St., Unit 225, New York, NY 10014 United States

STOCK TICKER/OTHER:

Stock Ticker: Subsidiary   Exchange:
Employees: 800   Fiscal Year Ends:
Parent Company: Lyft Inc

SALARIES/BONUSES:

Top Exec. Salary: $ Bonus: $
Second Exec. Salary: $ Bonus: $

OTHER THOUGHTS:

Estimated Female Officers or Directors:
Hot Spot for Advancement for Women/Minorities:

NeighborFavor Inc (Favor)

favordelivery.com

NAIC Code: 492210

TYPES OF BUSINESS:

Local Delivery Service
Food and Grocery Delivery Service
Online Ordering
Mobile Ordering
Restaurant Order and Delivery
Grocery Order and Delivery
Digital Payment Solutions

BRANDS/DIVISIONS/AFFILIATES:

HEB Grocery Company LP
Favor
Runners

CONTACTS: *Note: Officers with more than one job title may be intentionally listed here more than once.*

Jag Bath, CEO
Jason Lepes, COO
Angela Lee, CFO
Rachel Losh, Chief Product Officer
Daniel Guzman, Chief Legal Officer
Steve Romney, CTO

GROWTH PLANS/SPECIAL FEATURES:

NeighborFavor, Inc. has developed and operates an online and mobile food and grocery delivery platform called Favor. The app enables users throughout Texas to order food from local restaurants, with the items being delivered directly to their door primarily in under one hour's time. By entering an address, the app's screen of locally-connected restaurants display meals and beverages for users to order from. Orders can range from a single taco or soda to a five-course meal or more. Customer ratings are available as well. In addition, Favor will deliver personal goods such as dry cleaning, prescriptions, clothing purchases, groceries and more. Delivery persons, referred to as Runners, wear blue t-shirts with a tuxedo imprinted on the front. Payments are secure and cashless, and take place in the app. Favor charges a delivery fee based off the city and a 5%-to-9% processing fee for the cost of items paid for on the user's behalf. Tips are a suggested $2 minimum and go entirely to the Runner. The average delivery time is 35 minutes, but can vary depending on demand, traffic and restaurant/store wait times. NeighborFavor supplies Runners with the equipment and tools needed for their jobs, including laptops and monitors to photoshop and illustrate food offered by partner restaurants and stores. Favor offers its services in more than 130 cities across Texas. Gift cards are available on the company's website. NeighborFavor is owned by HEB Grocery Company LP.

NeighborFavor offers its employees health, dental and vision coverage, 401(k) options and other benefits and company perks.

FINANCIAL DATA: *Note: Data for latest year may not have been available at press time.*

In U.S. $	2021	2020	2019	2018	2017	2016
Revenue						
R&D Expense						
Operating Income						
Operating Margin %						
SGA Expense						
Net Income						
Operating Cash Flow						
Capital Expenditure						
EBITDA						
Return on Assets %						
Return on Equity %						
Debt to Equity						

CONTACT INFORMATION:

Phone: 512 761-6037   Fax:
Toll-Free:
Address: 2416 E. 6th St., Austin, TX 78702 United States

STOCK TICKER/OTHER:

Stock Ticker: Subsidiary   Exchange:
Employees: Fiscal Year Ends:
Parent Company: HEB Grocery Company LP

SALARIES/BONUSES:

Top Exec. Salary: $ Bonus: $
Second Exec. Salary: $ Bonus: $

OTHER THOUGHTS:

Estimated Female Officers or Directors:
Hot Spot for Advancement for Women/Minorities:

NetJets IP LLC

NAIC Code: 481211

www.netjets.com

TYPES OF BUSINESS:

Charter Aircraft
Fractional Aircraft Ownership
Aircraft Maintenance and Repair
Personal Security

BRANDS/DIVISIONS/AFFILIATES:

Berkshire Hathaway Inc
QS Partners LLC
Executive Jet Management Inc
QS Security
NetJets Share
NetJets Lease
NetJets Card Program

CONTACTS: *Note: Officers with more than one job title may be intentionally listed here more than once.*

Adam Johnson, CEO
Alan Bobo, COO
Pete Richards, CFO
Patrick Gallagher, Pres.-Sales & Mktg.
Chuck Suma, Sr. VP-Aircraft Mgmt.
Adam Johnson, Chmn.

GROWTH PLANS/SPECIAL FEATURES:

NetJets IP, LLC, owned by Berkshire Hathaway, Inc., is a leading provider of fractional aircraft ownership. NetJets manages more than 850 aircraft, of which individuals and businesses can buy a portion based on the number of actual flight hours they need. Owners are guaranteed use of an aircraft, within as little as four hours' notice, 24-hours-a-day, every day of the year. The company provides light, midsize and large cabin aircraft; flight crew management; ground support; and service in the U.S., Europe and China. The firm's NetJets Share interest ownership plan is for people who fly 50 or more hours per year and want the advantages of owning an asset. There is a 4-to-6-hour minimum booking notice requirement, as well as a minimum commitment of 36 months. The NetJets Lease program offers similar benefits to Share, but with a 24-month minimum commitment. A NetJets Lease starts at 50 hours of annual flying time and may be increased in 25-hour increments. The NetJets Card Program is for those who want the benefits of NetJets, but fly fewer than 50 hours, and have access to NetJets aircraft 25+ annual hours, with a 10-hour minimum booking notice and no long-term commitment. Flight times are pre-paid on the specific aircraft type, through the card program. The company operates select models of Embraer, Cessna and Bombardier aircraft. In addition, QS Security is a division of NetJets that orchestrates executive protection for the company's owners and guests, on the ground and in the air. NetJets subsidiaries include: QS Partners, LLC, a brokerage that works with individuals and businesses that own, or are considering ownership of, whole aircraft; and Executive Jet Management, Inc., offering worldwide aircraft management and private jet charter services.

NetJets offers pilots comprehensive benefits, 401(k), meal allowances, and paid hotel and travel expenses.

FINANCIAL DATA: *Note: Data for latest year may not have been available at press time.*

In U.S. $	2021	2020	2019	2018	2017	2016
Revenue	4,900,000,000	4,222,930,000	4,882,500,000	4,650,000,000	4,450,000,000	4,310,775,000
R&D Expense						
Operating Income						
Operating Margin %						
SGA Expense						
Net Income						
Operating Cash Flow						
Capital Expenditure						
EBITDA						
Return on Assets %						
Return on Equity %						
Debt to Equity						

CONTACT INFORMATION:

Phone: 614-239-5500   Fax:
Toll-Free: 877-356-5823
Address: 4151 Bridgeway Ave., Columbus, OH 43219 United States

STOCK TICKER/OTHER:

Stock Ticker: Subsidiary   Exchange:
Employees: 6,900   Fiscal Year Ends: 12/31
Parent Company: Berkshire Hathaway Inc

SALARIES/BONUSES:

Top Exec. Salary: $ Bonus: $
Second Exec. Salary: $ Bonus: $

OTHER THOUGHTS:

Estimated Female Officers or Directors:
Hot Spot for Advancement for Women/Minorities:

Neutron Holdings Inc (Lime)

www.li.me

NAIC Code: 532292

TYPES OF BUSINESS:

Recreational Goods Rental
Electric Scooter Rental
Electric Bike Rental
Micromobility Sharing
Mobile App
Online Booking
Insurance Solutions
Mobility Assistance Services

BRANDS/DIVISIONS/AFFILIATES:

Lime Access
Lime Hero
Lime Assist

CONTACTS: Note: Officers with more than one job title may be intentionally listed here more than once.

Wayne Ting, CEO

GROWTH PLANS/SPECIAL FEATURES:

Neutron Holdings, Inc. operates Lime, an online/mobile app mobility service that offers ride-sharing services through the distribution of shared e-scooters and e-bikes. Lime connects riders with these mobility options, and requests helmets for those riding its scooters and bikes. Users are encouraged to do a pre-ride safety check, are shown how to apply the brakes for slowing down or stopping, and shown the proper hand signals for traffic/vehicle communication. Lime Access provides low-income individuals with subsidized rides. Lime Hero is a community-empowerment program that allows riders to round up the cost of their rides to support a community organization in their hometown. Lime Assist is a program that extends access to shared electric vehicles for persons with varying abilities. Lime Assist vehicles are designed to meet a wide spectrum of abilities and are available to riders free of charge. Riders can access Lime Assist online or via mobile app, and select a vehicle and drop-off time. Lime then delivers the vehicle to the rider's door and picks it up 24 hours later. Lime has obtained insurance coverage with respect to its own activities and the key risks to riders arising from the use of Lime and JUMP vehicles. Riders in EMEA and Asia-Pacific benefit from the insurance coverage at no additional cost through an insurance policy obtained by Lime via Allianz. Bikes and scooters are unlocked via QR code through the apps. Lime is present across five continents.

FINANCIAL DATA: Note: Data for latest year may not have been available at press time.

In U.S. $	2021	2020	2019	2018	2017	2016
Revenue						
R&D Expense						
Operating Income						
Operating Margin %						
SGA Expense						
Net Income						
Operating Cash Flow						
Capital Expenditure						
EBITDA						
Return on Assets %						
Return on Equity %						
Debt to Equity						

CONTACT INFORMATION:

Phone: 510 710-2684   Fax:
Toll-Free: 888 546-3345
Address: 82 2nd St., San Francisco, CA 94105 United States

STOCK TICKER/OTHER:

Stock Ticker: Private   Exchange:
Employees: Fiscal Year Ends:
Parent Company:

SALARIES/BONUSES:

Top Exec. Salary: $ Bonus: $
Second Exec. Salary: $ Bonus: $

OTHER THOUGHTS:

Estimated Female Officers or Directors:
Hot Spot for Advancement for Women/Minorities:

Nuro Inc

NAIC Code: 336111

nuro.ai

TYPES OF BUSINESS:
Automobile Manufacturing
Self-Driving, Electric Delivery Vehicles
Cargo Delivery
Autonomous Delivery
Robotic Vehicles
Artificial Intelligence
Hot and Cold Flexibility Solutions

BRANDS/DIVISIONS/AFFILIATES:
R2
P2
Nuro

CONTACTS: Note: Officers with more than one job title may be intentionally listed here more than once.
Jiajun Zhu, CEO
Dave Ferguson, Pres.
Abishek Viswananthan, CFO
Sarah Eno Henderson, VP-Mktg. & Communications
Andrew Chapin, VP-People & Oper.
Andrew Clare, CTO
David Estrada, Chief Legal and Policy Officer

GROWTH PLANS/SPECIAL FEATURES:
Nuro, Inc. is a robotics company that develops autonomous delivery vehicles. To date, the firm's products are R2, P2 and Nuro. R2 are electric and self-driving vehicles, and designed for the delivery of local commerce. The vehicles carry only cargo. The R2 differs from the R1 in that it was designed with no steering wheel, side view mirrors or pedals. Nonetheless, R2 features 360-degree cameras, as well as LiDAR short- and long-range radar, and ultrasonic sensors. Nuro combines the advanced hardware with an autonomy stack that includes mapping, localization, perception and prediction. P2 is a small, self-driving EV sedan that performs autonomous deliveries with onboard safety operators. Nuro released its third-generation autonomous delivery EV in 2022 and named it Nuro, which is 20% smaller than the average passenger vehicle and yet holds nearly 500 pounds of groceries. Everything within the Nuro EV is accessible with the help of an intuitive touchscreen; and an innovative HVAC system keeps food cool or hot via separate compartments. Compartment inserts can be mixed and matched for new applications, such as mobile marketplaces or hot coffee dispensing. Nuro, Inc. has partnered with leading retail brands and are continuously testing its fleet for the benefit of customers, businesses and communities. The robots are human powered. Partners of Nuro include Domino's, Kroger, Walmart, Uber Eats, FedEx and 7-Eleven. Currently (late 2022), Nuro delivers in Houston, Texas and Silicon Valley, California.

FINANCIAL DATA: Note: Data for latest year may not have been available at press time.

In U.S. $	2021	2020	2019	2018	2017	2016
Revenue		7,300,000	9,273,000			
R&D Expense						
Operating Income						
Operating Margin %						
SGA Expense						
Net Income						
Operating Cash Flow						
Capital Expenditure						
EBITDA						
Return on Assets %						
Return on Equity %						
Debt to Equity						

CONTACT INFORMATION:
Phone: 650 476-2687   Fax:
Toll-Free:
Address: 1300 Terra Bella Ave., Ste. 100, Mountain View, CA 94043 United States

STOCK TICKER/OTHER:
Stock Ticker: Private
Employees: 992
Parent Company:

Exchange:
Fiscal Year Ends:

SALARIES/BONUSES:
Top Exec. Salary: $ Bonus: $
Second Exec. Salary: $ Bonus: $

OTHER THOUGHTS:
Estimated Female Officers or Directors:
Hot Spot for Advancement for Women/Minorities:

Observa Inc

NAIC Code: 541910

TYPES OF BUSINESS:

Information Collection & Analysis
Information Gathering Solutions
Analytics
Business Insights
Product Marketing Solutions
Data and Prediction Validation
Artificial Intelligence
Inventory Management

BRANDS/DIVISIONS/AFFILIATES:

CONTACTS: *Note: Officers with more than one job title may be intentionally listed here more than once.*

Hugh Holman, CEO
Joseph Peck, COO
Erik Chelstad, CTO

GROWTH PLANS/SPECIAL FEATURES:

Observa, Inc. provides an information gathering and analytic platform so clients can draw insight and understanding about their products within stores as well as about customers who shop there. Observa's solutions are related to product roll out, promotional display, stock check, product demonstrations, altruism and data and prediction validation. Product roll out solutions help clients launch products into the marketplace, and include insight on how the product should be priced, where promotional material should be displayed and which stores the product would have the best opportunity for success. Observa's technology enables clients to check on every aspect of retail execution in as many locations as they choose, in real-time. The firm's promotional display solutions include the ability to monitor pricing, in-store placement, display compliance as well as knowing if the product is out of stock or not. Scheduled in-store demonstrations of the product are checked via Observa, at the time they are supposed to be occurring. The company accomplishes this by sending live Observers to the stores during scheduled demo times. Is the demo occurring? Is the brand being represented as preferred? Is the agent speaking clearly about the product? Observa provides answers to these questions through verifiable quantitative data driven by machine learning and artificial intelligence (AI), which is conducted by on-site live Observers who take pictures, video and/or audio to verify if and where the product is being displayed, how many items are on the shelf, the listed price, and capturing live customer shopping interactions, demonstrations and other activities. Price plans vary per set services, with options for add-ons. Using both computers and humans, Observa makes sure all observation data is valid. Clients then sort through the data, current and historical, and interpret it for best product and marketing potential.

FINANCIAL DATA: *Note: Data for latest year may not have been available at press time.*

In U.S. $	2021	2020	2019	2018	2017	2016
Revenue						
R&D Expense						
Operating Income						
Operating Margin %						
SGA Expense						
Net Income						
Operating Cash Flow						
Capital Expenditure						
EBITDA						
Return on Assets %						
Return on Equity %						
Debt to Equity						

CONTACT INFORMATION:

Phone: 206 900-9833   Fax:
Toll-Free:
Address: 323 N. 46th St., Ste. B, Seattle, WA 98103 United States

STOCK TICKER/OTHER:

Stock Ticker: Private   Exchange:
Employees: Fiscal Year Ends:
Parent Company:

SALARIES/BONUSES:

Top Exec. Salary: $ Bonus: $
Second Exec. Salary: $ Bonus: $

OTHER THOUGHTS:

Estimated Female Officers or Directors:
Hot Spot for Advancement for Women/Minorities:

Sales, profits and employees may be estimates. Financial information, benefits and other data can change quickly and may vary from those stated here.

Ocado Group PLC

NAIC Code: 454111

www.ocado.com

TYPES OF BUSINESS:
Online Grocery Shopping
Ecommerce
Grocery
Home Delivery
Technology
Robotics
Automation
Warehouse

BRANDS/DIVISIONS/AFFILIATES:
Ocado Smart Platform
Ocado.com
Ocado Retail Limited
Ocado Engineering

GROWTH PLANS/SPECIAL FEATURES:
Ocado, one of the largest pure online grocers in the world, operates in two divisions. Ocado Retail is the group's online grocery business in the United Kingdom (joint venture with Marks & Spencer); it offers an extensive product range of over 55,000 items via its Ocado.com website and holds more than 15% of the U.K. online grocery market and approximately 2% of the total U.K. grocery market. Ocado Solutions is built on the Ocado Smart Platform, a modular, automated online retail fulfilment and delivery solution that involves the provision of software, fulfilment infrastructure, and support services to corporate clients for a variety of one-time and ongoing costs. OSP has allowed the company to work with 11 of the world's major grocers, including Ocado's retail operation.

CONTACTS: Note: Officers with more than one job title may be intentionally listed here more than once.
Tim Steiner, CEO
Neill Abrams, Dir.-Legal & Bus. Affairs
Mark Richardson, Dir.-Oper.
Jason Gissing, Dir.-Commercial

FINANCIAL DATA: Note: Data for latest year may not have been available at press time.

In U.S. $	2021	2020	2019	2018	2017	2016
Revenue	2,990,400,000	2,817,919,232	2,102,604,672	2,128,809,728	1,948,660,000	1,647,216,256
R&D Expense						
Operating Income						
Operating Margin %						
SGA Expense						
Net Income	-267,164,608	-162,298,032	-255,075,168	-59,784,560	-11,119,900	15,552,001
Operating Cash Flow						
Capital Expenditure						
EBITDA						
Return on Assets %						
Return on Equity %						
Debt to Equity						

CONTACT INFORMATION:
Phone: 44-1707-228080   Fax: 44-1707-227999
Toll-Free:
Address: Apollo Court, 2 Bishop Sq., Hatfield Bus. Park, Hatfield, Hertfordshire AL10 9EX United Kingdom

STOCK TICKER/OTHER:
Stock Ticker: OCDGF   Exchange: PINX
Employees: 20,132   Fiscal Year Ends: 11/30
Parent Company:

SALARIES/BONUSES:
Top Exec. Salary: $ Bonus: $
Second Exec. Salary: $ Bonus: $

OTHER THOUGHTS:
Estimated Female Officers or Directors: 2
Hot Spot for Advancement for Women/Minorities:

Penske Corporation Inc

www.penske.com

NAIC Code: 532120

TYPES OF BUSINESS:

Truck Rental
Auto Racing
Auto Sales & Service
Supply Chain Solutions
Auto Accessories Manufacturing & Retail
Fuel Management Systems
Fleet Management Services
Vehicle Components & Systems

BRANDS/DIVISIONS/AFFILIATES:

Penske Automotive Group
Penske Motor Group
Penske Truck Leasing
Penske Logistics
Premier Truck Group
Ilmor Engineering Inc
Team Penske
Penske Entertainment Corp

CONTACTS: Note: Officers with more than one job title may be intentionally listed here more than once.

Roger S. Penske, CEO
Robert H. Kurnick Jr., Pres.
Shelley Hulgrave, CFO
Robert H. Kurnick, Jr., Pres., Penske Automotive Group
Calvin C. Sharp, Exec. VP-Human Resources, Penske Automotive Group
Shane M. Spradlin, General Counsel
Roger S. Penske, Chmn.
Marc Althen, Pres., Penske Logistics

GROWTH PLANS/SPECIAL FEATURES:

Penske Corporation, Inc. is a diversified transportation company that participates in a variety of automotive markets through its network of subsidiaries. Penske Automotive Group is an international transportation services company that operates retail automotive dealerships, Hertz car rental franchises and commercial vehicle distribution. Penske Vehicle Services is a fleet solutions provider for automotive original equipment manufacturers. Penske Motor Group owns and operates automobile dealerships in California. Penske Truck Leasing operates over 390,000 vehicles, serving customers from more than 3,000 locations across North America, South America, Europe, Australia and Asia. Penske Truck Rental, which operates a truck rental fleet in North America and offers 24-hour roadside assistance, used for renting trucks commercially or for moving purposes. Penske Logistics focuses on supply chain solutions, providing services designed to cut costs, reduce cycle time, improve service and integrate technology into the operations of its customers. Premier Truck Group operates dealerships offering a selection of new Freightliner, Western Star and Isuzu commercial vehicles as well as Thomas Built buses, electric vehicles and a large selection of previously owned commercial trucks. Ilmor Engineering is a provider of high-performance motorsport engines for the top levels of racing, including IndyCar, NASCAR, and ARCA. Team Penske competes in a variety of disciplines, cars owned and prepared by Team Penske. Penske Entertainment Corp., a subsidiary of Penske Corporation, owns the Indianapolis Motor Speedway, the NTT INDYCAR SERIES and IMS Productions. Last, CarShop is an online used car marketplace for shopping for vehicles, obtaining financing and scheduling delivery of the vehicle online, available in the U.S. and the U.K. Penske Corporation offers parts and other related services.

FINANCIAL DATA: Note: Data for latest year may not have been available at press time.

In U.S. $	2021	2020	2019	2018	2017	2016
Revenue	33,000,000,000	32,000,000,000	32,000,000,000	27,000,000,000	26,500,000,000	26,000,000,000
R&D Expense						
Operating Income						
Operating Margin %						
SGA Expense						
Net Income						
Operating Cash Flow						
Capital Expenditure						
EBITDA						
Return on Assets %						
Return on Equity %						
Debt to Equity						

CONTACT INFORMATION:

Phone: 248-648-2000   Fax: 248-648-2525
Toll-Free:
Address: 2555 Telegraph Rd., Bloomfield Hills, MI 48302 United States

STOCK TICKER/OTHER:

Stock Ticker: Private
Employees: 60,000
Parent Company:

Exchange:
Fiscal Year Ends: 12/31

SALARIES/BONUSES:

Top Exec. Salary: $ Bonus: $
Second Exec. Salary: $ Bonus: $

OTHER THOUGHTS:

Estimated Female Officers or Directors:
Hot Spot for Advancement for Women/Minorities:

Postmates Inc

NAIC Code: 519130

TYPES OF BUSINESS:

Online Local Delivery Service Arrangement
On-Demand Delivery Platform
Logistics Development
Consumer Goods Delivery
Food Delivery
Payment Solutions
Mobile App
Online Ordering

BRANDS/DIVISIONS/AFFILIATES:

Uber Technologies Inc
Urban Logistics
Postmates Unlimited

GROWTH PLANS/SPECIAL FEATURES:

Postmates, Inc. has developed and operates a logistics and on-demand delivery platform connecting customers with local stores and restaurants as well as with couriers. Utilizing Postmates' integrated Urban Logistics network system, these couriers can deliver goods within minutes, via bike or car. Connected stores and restaurants sell their goods through the firm's application programming interface (API) software, from which users search, order and pay for. From that point, Postmates couriers receive the order, pick it up and deliver it to the consumer. Goods can include a Starbucks coffee, sushi and even a last-minute drugstore item. Revenue is derived from delivery fees paid by customers plus commission percentages paid by some restaurants. Unlimited free delivery is available for members who subscribe to Postmates Unlimited. Postmates operates throughout the U.S. and Puerto Rico. Gift cards are available on Postmates website. Postmates is a subsidiary of Uber Technologies, Inc.

CONTACTS:

Note: Officers with more than one job title may be intentionally listed here more than once.

Bastian Lehmann, CEO

FINANCIAL DATA:

Note: Data for latest year may not have been available at press time.

In U.S. $	2021	2020	2019	2018	2017	2016
Revenue	875,000,000	700,000,000	400,000,000	350,000,000	250,000,000	135,000,000
R&D Expense						
Operating Income						
Operating Margin %						
SGA Expense						
Net Income						
Operating Cash Flow						
Capital Expenditure						
EBITDA						
Return on Assets %						
Return on Equity %						
Debt to Equity						

CONTACT INFORMATION:

Phone: 415 989-5836   Fax:
Toll-Free:
Address: 201 3rd St., San Francisco, CA 94103 United States

STOCK TICKER/OTHER:

Stock Ticker: Subsidiary   Exchange:
Employees: 6,500   Fiscal Year Ends:
Parent Company: Uber Technologies Inc

SALARIES/BONUSES:

Top Exec. Salary: $ Bonus: $
Second Exec. Salary: $ Bonus: $

OTHER THOUGHTS:

Estimated Female Officers or Directors:
Hot Spot for Advancement for Women/Minorities:

Ramirent plc

www.ramirent.com

NAIC Code: 532412

TYPES OF BUSINESS:

Construction, Mining, and Forestry Machinery and Equipment Rental and Leasing
Equipment Rental Services
Unmanned Rental Equipment
Logistics Services
Equipment Handling Training
Mobile App
Online Measuring Tools
Artificial Intelligence

BRANDS/DIVISIONS/AFFILIATES:

Loxam SAS
Fortrent

CONTACTS: *Note: Officers with more than one job title may be intentionally listed here more than once.*

Erik Bengtsson, CEO

GROWTH PLANS/SPECIAL FEATURES:

Ramirent plc, a subsidiary of Loxam SAS, provides a broad product portfolio of unmanned rental equipment across Northern and Eastern Europe. In Russia, the firm operates through a 50-50 joint venture called Fortrent. Ramirent serves a broad range of customer industries including construction, industry, services, public sector and households. Ramirent fulfills customers' equipment rental and service needs through its fleet of access equipment, light equipment, safety equipment, heavy machinery and electrical and heating systems. Its services also include planning, on-site services, logistics services, training and accessories. Ramirent's equipment and services simplify the business processes of its customers. The firm delivers products throughout the project lifecycle. Ramirent has a mobile application that helps users with everyday measuring tasks. It contains a pocket-sized caliper and a unit converter. The caliper enables measuring small objects by swiping a finger on the touch screen; and the converter can convert measurements such as meters to miles and feet to inches. During 2022, Ramirent acquired the rental assets of Rolf Wee Transport A.S., including the ongoing business interests and personnel of the firm. The acquisition strengthens Ramirent's presence in the Haugesund region of Norway.

FINANCIAL DATA: *Note: Data for latest year may not have been available at press time.*

In U.S. $	2021	2020	2019	2018	2017	2016
Revenue		806,655,377	827,338,848	787,941,760	801,255,552	736,452,672
R&D Expense						
Operating Income						
Operating Margin %						
SGA Expense						
Net Income				52,959,480	70,252,440	24,447,520
Operating Cash Flow						
Capital Expenditure						
EBITDA						
Return on Assets %						
Return on Equity %						
Debt to Equity						

CONTACT INFORMATION:

Phone: 358 20750200   Fax: 358 207502810
Toll-Free:
Address: Tapulikaupungintie 37, Helsinki, 00750 Finland

STOCK TICKER/OTHER:

Stock Ticker: Subsidiary
Employees: 3,000
Parent Company: Loxam SAS

Exchange:
Fiscal Year Ends: 12/31

SALARIES/BONUSES:

Top Exec. Salary: $ Bonus: $
Second Exec. Salary: $ Bonus: $

OTHER THOUGHTS:

Estimated Female Officers or Directors:
Hot Spot for Advancement for Women/Minorities:

Sales, profits and employees may be estimates. Financial information, benefits and other data can change quickly and may vary from those stated here.

Randstad Holding NV

NAIC Code: 561320

www.randstad.nl

TYPES OF BUSINESS:

Staffing & Temporary Help Services
IT Staffing

GROWTH PLANS/SPECIAL FEATURES:

Established in 1960 and domiciled in the Netherlands, Randstad is one of only three global recruitment providers, placing over 200,000 permanent candidates and 2 million temporary candidates annually. Randstad has traditionally been focused on the general staffing market, but has in recent years begun diversifying into the professional space, as well as in-house services, in which consultants work remotely from clients' premises.

BRANDS/DIVISIONS/AFFILIATES:

twago
Randstad Sourceright
Monster
RiseSmart

CONTACTS: *Note: Officers with more than one job title may be intentionally listed here more than once.*

Jacques van den Broek, CEO
Robert Jan van de Kraats, CFO
Wout Dekker, Chmn.
Linda Galipeau, CEO-North America

FINANCIAL DATA: *Note: Data for latest year may not have been available at press time.*

In U.S. $	2021	2020	2019	2018	2017	2016
Revenue	25,982,177,280	21,127,450,624	24,970,733,568	26,891,933,696	25,156,519,936	24,414,371,840
R&D Expense						
Operating Income						
Operating Margin %						
SGA Expense						
Net Income	809,998,464	310,007,936	639,139,392	795,057,984	682,506,048	694,042,816
Operating Cash Flow						
Capital Expenditure						
EBITDA						
Return on Assets %						
Return on Equity %						
Debt to Equity						

CONTACT INFORMATION:

Phone: 31 20-5695911   Fax: 31 205695520
Toll-Free:
Address: Diemermere 25, Diemen, NL-1112 TC Netherlands

STOCK TICKER/OTHER:

Stock Ticker: RANJF   Exchange: PINX
Employees: 39,530   Fiscal Year Ends: 12/31
Parent Company:

SALARIES/BONUSES:

Top Exec. Salary: $ Bonus: $
Second Exec. Salary: $ Bonus: $

OTHER THOUGHTS:

Estimated Female Officers or Directors: 3
Hot Spot for Advancement for Women/Minorities: Y

Sales, profits and employees may be estimates. Financial information, benefits and other data can change quickly and may vary from those stated here.

Redde Northgate plc

reddenorthgate.co.uk

NAIC Code: 532120

TYPES OF BUSINESS:

Truck, Utility Trailer, and RV (Recreational Vehicle) Rental and Leasing
Vehicles for Rent
Vehicles for Sale
Integrated Mobility Solutions
Accident Management Solutions
Vehicle Maintenance and Repair
Electric Vehicle Charging Equipment

BRANDS/DIVISIONS/AFFILIATES:

Auxillis
FMG
NewLaw Solicitors
Northgate Espana Renting Flexible SA
Van Monster
Principia Law
ChargedEV
FMG Repair Services

CONTACTS: Note: Officers with more than one job title may be intentionally listed here more than once.

Martin Ward, CEO
Philip Vincent, CFO
Avril Palmer-Baunack, Chmn.

GROWTH PLANS/SPECIAL FEATURES:

Redde Northgate plc offers an integrated mobility solutions platform that spans vehicle rental and sales, incident and accident management, legal and other mobility-related services. The firm provides mobility solutions and automotive services to a wide range of businesses and customers, including vehicle supply, service, maintenance, repair, recovery and accident/incident management and disposal via sale or salvage. Redde Northgate comprises a network and diversified fleet of more than 125,000 owned vehicles and over 600,000 managed vehicles in more than 170 branches across the U.K., Ireland and Spain. Types of vehicles offered primarily consist of small vans, medium vans, passenger sedans and other passenger vehicle models such as trucks or SUVs. Businesses under Redde Northgate include: Auxillis, which delivers contact center support, sales, claims processing, customer service and general insurance products to insurance broker and automotive markets; FMG, which provides outsourced fleet management, specialist rapid response and recovery management, fleet risk and legal services; NewLaw Solicitors, which provides personal injury law; Northgate Vehicle Hire, a light commercial hire provider in the U.K. and Ireland; Northgate Espana Renting Flexible S.A., offering vehicle rental services in Spain; Van Monster, offering a range of used vans to businesses and private individuals; Principia Law, which provides legal advice and representation to victims of non-fault road traffic accidents; ChargedEV, which specializes in the supply and installation of electric vehicle charging equipment across the U.K.; and FMG Repair Services, offering automotive crash repair and accident administration network services in the U.K. to motorists, fleet operators and the automotive industry.

FINANCIAL DATA: Note: Data for latest year may not have been available at press time.

In U.S. $	2021	2020	2019	2018	2017	2016
Revenue	1,547,662,345	970,195,983	977,762,000	852,795,904	811,177,728	751,452,928
R&D Expense						
Operating Income						
Operating Margin %						
SGA Expense						
Net Income	106,334,752	59,155,453	66,683,800	52,543,172	74,017,664	74,720,152
Operating Cash Flow						
Capital Expenditure						
EBITDA						
Return on Assets %						
Return on Equity %						
Debt to Equity						

CONTACT INFORMATION:

Phone: 44 1325467558   Fax: 44 1325363204
Toll-Free:
Address: Northgate Centre, Lingfield Way, Darlington, DL1 4PZ United Kingdom

STOCK TICKER/OTHER:

Stock Ticker: REDD   Exchange: London
Employees: 6,000   Fiscal Year Ends: 04/30
Parent Company:

SALARIES/BONUSES:

Top Exec. Salary: $ Bonus: $
Second Exec. Salary: $ Bonus: $

OTHER THOUGHTS:

Estimated Female Officers or Directors:
Hot Spot for Advancement for Women/Minorities:

Rent Like A Champion Inc

rentlikeachampion.com

NAIC Code: 561510

TYPES OF BUSINESS:

Travel Agencies
Online Vacation Rental Services
Weekend Football Watching
Weekend Home Rental

BRANDS/DIVISIONS/AFFILIATES:

CONTACTS: *Note: Officers with more than one job title may be intentionally listed here more than once.*

Dave Longwell, CEO
Hank Greene, Dir.-Mktg
Mike Hostetler, CIO
Reuven Lerner, CTO

GROWTH PLANS/SPECIAL FEATURES:

Rent Like A Champion, Inc. started as a student housing company, listing a vacant apartment online as a weekend rental for football games. Being an immediate hit, the firm expanded the business to other college towns with major football programs. Currently, Rent Like A Champion offers internet-based weekend rentals at homeowners' vacation properties or homes near more than 20 college towns throughout the U.S. Homeowners rent their properties, with the average income deriving $1,200 per weekend. How the football weekend rental process works: owners set the dates and prices for renting out their properties; become notified via email from Rent Like A Champion, along with rental details and the renter's contact information; and get paid via direct deposit after the rental weekend. Renters are primarily aged between 35 and 55 years of age, and the groups are usually multi-generational families and groups of older alumni reuniting for a game weekend. The typical weekend begins at 5pm on Friday and ends at noon on Sunday. Every homeowner is covered up to $1 million for every rental. This becomes the primary insurance policy for rental weekends, and it covers liability, structural damage to the home, and damage to any items or property. The company claims that its incident rate is extremely low.

FINANCIAL DATA: *Note: Data for latest year may not have been available at press time.*

In U.S. $	2021	2020	2019	2018	2017	2016
Revenue						
R&D Expense						
Operating Income						
Operating Margin %						
SGA Expense						
Net Income						
Operating Cash Flow						
Capital Expenditure						
EBITDA						
Return on Assets %						
Return on Equity %						
Debt to Equity						

CONTACT INFORMATION:

Phone: 312 906-5038   Fax:
Toll-Free: 855 244-4263
Address: 1 W. Monroe, Chicago, IL 60603 United States

STOCK TICKER/OTHER:

Stock Ticker: Private   Exchange:
Employees: 12   Fiscal Year Ends:
Parent Company:

SALARIES/BONUSES:

Top Exec. Salary: $ Bonus: $
Second Exec. Salary: $ Bonus: $

OTHER THOUGHTS:

Estimated Female Officers or Directors:
Hot Spot for Advancement for Women/Minorities:

Rent the Runway Inc

www.renttherunway.com

NAIC Code: 454111

TYPES OF BUSINESS:
Online Rental of Luxury Apparel and Accessories

GROWTH PLANS/SPECIAL FEATURES:
Rent the Runway Inc is an e-commerce platform that allows users to rent, subscribe, or buy designer apparel and accessories.

Benefits for qualified employees at all levels include paid bereavement leave, paid family and parental sick leave and sabbatical packages. The main plant and logistics center is in New Jersey.

BRANDS/DIVISIONS/AFFILIATES:

CONTACTS: Note: Officers with more than one job title may be intentionally listed here more than once.
Jennifer Hyman, CEO
Scarlett O'Sullivan, CFO
Larry Steinberg, Chief Technology Officer
Anushka Salinas, COO
Cara Schembri, General Counsel
Sarah Tam, Other Executive Officer
Brian Donato, Other Executive Officer
Andrea Alexander, Other Executive Officer

FINANCIAL DATA: Note: Data for latest year may not have been available at press time.

In U.S. $	2021	2020	2019	2018	2017	2016
Revenue	157,500,000	256,900,000				
R&D Expense	37,700,000	40,200,000				
Operating Income	-130,500,000	-130,000,000				
Operating Margin %	- .83%	- .51%				
SGA Expense	85,300,000	121,800,000				
Net Income	-171,100,000	-153,900,000				
Operating Cash Flow	-42,800,000	-37,600,000				
Capital Expenditure	78,700,000	161,500,000				
EBITDA	-18,500,000	-23,200,000				
Return on Assets %						
Return on Equity %						
Debt to Equity						

CONTACT INFORMATION:
Phone: 646-832-3582 Fax:
Toll-Free: 800-509-0842
Address: 163 Varick St., Fl. 4, New York, NY 10013 United States

STOCK TICKER/OTHER:
Stock Ticker: RENT Exchange: NAS
Employees: 974 Fiscal Year Ends: 01/31
Parent Company:

SALARIES/BONUSES:
Top Exec. Salary: $616,477 Bonus: $
Second Exec. Salary: Bonus: $
$600,000

OTHER THOUGHTS:
Estimated Female Officers or Directors: 3
Hot Spot for Advancement for Women/Minorities: Y

Sales, profits and employees may be estimates. Financial information, benefits and other data can change quickly and may vary from those stated here.

Rent-A-Center Inc

www.rentacenter.com

NAIC Code: 532210

TYPES OF BUSINESS:

Consumer Electronics and Appliances Rental
Retail
Financing

BRANDS/DIVISIONS/AFFILIATES:

Rent-A-Center Franchising International Inc
Rent-A-Center
Get It Now
Home Choice

GROWTH PLANS/SPECIAL FEATURES:

Rent-A-Center Inc offers rent-to-own purchasing options for appliances, computers, smartphones, furniture, and related items. Customers make rental payments with the option to own the product after completing rent-to-own agreements. The company's operating segments are Rent-a-Center business, which includes company-owned stores and online platform; preferred lease, which provides lease-to-own options through third-party retailers; Mexico, which includes company-owned stores in Mexico; and franchising, which sells rental merchandise to intermediate franchisees for royalties and startup fees. The majority of revenue comes from repeat customers in the Rent-a-Center business segment of the U.S.

Rent-A-Center offers employee benefits, retirement options and employee assistance programs.

CONTACTS: *Note: Officers with more than one job title may be intentionally listed here more than once.*

Mitchell Fadel, CEO
Maureen Short, CFO
Jeffrey Brown, Chairman of the Board
Ann Davids, Chief Marketing Officer
Anthony Blasquez, Executive VP, Divisional
Jason Hogg, Executive VP, Divisional
Bryan Pechersky, Executive VP
Catherine Skula, Executive VP

FINANCIAL DATA: *Note: Data for latest year may not have been available at press time.*

In U.S. $	2021	2020	2019	2018	2017	2016
Revenue	4,583,451,000	2,814,191,000	2,669,852,000	2,660,465,000	2,702,540,000	2,963,252,000
R&D Expense						
Operating Income	280,539,000	237,336,000	253,859,000	56,137,000	-63,059,000	84,724,000
Operating Margin %	.06%	.08%	.10%	.02%	- .02%	.03%
SGA Expense	839,657,000	732,233,000	772,730,000	846,867,000	903,556,000	957,956,000
Net Income	134,940,000	208,115,000	173,546,000	8,492,000	6,653,000	-105,195,000
Operating Cash Flow	392,298,000	236,502,000	215,416,000	227,505,000	110,533,000	354,073,000
Capital Expenditure	62,450,000	34,545,000	21,157,000	27,962,000	65,460,000	61,143,000
EBITDA	1,651,746,000	928,466,000	935,482,000	742,395,000	632,779,000	670,534,000
Return on Assets %						
Return on Equity %						
Debt to Equity	3.64%	0.804	1.124	1.885	2.47	2.734

CONTACT INFORMATION:

Phone: 972 801-1100   Fax: 866 260-1424
Toll-Free: 800-275-2996
Address: 5501 Headquarters Dr., Plano, TX 75024 United States

STOCK TICKER/OTHER:

Stock Ticker: RCII   Exchange: NAS
Employees: 14,290   Fiscal Year Ends: 12/31
Parent Company:

SALARIES/BONUSES:

Top Exec. Salary: $1,078,846   Bonus: $
Second Exec. Salary: Bonus: $
$619,711

OTHER THOUGHTS:

Estimated Female Officers or Directors: 1
Hot Spot for Advancement for Women/Minorities: Y

Rentah Inc

www.rentah.com

NAIC Code: 532299

TYPES OF BUSINESS:

Consumer Goods Rental
Services Mobile App
Services Online Marketplace
Service Request
Service Fulfillment
Payment Solutions
Rental Solutions

BRANDS/DIVISIONS/AFFILIATES:

CONTACTS: *Note: Officers with more than one job title may be intentionally listed here more than once.*

Anup Desai, CEO

GROWTH PLANS/SPECIAL FEATURES:

Rentah, Inc. has developed and operates an online and mobile platform that gives people, freelancers and businesses a way to rent and use goods and services. The goods are physical products and individual property. Services are actions, skills or talents that can be helpful, entertaining and/or provide accommodations to others. Using the Rentah platform is free and designed to create a community that gives people an opportunity to earn or save money by utilizing under-used products, skills and talents. Listings include rental prices for goods and or one's skill/talent time. Renters search for what they need, when they need it and rent the goods or service offered via the web or mobile app. The Rentah dashboard is an all-in-one place for creating rental profiles, for handling deposits and payments, sorting through history transactions, for friend referrals, for communicating and messaging other providers and renters and for obtaining suggestions in relation to potential providers and renters. Rentah makes 5% on transactions that are paid by the renter. Rentah is an open platform, therefore pricing is entirely handled and operated by the providers. Each provider determines if their prices are negotiable.

FINANCIAL DATA: *Note: Data for latest year may not have been available at press time.*

In U.S. $	2021	2020	2019	2018	2017	2016
Revenue						
R&D Expense						
Operating Income						
Operating Margin %						
SGA Expense						
Net Income						
Operating Cash Flow						
Capital Expenditure						
EBITDA						
Return on Assets %						
Return on Equity %						
Debt to Equity						

CONTACT INFORMATION:

Phone: 718 966-3131 Fax:
Toll-Free:
Address: 67 West St., Brooklyn, NY 11222 United States

STOCK TICKER/OTHER:

Stock Ticker: Private Exchange:
Employees: 6 Fiscal Year Ends:
Parent Company:

SALARIES/BONUSES:

Top Exec. Salary: $ Bonus: $
Second Exec. Salary: $ Bonus: $

OTHER THOUGHTS:

Estimated Female Officers or Directors:
Hot Spot for Advancement for Women/Minorities:

Sales, profits and employees may be estimates. Financial information, benefits and other data can change quickly and may vary from those stated here.

ReserveBar Express Corp (Minibar Delivery)   minibardelivery.com
NAIC Code: 492210

TYPES OF BUSINESS:
Local Delivery Service
Alcohol Products
Online and Mobile App Ordering
On-Demand Delivery
Shipping Services
eGift Services
Bartending Services
Business and Brand Partnership

BRANDS/DIVISIONS/AFFILIATES:
Minibar Delivery

CONTACTS: Note: Officers with more than one job title may be intentionally listed here more than once.
Lindsey Andrews, CEO

GROWTH PLANS/SPECIAL FEATURES:
ReserveBar Express Corp. operates an online alcohol marketplace, Minibar Delivery, for the delivery of wine, beer and spirits to consumers. The company partners with local liquor stores, as well as vineyards, in a way that enables Minibar Delivery users to order, purchase and have the products directly delivered to them by Minibar Delivery. There are no up-front costs to business partners, and the firm has a full-service customer care team ready to help with any issue a partner or customer may have. Liquor store and vineyard owners can increase sales and boost business through the partnership. These businesses send product inventory to Minibar Delivery, which is subsequently integrated with all the firm's major point-of-sale systems. Customers are able to take their time when it comes to ordering alcohol, shopping by liquor type, brand or even particular stores or vineyards themselves. When a customer completes an order, the business is alerted, packs the order and makes it ready for delivery. Brand partnerships are also encouraged by ReserveBar, providing brands with a direct connection to Minibar Delivery consumers via advertising and customized programs. The firm has partnerships with more than 200 brands. Select partners include Stella Artois, Absolut, Bacardi, Heineken, Titos Handmade Vodka, Crown Royal and Veuve Clicquot. In addition, Minibar Delivery provides various services for events, including bar-stocking and the booking of a bartender. Corporate accounts can be set up through Minibar Delivery. Minibar Delivery currently serves in select cities in 22 U.S. states and the District of Columbia. The firm also offers statewide shipping, with orders primarily delivered within three to seven days. Orders can also be ready for customer pickup at the stores. They can be sent as a gift, and eGifts are available.

FINANCIAL DATA: Note: Data for latest year may not have been available at press time.

In U.S. $	2021	2020	2019	2018	2017	2016
Revenue						
R&D Expense						
Operating Income						
Operating Margin %						
SGA Expense						
Net Income						
Operating Cash Flow						
Capital Expenditure						
EBITDA						
Return on Assets %						
Return on Equity %						
Debt to Equity						

CONTACT INFORMATION:
Phone: 855 487-0740   Fax:
Toll-Free: 888 249-6070
Address: 79 Madison Ave., New York, NY 10016 United States

STOCK TICKER/OTHER:
Stock Ticker: Private   Exchange:
Employees: Fiscal Year Ends:
Parent Company:

SALARIES/BONUSES:
Top Exec. Salary: $ Bonus: $
Second Exec. Salary: $ Bonus: $

OTHER THOUGHTS:
Estimated Female Officers or Directors:
Hot Spot for Advancement for Women/Minorities:

RGF Staffing BV

rgfstaffing.com

NAIC Code: 561320

TYPES OF BUSINESS:

Temporary Help Services
Human Resources
Job Staffing
Recruitment

BRANDS/DIVISIONS/AFFILIATES:

Recruit Holdings Co Ltd
Advantage Group UK
Chandler Macleod Group
Recruit Staffing
Secretary Plus
Staffmark Group
StartPeople
USG Professionals

CONTACTS: *Note: Officers with more than one job title may be intentionally listed here more than once.*

Rob Zandbergen, CEO
Tom Dejonghe, CFO

GROWTH PLANS/SPECIAL FEATURES:

RGF Staffing BV, a subsidiary of Recruit Holdings Co. Ltd., offers a broad set of human resource services for people and businesses in various sectors. RFG helps people find jobs, and supports companies by developing smart workforce solutions. The company's HR and staffing services include: placement, such as temporary staffing, permanent placement, secondment and freelance/statement of work; talent acquisition, such as sourcing candidates, employee referrals, skills assessment/testing, onboarding and offboarding; advice, such as HR consulting, job search counseling, capacity building and process excellence; managed services, such as recruitment process outsourcing, and payrolling; and career management, such as training, outplacement and career transitions. Every day, more than 300,000 people are employed through the network of RFG Staffing. Its brands include Advantage Group UK, Bright Plus, Chandler Macleod Group, Recruit Staffing, Secretary Plus, Solvus, Staffmark Group, StartPeople, The CSI Companies, Unique, and USG Professionals, among many others.

FINANCIAL DATA: *Note: Data for latest year may not have been available at press time.*

In U.S. $	2021	2020	2019	2018	2017	2016
Revenue	11,300,000,000	1,900,000,000	2,800,000,000	2,700,000,000	2,700,000,000	2,650,000,000
R&D Expense						
Operating Income						
Operating Margin %						
SGA Expense						
Net Income						
Operating Cash Flow						
Capital Expenditure						
EBITDA						
Return on Assets %						
Return on Equity %						
Debt to Equity						

CONTACT INFORMATION:

Phone: 31 36-5299500   Fax: 31 365299509
Toll-Free:
Address: 61 PJ Oudweg, Almere, 1314 CK Netherlands

STOCK TICKER/OTHER:

Stock Ticker: Subsidiary   Exchange:
Employees: 17,000   Fiscal Year Ends: 12/31
Parent Company: Recruit Holdings Co Ltd

SALARIES/BONUSES:

Top Exec. Salary: $ Bonus: $
Second Exec. Salary: $ Bonus: $

OTHER THOUGHTS:

Estimated Female Officers or Directors:
Hot Spot for Advancement for Women/Minorities: Y

Roadie Inc

NAIC Code: 519130

www.roadie.com

TYPES OF BUSINESS:

Online Local Delivery Service Arrangement
On-the-Way Delivery
Shipping Services via Passenger Cars
Online Delivery Platform
Mobile App

BRANDS/DIVISIONS/AFFILIATES:

United Parcel Service Inc (UPS)

CONTACTS: *Note: Officers with more than one job title may be intentionally listed here more than once.*

Marc Gorlin, CEO

GROWTH PLANS/SPECIAL FEATURES:

Roadie, Inc. has developed and operates an on-the-way delivery platform utilizing unused capacity in passenger vehicles. Roadie app users connect people and businesses that have stuff to send with drivers heading in the same direction. This sharing program is usually cheaper than shipping charges, depending on the shape, size and type of item being shipped and where it needs to go. These items will not be in enclosed boxes or packages; but visible to the driver as to exactly what it is. Additional benefits to drivers by Roadie include no minimum vehicle standards, free roadside assistance, roadside discounts and tax write-offs on miles while driving. Since its 2015 inception, the firm has delivered items such as cupcakes to sofas to customers in more than 20,000 zip codes nationwide. The Roadie platform provides real-time tracking and the addresses of drop-off locations before offering to drive. Shipping charges can be calculated on the company's web or mobile app. Drivers create gig alerts and make offers on gigs they can take. Users display what they need shipped. Once an agreement has been accepted between the Roadie driver and app user, the driving/shipping will begin as scheduled. Roadie, Inc. has drivers in all 50 U.S. states. The firm is a subsidiary of United Parcel Service, Inc. (UPS).

Roadie offers its employees health plans, 401(k), education assistance, a bonus program and other plans and company perks.

FINANCIAL DATA: *Note: Data for latest year may not have been available at press time.*

In U.S. $	2021	2020	2019	2018	2017	2016
Revenue						
R&D Expense						
Operating Income						
Operating Margin %						
SGA Expense						
Net Income						
Operating Cash Flow						
Capital Expenditure						
EBITDA						
Return on Assets %						
Return on Equity %						
Debt to Equity						

CONTACT INFORMATION:

Phone: 470 785-9787   Fax:
Toll-Free: 844 476-2343
Address: 3565 Peidmont Rd., N.E. Bldg. 4, No. 120, Atlanta, GA 30305 United States

STOCK TICKER/OTHER:

Stock Ticker: Subsidiary   Exchange:
Employees: 80   Fiscal Year Ends:
Parent Company: United Parcel Service Inc (UPS)

SALARIES/BONUSES:

Top Exec. Salary: $ Bonus: $
Second Exec. Salary: $ Bonus: $

OTHER THOUGHTS:

Estimated Female Officers or Directors:
Hot Spot for Advancement for Women/Minorities:

Robert Half International Inc

www.rhi.com

NAIC Code: 561320

TYPES OF BUSINESS:

Staffing
Risk Consulting
Internal Audit Services
Litigation Consulting & Forensic Accounting

GROWTH PLANS/SPECIAL FEATURES:

Founded in 1948, Robert Half provides temporary, permanent, and project-based staffing to corporations seeking employees in the finance, accounting, and technology. It is one of the largest global staffing firms, operating hundreds of locations in several countries. Its Protiviti subsidiary provides risk and business consulting and internal audit services to corporations through scores of global offices. The firm generates annual revenue of over $5 billion and EBIT of over $400 million and has nearly 19,000 employees.

BRANDS/DIVISIONS/AFFILIATES:

Accountemps
Robert Half Finance & Accounting
Robert Half Management Resources
Robert Half Technology
OfficeTeam
Robert Half Legal
Creative Group (The)
Protiviti Inc

CONTACTS: *Note: Officers with more than one job title may be intentionally listed here more than once.*

Paul Gentzkow, CEO, Divisional
M. Waddell, CEO
Michael Buckley, CFO
Harold Messmer, Chairman of the Board
Robert Glass, Executive VP, Divisional

FINANCIAL DATA: *Note: Data for latest year may not have been available at press time.*

In U.S. $	2021	2020	2019	2018	2017	2016
Revenue	6,461,444,000	5,109,000,000	6,074,432,000	5,800,271,000	5,266,789,000	5,250,399,000
R&D Expense						
Operating Income	742,505,000	345,351,000	565,473,000	598,706,000	515,717,000	553,222,000
Operating Margin %	.11%	.07%	.09%	.10%	.10%	.11%
SGA Expense	1,951,282,000	1,666,041,000	1,958,295,000	1,810,601,000	1,646,532,000	1,606,217,000
Net Income	598,626,000	306,276,000	454,433,000	434,288,000	290,584,000	343,389,000
Operating Cash Flow	603,136,000	596,528,000	519,629,000	572,322,000	452,991,000	442,081,000
Capital Expenditure	36,611,000	33,377,000	59,464,000	42,484,000	40,753,000	82,956,000
EBITDA	796,956,000	408,851,000	631,098,000	664,655,000	581,210,000	617,537,000
Return on Assets %						
Return on Equity %						
Debt to Equity	.13%	0.186	0.177	0.00	0.001	0.001

CONTACT INFORMATION:

Phone: 650 234-6000   Fax:
Toll-Free:
Address: 2884 Sand Hill Rd., Menlo Park, CA 94025 United States

STOCK TICKER/OTHER:

Stock Ticker: RHI
Employees: 14,600
Parent Company:

Exchange: NYS
Fiscal Year Ends: 12/31

SALARIES/BONUSES:

Top Exec. Salary: $500,000   Bonus: $
Second Exec. Salary: Bonus: $
$450,000

OTHER THOUGHTS:

Estimated Female Officers or Directors: 1
Hot Spot for Advancement for Women/Minorities:

Sales, profits and employees may be estimates. Financial information, benefits and other data can change quickly and may vary from those stated here.

Rover Inc
NAIC Code: 519130

TYPES OF BUSINESS:
Online Pet Care Arrangement Services
Pet Sitting
Dog Walking
Pet Boarding

BRANDS/DIVISIONS/AFFILIATES:

GROWTH PLANS/SPECIAL FEATURES:
Rover Group Inc is an online marketplace for pet care based on gross booking value or GBV. The company connects pet parents with loving pet care providers who offer overnight services, including boarding and in-home pet sitting, as well as daytime services, including doggy daycare, dog walking, and drop-in visits. The user-based platform extends across the U.S., Canada, the U.K., Spain, France, Norway, Sweden, Netherlands, Italy and Germany. For pet care providers, the company built tools to easily create a listing in the marketplace along with simple tools for scheduling and booking care, communicating with pet parents, and receiving payment. The company generates revenue from facilitating the connection between pet care providers and pet parents.

CONTACTS: Note: Officers with more than one job title may be intentionally listed here more than once.
Aaron Easterly, CEO
Tracy Knox, CFO
Adam Clammer, Chairman of the Board
Brent Turner, COO

FINANCIAL DATA: Note: Data for latest year may not have been available at press time.

In U.S. $	2021	2020	2019	2018	2017	2016
Revenue	109,837,000	48,800,000	95,052,000			
R&D Expense	22,712,000	22,567,000	22,066,000			
Operating Income	-17,162,000	-53,005,000	-53,676,000			
Operating Margin %	-.16%	-1.09%	-.56%			
SGA Expense	55,496,000	38,145,000	74,868,000			
Net Income	-64,049,000	-57,485,000	-51,714,000			
Operating Cash Flow	14,334,000	-56,955,000	-24,721,000			
Capital Expenditure	7,221,000	7,667,000	28,273,000			
EBITDA	-46,640,000	-35,712,000	-38,382,000			
Return on Assets %						
Return on Equity %						
Debt to Equity	.09%					

CONTACT INFORMATION:
Phone: 888-453-7889   Fax:
Toll-Free:
Address: 711 Capitol Way S., Ste. 204, Olympia, WA 98501 United States

STOCK TICKER/OTHER:
Stock Ticker: ROVR   Exchange: NAS
Employees: 372   Fiscal Year Ends: 12/31
Parent Company:

SALARIES/BONUSES:
Top Exec. Salary: $423,333   Bonus: $43,000
Second Exec. Salary: $415,000   Bonus: $35,000

OTHER THOUGHTS:
Estimated Female Officers or Directors:
Hot Spot for Advancement for Women/Minorities:

RVshare LLC

NAIC Code: 532120

TYPES OF BUSINESS:

RV (Recreational Vehicle) Rental
Recreational Vehicle Sharing
Online Booking
Roadside Assistance

BRANDS/DIVISIONS/AFFILIATES:

RVshare.com

CONTACTS: Note: Officers with more than one job title may be intentionally listed here more than once.

Jon Gray, CEO
Morgan Larkin, COO
Tom Klenotic, VP-Finance
Martijn Scheijbeler, Sr. VP-Mktg.
Maddi Bourgerie, Dir.-Communications & PR
Tony Cassandra, VP-Engineering
Melissa Fortenberry, Chief Product Officer

GROWTH PLANS/SPECIAL FEATURES:

RVshare, LLC, an online recreational vehicle rental sharing marketplace. RV owners throughout the U.S. list their Luxury Class A Diesel Pushers, Class B Camper Vans, Class C motorhomes and travel trailers, consisting of thousands of options for renters to choose from. Whether it be a cross country road trip, week-long camping trip or attending a family reunion or event, RVshare's process is simple and convenient through its online and mobile channels. Owners listing their RVs attach photos and detailed descriptions, set the prices and dates of availability and review reservation requests. Owners decide who rents the RV. Renters search and locate the type of trip and RV preferred, and the firm's search tools can be filtered by location, features and type of RV. Renters can talk directly with the RV dealer or owner to arrange the trip and will go through a quick demonstration of where everything is and how the RV works when picking up the vehicle. Bookings through the RVshare payment system are backed by a guarantee. Every rental booked through Rvshare.com comes with a 24-hour travel concierge and roadside assistance. Investors of the firm include KKR & Co., Inc. and Tritium Partners.

RVshare offers its employees comprehensive benefits, 401(k) and other benefits and company perks.

FINANCIAL DATA: Note: Data for latest year may not have been available at press time.

In U.S. $	2021	2020	2019	2018	2017	2016
Revenue						
R&D Expense						
Operating Income						
Operating Margin %						
SGA Expense						
Net Income						
Operating Cash Flow						
Capital Expenditure						
EBITDA						
Return on Assets %						
Return on Equity %						
Debt to Equity						

CONTACT INFORMATION:

Phone: Fax:
Toll-Free: 800 549-7104
Address: 543 N Cleveland Massillon Rd, Akron, OH 44333 United States

STOCK TICKER/OTHER:

Stock Ticker: Private   Exchange:
Employees: Fiscal Year Ends:
Parent Company:

SALARIES/BONUSES:

Top Exec. Salary: $ Bonus: $
Second Exec. Salary: $ Bonus: $

OTHER THOUGHTS:

Estimated Female Officers or Directors:
Hot Spot for Advancement for Women/Minorities:

Ryder System Inc

NAIC Code: 532120

www.ryder.com

TYPES OF BUSINESS:

Truck Rental & Leasing
Trucking
Logistics & Consulting Services
Supply Chain Management
Dedicated Fleet Services
Fleet Management Services

BRANDS/DIVISIONS/AFFILIATES:

GROWTH PLANS/SPECIAL FEATURES:

Ryder System Inc is a provider of supply chain and fleet management solutions in the United States. The company offers fleet leasing, fleet maintenance, truck rental, dedicated transportation, transportation management, freight brokerage, supply-chain optimization, warehouse and distribution, and small-business solutions. Ryder serves the automotive, consumer packaged goods, energy, food and beverage, healthcare, industrial manufacturing, metals, retail, technology and electronics, and transportation and logistics industries. The segment of the company are Finance, corporate services, and health and safety; Human resources; Information technology and other.

Ryder offers comprehensive health benefits and retirement/savings plans.

CONTACTS: Note: Officers with more than one job title may be intentionally listed here more than once.

Robert Sanchez, CEO
John Diez, CFO
Cristina Gallo-Aquino, Chief Accounting Officer
Rajeev Ravindran, Chief Information Officer
Robert Fatovic, Chief Legal Officer
Karen Jones, Chief Marketing Officer
John Gleason, Executive VP
Francisco Lopez, Executive VP
Timothy Fiore, Other Executive Officer
Thomas Havens, President, Divisional
John Sensing, President, Divisional

FINANCIAL DATA: Note: Data for latest year may not have been available at press time.

In U.S. $	2021	2020	2019	2018	2017	2016
Revenue	9,662,953,000	8,420,091,000	8,925,801,000	8,413,946,000	7,280,074,000	6,758,138,000
R&D Expense						
Operating Income	872,356,000	230,909,000	282,442,000	593,928,000	439,073,000	584,698,000
Operating Margin %	.09%	.03%	.03%	.07%	.06%	.09%
SGA Expense	1,054,537,000	921,573,000	907,449,000	849,410,000	870,918,000	804,229,000
Net Income	519,041,000	-122,250,000	-24,410,000	284,613,000	719,644,000	263,069,000
Operating Cash Flow	2,175,307,000	2,181,303,000	2,140,539,000	1,717,993,000	1,628,098,000	1,601,022,000
Capital Expenditure	1,941,409,000	1,146,521,000	3,735,174,000	3,050,409,000	1,860,436,000	1,905,157,000
EBITDA	2,717,887,000	2,273,914,000	2,179,328,000	2,026,463,000	1,737,032,000	1,781,006,000
Return on Assets %						
Return on Equity %						
Debt to Equity	1.97%	2.784	2.795	2.306	1.613	2.241

CONTACT INFORMATION:

Phone: 305 500-3726   Fax: 305 500-4129
Toll-Free:
Address: 11690 NW 105th St., Miami, FL 33178 United States

STOCK TICKER/OTHER:

Stock Ticker: R   Exchange: NYS
Employees: 42,800   Fiscal Year Ends: 12/31
Parent Company:

SALARIES/BONUSES:

Top Exec. Salary: $962,000   Bonus: $
Second Exec. Salary: Bonus: $
$650,000

OTHER THOUGHTS:

Estimated Female Officers or Directors: 4
Hot Spot for Advancement for Women/Minorities: Y

Sailo Inc

NAIC Code: 532292

TYPES OF BUSINESS:

Recreational Goods Rental
Boat-Sharing
Online Booking
Payment Solutions

BRANDS/DIVISIONS/AFFILIATES:

CONTACTS: *Note: Officers with more than one job title may be intentionally listed here more than once.*

Adrian Gradinaru, CEO
Magda Marcu, Dir.-Operations

GROWTH PLANS/SPECIAL FEATURES:

Sailo, Inc. operates an online platform that enables boat owners to rent out their boats. Boat rentals can include motorboats, sailboats, catamarans and luxury yachts, and are offered at a variety of price points. The peer-to-peer boat rental marketplace provides a means of connecting owners, captains and renters. Sailo users search through thousands of options, which can be filtered by boat type, length, price, crew or trip duration. Once a boat is found and preferred, the user then chooses a date, the amount of time for renting the boat, as well as the option to rent the boat themselves or to charter a yacht per one's own terms. During the booking process, users can communicate or ask questions directly to the boat representative from Sailo's web-based boat page; payment information will be requested; and the booking would be submitted. Renters receive a reply within 24 hours. Sailo's captains are licensed and each trip is completely insured. This boat-sharing opportunity is a way for boat owners to monetize their underutilized boats, and captains can generate additional income doing what they enjoy doing. The most popular destinations on Sailo include New York, Miami, British Virgin Islands, Croatia and Greece. Sailo's inventory over more than 30,000 boats spans three continents, over 50 countries and 500 locations worldwide.

FINANCIAL DATA: *Note: Data for latest year may not have been available at press time.*

In U.S. $	2021	2020	2019	2018	2017	2016
Revenue						
R&D Expense						
Operating Income						
Operating Margin %						
SGA Expense						
Net Income						
Operating Cash Flow						
Capital Expenditure						
EBITDA						
Return on Assets %						
Return on Equity %						
Debt to Equity						

CONTACT INFORMATION:

Phone: 910 447-2456 Fax:
Toll-Free:
Address: 32 W. 39th St., Fl 4, New York, NY 10018 United States

STOCK TICKER/OTHER:

Stock Ticker: Private Exchange:
Employees: 9 Fiscal Year Ends:
Parent Company:

SALARIES/BONUSES:

Top Exec. Salary: $ Bonus: $
Second Exec. Salary: $ Bonus: $

OTHER THOUGHTS:

Estimated Female Officers or Directors:
Hot Spot for Advancement for Women/Minorities:

Saucey

NAIC Code: 492210

TYPES OF BUSINESS:

Local Delivery Service
Online Alcohol Delivery Service
Mobile App Delivery Service
Online Ordering
Payment Solutions
On-Demand Services
Retail Partnerships
Bartending Services

BRANDS/DIVISIONS/AFFILIATES:

Saucey.com

CONTACTS: *Note: Officers with more than one job title may be intentionally listed here more than once.*

Chris Vaughn, CEO

GROWTH PLANS/SPECIAL FEATURES:

Saucey has developed and operates an online and mobile platform for ordering alcohol and having it delivered within an hour. The firm also offers a two-day shipping option. With the user's payment information on file, locating and ordering from a range of craft beer, wine, spirits and mixers proves both fast and convenient. Saucey couriers prepare the orders and deliver them directly to the address provided by customers through the app. The price presented on the webpage or mobile app is exactly as-is, with no extra delivery fees or order minimums; on the other hand, shipping orders placed outside of Saucey's on-demand services areas are subject to shipping costs. Saucey serves approximately 45 cities nationwide, including Atlanta, Boston, Chicago, Houston, Los Angeles, New York City, Orlando, San Diego, Seattle, St. Louis, Tampa and Washington DC. The app's most common hours are Monday through Thursday, 12pm-11pm; Friday and Saturday, 12pm-1am; and Sunday, 12pm-10pm; but hours do vary by location and are subject to change. Saucey couriers are required to go through ID verification training and are provided with an identification scanning app. This process occurs prior to delivery. Users can schedule an order at checkout by selecting the dates and times provided. For orders that need to be cancelled, users contact the customer support department by phone (the number is provided on the app and online). Once an order has been delivered, users receive a notification in the app with the option to rate and tip the courier. There is also an option to rate and tip the courier through the receipt sent to the user's email inbox. Retailers interested in becoming a partner of the app can apply on the Saucey.com website. For customers planning a party and need a professional mixologist, the company can provide bartenders for such occasions.

FINANCIAL DATA: *Note: Data for latest year may not have been available at press time.*

In U.S. $	2021	2020	2019	2018	2017	2016
Revenue						
R&D Expense						
Operating Income						
Operating Margin %						
SGA Expense						
Net Income						
Operating Cash Flow						
Capital Expenditure						
EBITDA						
Return on Assets %						
Return on Equity %						
Debt to Equity						

CONTACT INFORMATION:

Phone: 213 456-7890   Fax:
Toll-Free:
Address: 5700 Melrose Ave., Ste. 406, Los Angeles, CA 90038 United States

STOCK TICKER/OTHER:

Stock Ticker: Private   Exchange:
Employees: 25   Fiscal Year Ends:
Parent Company:

SALARIES/BONUSES:

Top Exec. Salary: $ Bonus: $
Second Exec. Salary: $ Bonus: $

OTHER THOUGHTS:

Estimated Female Officers or Directors:
Hot Spot for Advancement for Women/Minorities:

Schlep Inc

www.schlep.it

NAIC Code: 519130

TYPES OF BUSINESS:

Online Local Delivery Service Arrangement
Truck Sharing
Moving Goods
Heavy Lifting Help
Transportation Solutions
Short-term Warehousing Services
Transportation and Logistics Tracking

BRANDS/DIVISIONS/AFFILIATES:

Schleppers
schlep.it

CONTACTS: *Note: Officers with more than one job title may be intentionally listed here more than once.*

Hunter I. Riley, CEO

GROWTH PLANS/SPECIAL FEATURES:

Schlep, Inc. has developed and operates an online and mobile marketplace that connects individuals and businesses with truck owners who will transport or heavy-lift goods locally. Schlep users include people with items too big to transport in their own vehicles, but not enough items or reasons to hire a traditional moving company; and businesses that need additional hands in relation to heavy lifting and local delivery. Truck-owning movers, referred to as Schleppers, are able to respond to loading and moving requests in real-time at reasonable prices. Schlep also offers short-term warehousing services. The firm is fully insured. On the mobile app or website (schlep.it), the company's service is by-the-item, with the requester stating exactly what is needed, where it is and/or where it is going. Transportation and logistics services include a tracking system for tracking Schleppers while on the move. For heavy lifting only or other single location jobs, users select the same location for the drop-off address. Schleppers operate between 8am and 8pm daily. Whether users need help within three hours from submitting a request or in 2 weeks (scheduling ahead of time), Schlep strives to get the job done. Schlep's integrated platform seamlessly serves businesses and their customers, whether it be delivering for furniture boutiques or home staging for interior designers. In addition, the company's same-day logistic services are not only ready to serve everyday consumers with completing tasks, but for event planners as well. Payment cards previously entered into the Schlep platform by account holders are not charged until the job is complete. First-time users must create an account.

FINANCIAL DATA: *Note: Data for latest year may not have been available at press time.*

In U.S. $	2021	2020	2019	2018	2017	2016
Revenue						
R&D Expense						
Operating Income						
Operating Margin %						
SGA Expense						
Net Income						
Operating Cash Flow						
Capital Expenditure						
EBITDA						
Return on Assets %						
Return on Equity %						
Debt to Equity						

CONTACT INFORMATION:

Phone: 501 350-5283   Fax:
Toll-Free: 844 972-4537
Address: 1500 S. Western Ave. #1AS1, Chicago, IL 60608 United States

STOCK TICKER/OTHER:

Stock Ticker: Private   Exchange:
Employees: Fiscal Year Ends:
Parent Company:

SALARIES/BONUSES:

Top Exec. Salary: $ Bonus: $
Second Exec. Salary: $ Bonus: $

OTHER THOUGHTS:

Estimated Female Officers or Directors:
Hot Spot for Advancement for Women/Minorities:

Share Now GmbH

www.share-now.com

NAIC Code: 532111

TYPES OF BUSINESS:

Car Sharing Service
Car-Sharing
Mobile App Car Sharing Management
Payment Solutions
Online and Mobile Car-Sharing Platform

BRANDS/DIVISIONS/AFFILIATES:

Stellantis NV
Free2Move

CONTACTS: *Note: Officers with more than one job title may be intentionally listed here more than once.*

Olivier Reppert, CEO

GROWTH PLANS/SPECIAL FEATURES:

Share Now GmbH operates the ShareNow online and mobile car-sharing platform. The firm owns the vehicles, which are used specifically for car-sharing. ShareNow cars are currently (late-2022) available in major European cities within the countries of Austria, Denmark, France, Germany, Hungary, Italy, Netherlands and Spain. How it works: download the ShareNow app; upload driver's license and wait for validation; ShareNow cars are parked in normal parking spaces within a city; choose a preferred rate and type of car (smart, Mini, Mercedes-Benz or BMW); open the vehicle and drive; and park the car on any legal public street inside the home area/city and at dedicated car-sharing parking spots. Rates are all-inclusive, including insurance and fuel. Rates are per-minute, per hour or per day, and a long-distance fee does apply for each additional mile beyond the mileage package. Drivers are responsible for parking costs incurred in private parking garages. If drivers must refuel the vehicle, ShareNow gives credit for it. For corporations, the ShareNow fleet can be used for business travel through its corporate car-sharing division. During 2022, Share Now GmbH was acquired by Stellantis N.V., and operates under Stellantis' subsidiary Free2Move. Free2Move is a global mobility player for businesses and individuals.

FINANCIAL DATA: *Note: Data for latest year may not have been available at press time.*

In U.S. $	2021	2020	2019	2018	2017	2016
Revenue						
R&D Expense						
Operating Income						
Operating Margin %						
SGA Expense						
Net Income						
Operating Cash Flow						
Capital Expenditure						
EBITDA						
Return on Assets %						
Return on Equity %						
Debt to Equity						

CONTACT INFORMATION:

Phone: 49 30-233-40110   Fax:
Toll-Free: 877 488-4224
Address: Brunnenstrasse 19, Kaufhaus Jandorf, Berlin, DEU 10115 Germany

STOCK TICKER/OTHER:

Stock Ticker: Subsidiary   Exchange:
Employees: 500   Fiscal Year Ends:
Parent Company: Stellantis NV

SALARIES/BONUSES:

Top Exec. Salary: $ Bonus: $
Second Exec. Salary: $ Bonus: $

OTHER THOUGHTS:

Estimated Female Officers or Directors:
Hot Spot for Advancement for Women/Minorities:

Shipt Inc

NAIC Code: 492210

TYPES OF BUSINESS:

Local Delivery Service
Shopping Services
Delivery Services
Online Ordering
Online Payment
Mobile App

BRANDS/DIVISIONS/AFFILIATES:

Target Corporation

CONTACTS: *Note: Officers with more than one job title may be intentionally listed here more than once.*

Kamau Witherspoon, CEO

GROWTH PLANS/SPECIAL FEATURES:

Shipt, Inc., owned by Target Corporation, operates a shopping order and delivery platform that enables members to order products and groceries from a variety of retailers via online or mobile app. Customers can either purchase products on-demand or schedule frequently-purchased items for delivery through Shipt's autopilot feature. Shipt offers a monthly and annual membership plans ($10.99/month or $99/year for unlimited free deliveries on orders $35 or more), as well as a pay-per-order plan. Products are hand-selected by Shipt shoppers, according to the user's preferences. All grocery items are available for delivery, including fresh produce, meat and perishable items as well as household goods such as paper towels and cleaning products. How it works: once users are signed up (www.shipt.com) and/or download the Shipt app, they select groceries, choose delivery options and pay/checkout. Shipt sends out a shopper to fulfill the order within one hour after the order has been submitted. Shipt is available in more than 5,000 U.S. cities, and utilizes vetted shoppers who set their own working schedules. By partnering with retailers in each city, shoppers are able to move efficiently through stores. Partner retailers include H-E-B, Meijer, Costco, CVS, Office Depot, Petco, Bed Bath & Beyond, buy buy Baby and Sur la Table. Headquartered in Alabama, Shipt has an additional office in San Francisco, California.

Shipt offers its employees comprehensive health benefits, 401(k) and a variety of company plans, programs and perks.

FINANCIAL DATA: *Note: Data for latest year may not have been available at press time.*

In U.S. $	2021	2020	2019	2018	2017	2016
Revenue	3,150,000,000	3,000,000,000	1,175,000,000	1,000,000,000	40,000,000	35,000,000
R&D Expense						
Operating Income						
Operating Margin %						
SGA Expense						
Net Income						
Operating Cash Flow						
Capital Expenditure						
EBITDA						
Return on Assets %						
Return on Equity %						
Debt to Equity						

CONTACT INFORMATION:

Phone: 205 502-2500   Fax:
Toll-Free: 888 807-5537
Address: 420 20th St. N, Ste. 100, Birmingham, AL 35203 United States

STOCK TICKER/OTHER:

Stock Ticker: Subsidiary   Exchange:
Employees: 3,500   Fiscal Year Ends: 01/31
Parent Company: Target Corporation

SALARIES/BONUSES:

Top Exec. Salary: $ Bonus: $
Second Exec. Salary: $ Bonus: $

OTHER THOUGHTS:

Estimated Female Officers or Directors:
Hot Spot for Advancement for Women/Minorities:

Sixt SE
NAIC Code: 532111

TYPES OF BUSINESS:
Automobile Rental
Ecommerce
Automobile Leasing
Used Car Sales
Fleet Management
Insurance Services
Passenger and Commercial Vehicle Rental

BRANDS/DIVISIONS/AFFILIATES:
Sixt rent
Sixt share
Sixt ride
Sixt Van & Truck

GROWTH PLANS/SPECIAL FEATURES:
Sixt SE provides automotive rental services mainly across Europe and the U.S., but has a presence in more than 100 countries worldwide. The company offers rental solutions from passenger vehicles, including sports utilities vehicles, electric vehicles, and luxury sports cars to commercial vans and trucks. With its products SIXT rent, SIXT share, SIXT ride, SIXT Van & Truck and others, the company offers mobility services in the areas of car rental, car sharing, ride services, and car subscriptions. These products can be booked via a single app that also integrates the services of mobility partners. During 2022, Sixt SE announced that its strategy to expand into the Canadian market, with plans to open in Vancouver first and then in Toronto. The firm wants its network to cover the North American continent.

CONTACTS: Note: Officers with more than one job title may be intentionally listed here more than once.
Alexander Sixt, Co-CEO
Konstantin Sixt, Co-CEO
Kai Andrejewski, CFO
James Adams, CCO
Vinzenz Pflanz, Chief Business Officer
Nico Gabriel, COO
Frank Elsner, Head-Press Rel.
Julian zu Pulitz, Controller
Erich Sixt, Chmn.

FINANCIAL DATA: Note: Data for latest year may not have been available at press time.

In U.S. $	2021	2020	2019	2018	2017	2016
Revenue	2,584,136,800	1,730,254,080	3,734,172,928	3,308,450,816	3,118,040,000	2,050,000,000
R&D Expense						
Operating Income						
Operating Margin %						
SGA Expense						
Net Income	354,441,200	-37,546,164	264,658,336	481,125,312	244,364,000	184,938,989
Operating Cash Flow						
Capital Expenditure						
EBITDA						
Return on Assets %						
Return on Equity %						
Debt to Equity						

CONTACT INFORMATION:
Phone: 49-89-74444-0   Fax: 49-89-74444-86666
Toll-Free:
Address: Zugspitzstrasse 1, Pullach, BY 82049 Germany

STOCK TICKER/OTHER:
Stock Ticker: SIXG   Exchange: Frankfurt
Employees: 6,399   Fiscal Year Ends: 12/31
Parent Company:

SALARIES/BONUSES:
Top Exec. Salary: $ Bonus: $
Second Exec. Salary: $ Bonus: $

OTHER THOUGHTS:
Estimated Female Officers or Directors:
Hot Spot for Advancement for Women/Minorities:

Skillshare Inc

www.skillshare.com

NAIC Code: 519130

TYPES OF BUSINESS:

Online Educative Services Arrangement
Online Creative Learning Platform
Creative Lessons
Video Classes
Software Development
Online Technology
Business Training and Collaboration
Online Education

BRANDS/DIVISIONS/AFFILIATES:

Skillshare for Teams

GROWTH PLANS/SPECIAL FEATURES:

Skillshare, Inc. has developed and operates a global online learning platform focused on creativity. 830,000+ subscribers can explore more than 40,000 video-based classes across a range of creative disciplines, from graphic design to photography to web development to painting and illustration to interior design. Industry experts are part of the community, such as Jonathan Van Ness, Aaron Draplin, Emily Henderson, Thomas Frank, Rebecca Minkoff, Jeff Staple and others. Skillshare is both a publisher of original content and an open platform, in which those who meet the firm's standards and guidelines can upload a class and earn income. Skillshare for Teams is a business solution for training and supporting employees, as well as to enable administrative and employee members to collaborate through a personalized, on-demand format. The Skillshare website has a link that offers free classes, scholarships, eGifts and more.

CONTACTS: *Note: Officers with more than one job title may be intentionally listed here more than once.*

Matt Cooper, CEO
James Rosenstock, CFO

FINANCIAL DATA: *Note: Data for latest year may not have been available at press time.*

In U.S. $	2021	2020	2019	2018	2017	2016
Revenue						
R&D Expense						
Operating Income						
Operating Margin %						
SGA Expense						
Net Income						
Operating Cash Flow						
Capital Expenditure						
EBITDA						
Return on Assets %						
Return on Equity %						
Debt to Equity						

CONTACT INFORMATION:

Phone: 212 219-3670   Fax:
Toll-Free: 888 364-6223
Address: 210 Elizabeth St., New York, NY 10012 United States

STOCK TICKER/OTHER:

Stock Ticker: Private   Exchange:
Employees: Fiscal Year Ends:
Parent Company:

SALARIES/BONUSES:

Top Exec. Salary: $ Bonus: $
Second Exec. Salary: $ Bonus: $

OTHER THOUGHTS:

Estimated Female Officers or Directors:
Hot Spot for Advancement for Women/Minorities:

Social Travel Club Limited (Love Home Swap)

www.lovehomeswap.com
NAIC Code: 519130

TYPES OF BUSINESS:
Online Vacation Rental Services
Home Swapping
Online Booking
Mobile App
Payment Solutions

BRANDS/DIVISIONS/AFFILIATES:
Wyndham Destinations Inc
www.lovehomeswap.com
Love Home Swap

CONTACTS: *Note: Officers with more than one job title may be intentionally listed here more than once.*
Celia Pronto, Managing Dir.

GROWTH PLANS/SPECIAL FEATURES:

Social Travel Club Limited operates the Love Home Swap platform that lets people book time to stay in other people's homes, while at the same time list their properties for people to book. How it works: users search online at www.lovehomeswap.com or via mobile app for a place to rent, whether it be in a city or a chateau, with a variety of locations and price points; and list their own home for other members to rent in an effort to create a home-swapping chain reaction. There are different ways to swap: the classic way, two homeowners switch with each other, staying at each other's homes, either at the same time or on different dates; or points swap, in which members they earn points for renting out their homes and then use the points in the future when convenient. Each member's identities are verified through Social Travel's ID verification service, and includes a special member profile badge. Love Home Swap requires that users purchase a monthly plan ranging from $11 to $15 per month. Members leave a review after a swap, with the average trip rating about 4.5 out of 5 stars. The firm's on-site messaging service enables members to arrange trips, which also helps them get to know each other before swapping homes. After-use cleaning expectations are agreed upon beforehand, including what to do with sheets and towels. The marketplace comprises a pet-friendly filter. Photos are primarily attached to each listed home. Most swappers leave a guide covering the nearest shops, cafes and attractions. Love Home Swap has homes in over 100 countries, with popular destinations including Spain, the U.S., Australia and Italy. Social Travel Club operates as a subsidiary of Wyndham Destinations, Inc.

FINANCIAL DATA: *Note: Data for latest year may not have been available at press time.*

In U.S. $	2021	2020	2019	2018	2017	2016
Revenue						
R&D Expense						
Operating Income						
Operating Margin %						
SGA Expense						
Net Income						
Operating Cash Flow						
Capital Expenditure						
EBITDA						
Return on Assets %						
Return on Equity %						
Debt to Equity						

CONTACT INFORMATION:
Phone: 44 20-3170-6101   Fax:
Toll-Free:
Address: Haylock House, Kettering Pkwy., Kettering, NN15 6EY United Kingdom

STOCK TICKER/OTHER:
Stock Ticker: Subsidiary   Exchange:
Employees: 43   Fiscal Year Ends: 12/31
Parent Company: Wyndham Destinations Inc

SALARIES/BONUSES:
Top Exec. Salary: $ Bonus: $
Second Exec. Salary: $ Bonus: $

OTHER THOUGHTS:
Estimated Female Officers or Directors:
Hot Spot for Advancement for Women/Minorities:

Soothe Inc

www.soothe.com

NAIC Code: 519130

TYPES OF BUSINESS:

Online Massage Arrangement Services
Massage Therapy
Skin Facials
Haircut
Beauty
Spray Tans
Online Booking
Mobile App

BRANDS/DIVISIONS/AFFILIATES:

CONTACTS: *Note: Officers with more than one job title may be intentionally listed here more than once.*

John Ellis, CEO

GROWTH PLANS/SPECIAL FEATURES:

Soothe, Inc. operates an online and mobile platform that connects licensed massage, personal care and wellness professionals with consumers. The professionals go to the Soothe member's home, office or hotel, along with supplies and products, including massage tables, blow dryers and beauty products. Booking can be completed in seconds, with scheduling ranging between 8am to midnight, seven days a week. Professionals can often arrive in as little as one hour after booking a request. Soothe hand-selects each professional in person after demonstrating their services. Customers are able to receive care in the comfort and convenience of their home or office. Price plans range from one-hour, 90-minutes to two-hours, and billed as a one-time/no-commitment monthly plan or as an annual plan. Types of massages include: Swedish, comprising long, gliding strokes, kneading and circular movements; deep tissue, focusing on chronically-tense areas; sports, offering trigger point therapy for improving flexibility and muscle recovery; prenatal, a gentle, nurturing massage to promote wellness; couples massage, in which couples can share relaxation or schedule back-to-back sessions; and soothe at work, for in-office stress relief. Skincare services include acne facial, age-defying facial, hydration facial, anti-stress facial and facials for men. Hair services are primarily haircuts, and beauty services primarily consist of spray tans. Soothe does not accept insurance as a form of coverage; however, some companies allow clients a self-claim reimbursement. Products are available from Sooth, including candles, workout equipment and related accessories. Soothe offers gift cards, and its services are available in over 70 major cities across the U.S., U.K., Ireland, Canada and Australia.

FINANCIAL DATA: *Note: Data for latest year may not have been available at press time.*

In U.S. $	2021	2020	2019	2018	2017	2016
Revenue						
R&D Expense						
Operating Income						
Operating Margin %						
SGA Expense						
Net Income						
Operating Cash Flow						
Capital Expenditure						
EBITDA						
Return on Assets %						
Return on Equity %						
Debt to Equity						

CONTACT INFORMATION:

Phone: Fax:
Toll-Free: 833 276-6843
Address: 7998 Santa Monica Blvd, West Hollywood, CA 90046-55109
United States

STOCK TICKER/OTHER:

Stock Ticker: Private   Exchange:
Employees: 100   Fiscal Year Ends:
Parent Company:

SALARIES/BONUSES:

Top Exec. Salary: $ Bonus: $
Second Exec. Salary: $ Bonus: $

OTHER THOUGHTS:

Estimated Female Officers or Directors:
Hot Spot for Advancement for Women/Minorities:

Sales, profits and employees may be estimates. Financial information, benefits and other data can change quickly and may vary from those stated here.

Spinlister LLC

NAIC Code: 532292

www.spinlister.com

TYPES OF BUSINESS:

Recreational Goods Rental
Bike-Sharing
Surfboard Sharing
Snowboard Sharing
Ski Sharing

BRANDS/DIVISIONS/AFFILIATES:

www.spinlister.com

CONTACTS: *Note: Officers with more than one job title may be intentionally listed here more than once.*

Mark Gustafson, CEO

GROWTH PLANS/SPECIAL FEATURES:

Spinlister, LLC operates an online and mobile platform that helps active people searching for a local bike to connect with trusted bike owners. The company's global bike rental and sharing service platform enables people to rent or borrow these bikes. Owners and bike shops list bikes on the platform. Renters must complete the rental process through the www.spinlister.com website, mobile app or at an in-store kiosk. Finding a preferred bike includes searching by city, zip code, ride type, available date and more; and booking and paying for the selected bike through Spinlister. Bike owners can make up to $500 per month by sharing their bikes. The company's marketplace for active people also enables the rental-sharing of surfboards, stand-up paddling boards, snowboards, skis and more. Moreover, Spinlister offers various protection options and delivery services. Listers' rides are protected against damage up to $1,000. Messages, reviews, identity verification and payment are all handled by Spinlister. Popular cities in which Spinlister is present includes New York, San Francisco, Portland, Los Angeles, London, Amsterdam, Boston, Santa Monica, Denver, Chicago, Seattle, Austin, Miami and Brooklyn.

FINANCIAL DATA: *Note: Data for latest year may not have been available at press time.*

In U.S. $	2021	2020	2019	2018	2017	2016
Revenue						
R&D Expense						
Operating Income						
Operating Margin %						
SGA Expense						
Net Income						
Operating Cash Flow						
Capital Expenditure						
EBITDA						
Return on Assets %						
Return on Equity %						
Debt to Equity						

CONTACT INFORMATION:

Phone: 213 443-8185   Fax:
Toll-Free:
Address: 12655 W. Jefferson Blvd., Los Angeles, CA 90066 United States

STOCK TICKER/OTHER:

Stock Ticker: Private   Exchange:
Employees: Fiscal Year Ends:
Parent Company:

SALARIES/BONUSES:

Top Exec. Salary: $ Bonus: $
Second Exec. Salary: $ Bonus: $

OTHER THOUGHTS:

Estimated Female Officers or Directors:
Hot Spot for Advancement for Women/Minorities:

SpotHero Inc

spothero.com

NAIC Code: 519130

TYPES OF BUSINESS:

Online Parking Reservation Service
Vehicle Parking Space Solutions
Online Parking Space Booking
Mobile Parking Space App
Payment Solution
Parking Reservations
Purchase and Sell Parking Spots

BRANDS/DIVISIONS/AFFILIATES:

SpotHero for Business
Parking Panda

CONTACTS: *Note: Officers with more than one job title may be intentionally listed here more than once.*

Mark Lawrence, CEO
Larry Kiss, Chief Architect Officer
Varvara Alva, CFO
Chris Stevens, CMO
Beth Hayden, Chief People Officer
Eric Brooke, CTO
Matt Dibari, Chief Product Officer

GROWTH PLANS/SPECIAL FEATURES:

SpotHero, Inc. operates an online and mobile platform that provides parking reservation services, connecting drivers looking to reserve and pre-pay for spaces. The parking marketplace connects drivers with available parking lots, parking garages and valet services. SpotHero's network comprises more than 8,000 parking facilities in over 300 North American cities. This includes city parking lots, airports and stadiums. SpotHero users can save up to 50% when booking a parking spot through its spothero.com website or the iOS/Android mobile app. Hourly as well as monthly rates are offered. How it works: drivers search for a parking space; compare locations by distance and price; pre-pay to reserve preferred spot; and drive there via the app's map and driving directions. Parking lot owners and managers can partner with the firm to list available spaces and connect with drivers. The SpotHero for Business product is designed to help businesses integrate parking reservations into their existing apps. This business-focused service includes features and tools for paying, managing and organizing parking expenses. SpotHero also enables parking spot owners or parking spot sellers to purchase and sell spots through SpotHero. Subsidiary Parking Panda offers an online parking service for drivers who need to find or reserve a parking space. During 2022, SpotHero partnered with Lyft, enabling Lyft riders to book parking in select cities via SpotHero directly within the Lyft app.

SpotHero offers its employees comprehensive benefits and insurance; flexible vacation time; and other perks.

FINANCIAL DATA: *Note: Data for latest year may not have been available at press time.*

In U.S. $	2021	2020	2019	2018	2017	2016
Revenue						
R&D Expense						
Operating Income						
Operating Margin %						
SGA Expense						
Net Income						
Operating Cash Flow						
Capital Expenditure						
EBITDA						
Return on Assets %						
Return on Equity %						
Debt to Equity						

CONTACT INFORMATION:

Phone: 312 556-7768   Fax:
Toll-Free:
Address: 125 S. Clark St., Chicago, IL 60603 United States

STOCK TICKER/OTHER:

Stock Ticker: Private   Exchange:
Employees: 200   Fiscal Year Ends:
Parent Company:

SALARIES/BONUSES:

Top Exec. Salary: $ Bonus: $
Second Exec. Salary: $ Bonus: $

OTHER THOUGHTS:

Estimated Female Officers or Directors:
Hot Spot for Advancement for Women/Minorities:

Staffing 360 Solutions Inc

NAIC Code: 561320

www.staffing360solutions.com

TYPES OF BUSINESS:

Temporary Staffing
Professional Staffing
Recruitment
Accounting
Information Technology
Engineering
Administration
Light Industrial

BRANDS/DIVISIONS/AFFILIATES:

GROWTH PLANS/SPECIAL FEATURES:

Staffing 360 Solutions Inc operates in the international staffing sector. It is engaged in the execution of an international buy-integrate-build process through the acquisition of domestic and international staffing organizations. The company carries its business through the reportable segments of Commercial- US; Professional- US and Professional-UK. Geographically, the group has business operations in the US, UK and Canada.

CONTACTS: *Note: Officers with more than one job title may be intentionally listed here more than once.*

Brendan Flood, CEO
Khalid Anwar, CFO
Alicia Barker, COO

FINANCIAL DATA: *Note: Data for latest year may not have been available at press time.*

In U.S. $	2021	2020	2019	2018	2017	2016
Revenue	197,770,000	204,527,000	278,478,000	260,926,000	192,650,000	109,422,000
R&D Expense						
Operating Income	-4,196,000	-5,811,000	623,000	1,601,000	356,000	-629,000
Operating Margin %	- .02%	- .03%	.00%	.01%	.00%	
SGA Expense	35,305,000	37,506,000	44,317,000	43,579,000	32,819,000	17,993,000
Net Income	8,158,000	-15,642,000	-4,894,000	-6,501,000	-18,491,000	-3,610,000
Operating Cash Flow	-14,634,000	-14,256,000	-10,840,000	1,971,000	-7,233,000	-1,208,000
Capital Expenditure	249,000	257,000	510,000	425,000	698,000	221,000
EBITDA	16,073,000	-3,151,000	8,158,000	5,611,000	-7,503,000	-439,000
Return on Assets %						
Return on Equity %						
Debt to Equity	.21%			8.504		

CONTACT INFORMATION:

Phone: 646-507-5710   Fax:
Toll-Free:
Address: 641 Lexington Ave., Ste. 2701, New York, NY 10022 United States

STOCK TICKER/OTHER:

Stock Ticker: STAF   Exchange: NAS
Employees: 200   Fiscal Year Ends: 05/31
Parent Company:

SALARIES/BONUSES:

Top Exec. Salary: $359,532   Bonus: $
Second Exec. Salary: $254,803   Bonus: $

OTHER THOUGHTS:

Estimated Female Officers or Directors:
Hot Spot for Advancement for Women/Minorities:

Staffmark Group

www.staffmark.com

NAIC Code: 561320

TYPES OF BUSINESS:

Staffing
Human Resources Consulting
Human Resources Outsourcing
Training Services
Executive Searches

BRANDS/DIVISIONS/AFFILIATES:

Recruit Holdings Co Ltd
RGF Staffing BV
Employee Management Services
Advantage Technical
Digital People
Hunter Hamilton
Advantage xPO
Workforce Solutions

CONTACTS: *Note: Officers with more than one job title may be intentionally listed here more than once.*

Stacey Lane, CEO
Tom Simeur, CFO
Sally Lynch, Sr. VP-Sales
Suzanne M. Perry, Chief Human Resources Officer
Forrest Wagner, CIO
William E. Aglinsky, Chief Admin. Officer
Kathryn S. Bernard, General Counsel
Mary B. Lucas, Chief Resource Officer
Rob Zandbergen, Chmn.

GROWTH PLANS/SPECIAL FEATURES:

Staffmark Group is a leading human resources and staffing firm based in the U.S. The company focuses on light industrial, clerical, transportation, professional, direct hire and managed services. It specializes in a wide range of industries, including accounting and finance, administrative and office, call centers, electronics, engineering, healthcare and medical office, industrial, IT, legal, logistics, mortgage and transportation. Staffmark operates from over 400 offices throughout the U.S. In addition to providing temporary staffing services, the firm offers employee leasing services, temporary placement services and permanent staffing. Affiliate Employee Management Services is a human resources consulting firm that offers assistance in employee selection and retention strategies, manager training and development, human resources and offers expertise in administration, compensation analysis, workplace safety plans and training and regulatory compliance processes. Other brands within Staffmark include Advantage Technical, Digital People, Hunter Hamilton, Advantage xPO and Workforce Solutions. Staffmark operates under RGF Staffing BV, a subsidiary of Recruit Holdings Co., Ltd.

FINANCIAL DATA: *Note: Data for latest year may not have been available at press time.*

In U.S. $	2021	2020	2019	2018	2017	2016
Revenue	1,300,000,000	1,250,000,000	1,680,000,000	1,600,000,000	1,500,000,000	1,400,000,000
R&D Expense						
Operating Income						
Operating Margin %						
SGA Expense						
Net Income						
Operating Cash Flow						
Capital Expenditure						
EBITDA						
Return on Assets %						
Return on Equity %						
Debt to Equity						

CONTACT INFORMATION:

Phone: 513-651-3600　　Fax: 513-651-1356
Toll-Free:
Address: 201 E. 4th St., Ste. 800, Cincinnati, OH 45202 United States

STOCK TICKER/OTHER:

Stock Ticker: Subsidiary　　　　Exchange:
Employees: 1,300　　　　Fiscal Year Ends: 12/31
Parent Company: Recruit Holdings Co Ltd

SALARIES/BONUSES:

Top Exec. Salary: $　　Bonus: $
Second Exec. Salary: $　　Bonus: $

OTHER THOUGHTS:

Estimated Female Officers or Directors: 4
Hot Spot for Advancement for Women/Minorities: Y

StyleSeat Inc

NAIC Code: 519130

TYPES OF BUSINESS:

Online Personal Care Services Arrangement
Beauty Booking
Wellness Booking
Mobile App
Product Order
Product Delivery

BRANDS/DIVISIONS/AFFILIATES:

GROWTH PLANS/SPECIAL FEATURES:

StyleSeat, Inc. operates an online and mobile platform that connects beauty and wellness professionals with clients. Professionals can showcase their work, connect with new and existing clients and build their businesses. Clients can discover new services and providers, and book appointments online. StyleSeat offerings are grouped into the following categories: haircut, barber, braids, weaves, natural hair, nails, eyelashes, color, eyebrows and facial. StyleSeat also offers products that can be ordered online and delivered to the consumer's provided address. The company serves customers throughout the U.S. Popular locations include Dallas, Chicago, Atlanta, Los Angeles, Houston, Detroit, Charlotte, Columbus and Washington DC.

CONTACTS: *Note: Officers with more than one job title may be intentionally listed here more than once.*

Melody McCloskey, CEO

FINANCIAL DATA: *Note: Data for latest year may not have been available at press time.*

In U.S. $	2021	2020	2019	2018	2017	2016
Revenue						
R&D Expense						
Operating Income						
Operating Margin %						
SGA Expense						
Net Income						
Operating Cash Flow						
Capital Expenditure						
EBITDA						
Return on Assets %						
Return on Equity %						
Debt to Equity						

CONTACT INFORMATION:

Phone: 415 638-6658   Fax:
Toll-Free: 888 496-6833
Address: 218 Clara St., San Francisco, CA 94107 United States

STOCK TICKER/OTHER:

Stock Ticker: Private   Exchange:
Employees: Fiscal Year Ends:
Parent Company:

SALARIES/BONUSES:

Top Exec. Salary: $ Bonus: $
Second Exec. Salary: $ Bonus: $

OTHER THOUGHTS:

Estimated Female Officers or Directors:
Hot Spot for Advancement for Women/Minorities:

Swiggy (Bundl Technologies Private Ltd)   www.swiggy.com

NAIC Code: 492210

TYPES OF BUSINESS:

Online Restaurant Delivery Services
Food Delivery
Online Food Order
Technology
Order Tracking
Shopping and Delivery Services
Tasks Services

BRANDS/DIVISIONS/AFFILIATES:

Swiggy One
Swiggy Instamart
Swiggy Corporate
Swiggy Genie

CONTACTS: *Note: Officers with more than one job title may be intentionally listed here more than once.*

Sriharsha Majety, CEO

GROWTH PLANS/SPECIAL FEATURES:

Bundl Technologies Private Ltd. is a technology product innovator and software solutions firm that has developed and operates Swiggy, a food ordering and delivery platform that serves the India market. Deliverers are called Hunger Saviors, which oftentimes deliver food within 40 minutes after the order has been placed. Bundl's technology was developed in-house, both online and mobile app formats, and features live order tracking. There are no restrictions on order amount. The company offers membership programs. Swiggy One is a single membership that offers unlimited benefits across restaurants and Instamart orders on Swiggy, including free delivery and discounts from select restaurants. Swiggy Instamart enables users to order groceries from the company's stores for fast delivery, usually in 15 to 30 minutes. Swiggy Corporate caters to businesses and offers gift vouchers, sponsored meals, exclusive discounts and more. Swiggy Genie is a local shopping and delivery service that will purchase, pick up, send and/or deliver items needed. Genie will do tasks such as taking a baked cake and delivering it to a specific location, or picking up a pair of reading glasses and delivering them to the person who needs them. Live tracking is available on Swiggy.

Bundl employees receive group personal accident and medical insurance, vehicle leasing, assistance on tax and investment planning, and other employee incentives and perks.

FINANCIAL DATA: *Note: Data for latest year may not have been available at press time.*

In U.S. $	2021	2020	2019	2018	2017	2016
Revenue	311,032,000	368,966,488	162,177,000	64,103,500		
R&D Expense						
Operating Income						
Operating Margin %						
SGA Expense						
Net Income		-500,816,184	-339,648,000	-59,184,300		
Operating Cash Flow						
Capital Expenditure						
EBITDA						
Return on Assets %						
Return on Equity %						
Debt to Equity						

CONTACT INFORMATION:

Phone: 91 80-6000-6600   Fax:
Toll-Free:
Address: No. 55 Sy No. 8 to 14 I&J Block, Ground Fl., Outer Ring Rd., Devarbinsanahalli, Varthur, Bengaluru, 560130 India

STOCK TICKER/OTHER:

Stock Ticker: Private
Employees: 11,000
Parent Company:

Exchange:
Fiscal Year Ends:

SALARIES/BONUSES:

Top Exec. Salary: $ Bonus: $
Second Exec. Salary: $ Bonus: $

OTHER THOUGHTS:

Estimated Female Officers or Directors:
Hot Spot for Advancement for Women/Minorities:

TakeLessons

NAIC Code: 519130

TYPES OF BUSINESS:

Online Educative Services Arrangement
Education Technology
Online and In-Person Education
Instructor Services
Flexible Lessons and Courses
Payment Solutions

BRANDS/DIVISIONS/AFFILIATES:

Microsoft Corporation

GROWTH PLANS/SPECIAL FEATURES:

TakeLessons is an education technology company that operates a platform where instructors offer their services for sale. Consumers purchase lessons and courses, which can be given online or in person. More than 300 subjects are offered on TakeLessons by more than 5,000 experts. How it works: Users pick a subject, choose how they want to learn and begin learning. The lessons are backed by the company's satisfaction guarantee. Private lessons and group lessons are available. Subject categories include, but are not limited to, music, language, academic tutoring, computer skills, crafts and hobbies, performing arts and wellness. Teachers set their own hourly rates and/or cost of lessons. Through the TakeLessons platform, qualified teachers create a profile, offer private or group lessons (online or in person) or provide pre-recorded learning content. TakeLessons pays teachers every week for any lesson taught, via direct-deposit. TakeLessons is owned by Microsoft Corporation.

CONTACTS: *Note: Officers with more than one job title may be intentionally listed here more than once.*

Steven Cox, CEO

FINANCIAL DATA: *Note: Data for latest year may not have been available at press time.*

In U.S. $	2021	2020	2019	2018	2017	2016
Revenue						
R&D Expense						
Operating Income						
Operating Margin %						
SGA Expense						
Net Income						
Operating Cash Flow						
Capital Expenditure						
EBITDA						
Return on Assets %						
Return on Equity %						
Debt to Equity						

CONTACT INFORMATION:

Phone: 619 238-2430   Fax:
Toll-Free: 877 310-1872
Address: 1320 Columbia St., Ste. 310, San Diego, CA 92101 United States

STOCK TICKER/OTHER:

Stock Ticker: Subsidiary   Exchange:
Employees: Fiscal Year Ends:
Parent Company: Microsoft Corporation

SALARIES/BONUSES:

Top Exec. Salary: $ Bonus: $
Second Exec. Salary: $ Bonus: $

OTHER THOUGHTS:

Estimated Female Officers or Directors:
Hot Spot for Advancement for Women/Minorities:

TaskEasy

www.taskeasy.com

NAIC Code: 519130

TYPES OF BUSINESS:

Online Lawn Care Arrangement Services
Lawn Care Services
Online Platform
Automated Pricing
Technology
Online Booking
Home Services

BRANDS/DIVISIONS/AFFILIATES:

WorkWave LLC

CONTACTS: *Note: Officers with more than one job title may be intentionally listed here more than once.*

Ken Davis, CEO
Karl Sowa, Pres.
Jeff Davis, CFO
Alex Smith, VP-Engineering
Amy Ames, VP-Oper.
Kyle Lewis, CTO
Chris Griego, COO

GROWTH PLANS/SPECIAL FEATURES:

TaskEasy operates a software-as-a-service (SaaS) platform that connects property owners, renters, property managers and businesses with contractors offering lawn care services. TaskEasy comprises a patent-pending formula that establishes fair market pricing for these services in statistical metropolitan areas throughout the U.S. The pricing system helps contractors and property owners to feel comfortable with the stated rates presented on TaskEasy. The platform is accessible online and through mobile app. Users answer a few questions about their home and task in order to see an instant price. There is no bidding process or waiting for calls; instead, services are purchased instantly through the app. From that point, TaskEasy arranges the service and ensures satisfaction with its 100% money back guarantee. The company also offers weekly and bi-weekly plans for lawn care and related needs. Each contractor must carry insurance. In late-2022, TaskEasy was acquired by WorkWave LLC, a provider of SaaS software solutions that support every stage of a service business' lifecycle. As part of the WorkWave family, TaskEasy will expand its service offerings to include any home service.

FINANCIAL DATA: *Note: Data for latest year may not have been available at press time.*

In U.S. $	2021	2020	2019	2018	2017	2016
Revenue						
R&D Expense						
Operating Income						
Operating Margin %						
SGA Expense						
Net Income						
Operating Cash Flow						
Capital Expenditure						
EBITDA						
Return on Assets %						
Return on Equity %						
Debt to Equity						

CONTACT INFORMATION:

Phone: Fax:
Toll-Free: 800 518-4461
Address: 669 SW Temple, Ste. 300, Salt Lake City, UT 84101 United States

STOCK TICKER/OTHER:

Stock Ticker: Subsidiary Exchange:
Employees: Fiscal Year Ends:
Parent Company: WorkWave LLC

SALARIES/BONUSES:

Top Exec. Salary: $ Bonus: $
Second Exec. Salary: $ Bonus: $

OTHER THOUGHTS:

Estimated Female Officers or Directors:
Hot Spot for Advancement for Women/Minorities:

TaskRabbit Inc

www.taskrabbit.com

NAIC Code: 519130

TYPES OF BUSINESS:

Online Labor Arrangement Services
Furniture Assembly
Personal Assistants
Shopping
Repairs
Online Booking
Mobile App Booking
On-Demand Services

BRANDS/DIVISIONS/AFFILIATES:

IKEA (Inter IKEA Systems BV)

CONTACTS: *Note: Officers with more than one job title may be intentionally listed here more than once.*

Ania Smith, CEO
Zac Jacobson, Sr. VP-Oper.
Amy Ming Zhang, CFO
Tamara Rosenthal, VP-Mktg.
Jessica Davila, VP-People
Chi-Yi Kuan, VP-Data
Jeff Prus, Chief Product Officer

GROWTH PLANS/SPECIAL FEATURES:

TaskRabbit, Inc. operates a same-day service platform that connects clients and taskers. This online and mobile marketplace enables clients to book a tasker for various home services, including minor home repair, mounting and installation, furniture assembly, moving and packing, housecleaning, yard work and home improvement. TaskRabbit has tens of thousands of vetted, background-checked taskers available. How the same-day system works: users pick a task or type what task they need completed; the TaskRabbit platform automatically searches for related contractors in the local area; users choose a contractor for that day or schedule a preferred date and time; and book the contractor directly through the app. Tasks are priced at a set hourly rate, and users pay for the task directly in the app with a credit or debit card when it is completed. Cancellations or reschedules are free with at least 24 hours' notice. For contractors, TaskRabbit provides notifications of potential jobs nearby and select the ones they want to complete. When a client chooses a contractor, the details of the task are communicated and confirmed between the two parties. Once the task is complete, the contractor submits an invoice to TaskRabbit. Contractors can register online to be a tasker, and attend a local onboarding orientation. TaskRabbit operates as a subsidiary of IKEA (Inter IKEA Systems BV), and is present in thousands of cities across the U.S., U.K., Canada, France, Germany, Italy, Portugal and Spain.

TaskRabbit offers its employees health coverage, 401(k) matching, generous time off, as well as company perks.

FINANCIAL DATA: *Note: Data for latest year may not have been available at press time.*

In U.S. $	2021	2020	2019	2018	2017	2016
Revenue		121,500,000	300,000,000	250,000,000	200,000,000	150,000,000
R&D Expense						
Operating Income						
Operating Margin %						
SGA Expense						
Net Income						
Operating Cash Flow						
Capital Expenditure						
EBITDA						
Return on Assets %						
Return on Equity %						
Debt to Equity						

CONTACT INFORMATION:

Phone: 877-617-8275   Fax:
Toll-Free: 877 617-8275
Address: 452 2nd St., Fl. 5, San Francisco, CA 94107 United States

STOCK TICKER/OTHER:

Stock Ticker: Subsidiary   Exchange:
Employees: 350   Fiscal Year Ends:
Parent Company: IKEA (Inter IKEA Systems BV)

SALARIES/BONUSES:

Top Exec. Salary: $ Bonus: $
Second Exec. Salary: $ Bonus: $

OTHER THOUGHTS:

Estimated Female Officers or Directors:
Hot Spot for Advancement for Women/Minorities:

Thumbtack Inc

www.thumbtack.com

NAIC Code: 519130

TYPES OF BUSINESS:

Online Freelance Work Arrangement Services
Online and Mobile Hire Platform
Job Tasks
Software and Innovative Technology
Professional Services

BRANDS/DIVISIONS/AFFILIATES:

CONTACTS: Note: Officers with more than one job title may be intentionally listed here more than once.

Marco Zappacosta, CEO
Jeff Grant, COO
Larry Roseman, CFO
Jelena Djordjevic, VP-People
Shelton Mar, VP-Engineering

GROWTH PLANS/SPECIAL FEATURES:

Thumbtack, Inc. operates a platform that connects users with qualified professionals that help them get whatever it is they need done. Jobs and tasks can include painting or remodeling a home, learning a new language, tutoring, disc jockeying an event, photographing weddings, catering, helping someone move and more. There are more than 500 different categories on the Thumbtack web and mobile platform. How it works: users answer questions about what is needed; Thumbtack takes those details and matches them with related professionals (keeping email and phone number private during the process); users compare the listed professionals, who have paid to send a custom quote; and hire the preferred professional. Along with the listed quote, each professional includes customer reviews, contact information, business profile and a customized message. When professionals register on the marketplace, they each describe the kind of jobs sought, how far they are willing to drive, as well as what projects they are able to work on and when they are available, in real-time. The firm's proprietary platform matches professionals with customers that fit and sends customer job prompts. If interested, each professional presents a quote in response to the request. Thumbtack's network comprises professionals throughout the U.S. Thumbtack also offers a membership plan for $49 year, and includes a $10,000 money-back guarantee, 20% off on on-demand bookings, and additional support from home specialists.

Thumbtack offers its employees career development and physical/emotional wellness benefits.

FINANCIAL DATA: Note: Data for latest year may not have been available at press time.

In U.S. $	2021	2020	2019	2018	2017	2016
Revenue		185,000,000	155,000,000	101,850,000	97,000,000	60,000,000
R&D Expense						
Operating Income						
Operating Margin %						
SGA Expense						
Net Income						
Operating Cash Flow						
Capital Expenditure						
EBITDA						
Return on Assets %						
Return on Equity %						
Debt to Equity						

CONTACT INFORMATION:

Phone: 415 779-2191   Fax:
Toll-Free:
Address: 1355 Market St., San Francisco, CA 94103 United States

STOCK TICKER/OTHER:

Stock Ticker: Private   Exchange:
Employees: 550   Fiscal Year Ends:
Parent Company:

SALARIES/BONUSES:

Top Exec. Salary: $ Bonus: $
Second Exec. Salary: $ Bonus: $

OTHER THOUGHTS:

Estimated Female Officers or Directors:
Hot Spot for Advancement for Women/Minorities:

Sales, profits and employees may be estimates. Financial information, benefits and other data can change quickly and may vary from those stated here.

Toromont Industries Ltd

www.toromont.com

NAIC Code: 532412

TYPES OF BUSINESS:

Construction, Mining, and Forestry Machinery and Equipment Rental and Leasing

BRANDS/DIVISIONS/AFFILIATES:

Toromont CAT
Battlefield - The CAT Rental Store
Toromont Energy
AgWest Ltd
SITECH Mid-Canada Ltd
Toromont Material Handling
CIMCO Refrigeration

GROWTH PLANS/SPECIAL FEATURES:

Toromont Industries Ltd is a Canadian industrial company. The company operates two business segments: Equipment Group and CIMCO. The larger segment by revenue, Equipment Group includes a Caterpillar dealership and rental operation of construction equipment. CIMCO offers solutions for the design, engineering, fabrication, and installation of industrial and recreational refrigeration systems. The company operates primarily in Canada and derives a smaller portion of sales from the United States of America.

CONTACTS: Note: Officers with more than one job title may be intentionally listed here more than once.

Scott Medhurst, CEO
Michael McMillan, CFO
Robert M. Ogilvie, Chairman of the Board
Michael Cuddy, Chief Information Officer
Lynn Korbak, General Counsel
Colin Goheen, President, Divisional
David Malinauskas, President, Divisional
Miles Gregg, Senior VP, Subsidiary
Jennifer Cochrane, Vice President, Divisional

FINANCIAL DATA: Note: Data for latest year may not have been available at press time.

In U.S. $	2021	2020	2019	2018	2017	2016
Revenue	2,842,262,000	2,544,151,000	2,690,272,000	2,562,681,000	1,718,696,000	1,398,293,000
R&D Expense						
Operating Income	348,057,300	272,364,500	301,661,600	270,273,000	182,521,700	154,762,700
Operating Margin %	.12%	.11%	.11%	.11%	.11%	.11%
SGA Expense	361,143,400	338,824,500	360,994,200	361,140,400	224,049,100	187,535,600
Net Income	243,314,000	186,421,800	209,739,600	184,278,300	128,688,600	113,900,000
Operating Cash Flow	396,899,200	255,247,500	106,793,100	370,176,500	191,244,800	138,080,800
Capital Expenditure	52,071,440	31,658,390	41,832,370	36,202,750	27,290,280	18,155,490
EBITDA	470,469,000	400,629,000	427,969,000	380,300,700	251,531,000	217,414,700
Return on Assets %						
Return on Equity %						
Debt to Equity						

CONTACT INFORMATION:

Phone: 416 667-5662   Fax: 416 667-5555
Toll-Free:
Address: 3131 Highway 7 West, Concord, ON L4K 1B7 Canada

STOCK TICKER/OTHER:

Stock Ticker: TMTNF   Exchange: PINX
Employees: 6,400   Fiscal Year Ends: 12/31
Parent Company:

SALARIES/BONUSES:

Top Exec. Salary: $ Bonus: $
Second Exec. Salary: $ Bonus: $

OTHER THOUGHTS:

Estimated Female Officers or Directors:
Hot Spot for Advancement for Women/Minorities:

Trueblue Inc

www.trueblueinc.com

NAIC Code: 561320

TYPES OF BUSINESS:

Temporary Staffing Services

BRANDS/DIVISIONS/AFFILIATES:

PeopleReady
PeopleScout
Staff Management SMX
Centerline
SIMOS

GROWTH PLANS/SPECIAL FEATURES:

TrueBlue Inc is a provider of staffing and workforce management solutions. The company's reportable segments include PeopleReady offers industrial staffing services. PeopleManagement offers contingent and productivity-based on-site industrial staffing services and PeopleScout offers recruitment process outsourcing and managed service provider services. It generates maximum revenue from the PeopleReady segment.

CONTACTS: *Note: Officers with more than one job title may be intentionally listed here more than once.*

A. Patrick Beharelle, CEO
Derrek Gafford, CFO
Steven Cooper, Chairman of the Board
Richard Christensen, Chief Accounting Officer
Garrett Ferencz, Chief Legal Officer
Taryn Owen, Executive VP
Carl Schweihs, Executive VP

FINANCIAL DATA: *Note: Data for latest year may not have been available at press time.*

In U.S. $	2021	2020	2019	2018	2017	2016
Revenue	2,173,622,000	1,846,360,000	2,368,779,000	2,499,207,000	2,508,771,000	2,750,640,000
R&D Expense						
Operating Income	68,442,000	307,000	66,179,000	73,919,000	77,564,000	86,549,000
Operating Margin %	.03%	.00%	.03%	.03%	.03%	.03%
SGA Expense	464,322,000	408,307,000	516,220,000	540,479,000	510,794,000	546,477,000
Net Income	61,634,000	-141,841,000	63,073,000	65,754,000	55,456,000	-15,251,000
Operating Cash Flow	20,440,000	152,531,000	93,531,000	125,692,000	100,134,000	260,703,000
Capital Expenditure	35,006,000	27,066,000	28,119,000	17,054,000	21,958,000	29,042,000
EBITDA	95,998,000	32,338,000	103,728,000	114,968,000	129,159,000	33,518,000
Return on Assets %						
Return on Equity %						
Debt to Equity	.11%	0.125	0.105	0.135	0.21	0.258

CONTACT INFORMATION:

Phone: 253 383-9101   Fax: 253 383-9311
Toll-Free:
Address: 1015 A St., Tacoma, WA 98402 United States

STOCK TICKER/OTHER:

Stock Ticker: TBI
Employees: 6,400
Parent Company:

Exchange: NYS
Fiscal Year Ends: 12/31

SALARIES/BONUSES:

Top Exec. Salary: $876,750   Bonus: $
Second Exec. Salary: Bonus: $
$521,250

OTHER THOUGHTS:

Estimated Female Officers or Directors: 4
Hot Spot for Advancement for Women/Minorities: Y

TSR Inc
NAIC Code: 561320

www.tsrconsulting.com

TYPES OF BUSINESS:
Temporary Staffing Services
IT Business Process Outsourcing

GROWTH PLANS/SPECIAL FEATURES:
TSR Inc is primarily engaged in the business of providing contract computer programming services to its customers. The company offers technical computer personnel to supplement its in-house information technology capabilities. It also gives staffing capabilities in the areas of mainframe and mid-range computer operations, personal computers and client-server support, internet and e-commerce operations, voice and data communications and helps desk support. Additionally, the company renders services on day-to-day operations, special projects, and on a short-term or long-term basis. It caters to various industries such as insurance, pharmaceutical and biotechnology, publishing and new media, financial services and project utilities.

BRANDS/DIVISIONS/AFFILIATES:

CONTACTS: Note: Officers with more than one job title may be intentionally listed here more than once.
Thomas Salerno, CEO
John Sharkey, CFO
Bradley Tirpak, Chairman of the Board

FINANCIAL DATA: Note: Data for latest year may not have been available at press time.

In U.S. $	2021	2020	2019	2018	2017	2016
Revenue	68,821,220	59,121,400	63,340,030	64,990,000	62,572,580	
R&D Expense						
Operating Income	-488,036	-1,750,652	-1,847,554	909,377	562,463	
Operating Margin %	-.01%	-.03%	-.03%	.01%	.01%	
SGA Expense	11,808,950	10,928,650	11,672,950	9,471,523	9,683,601	
Net Income	-600,974	-1,126,428	-1,335,995	486,208	268,189	
Operating Cash Flow	1,303,674	-1,567,054	-1,583,504	1,130,665	750,371	
Capital Expenditure	125,951	21,476	3,244	21,415	12,628	
EBITDA	-334,530	-1,722,876	-1,825,469	923,716	582,439	
Return on Assets %						
Return on Equity %						
Debt to Equity	1.36%	1.189				

CONTACT INFORMATION:
Phone: 212-986-4600   Fax:
Toll-Free:
Address: 400 Oser Ave., Ste. 150, Hauppauge, NY 11788 United States

STOCK TICKER/OTHER:
Stock Ticker: TSRI   Exchange: NAS
Employees: 606   Fiscal Year Ends: 05/31
Parent Company:

SALARIES/BONUSES:
Top Exec. Salary: $350,000   Bonus: $64,000
Second Exec. Salary: $310,000   Bonus: $41,000

OTHER THOUGHTS:
Estimated Female Officers or Directors:
Hot Spot for Advancement for Women/Minorities:

Tujia Online Information Technology (Beijing) Co Ltd

www.tujia.com
NAIC Code: 561510

TYPES OF BUSINESS:

Online Homestay Reservations
Room Rental Reservations
Home Rental
Online Booking

BRANDS/DIVISIONS/AFFILIATES:

CONTACTS:
Note: Officers with more than one job title may be intentionally listed here more than once.

Gang Chen, CEO

GROWTH PLANS/SPECIAL FEATURES:

Tujia Online Information Technology (Beijing) Co., Ltd. operates Tujia, an online short-term home rental platform in China. Tujia offers destinations in China and overseas. The platform's online listings include accommodation products and extension services such as homestays, apartments, villas and more. Short-term rentals primarily serve the vacation traveler's accommodation needs, but are also used by business travelers, group travelers, holiday gatherings and more. Users can book via online or mobile channels, as well as WeChat and telephone. Tujia takes care of verifying that the listed properties are what and where they say they are, and provides tenants with an advanced payment guarantee fund. Tujia members also receive benefits of the local culture, as well as discounts at nearby coffee houses, attractions and more. The company welcomes landlords who have idle houses to rent/share, as well as new-home builders desiring to share a portion of their rooms for advertising/accommodation purposes. Owners and landlords publish their homes on Tujia's multiple website portals for free. The company also guides landlords through the process for a worry-free, seamless process. Tujia has signed contracts with government agencies in China, as well as partnership agreements with top-tier real estate development companies.

FINANCIAL DATA:
Note: Data for latest year may not have been available at press time.

In U.S. $	2021	2020	2019	2018	2017	2016
Revenue						
R&D Expense						
Operating Income						
Operating Margin %						
SGA Expense						
Net Income						
Operating Cash Flow						
Capital Expenditure						
EBITDA						
Return on Assets %						
Return on Equity %						
Debt to Equity						

CONTACT INFORMATION:

Phone: 86 10-5975-6798   Fax: 86-10-5975-6717
Toll-Free:
Address: 10 Jiuxianqiao Rd., Chaoyang Dist., Beijing, Beijing 100015 China

STOCK TICKER/OTHER:

Stock Ticker: Private   Exchange:
Employees: Fiscal Year Ends:
Parent Company:

SALARIES/BONUSES:

Top Exec. Salary: $ Bonus: $
Second Exec. Salary: $ Bonus: $

OTHER THOUGHTS:

Estimated Female Officers or Directors:
Hot Spot for Advancement for Women/Minorities:

TurningArt.com
NAIC Code: 541410

www.turningart.com

TYPES OF BUSINESS:
Interior Design Services
Online Art Rental Services
Online Art Sales
Bespoke Artwork
Painting Services
Design Services
Installation Services

BRANDS/DIVISIONS/AFFILIATES:

CONTACTS: *Note: Officers with more than one job title may be intentionally listed here more than once.*
Jason Gracilieri, CEO

GROWTH PLANS/SPECIAL FEATURES:
TurningArt.com is an online rental services marketplace that primarily connects talented artists with workplaces in which art is displayed. Reproduction artwork is offered in rotating collections that are engaging and fresh within a business environment. TurningArt works with more than 1,000 painters, photographers and mixed-media artists to offer clients these collections of art. In return, employees and visitors are provided with a way to learn about current artists, and workspaces appear less redundant and dull. Through its dedicated Art Advisors, the firm handles everything, from design and curation to installation and rotation. TurningArt also offers technology that lets employees participate in artwork selection. Artwork is rotated at the frequency of each client's choosing. The company is able to draw from a proprietary catalogue of more than 25,000 pieces in a variety of sizes and styles. It can also arrange commissions and sculpture installations as well. TurningArt primarily serves the general business, real estate and designer industries, but also serves individuals desiring rotated artwork in their homes. Every dollar a member spends on the company's service is banked as ArtCredit which can be used toward the purchase of original artwork or prints. There are three ways for artists to earn money through the marketplace: royalties when a print is displayed; a fair cut of the revenue from any prints sold at the displayed sites; and a larger share of the revenue from original sales through TurningArt. Artists submit artwork to TurningArt, which is then reviewed by its team and published online; and each month, members pay a fee to have the art displayed. A photo gallery of examples is provided on TurningArt.com.

FINANCIAL DATA: *Note: Data for latest year may not have been available at press time.*

In U.S. $	2021	2020	2019	2018	2017	2016
Revenue						
R&D Expense						
Operating Income						
Operating Margin %						
SGA Expense						
Net Income						
Operating Cash Flow						
Capital Expenditure						
EBITDA						
Return on Assets %						
Return on Equity %						
Debt to Equity						

CONTACT INFORMATION:
Phone: Fax:
Toll-Free: 888 543-4546
Address: 184 South St., Boston, MA 02111 United States

STOCK TICKER/OTHER:
Stock Ticker: Private   Exchange:
Employees: Fiscal Year Ends:
Parent Company:

SALARIES/BONUSES:
Top Exec. Salary: $ Bonus: $
Second Exec. Salary: $ Bonus: $

OTHER THOUGHTS:
Estimated Female Officers or Directors:
Hot Spot for Advancement for Women/Minorities:

Turo Inc

turo.com

NAIC Code: 532111

TYPES OF BUSINESS:

Peer-to-Peer Passenger Car Rental
Vehicle Rental
Vehicle Sharing
Car Owner Rental Services
Insurance Coverage
Mobile App Booking
Online Booking

BRANDS/DIVISIONS/AFFILIATES:

Turo Go

CONTACTS: *Note: Officers with more than one job title may be intentionally listed here more than once.*

Andre Haddad, CEO
Alex Benn, Pres.
Chuck Fisher, CFO
Andrew Mok, CMO
Lorie Boyd, Chief People Officer
Avinash Gangadharan, CTO
Tom Wang, Chief Product Officer

GROWTH PLANS/SPECIAL FEATURES:

Turo, Inc. operates an online and mobile car-sharing marketplace that connects local car owners with people looking to rent a vehicle. Turo users choose from a unique selection of nearby cars through the app, whether it be for sight-seeing in a luxurious Tesla or utilizing an F-150 truck for moving furniture. Turo has more than 125,000 active hosts and 2.3 million active guests (as of mid-2022), with vehicles located across the U.S., Canada, the U.K. and France. For hosts/vehicle owners, each trip is covered up to $750,000 insurance policy issued to Turo by Travelers' insurance company. Car owners create listings for free and provide vehicle descriptions and photos. Car owners create listings for free and provide vehicle descriptions and photos. They are notified when someone requests and can confirm the trip. Users must sign up on Turo to rent a car, with identity verified through the company's technology. Approved members enter rental dates and location into the app, as well as features desired, and Turo automatically displays locally-owned cars to choose from. When a vehicle is chosen for booking, the owner will either confirm or decline the trip within eight hours. Cars can also be booked instantly if they display a Book Instantly badge. When a car is confirmed as booked, the renter and owner either meet to hand over the keys or the owner will deliver it directly to the renter. Used gasoline must be replaced when trips are completed, and renters drop cars off at agreed-upon destinations. Turo Go-enabled cars lets approved guests book, locate and unlock cars directly from the Turo app. During 2022, Turo filed an S-1 registration statement with the Securities and Exchange Commission. The firm was approved to list its common stock on the New York Stock Exchange under symbol TURO.

FINANCIAL DATA: *Note: Data for latest year may not have been available at press time.*

In U.S. $	2021	2020	2019	2018	2017	2016
Revenue	170,000,000	150,000,000				
R&D Expense						
Operating Income						
Operating Margin %						
SGA Expense						
Net Income						
Operating Cash Flow						
Capital Expenditure						
EBITDA						
Return on Assets %						
Return on Equity %						
Debt to Equity						

CONTACT INFORMATION:

Phone: 415-965-4525   Fax:
Toll-Free:
Address: 11 Sutter St., Fl. 12, San Francisco, CA 94104 United States

STOCK TICKER/OTHER:

Stock Ticker: TURO   Exchange: NYS
Employees: 220   Fiscal Year Ends:
Parent Company:

SALARIES/BONUSES:

Top Exec. Salary: $ Bonus: $
Second Exec. Salary: $ Bonus: $

OTHER THOUGHTS:

Estimated Female Officers or Directors:
Hot Spot for Advancement for Women/Minorities:

Uber Technologies Inc

NAIC Code: 561599

TYPES OF BUSINESS:

Car Ride Dispatch Service, Mobile App-Based
Freight Truck Dispatch Service
Restaurant Meal Delivery Service
Transportation Marketplace Technologies
Self-Driving Truck Technologies
Self-Driving Car Technologies

BRANDS/DIVISIONS/AFFILIATES:

UberEATS
Uber Freight
JUMP Bikes
Uber for Business
Postmates

GROWTH PLANS/SPECIAL FEATURES:

Uber Technologies is a technology provider that matches riders with drivers, hungry people with restaurants and food delivery service providers, and shippers with carriers. The firm's on-demand technology platform could eventually be used for additional products and services, such as autonomous vehicles, delivery via drones, and Uber Elevate, which, as the firm refers to it, provides "aerial ride-sharing." Uber Technologies is headquartered in San Francisco and operates in over 63 countries with over 110 million users that order rides or foods at least once a month. Approximately 76% of its gross revenue comes from ride-sharing and 22% from food delivery.

CONTACTS: Note: Officers with more than one job title may be intentionally listed here more than once.

Dara Khosrowshahi, CEO
Nelson Chai, CFO
Ronald Sugar, Chairman of the Board
Glen Ceremony, Chief Accounting Officer
Tony West, Chief Legal Officer
Nikki Krishnamurthy, Other Executive Officer
Jill Hazelbaker, Senior VP, Divisional

FINANCIAL DATA: Note: Data for latest year may not have been available at press time.

In U.S. $	2021	2020	2019	2018	2017	2016
Revenue	17,455,000,000	11,139,000,000	13,000,000,000	10,433,000,000	7,932,000,000	3,845,000,000
R&D Expense	2,054,000,000	2,205,000,000	4,836,000,000	1,505,000,000	1,201,000,000	864,000,000
Operating Income	-3,834,000,000	-4,863,000,000	-8,596,000,000	-3,033,000,000	-4,080,000,000	-3,023,000,000
Operating Margin %	- .22%	- .44%	- .66%	- .29%	- .51%	- .79%
SGA Expense	7,105,000,000	6,249,000,000	7,925,000,000	5,233,000,000	4,787,000,000	2,575,000,000
Net Income	-496,000,000	-6,768,000,000	-8,506,000,000	997,000,000	-4,033,000,000	-370,000,000
Operating Cash Flow	-445,000,000	-2,745,000,000	-4,321,000,000	-1,541,000,000	-1,418,000,000	-2,913,000,000
Capital Expenditure	298,000,000	616,000,000	588,000,000	558,000,000	829,000,000	1,635,000,000
EBITDA	360,000,000	-5,913,000,000	-7,402,000,000	2,386,000,000	-3,586,000,000	-2,537,000,000
Return on Assets %						
Return on Equity %						
Debt to Equity	.76%	0.742	0.52			

CONTACT INFORMATION:

Phone: 415-986-2715   Fax: 415-986-2104
Toll-Free:
Address: 1455 Market St., Ste. 400, San Francisco, CA 94103 United States

STOCK TICKER/OTHER:

Stock Ticker: UBER   Exchange: NYS
Employees: 29,300   Fiscal Year Ends: 12/31
Parent Company:

SALARIES/BONUSES:

Top Exec. Salary: $1,000,000   Bonus: $
Second Exec. Salary: $800,000   Bonus: $

OTHER THOUGHTS:

Estimated Female Officers or Directors: 1
Hot Spot for Advancement for Women/Minorities:

Ucommune International Ltd

www.ucommune.com

NAIC Code: 531120

TYPES OF BUSINESS:

Shared Office Space
Co-Working Spaces
Work Spaces
Online Booking
Office S[ace Management
Customized Office Services
Landlord Office Sharing Services

BRANDS/DIVISIONS/AFFILIATES:

U Space
U Studio
U Design
U Brand
U Partner

GROWTH PLANS/SPECIAL FEATURES:

Ucommune International Limited is an agile officer space manager and provider based in China. Founded in 2015, Ucommune offers flexible and cost-efficient office space solutions on a regular or as-needed basis. Offices consists of self-operated models such as: U Space and U Studio, which are leased with landlords for small office spaces, including co-working spaces; U Design, which is a customized service from location selection to daily operations in accordance to the specification of the renter; and asset light models U Brand and U Partner, through which Ucommune either charges or shares revenue with landlords for select spaces and services. Leveraging its expertise in real estate and retail industries, Ucommune transforms older and under-utilized buildings to serve China's commercial real estate sector and to provide flexible office and meeting space solutions. When Ucommune leases an office space, it designs (and sometimes builds) the space for work or meeting purposes.

CONTACTS: *Note: Officers with more than one job title may be intentionally listed here more than once.*

Xin Guan, CEO

FINANCIAL DATA: *Note: Data for latest year may not have been available at press time.*

In U.S. $	2021	2020	2019	2018	2017	2016
Revenue	16,594,500	35,000,000	70,000,000	62,748,000	25,702,800	
R&D Expense						
Operating Income						
Operating Margin %						
SGA Expense						
Net Income	-33,939,600	-49,470,000	-70,570,000	-62,279,000	-57,253,900	
Operating Cash Flow						
Capital Expenditure						
EBITDA						
Return on Assets %						
Return on Equity %						
Debt to Equity						

CONTACT INFORMATION:

Phone: 86 10 6506-7789   Fax:
Toll-Free: 400-1188-891
Address: Guang Hua Rd., No. 2, Tower D., Fl. 8, Chaoyang Dist., Beijing, Beijing 100026 China

STOCK TICKER/OTHER:

Stock Ticker: UK
Employees: 751
Parent Company:

Exchange: NAS
Fiscal Year Ends: 12/31

SALARIES/BONUSES:

Top Exec. Salary: $ Bonus: $
Second Exec. Salary: $ Bonus: $

OTHER THOUGHTS:

Estimated Female Officers or Directors:
Hot Spot for Advancement for Women/Minorities:

Sales, profits and employees may be estimates. Financial information, benefits and other data can change quickly and may vary from those stated here.

United Rentals Inc

www.unitedrentals.com

NAIC Code: 532490

TYPES OF BUSINESS:

Construction, Mining, and Forestry Machinery and Equipment Rental and Leasing

BRANDS/DIVISIONS/AFFILIATES:

GROWTH PLANS/SPECIAL FEATURES:

United Rentals is the world's largest equipment rental company, and principally operates in the United States and Canada, where it commands approximately 15% share in a highly fragmented market. It serves three end markets: general industrial, commercial construction, and residential construction. Like its peers, United Rentals historically has provided its customers with equipment that was intermittently used, such as aerial equipment and portable generators. As the company has grown organically and through hundreds of acquisitions since it went public in 1997, its catalog (fleet size of $16.6 billion) now includes a range of specialty equipment and other items that can be rented for indefinitely long time periods.

CONTACTS: Note: Officers with more than one job title may be intentionally listed here more than once.

Matthew Flannery, CEO
Jessica Graziano, CFO
Michael Kneeland, Chairman of the Board
Andrew Limoges, Chief Accounting Officer
Craig Pintoff, Chief Administrative Officer
Dale Asplund, COO
Jeffrey Fenton, Senior VP, Divisional

FINANCIAL DATA: Note: Data for latest year may not have been available at press time.

In U.S. $	2021	2020	2019	2018	2017	2016
Revenue	9,716,000,000	8,530,000,000	9,351,000,000	8,047,000,000	6,641,000,000	5,762,000,000
R&D Expense						
Operating Income	2,282,000,000	1,817,000,000	2,171,000,000	2,018,000,000	1,607,000,000	1,429,000,000
Operating Margin %	.23%	.21%	.23%	.25%	.24%	.25%
SGA Expense	1,199,000,000	979,000,000	1,092,000,000	1,038,000,000	903,000,000	719,000,000
Net Income	1,386,000,000	890,000,000	1,174,000,000	1,096,000,000	1,346,000,000	566,000,000
Operating Cash Flow	3,689,000,000	2,658,000,000	3,024,000,000	2,853,000,000	2,209,000,000	1,941,000,000
Capital Expenditure	3,198,000,000	1,158,000,000	2,350,000,000	2,291,000,000	1,889,000,000	1,339,000,000
EBITDA	4,253,000,000	3,796,000,000	4,200,000,000	3,628,000,000	2,895,000,000	2,665,000,000
Return on Assets %						
Return on Equity %						
Debt to Equity	1.57%	2.096	2.863	3.187	2.807	4.365

CONTACT INFORMATION:

Phone: 203 622-3131   Fax: 203 622-6080
Toll-Free:
Address: 5 Greenwich Office Park, Greenwich, CT 06831 United States

STOCK TICKER/OTHER:

Stock Ticker: URI
Employees: 20,400
Parent Company:

Exchange: NYS
Fiscal Year Ends: 12/31

SALARIES/BONUSES:

Top Exec. Salary: $987,681   Bonus: $
Second Exec. Salary: $659,347   Bonus: $

OTHER THOUGHTS:

Estimated Female Officers or Directors:
Hot Spot for Advancement for Women/Minorities:

UpCounsel Technologies Inc

www.upcounsel.com

NAIC Code: 541110

TYPES OF BUSINESS:

Online Legal Services
Business Legal Marketplace
Lawyers for Hire
Online Search
Online Communication

BRANDS/DIVISIONS/AFFILIATES:

Enduring Ventures

CONTACTS: *Note: Officers with more than one job title may be intentionally listed here more than once.*

Xavier Helgesen, CEO

GROWTH PLANS/SPECIAL FEATURES:

UpCounsel Technologies, Inc. operates an online and mobile on-demand marketplace that connects businesses with legal help based on their preferences. Users can access lawyers for legal purposes such as agreements, business formation, patents, trademarks, immigration, general counsel, labor and employment, securities and finance. Tens of thousands of businesses have utilized UpCounsel, from startups to small businesses to Fortune 500 companies. How it works: users post their business and legal needs (posting is free); UpCounsel's proprietary algorithm matches the request with attorneys most qualified to handle the work; users review proposals and schedule free consultations with no obligation attached; and when ready, can instantly hire the preferred attorney. Displayed pricing is also provided, as well as flexible payment options. UpCounsel users generally save 60% in comparison to law firm prices. UpCounsel's dashboard makes it convenient for users to return to their lawyers anytime a need arises; and comprises free tools for managing ongoing projects. For lawyers, the marketplace provides direct access to clients; free access to UpCounsel's document collaboration software (including e-signature); and a full-service billing platform to track income and send invoices and receive payment. UpCounsel is privately owned by Enduring Ventures.

FINANCIAL DATA: *Note: Data for latest year may not have been available at press time.*

In U.S. $	2021	2020	2019	2018	2017	2016
Revenue						
R&D Expense						
Operating Income						
Operating Margin %						
SGA Expense						
Net Income						
Operating Cash Flow						
Capital Expenditure						
EBITDA						
Return on Assets %						
Return on Equity %						
Debt to Equity						

CONTACT INFORMATION:

Phone: 510 698-2462   Fax:
Toll-Free:
Address: 28 N. Main St., Yerington, NV 89447 United States

STOCK TICKER/OTHER:

Stock Ticker: Private   Exchange:
Employees: Fiscal Year Ends:
Parent Company: Enduring Ventures

SALARIES/BONUSES:

Top Exec. Salary: $ Bonus: $
Second Exec. Salary: $ Bonus: $

OTHER THOUGHTS:

Estimated Female Officers or Directors:
Hot Spot for Advancement for Women/Minorities:

Sales, profits and employees may be estimates. Financial information, benefits and other data can change quickly and may vary from those stated here.

Upwork Inc

NAIC Code: 519130

www.upwork.com

TYPES OF BUSINESS:

Online Freelance Work Arrangement Services

GROWTH PLANS/SPECIAL FEATURES:

Upwork Inc is a United States-based company that operates an online marketplace that enables businesses to find and work with highly-skilled independent professionals. The develops platform for hiring and freelancing purposes. Its products offering include Upwork Basic, Upwork Plus, Upwork Business, Upwork Enterprise, and Upwork Payroll. The business generates revenue from Talent and Clients across the USA, India, the Philippines and the rest of the world. Substantial income is derived from providing services to Clients.

BRANDS/DIVISIONS/AFFILIATES:

Upwork Standard
Upwork Enterprise
Upwork Payroll

CONTACTS: *Note: Officers with more than one job title may be intentionally listed here more than once.*

Hayden Brown, CEO
Jeff McCombs, CFO
Thomas Layton, Chairman of the Board
Brian Levey, Chief Legal Officer
Zoe Harte, Other Executive Officer
Sam Bright, Other Executive Officer
Jessica Tiwari, Senior VP, Divisional
Lars Asbjornsen, Senior VP, Divisional
Eric Gilpin, Senior VP, Divisional

FINANCIAL DATA: *Note: Data for latest year may not have been available at press time.*

In U.S. $	2021	2020	2019	2018	2017	2016
Revenue	502,797,000	373,628,000	300,562,000	253,354,000	202,552,000	164,445,000
R&D Expense	119,083,000	83,471,000	64,027,000	55,488,000	45,604,000	37,902,000
Operating Income	-54,217,000	-22,408,000	-18,732,000	-11,712,000	-3,123,000	-14,468,000
Operating Margin %	-.11%	-.06%	-.06%	-.05%	-.02%	-.09%
SGA Expense	296,375,000	204,743,000	163,218,000	122,299,000	90,378,000	72,883,000
Net Income	-56,240,000	-22,867,000	-16,659,000	-19,907,000	-4,123,000	-16,233,000
Operating Cash Flow	10,836,000	22,365,000	1,058,000	13,744,000	-4,001,000	3,148,000
Capital Expenditure	6,137,000	14,365,000	16,638,000	6,841,000	2,319,000	846,000
EBITDA	-40,132,000	-7,907,000	-4,719,000	-12,905,000	1,001,000	-6,914,000
Return on Assets %						
Return on Equity %						
Debt to Equity	2.23%	0.079	0.123	0.075		

CONTACT INFORMATION:

Phone: 650-316-7500   Fax: 650-316-7501
Toll-Free:
Address: 2625 Augustine Dr., Ste. 601, Santa Clara, CA 95054 United States

STOCK TICKER/OTHER:

Stock Ticker: UPWK   Exchange: NAS
Employees: 650   Fiscal Year Ends: 12/31
Parent Company:

SALARIES/BONUSES:

Top Exec. Salary: $500,000   Bonus: $
Second Exec. Salary: $415,000   Bonus: $

OTHER THOUGHTS:

Estimated Female Officers or Directors:
Hot Spot for Advancement for Women/Minorities:

Sales, profits and employees may be estimates. Financial information, benefits and other data can change quickly and may vary from those stated here.

Urban Massage Ltd

www.urbanmassage.com

NAIC Code: 519130

TYPES OF BUSINESS:

Online Massage Arrangement Services
Masseuse
Spa Services
Exercise
Nutrition
Online Booking Services
Mobile Booking Services

BRANDS/DIVISIONS/AFFILIATES:

CONTACTS: *Note: Officers with more than one job title may be intentionally listed here more than once.*

Jack Tang, CEO

GROWTH PLANS/SPECIAL FEATURES:

Urban Massage Ltd. provides mobile, professional treatment services at the convenience of the customer, whether in-home or in-office. The company utilizes cutting-edge technology to seamlessly connect users to wellness services, whenever and wherever they want them. Users have access to accredited massage therapists and other professionals via the Urban Massage website or mobile app, who can provide service within an hour's time. Being mobile reduces overhead costs when compared to working at a spa, enabling therapists to generate up to 20% more of the treatment price. Each service professional must have their own public liability insurance and equipment or products. Available treatments by Urban Massage include massages, physiotherapy, osteopathy, pregnancy massages and facials, nails, lashes, hair removal, hair styling, makeup, facials, and fitness and nutrition services. Popular treatments include classic massages, deep tissue massages, sports massages, reflexology massages, luxury manicures, gel polish manicures, luxury mani/pedi's, osteopathy consultation and treatment and physiotherapy consultation and treatment. Customer reviews are provided on Urban's website and mobile app. Urban Massage operates in the U.K. and France.

FINANCIAL DATA: *Note: Data for latest year may not have been available at press time.*

In U.S. $	2021	2020	2019	2018	2017	2016
Revenue						
R&D Expense						
Operating Income						
Operating Margin %						
SGA Expense						
Net Income						
Operating Cash Flow						
Capital Expenditure						
EBITDA						
Return on Assets %						
Return on Equity %						
Debt to Equity						

CONTACT INFORMATION:

Phone: 44 330-102-7667   Fax:
Toll-Free:
Address: 27-45 Stamford St., London, SE1 9PY United Kingdom

STOCK TICKER/OTHER:

Stock Ticker: Private
Employees: 62
Parent Company:

Exchange:
Fiscal Year Ends: 12/31

SALARIES/BONUSES:

Top Exec. Salary: $ Bonus: $
Second Exec. Salary: $ Bonus: $

OTHER THOUGHTS:

Estimated Female Officers or Directors:
Hot Spot for Advancement for Women/Minorities:

UrbanSitter Inc

www.urbansitter.com

NAIC Code: 519130

TYPES OF BUSINESS:

Online Sitter Arrangement Services
On-Demand Childcare
Nanny
Babysitters
Employer Childcare
Senior Care
Online Platform
Online Payment Solutions

BRANDS/DIVISIONS/AFFILIATES:

CONTACTS: *Note: Officers with more than one job title may be intentionally listed here more than once.*

Lynn Perkins, CEO

GROWTH PLANS/SPECIAL FEATURES:

UrbanSitter, Inc. has developed and operates an online and mobile marketplace that connects people with caregivers through people they know and other trusted sources. How the system works: post a job or search for a sitter, whether for occasional, last-minute, part- or full-time help; select a date and time; click Book. UrbanSitter's platform helps keep users organized via reminders and contact details; and sends summaries of the hours, rates and amount due. Payments are conveniently made through UrbanSitters' online and mobile channels via credit card, not cash. How UrbanSitter works for sitters, nannies and caregivers: create a free profile with information about childcare or senior care experience, preferred area to work in, preferred schedule and hourly rate; browse the Job Board to apply for positions; and accept jobs with a simple tap. Sitters, nannies and caregivers keep 100% of what they earn; UrbanSitter does not take a cut from wages. Users can read reviews about caregivers, and those with repeat family badges mean local parents book them over and over again. For employers, UrbanSitter provides access to sitters and nannies when employees need them, whether they need to hire a full-time nanny or need a backup plan as soon as possible. Other services offered include pet sitting and household services such as housekeeping. Pricing plans include: monthly at $34.95 per month; quarterly at $64.95 spread across a three-month time span and billed every three months; and $59.95 for a 3-month pass that does not auto-renew. Gift cards are available through UrbanSitter. The company offers its services in more than 60 cities throughout the U.S.

FINANCIAL DATA: *Note: Data for latest year may not have been available at press time.*

In U.S. $	2021	2020	2019	2018	2017	2016
Revenue						
R&D Expense						
Operating Income						
Operating Margin %						
SGA Expense						
Net Income						
Operating Cash Flow						
Capital Expenditure						
EBITDA						
Return on Assets %						
Return on Equity %						
Debt to Equity						

CONTACT INFORMATION:

Phone: 415 677-7331   Fax:
Toll-Free:
Address: 268 Bush St., San Francisco, CA 94104 United States

STOCK TICKER/OTHER:

Stock Ticker: Private   Exchange:
Employees: Fiscal Year Ends:
Parent Company:

SALARIES/BONUSES:

Top Exec. Salary: $ Bonus: $
Second Exec. Salary: $ Bonus: $

OTHER THOUGHTS:

Estimated Female Officers or Directors:
Hot Spot for Advancement for Women/Minorities:

UZURV Holdings Inc

uzurv.com

NAIC Code: 561599

TYPES OF BUSINESS:

Car Ride Dispatch Service, Mobile App-Based
Transportation Services
ADA Paratransit Services
Non-Emergency Medical Transportation
Vehicle Sharing Services
Ride Sharing Services
Compliant Drivers
Online and Mobile App Booking

BRANDS/DIVISIONS/AFFILIATES:

CONTACTS: *Note: Officers with more than one job title may be intentionally listed here more than once.*

John Donlon, CEO
Ned Freeman, COO
Mike Page, CFO
John Duncan, Exec. VP
Phil Bayer, CTO

GROWTH PLANS/SPECIAL FEATURES:

UZURV Holdings, Inc. operates an online and mobile reservation platform for adaptive transportation. UZURV stands for user reservation, and is a stand-alone reservation services app that provides on-demand paratransit and assisted mobility services. The company helps agencies, organizations, non-profits and communities ensure that everyone has access to safe, reliable and affordable transportation. URZURV integrates technology and a network of fully FTA compliant drivers to offers its services. URZURV help older adults and people with disabilities with transportation. Rides can be scheduled with specialty credentialed drivers, including door-to-door and wheelchair accessible transportation. Live trip monitoring is provided. How it works for those who want to drive for UZURV: download the drive app, present pictures of their vehicle and create a driver profile; upload required documents; complete a background check and screenings; and review the UZURV learning center modules in the app. Drivers must be 21 years of age, have a valid U.S. driver's license, must have no DUI/DWI nor state law determined moving violation regulations, and must go through required drug/alcohol screening to FTA and state compliance standards. General vehicle requirements include: 4-door vehicle, 10-years old or less, a typical sedan or SUV that can hold two-to-seven passengers (not including the driver), valid personal vehicle insurance, valid vehicle registration, vehicle inspection, no cosmetic or major damage, clean and tidy interior, no smoking and no vaping (with passengers in the vehicle). Partners of UZURV include Americans with Disabilities Act (ADA) Paratransit, healthcare non-emergency medical transportation (NEMT) and others. UZURV operates in select cities within Virginia, Maryland, Ohio, North Carolina, Indiana, Florida, Nevada, Tennessee, Arizona and California.

FINANCIAL DATA: *Note: Data for latest year may not have been available at press time.*

In U.S. $	2021	2020	2019	2018	2017	2016
Revenue						
R&D Expense						
Operating Income						
Operating Margin %						
SGA Expense						
Net Income						
Operating Cash Flow						
Capital Expenditure						
EBITDA						
Return on Assets %						
Return on Equity %						
Debt to Equity						

CONTACT INFORMATION:

Phone: 804 662-9909   Fax:
Toll-Free:
Address: 413 Stuart Circle, Ste. 100, Richmond, VA 23220 United States

STOCK TICKER/OTHER:

Stock Ticker: Private   Exchange:
Employees: Fiscal Year Ends:
Parent Company:

SALARIES/BONUSES:

Top Exec. Salary: $ Bonus: $
Second Exec. Salary: $ Bonus: $

OTHER THOUGHTS:

Estimated Female Officers or Directors:
Hot Spot for Advancement for Women/Minorities:

Vacasa LLC
NAIC Code: 561510

TYPES OF BUSINESS:
Travel Agencies
Vacation-Rental Property Management
Home Vacation Rental

GROWTH PLANS/SPECIAL FEATURES:
Vacasa Inc is a vacation rental management platform in North America, transforming the vacation rental experience by integrating purpose-built technology with expert local and national teams.

Vacasa offers its full-time employees health benefits, 401(k) with 6% match and a variety of assistance programs and perks.

BRANDS/DIVISIONS/AFFILIATES:
Wyndham Vacation Rentals

CONTACTS: Note: Officers with more than one job title may be intentionally listed here more than once.
Matthew Roberts, CEO
Jamie Cohen, CFO
Craig Smith, COO

FINANCIAL DATA: Note: Data for latest year may not have been available at press time.

In U.S. $	2021	2020	2019	2018	2017	2016
Revenue	889,058,000	491,760,000	299,281,000			
R&D Expense	48,709,000	27,030,000	16,929,000			
Operating Income	-125,400,000	-79,406,000	-81,458,000			
Operating Margin %	-.14%	-.16%	-.27%			
SGA Expense	276,739,000	137,558,000	106,873,000			
Net Income	-142,033,000	-92,338,000	-84,872,000			
Operating Cash Flow	63,265,000	-2,427,000	-35,456,000			
Capital Expenditure	11,240,000	9,475,000	21,468,000			
EBITDA	-60,811,000	-50,446,000	-70,073,000			
Return on Assets %						
Return on Equity %						
Debt to Equity						

CONTACT INFORMATION:
Phone: 503 345-9399   Fax:
Toll-Free:
Address: 850 N.W. 13th Ave., Portland, OR 97209 United States

STOCK TICKER/OTHER:
Stock Ticker: VCSA   Exchange: NAS
Employees: 8,200   Fiscal Year Ends: 12/31
Parent Company:

SALARIES/BONUSES:
Top Exec. Salary: $500,000   Bonus: $
Second Exec. Salary: $330,769   Bonus: $50,000

OTHER THOUGHTS:
Estimated Female Officers or Directors:
Hot Spot for Advancement for Women/Minorities:

Volt Information Sciences Inc

www.volt.com

NAIC Code: 561320

TYPES OF BUSINESS:
Temporary Staffing Services
Staffing Services

BRANDS/DIVISIONS/AFFILIATES:
Volt Workforce Solutions
Volt Consulting Group
Design Technical Services
Volt Asia
Volt Europe
Volt Customer Care Solutions

GROWTH PLANS/SPECIAL FEATURES:
Volt Information Sciences Inc offers recruitment services. The company provides staffing services, outsourcing solutions, and information technology infrastructure services. Staffing services include contingent workers and personnel recruitment services. Outsourcing solutions consist of project-based IT and technology services, and Information technology infrastructure services provide server, storage, network, and desktop IT hardware maintenance. Its geographical segments are North American Staffing, International Staffing, and North American MSP. The company generates a majority of its revenue from the North American Staffing segment.

CONTACTS: Note: Officers with more than one job title may be intentionally listed here more than once.
Linda Perneau, CEO
Herbert Mueller, CFO
William Grubbs, Chairman of the Board
Leonard Naujokas, Chief Accounting Officer
Nancy Avedissian, Chief Legal Officer
Lori Schultz, Other Executive Officer

FINANCIAL DATA: Note: Data for latest year may not have been available at press time.

In U.S. $	2021	2020	2019	2018	2017	2016
Revenue		822,054,976	997,089,984	1,039,169,984	1,194,435,968	1,334,747,008
R&D Expense						
Operating Income						
Operating Margin %						
SGA Expense						
Net Income		-33,587,000	-15,186,000	-32,685,000	27,132,000	-14,570,000
Operating Cash Flow						
Capital Expenditure						
EBITDA						
Return on Assets %						
Return on Equity %						
Debt to Equity						

CONTACT INFORMATION:
Phone: 516-228-6700 Fax:
Toll-Free:
Address: 50 Charles Lindbergh Blvd., Uniondale, NY 11553 United States

STOCK TICKER/OTHER:
Stock Ticker: Subsidiary
Employees: 15,600
Parent Company: Vega Consulting Inc

Exchange:
Fiscal Year Ends: 10/31

SALARIES/BONUSES:
Top Exec. Salary: $ Bonus: $
Second Exec. Salary: $ Bonus: $

OTHER THOUGHTS:
Estimated Female Officers or Directors: 3
Hot Spot for Advancement for Women/Minorities: Y

Sales, profits and employees may be estimates. Financial information, benefits and other data can change quickly and may vary from those stated here.

Vrbo

NAIC Code: 519130

TYPES OF BUSINESS:

Online Vacation Rental Services
Vacation Homes for Rent
Online Platform
Online Booking
Mobile App Booking
Property Search

BRANDS/DIVISIONS/AFFILIATES:

Expedia Group Inc

CONTACTS: *Note: Officers with more than one job title may be intentionally listed here more than once.*

Barry Diller, Chmn.-Expedia

GROWTH PLANS/SPECIAL FEATURES:

Vrbo, which stands for vacation rentals by owners, is an online marketplace for searching and booking vacation homes to rent. These owned homes include houses, condos and other types of properties at destinations such as a chalet in Colorado, a flat in London or a mountainside luxury home in Spain. How it works: users enter the destination and travel dates; search through the available rental properties; and inquire on three or more to increase chances of booking, or select the Book It Now option. Once a booking has been confirmed by Vrbo and the property owner, payment is securely transacted via Vrbo's payment platform. When listing their homes, owners provide detailed information and photos of their properties, including the number of bedrooms and bathrooms, and other features. Property managers, those who manage more than 10 properties, can also list available homes on the site. The average vacation rental is 1,850 square feet versus the average 325 square foot hotel room. There are over 2 million bookable vacation rentals on the Vrbo platform, offering properties throughout the world. Many of the homes are dog-friendly (look for the purple paw print icon on the listing). Some vacation rentals include free amenities such as playpens, cribs, highchairs and more. The Vrbo dashboard enables lessors to manage all aspects of their listings, including property availability, online booking, online payments and more. Vrbo has an affiliate program, offering monetary and other incentives for referrals. Vrbo operates as a subsidiary of Expedia Group, Inc.

Vrbo offers employees comprehensive health benefits, paid vacation and holidays and more.

FINANCIAL DATA: *Note: Data for latest year may not have been available at press time.*

In U.S. $	2021	2020	2019	2018	2017	2016
Revenue						
R&D Expense						
Operating Income						
Operating Margin %						
SGA Expense						
Net Income						
Operating Cash Flow						
Capital Expenditure						
EBITDA						
Return on Assets %						
Return on Equity %						
Debt to Equity						

CONTACT INFORMATION:

Phone: 512 684-1100   Fax:
Toll-Free:
Address: 1011 W. Fifth St., Ste. 300, Austin, TX 78703 United States

STOCK TICKER/OTHER:

Stock Ticker: Subsidiary   Exchange:
Employees: 2,500   Fiscal Year Ends:
Parent Company: Expedia Group Inc

SALARIES/BONUSES:

Top Exec. Salary: $ Bonus: $
Second Exec. Salary: $ Bonus: $

OTHER THOUGHTS:

Estimated Female Officers or Directors:
Hot Spot for Advancement for Women/Minorities:

Wag! Group Co

www.wagwalking.com

NAIC Code: 812910

TYPES OF BUSINESS:

Dog Walking Service
Mobile Pet Grooming Service
Online Booking
Digital Payment Solutions
Dog Walking and Sitting Services
Dog Daycare and Boarding Services
Dog Training Services

BRANDS/DIVISIONS/AFFILIATES:

Wag!
Wagwalking.com
Wag Labs Inc
CHW Merger Sub Inc

CONTACTS: *Note: Officers with more than one job title may be intentionally listed here more than once.*

Garrett Smallwood, CEO
Dylan Allread, COO
Alec Davidian, CFO
Patrick McCarthy, CMO
David Cane, Chief Customer Care
Mazi Arjomand, CTO
Adam Storm, Pres.

GROWTH PLANS/SPECIAL FEATURES:

Wag! Group Co. owns and operates the Wag! website and mobile app for dog services, which are available in over 5,000 cities across all 50 U.S. states Services include dog walking, dropping by for a 20-minute visit with the dog, a dog sleepover in a pet caregiver's home for as many nights as needed, dog sitting in the comfort of the dog owner's home, daytime dog daycare for those who need some company while their owners are running errands or taking care of business and both in-person and digital dog training. Wag! also offers an insurance marketplace, wherein users can compare and select different insurance plans for their dogs. Wag! users can also make use of their Wag! app to get in contact with a licensed veterinarian to ask questions regarding their pet's health. Users set up accounts for dog services, which are performed by background-checked, insured and bonded dog lovers. The app uses GPS to track walks, including distance, duration and whether or not the dog peed or pooped, and the walker sends a report card at the conclusion of the walk with a photo or video. Wag! provides lock boxes for key storage to allow walkers access to homes and pets when owners are away from home. Services are offered seven days per week. During peak hours, most on-demand requests are filled within 30 minutes of booking. Wagwalking.com offers resources and services in regards to dog health, training, grooming, breeds, names, activities, senses and behavior. It also provides information on dog-friendly locations such as beaches, trails, campgrounds and dog parks. During 2022, former Wag Labs Inc. was acquired by and merged with and into CHW Merger Sub, Inc. and eventually formed Wag! Group Co., a public company trading on Nasdaq under ticker symbol PET.

FINANCIAL DATA: *Note: Data for latest year may not have been available at press time.*

In U.S. $	2021	2020	2019	2018	2017	2016
Revenue	27,500,000	25,000,000	47,531,250	48,750,000	50,000,000	30,000,000
R&D Expense						
Operating Income						
Operating Margin %						
SGA Expense						
Net Income						
Operating Cash Flow						
Capital Expenditure						
EBITDA						
Return on Assets %						
Return on Equity %						
Debt to Equity						

CONTACT INFORMATION:

Phone: 707 324-4219   Fax:
Toll-Free:
Address: 55 Francisco St., Ste. 360, San Francisco, CA 94133 United States

STOCK TICKER/OTHER:

Stock Ticker: PET   Exchange: NAS
Employees: Fiscal Year Ends:
Parent Company:

SALARIES/BONUSES:

Top Exec. Salary: $ Bonus: $
Second Exec. Salary: $ Bonus: $

OTHER THOUGHTS:

Estimated Female Officers or Directors: 1
Hot Spot for Advancement for Women/Minorities: Y

Waitr Holdings Inc

waitrapp.com

NAIC Code: 492210

TYPES OF BUSINESS:

Online Restaurant Delivery Services
Online Food Order Platform
Food Delivery

BRANDS/DIVISIONS/AFFILIATES:

BiteSquad.com LLC

GROWTH PLANS/SPECIAL FEATURES:

Waitr Holdings Inc provides a restaurant platform for online food ordering and delivery services across the United States. It partners with independent local restaurants and regional and national chains in small and mid-size markets. The company provides an online platform for consumers to order food from restaurant partners for pick-up and delivery through a network of drivers. This platform benefits the consumer by providing a single location to browse local restaurants and menus, track order and delivery status, and securely store previous orders and payment information for ease of use and convenience.

Waitr offers its full-time employees medical, dental and vision insurance packages.

CONTACTS: Note: Officers with more than one job title may be intentionally listed here more than once.

Carl Grimstad, CEO
Leo Bogdanov, CFO
Armen Yeghyazarians, Chief Accounting Officer
Thomas Pritchard, General Counsel
Mark DAmbrosio, Other Executive Officer
David Cronin, Other Executive Officer

FINANCIAL DATA: Note: Data for latest year may not have been available at press time.

In U.S. $	2021	2020	2019	2018	2017	2016
Revenue	182,194,000	204,328,000	191,675,008	69,273,000		
R&D Expense						
Operating Income						
Operating Margin %						
SGA Expense						
Net Income	-5,229,000	15,836,000	-289,408,992	-34,311,000	869,840	-4,518
Operating Cash Flow						
Capital Expenditure						
EBITDA						
Return on Assets %						
Return on Equity %						
Debt to Equity						

CONTACT INFORMATION:

Phone: 337-534-6881   Fax:
Toll-Free: 800-661-9036
Address: 214 Jefferson St., Ste. 200, Lafayette, LA 70501 United States

STOCK TICKER/OTHER:

Stock Ticker: WTRH   Exchange: NAS
Employees: 1,034   Fiscal Year Ends: 12/31
Parent Company:

SALARIES/BONUSES:

Top Exec. Salary: $ Bonus: $
Second Exec. Salary: $ Bonus: $

OTHER THOUGHTS:

Estimated Female Officers or Directors:
Hot Spot for Advancement for Women/Minorities:

WeWork

NAIC Code: 531120

www.wework.com

TYPES OF BUSINESS:

Shared Office Space
Shared Work Spaces
Shared Living Spaces
HR Services

GROWTH PLANS/SPECIAL FEATURES:

WeWork Inc is a commercial real estate company that provides flexible shared workspaces for technology startups and services for other enterprises. It designs and builds physical and virtual shared spaces and office services for entrepreneurs and companies.

BRANDS/DIVISIONS/AFFILIATES:

SoftBank Group Corp
WeWork
WeLive
We Company (The)

CONTACTS: *Note: Officers with more than one job title may be intentionally listed here more than once.*

Sandeep Mathrani, CEO
Benjamin Dunham, CFO
Jared DeMatteis, Chief Legal Officer
Roger Rafols, Chief Marketing Officer
Anthony Yazbeck, COO
Peter Greenspan, Other Corporate Officer
Maral Kazanjian, Other Executive Officer
Lauren Fritts, Other Executive Officer
Hamid Hashemi, Other Executive Officer
Scott Morey, President, Divisional

FINANCIAL DATA: *Note: Data for latest year may not have been available at press time.*

In U.S. $	2021	2020	2019	2018	2017	2016
Revenue	2,570,127,000	3,415,865,000	3,458,592,000	1,821,751,000		
R&D Expense						
Operating Income	-2,393,670,000	-2,784,139,000	-3,255,271,000	-1,690,999,000		
Operating Margin %	-.93%	-.82%	-.94%	-.93%		
SGA Expense	1,010,582,000	1,604,669,000	2,793,663,000	1,349,622,000		
Net Income	-4,439,027,000	-3,129,358,000	-3,264,738,000	-1,610,792,000		
Operating Cash Flow	-1,911,937,000	-857,008,000	-448,244,000	-176,729,000		
Capital Expenditure	336,892,000	1,463,846,000	3,528,821,000	2,063,911,000		
EBITDA	-3,463,955,000	-2,703,766,000	-3,039,749,000	-1,431,058,000		
Return on Assets %						
Return on Equity %						
Debt to Equity						

CONTACT INFORMATION:

Phone: 646 491-9060   Fax:
Toll-Free:
Address: 115 W. 18th St., New York, NY 10011 United States

STOCK TICKER/OTHER:

Stock Ticker: WE
Employees: 4,400
Parent Company: SoftBank Group Corp

Exchange: NYS
Fiscal Year Ends: 12/31

SALARIES/BONUSES:

Top Exec. Salary: $1,500,000   Bonus: $10,750,000
Second Exec. Salary: $877,435   Bonus: $4,345,304

OTHER THOUGHTS:

Estimated Female Officers or Directors:
Hot Spot for Advancement for Women/Minorities:

Sales, profits and employees may be estimates. Financial information, benefits and other data can change quickly and may vary from those stated here.

Wheels Up Experience Inc

wheelsup.com

NAIC Code: 481211

TYPES OF BUSINESS:

Passenger Air Charter
Private Flight Agency
Private Jets
Membership Aviation

GROWTH PLANS/SPECIAL FEATURES:

Wheels Up Experience Inc is the provider of on-demand private aviation in the United States. It is pioneering data and technology-driven solutions that connect consumers to safety-vetted and verified private aircraft. Its offerings consist of multi-tiered membership programs, on-demand flights across all private aircraft cabin categories, aircraft management, retail and wholesale charter, aircraft sales, corporate flight solutions, special missions, signature events and experiences, and commercial travel benefits through its strategic partnership with Delta.

BRANDS/DIVISIONS/AFFILIATES:

Mountain Aviation

CONTACTS: Note: Officers with more than one job title may be intentionally listed here more than once.

Kenny Dichter, CEO
Eric Jacobs, CFO
Laura Heltebran, Chief Legal Officer
Lee Applbaum, Chief Marketing Officer
Thomas Bergeson, COO
Jason Horowitz, Other Executive Officer
Francesca Molinari, Other Executive Officer
Vinayak Hegde, President

FINANCIAL DATA: Note: Data for latest year may not have been available at press time.

In U.S. $	2021	2020	2019	2018	2017	2016
Revenue	1,194,259,000	694,981,000	384,912,000			
R&D Expense	33,579,000	21,010,000	13,965,000			
Operating Income	-204,553,000	-62,966,000	-78,128,000			
Operating Margin %	-.17%	-.09%	-.20%			
SGA Expense	193,402,000	120,009,000	69,050,000			
Net Income	-190,020,000	-78,641,000	-96,274,000			
Operating Cash Flow	126,490,000	209,644,000	-24,879,000			
Capital Expenditure	60,082,000	15,524,000	8,069,000			
EBITDA	-133,455,000	-3,887,000	-38,161,000			
Return on Assets %						
Return on Equity %						
Debt to Equity	.11%	0.765				

CONTACT INFORMATION:

Phone: 212 257-5252   Fax:
Toll-Free: 855-359-8760
Address: 601 W. 26th St., New York, NY 10001 United States

STOCK TICKER/OTHER:

Stock Ticker: UP   Exchange: NYS
Employees: 2,171   Fiscal Year Ends:
Parent Company:

SALARIES/BONUSES:

Top Exec. Salary: $950,000   Bonus: $
Second Exec. Salary: Bonus: $250,000
$312,692

OTHER THOUGHTS:

Estimated Female Officers or Directors:
Hot Spot for Advancement for Women/Minorities:

Wimdu

www.wimdu.com

NAIC Code: 519130

TYPES OF BUSINESS:

Online Vacation Rental Services
Vacation Rental Services
Online Platform
Home-Sharing
Online Booking
Mobile App Booking
Rental Payments Solution

BRANDS/DIVISIONS/AFFILIATES:

HomeToGo SE
Rocket Internet SE

CONTACTS: Note: Officers with more than one job title may be intentionally listed here more than once.

Arne Bleckwenn, Managing Dir.

GROWTH PLANS/SPECIAL FEATURES:

Wimdu is an online platform that connects guests with hosts for private accommodations in Germany and internationally. These properties can include vacation rentals, holiday apartments, homes, penthouses and city studios or flats. Bookings can be made through www.windu.com, which is one of the largest portals for city and holiday bookings in Europe. Rental properties are located throughout the world, with over 350,000 properties listed. The company ensures quality through its Wimdu Triple Check standards. The triple check process consists of initial on-site property checks, continual spot-checks throughout the year and customer ratings and reviews. Hosts create listings through the Wimdu online platform, accept bookings, welcome guests/hand over the keys and receive payment. Payments are securely processed through encrypted connections, and the total cost is immediately transacted when hosts accept and confirm the request. Guests search for accommodations, enter the dates preferred, submit the booking and receive a reply or confirmation. Guest ratings and reviews help other searchers make informed decisions of where to stay. Deals for popular cities and destinations can cost up to 70% less than renting a hotel room in the same areas. For both hosts and guests, Wimdu offers 24/7 support to help with any questions or queries. Wimdu is jointly owned by HomeToGo SE and Rocket Internet SE.

FINANCIAL DATA: Note: Data for latest year may not have been available at press time.

In U.S. $	2021	2020	2019	2018	2017	2016
Revenue						
R&D Expense						
Operating Income						
Operating Margin %						
SGA Expense						
Net Income						
Operating Cash Flow						
Capital Expenditure						
EBITDA						
Return on Assets %						
Return on Equity %						
Debt to Equity						

CONTACT INFORMATION:

Phone: 49 30-695-805   Fax:
Toll-Free:
Address: Ohlauer Strausse 43, Berlin, 1099 Germany

STOCK TICKER/OTHER:

Stock Ticker: Joint Venture   Exchange:
Employees: Fiscal Year Ends:
Parent Company:

SALARIES/BONUSES:

Top Exec. Salary: $ Bonus: $
Second Exec. Salary: $ Bonus: $

OTHER THOUGHTS:

Estimated Female Officers or Directors:
Hot Spot for Advancement for Women/Minorities:

Wingz Inc

NAIC Code: 561599

www.wingz.me

TYPES OF BUSINESS:

Car Ride Dispatch Service, Mobile App-Based
Ride Sharing
Ride Hailing
Mobile App Booking
Online Booking
Airport Transportation
Non-Emergency Medical Transportation
Rides to Events

BRANDS/DIVISIONS/AFFILIATES:

www.wingz.me

CONTACTS: *Note: Officers with more than one job title may be intentionally listed here more than once.*

Christof Baumbach, CEO

GROWTH PLANS/SPECIAL FEATURES:

Wingz, Inc. has developed and operates a mobile app that enables passengers to conveniently schedule private, fixed-price, point-to-point vehicle rides. Wingz is primarily known for serving app users looking to navigate routes to and from airports, but also serves senior and non-emergency medical transportation (NEMT) rides and rides to events. The company's ride-sharing system and technology connects riders with drivers in a more affordable way versus the cost of traditional ground transportation modes. Based in San Francisco, Wingz is currently available in 16 metropolitan areas and at 22 airports in the U.S. The Wingz app enables riders to schedule rides up to two months in advance, know the fixed-rate fare up front and book with favorite drivers as often as they would like. Rides can be booked through the app, the www.wingz.me website or by telephone. Drivers have an opportunity to grow their business through direct bookings and pre-scheduled rides, building a clientele. The company's platform technology enables drivers to plan their calendars weeks and even months in advance. In addition to airport transfer, drivers can also provide event transportation services, as well as senior transportation services. Drivers must: be 21 years or older; have a personal or commercial driver's license, auto insurance, a 4-door vehicle 5 years old or younger (less than 7 years old for NEMT drivers) ; and stay connected via mobile app (iPhone or Android). Wingz's driver acceptance process includes criminal background check, motor vehicle record check, in-person and online orientation and knowledge tests, and training in transporting disabled persons. In addition, Wingz offers rides to events, doctor's appointments, business meetings or order pick-ups and errand fulfillment (for a fixed rate).

FINANCIAL DATA: *Note: Data for latest year may not have been available at press time.*

In U.S. $	2021	2020	2019	2018	2017	2016
Revenue						
R&D Expense						
Operating Income						
Operating Margin %						
SGA Expense						
Net Income						
Operating Cash Flow						
Capital Expenditure						
EBITDA						
Return on Assets %						
Return on Equity %						
Debt to Equity						

CONTACT INFORMATION:

Phone: 415 420-2222   Fax:
Toll-Free: 888 982-9716
Address: 95 3rd St., Fl. 2, San Francisco, CA 94103 United States

STOCK TICKER/OTHER:

Stock Ticker: Private   Exchange:
Employees: Fiscal Year Ends:
Parent Company:

SALARIES/BONUSES:

Top Exec. Salary: $ Bonus: $
Second Exec. Salary: $ Bonus: $

OTHER THOUGHTS:

Estimated Female Officers or Directors:
Hot Spot for Advancement for Women/Minorities:

Wonder Distribution LLC

www.wonder.com

NAIC Code: 492210

TYPES OF BUSINESS:

Online Restaurant Meals Delivery Services
Chef-Prepared Meals On-Demand
Restaurant Partnership
Food Delivery Services
Food Order Platform

BRANDS/DIVISIONS/AFFILIATES:

GROWTH PLANS/SPECIAL FEATURES:

Wonder Distribution, LLC has developed and operates an online and mobile application in which users order meals prepared by restaurant chefs and have them delivered. The company partners with chefs to craft exclusive menus, delivering unique recipes through its mobile restaurant-to-door platform. Wonder has partnered with restaurants across the U.S., and include Alanza, Barrio Cafe, Bar Nakazawa, Bobby Flay Steak, Chai Pani, Chios Taverna, Chuko, Di Fara Pizza, Fred's Meat & Bread, JBird, Jota, The Mainstay, Maydan, Pizzeria Mozza, The Regular, Taqueria del Dia, and Tejas Barbecue. Delivery by Wonder is the firm's delivery and pickup platform for restaurant partners.

CONTACTS: *Note: Officers with more than one job title may be intentionally listed here more than once.*

Marc Lore, CEO

FINANCIAL DATA: *Note: Data for latest year may not have been available at press time.*

In U.S. $	2021	2020	2019	2018	2017	2016
Revenue						
R&D Expense						
Operating Income						
Operating Margin %						
SGA Expense						
Net Income						
Operating Cash Flow						
Capital Expenditure						
EBITDA						
Return on Assets %						
Return on Equity %						
Debt to Equity						

CONTACT INFORMATION:

Phone: 424 320-0944   Fax:
Toll-Free:
Address: 4 World Trade Ctr., 150 Greenwich St., Fl. 57, New York, NY 10007 United States

STOCK TICKER/OTHER:

Stock Ticker: Private
Employees:
Parent Company:

Exchange:
Fiscal Year Ends:

SALARIES/BONUSES:

Top Exec. Salary: $ Bonus: $
Second Exec. Salary: $ Bonus: $

OTHER THOUGHTS:

Estimated Female Officers or Directors:
Hot Spot for Advancement for Women/Minorities:

Wonolo Inc

www.wonolo.com

NAIC Code: 561320

TYPES OF BUSINESS:

On-Demand Staffing Platform
Online and Mobile App Staffing Platforms
Job Seeking
Job Postings
On-Demand Staffing Solutions
Flexible Work

BRANDS/DIVISIONS/AFFILIATES:

CONTACTS: *Note: Officers with more than one job title may be intentionally listed here more than once.*

Yong Kim, CEO
Rolf leuter, Sr. Dir.-Oper. & Strategy
Angela Shi, Sr. Dir.-Finance
Susan Dimaculangan, Sr. Dir.-Mktg.
Jennifer Shewan, VP-People
Waynn Lue, VP-Engineering
Matthew Himelstein, VP-Product

GROWTH PLANS/SPECIAL FEATURES:

Wonolo, Inc. provides an online and mobile staffing platform that connects job seekers with businesses and businesses with job seekers. Nearly 600,000 pre-screened workers are connected to Wonolo's staffing marketplace. There are no up-front costs, businesses only pay when a job is successfully completed. The average time-to-fill a staff person is four minutes through the Wonolo app, versus days or weeks for many temp/contract staffing companies. Moreover, the average fill rate is 90%. On-demand staffing is 40% less than the cost of traditional temp staffing solutions. For businesses, Wonolo's platform is human resources and legal compliant. The pre-screened workers are ready to accept a job. Types of work include warehouse operations, delivery drivers, general labor, administrative tasks, event staff and merchandising. Job opportunities range from hourly to daily or more. Wonoloers range from people looking to supplement a part-time job, to college students who need to be in class most of the time to those who would rather work Wonolo jobs than a traditional one. The firm is designed to make work flexible and obtainable for anyone.

Wonolo offers its employees health benefits, a 401(k) and a variety of assistance programs.

FINANCIAL DATA: *Note: Data for latest year may not have been available at press time.*

In U.S. $	2021	2020	2019	2018	2017	2016
Revenue						
R&D Expense						
Operating Income						
Operating Margin %						
SGA Expense						
Net Income						
Operating Cash Flow						
Capital Expenditure						
EBITDA						
Return on Assets %						
Return on Equity %						
Debt to Equity						

CONTACT INFORMATION:

Phone: 404 585-1239   Fax:
Toll-Free:
Address: 535 Mission St., San Francisco, CA 94105-2997 United States

STOCK TICKER/OTHER:

Stock Ticker: Private   Exchange:
Employees: 89   Fiscal Year Ends:
Parent Company:

SALARIES/BONUSES:

Top Exec. Salary: $ Bonus: $
Second Exec. Salary: $ Bonus: $

OTHER THOUGHTS:

Estimated Female Officers or Directors:
Hot Spot for Advancement for Women/Minorities:

Yandex NV

yandex.com/company

NAIC Code: 561599

TYPES OF BUSINESS:
Car Ride Dispatch Services, Mobile App-Based
Technology and Machine Learning
Information Search Technology
Ride-Hailing and Ride-Sharing Services
Food Delivery Services
Ecommerce and Marketing Services
Media and Entertainment Information
Self-Driving Vehicles and Robotic Services

BRANDS/DIVISIONS/AFFILIATES:
MLU BV
Yandex Drive
Yandex Eats
Yandex Delivery
Yandex Market
Yandex Plus
Yandex Studio
Yandex Realty

CONTACTS: Note: Officers with more than one job title may be intentionally listed here more than once.
Arkady Volozh, CEO
Svetlana Demyashkevich, CFO

GROWTH PLANS/SPECIAL FEATURES:
Yandex NV is a technology company that builds intelligent products and services powered by machine learning. The firm's products and services help consumers and businesses better navigate the world through its search information services, including transportation services, navigation products and mobile applications. Yandex has offices worldwide. Primary business segments within Yandex include: search and portal, MLU (taxi), Yandex Market, media services and classifieds. The search and portal segment includes services offered in Russia, Belarus and Kazakhstan, such as locally relevant search and information such as navigation help, weather, news travel, voice assistance and more. These online/app services are free to users. The MLU (taxi) segment consists of majority-owned MLU B.V. (minority-owned by Uber), which operates the company's mobility businesses, including its Yandex brand of ride-hailing services in Russia and 19 other countries within the CIS and EMEA, and its Yandex Drive car-sharing business; its FoodTech business, including Yandex Eats ready-to-eat and grocery delivery service, and Yandex Lavka hyper-local convenience store delivery service; and the Yandex Delivery business, a last-mile logistics solution for individuals. The Yandex Market segment offers a multi-category ecommerce marketplace. This unified platform provides a full suite of services to its partners, including access to consumers, fulfillment, logistics, advertising and marketing, support and analytics. The media services segment consists of: Yandex Plus, a media subscription service; Yandex Music, Kinopoisk and Yandex Afisha, each of which offer entertainment services; and Yandex Studio, a production center. Last, the classifieds segment consists of Auto.ru, Yandex Realty, and Yandex Rent, for listing or shopping for vehicles, land and houses, and places to rent. Other businesses within Yandex include self-driving vehicles and robotic delivery services, cloud services, education services, FinTech services and more.

FINANCIAL DATA: Note: Data for latest year may not have been available at press time.

In U.S. $	2021	2020	2019	2018	2017	2016
Revenue	4,878,052,352	400,000,000	2,402,122,752	110,055,000	84,820,600	38,000,500
R&D Expense						
Operating Income						
Operating Margin %						
SGA Expense						
Net Income	-19,720,000		12,064,500	-63,880,500	-138,096,000	-34,271,100
Operating Cash Flow						
Capital Expenditure						
EBITDA						
Return on Assets %						
Return on Equity %						
Debt to Equity						

CONTACT INFORMATION:
Phone: 31 20-2066970   Fax: 31 204466372
Toll-Free:
Address: Schiphol Blvd. 165, Schiphol, 1118 BG Netherlands

STOCK TICKER/OTHER:
Stock Ticker: YNDX   Exchange: NAS
Employees: Fiscal Year Ends: 12/31
Parent Company:

SALARIES/BONUSES:
Top Exec. Salary: $ Bonus: $
Second Exec. Salary: $ Bonus: $

OTHER THOUGHTS:
Estimated Female Officers or Directors:
Hot Spot for Advancement for Women/Minorities:

YourMechanic Inc

NAIC Code: 811112

www.yourmechanic.com

TYPES OF BUSINESS:

Mobile Auto Repair Services
Vehicle Service
On-Demand Auto Mechanic
Fleet Service
Online Booking
Online Mechanic Services Quotes

BRANDS/DIVISIONS/AFFILIATES:

www.yourmechanic.com

CONTACTS: Note: Officers with more than one job title may be intentionally listed here more than once.

Anthony Rodio, CEO
Yu Chen, Chief Product Officer
Paul Bruso, VP-Finance
Valerie Demicheva, Dir.-Communications
Katrina Durant, Dir.-Talent
John Wall, CTO
Rajat Agarwal, VP-Engineering

GROWTH PLANS/SPECIAL FEATURES:

YourMechanic, Inc. provides an online and mobile platform for requesting quotes, booking services and accessing advice from auto mechanics. The mobile mechanic marketplace provides over 500 repair, maintenance and diagnostic services to car owners and fleets at reasonable and transparent prices across the U.S. and Canada. Quotes are provided once a user enters the vehicle make and model, desired service and location into the web or mobile portal. When consumers book a service online, the mechanic goes to their home, office or other location to service the vehicle. Scheduling maintenance services via the www.yourmechanic.com website or mobile app is convenient, as well as for making payments, accessing service histories and receiving maintenance reminders. All repairs and parts come with a 12-month/12,000-mile (whichever comes first) warranty. Mechanics undergo extensive screenings before joining the network system. They are able to choose when they can work and the types of cars and services they want to work on. By working directly with car owners, mechanics can earn additional or a better income. YourMechanic service teams are available 7 days a week, from 6am to 5pm Monday through Friday and from 7am to 4pm on Saturday through Sunday. Services span battery, belts, brakes, pre-purchase car inspection, clutch, transmission, diagnostics, doors, engine (under the hood), exhaust system, filters, fluids, fuel system, heating/air conditioning, hoses, ignition, lights, mirrors, sensors, suspension, steering, switches, tires, windows and wiper systems. Fleet solutions for government, rental, rideshare and corporate customers are provided.

YourMechanic offers employees medical and dental insurance benefits.

FINANCIAL DATA: Note: Data for latest year may not have been available at press time.

In U.S. $	2021	2020	2019	2018	2017	2016
Revenue						
R&D Expense						
Operating Income						
Operating Margin %						
SGA Expense						
Net Income						
Operating Cash Flow						
Capital Expenditure						
EBITDA						
Return on Assets %						
Return on Equity %						
Debt to Equity						

CONTACT INFORMATION:

Phone: 215 253-7941   Fax: 650-434-3797
Toll-Free: 800 701-6230
Address: 2525 E. Charleston Rd., Ste. 100, Mountain View, CA 94043 United States

STOCK TICKER/OTHER:

Stock Ticker: Private   Exchange:
Employees: 1,000   Fiscal Year Ends:
Parent Company:

SALARIES/BONUSES:

Top Exec. Salary: $ Bonus: $
Second Exec. Salary: $ Bonus: $

OTHER THOUGHTS:

Estimated Female Officers or Directors:
Hot Spot for Advancement for Women/Minorities:

Sales, profits and employees may be estimates. Financial information, benefits and other data can change quickly and may vary from those stated here.

Zeel Networks Inc

www.zeel.com

NAIC Code: 519130

TYPES OF BUSINESS:

Online Massage Arrangement Services
Online Booking
Mobile App Booking
Massage Treatments
At-Home Massages
At-Business Massages
Physical Recovery Services
Healthcare Partnering Services

BRANDS/DIVISIONS/AFFILIATES:

Zeel
www.zeel.com

CONTACTS: *Note: Officers with more than one job title may be intentionally listed here more than once.*

Samer Hamadeh, CEO
Missy Leiting, COO
Todd Colwell, CFO
Samantha Merley, Sr. VP-Mktg. & Brand
Marcy Lerner, Sr. VP-People & Culture
Joseph Loria, CTO
Ben Robinson, Sr. VP-Sales

GROWTH PLANS/SPECIAL FEATURES:

Zeel Networks, Inc. operates the Zeel online platform that offers same-day massages with licensed, vetted and insured massage therapists. Customers can book 5-star massages through the company's www.zeel.com website or mobile app. A licensed massage therapist is usually able to arrive at the customer's home, hotel or office in as little as one hour. Appointments can also be scheduled in advance, and Zeel's massage services are available within a daily time-frame seven days a week, 365 days a year. Massage services are offered throughout the U.S., with prices and availability obtained by entering one's zip code. Both the customer and the therapist are protected by Zeel's customer identification and mobile phone verification for enhanced security purposes. Massage techniques include: Swedish, with a combination of gliding and kneading strokes to release overall muscular stress and physical tension; deep tissue, which targets the deeper layers of muscles, tendons and fascia for easing persistent muscle discomfort; sports, offering a combination of deep tissue and assisted stretching for decreasing muscle soreness, improving flexibility and increasing motion; prenatal, providing a combination of techniques aimed at easing pelvic and back pain, reducing swelling and enhancing overall well-being during pregnancy; sleep, which consists of a combination of relaxing techniques such as reflexology, scalp, face, neck and back massages, as well as lavender oil to promote a better night's sleep; and couples, which offers massages for two people at the same time and place, providing the preferred massage technique of each individual. Each technique session can be booked for varied time-lengths, such as 30 or 90 minutes. Other in-home services include physical therapy, pain treatment, injury recovery, assisted stretching for recovery/flexibility/balance, orthopedic care and more. Zeel offers at-home solutions for healthcare partners, reducing payer costs and improving patient outcomes; and offers workplace wellness services and solutions.

FINANCIAL DATA: *Note: Data for latest year may not have been available at press time.*

In U.S. $	2021	2020	2019	2018	2017	2016
Revenue						
R&D Expense						
Operating Income						
Operating Margin %						
SGA Expense						
Net Income						
Operating Cash Flow						
Capital Expenditure						
EBITDA						
Return on Assets %						
Return on Equity %						
Debt to Equity						

CONTACT INFORMATION:

Phone: 917 972-2215   Fax:
Toll-Free: 877 438-9335
Address: 45 W. 45th St., New York, NY 10036 United States

STOCK TICKER/OTHER:

Stock Ticker: Private   Exchange:
Employees: Fiscal Year Ends:
Parent Company:

SALARIES/BONUSES:

Top Exec. Salary: $ Bonus: $
Second Exec. Salary: $ Bonus: $

OTHER THOUGHTS:

Estimated Female Officers or Directors:
Hot Spot for Advancement for Women/Minorities:

Sales, profits and employees may be estimates. Financial information, benefits and other data can change quickly and may vary from those stated here.

Zipcar Inc

NAIC Code: 532111

TYPES OF BUSINESS:

Car Sharing Service
Car Rental
Fleet Management Software
Mobile App Booking
Online Booking
Car-Sharing Services

BRANDS/DIVISIONS/AFFILIATES:

Avis Budget Group Inc
Zipcard

CONTACTS: *Note: Officers with more than one job title may be intentionally listed here more than once.*

Angelo Adams, Managing Dir.
Dean Breda, General Counsel
Gretchen Effgen, VP-Strategy & Corp. Dev.

GROWTH PLANS/SPECIAL FEATURES:

Zipcar, Inc., a subsidiary of Avis Budget Group, Inc., provides membership-based car-sharing services for users in a growing number of urban areas across the U.S., Canada, Costa Rica, Iceland, Taiwan, Turkey and the U.K. Zipcar members must be 21 or older (18 if a student or where required by law), can reserve vehicles ahead of time, then pay an hourly, monthly or annual fee for the use of the vehicle. The rental price includes all gas and insurance costs. Driving rates vary by city and car model. The program is marketed to drivers who normally use public transportation but occasionally want access to a car, and to those who need a car as a primary mode of transportation but wish to avoid the costs associated with car ownership. To become a member, users need to create a Zipcar log-in account, enter their driver's license number as well as credit or debit card information. Once approved, members can book cars instantly through the Zipcar app. A Zipcard will also be sent as a backup way to access cars. Zipcar, Inc.'s global positioning system (GPS) technology combined with embedded smartphone software allows members to locate cars nearby and make reservations from their mobile phones. To unlock and lock the car, members use the app or tap the Zipcard to the reader on the driver's side windshield of the car. The keys should stay in the car at all times. Zipcar has cars and related plans specifically for universities, businesses and commuters.

FINANCIAL DATA: *Note: Data for latest year may not have been available at press time.*

In U.S. $	2021	2020	2019	2018	2017	2016
Revenue	275,000,000	250,000,000	420,000,000	400,000,000	385,000,000	380,000,000
R&D Expense						
Operating Income						
Operating Margin %						
SGA Expense						
Net Income						
Operating Cash Flow						
Capital Expenditure						
EBITDA						
Return on Assets %						
Return on Equity %						
Debt to Equity						

CONTACT INFORMATION:

Phone: 617 995-4231   Fax: 617 995-4300
Toll-Free: 866-494-7227
Address: 35 Thomson Pl., Boston, MA 02210 United States

STOCK TICKER/OTHER:

Stock Ticker: Subsidiary   Exchange:
Employees: 500   Fiscal Year Ends: 12/31
Parent Company: Avis Budget Group Inc

SALARIES/BONUSES:

Top Exec. Salary: $ Bonus: $
Second Exec. Salary: $ Bonus: $

OTHER THOUGHTS:

Estimated Female Officers or Directors: 2
Hot Spot for Advancement for Women/Minorities: Y

Zomato Limited

www.zomato.com

NAIC Code: 492210

TYPES OF BUSINESS:

Local Messengers and Local Delivery
Restaurant Aggregator
Food Order Mobile App
Online Ordering
Food Delivery Services
Restaurant Search and Ratings
Technology Platform

BRANDS/DIVISIONS/AFFILIATES:

Zomato
Hyperpure

CONTACTS: *Note: Officers with more than one job title may be intentionally listed here more than once.*

Deepinder Goyal, CEO
Akshant Goyal, CFO
Daminee Sawhney, Dir.-Human Resources
Gunjan Patidar, CTO

GROWTH PLANS/SPECIAL FEATURES:

Zomato Limited is an India-based company that operates Zomato, a food and beverage aggregate platform that connects customers, restaurants and delivery partners. Launched in 2010, Zomato is currently used throughout India and the United Arab Emirates. Customers use Zomato's online or mobile platform to search restaurants, read and write customer reviews, view and upload pictures, order food to be delivered to them, or book a table at a restaurant and make payments. For restaurants, Zomato provides industry-specific marketing tools that enable them to engage and acquire customers and to provide food service. For workplaces, Zomato offers a corporate recurring meal program, as well as food delivery services for company celebrations, corporate get-togethers and other occasions. Zomato also operates Hyperpure, which supplies ingredients and kitchen products to restaurant partners. Delivery partners deliver the orders to customers.

Zomato offers its employees medical coverage and a variety of employee assistance programs and company perks.

FINANCIAL DATA: *Note: Data for latest year may not have been available at press time.*

In U.S. $	2021	2020	2019	2018	2017	2016
Revenue	295,328,000	346,105,452	200,799,000	74,556,800		
R&D Expense						
Operating Income						
Operating Margin %						
SGA Expense						
Net Income	-9,970,000	-325,769,763	-143,880,000	-16,294,900		
Operating Cash Flow						
Capital Expenditure						
EBITDA						
Return on Assets %						
Return on Equity %						
Debt to Equity						

CONTACT INFORMATION:

Phone: 91 11-4059-2373   Fax:
Toll-Free:
Address: Ground Fl. 12A, 94 Meghdoot, Nehru Pl., New Delhi, 110019 India

STOCK TICKER/OTHER:

Stock Ticker: ZOMATO
Employees:
Parent Company:

Exchange: Mumbai
Fiscal Year Ends: 12/31

SALARIES/BONUSES:

Top Exec. Salary: $ Bonus: $
Second Exec. Salary: $ Bonus: $

OTHER THOUGHTS:

Estimated Female Officers or Directors:
Hot Spot for Advancement for Women/Minorities:

ADDITIONAL INDEXES

Contents:

INDEX OF FIRMS NOTED AS HOT SPOTS FOR ADVANCEMENT FOR WOMEN & MINORITIES

INDEX OF SUBSIDIARIES, BRAND NAMES AND AFFILIATIONS

Brand or subsidiary, followed by the name of the related corporation

99 Marketplace; **99 Technology Limited**
9flats.com; **9flats PTE Ltd**
Access Data Consulting Corporation; **GEE Group Inc**
Accor SA; **Lifealike Limited (onefinestay)**
Accountemps; **Robert Half International Inc**
Actalent; **Allegis Group**
Adecco; **Adecco Group AG**
Advantage Group UK; **RGF Staffing BV**
Advantage Technical; **Staffmark Group**
Advantage xPO; **Staffmark Group**
Aerotek; **Allegis Group**
Agile Resources Inc; **GEE Group Inc**
AgWest Ltd; **Toromont Industries Ltd**
Airbnb Citizen; **Airbnb Inc**
Airbnb Experiences; **Airbnb Inc**
Airbnb for Business; **Airbnb Inc**
Airbnb Plus; **Airbnb Inc**
Airbnb.com; **Airbnb Inc**
AirCover; **Airbnb Inc**
Alamo Rent A Car; **Enterprise Holdings Inc**
Allegis Global Solutions; **Allegis Group**
Amazon.com Inc; **Amazon Flex**
AmberLeaf Partners Inc; **Mastech Digital Inc**
Amerco Real Estate Company; **AMERCO (U-Haul)**
American Mobile; **AMN Healthcare Services Inc**
AMN Revenue Cycle Solutions; **AMN Healthcare Services Inc**
Analysts International Corporation; **Innova Solutions Inc**
AND CO; **Fiverr International Limited**
Angi Inc; **Handy Technologies Inc**
Apex; **Avis Budget Group Inc**
Apollo Tourism & Leisure Ltd; **CanaDream Corporation**
Argo Autonomy Platform; **Argo AI**
Argo Hub; **Argo AI**
Argo Lidar; **Argo AI**
Ashley Ellis; **GEE Group Inc**
Aston Carter; **Allegis Group**
Auxillis; **Redde Northgate plc**
Avis; **Avis Budget Group Inc**
Avis Budget Group Inc; **Zipcar Inc**
Badenoch + Clark; **Adecco Group AG**
Basepoint Business Centres; **IWG plc**
Battlefield - The CAT Rental Store; **Toromont Industries Ltd**
Berkshire Hathaway Inc; **NetJets IP LLC**
Bestway Rental Inc; **Bestway Rental Inc**
Bestway Rent-To-Own; **Bestway Rental Inc**
BevMo!; **Gopuff (GoBrands Inc)**
Beyond by Airbnb; **Airbnb Inc**
BG California Multifamily Staffing Inc; **BGSF Inc**
BG Finance and Accounting Inc; **BGSF Inc**

BG Personal LP; **BGSF Inc**
BG Staff Services Inc; **BGSF Inc**
BG Talent; **BGSF Inc**
Bikeshare Holdings LLC; **Motivate LLC**
BiteSquad.com LLC; **Waitr Holdings Inc**
bizDojo; **IWG plc**
BMCH Inc; **GEE Group Inc**
Breedlove and Associates LLC; **Care.com Inc**
Budget; **Avis Budget Group Inc**
BxB Digital; **Brambles Limited**
Cabify; **Cabify Espana SLU**
Capital Bikeshare; **Motivate LLC**
Care.com HomePay; **Care.com Inc**
CareDriver; **HopSkipDrive Inc**
Careem BUS; **Careem Networks FZ LLC**
Careem for Business; **Careem Networks FZ LLC**
Careem NOW; **Careem Networks FZ LLC**
Careem NOW for Business; **Careem Networks FZ LLC**
Careem PAY; **Careem Networks FZ LLC**
Castlerock Recruitment Group Ltd; **Healthcare Locum Limited**
Caviar Inc; **DoorDash Inc**
Centerline; **Trueblue Inc**
Cera; **Allied Healthcare International Inc**
Certares Management LLC; **Hertz Global Holdings Inc**
Certes Financial Professionals; **GEE Group Inc**
Chandler Macleod Group; **RGF Staffing BV**
ChargedEV; **Redde Northgate plc**
Chefs Plate; **HelloFresh SE**
CHEP; **Brambles Limited**
CHW Merger Sub Inc; **Wag! Group Co**
CIMCO Refrigeration; **Toromont Industries Ltd**
CityPantry; **Just Eat Takeaway.com NV**
Clarity Workforce Technology; **Healthcare Locum Limited**
ClearVoice; **Fiverr International Limited**
Connell Equipment Leasing Company; **Connell Company (The)**
Connell Real Estate & Development Company; **Connell Company (The)**
Creative Group (The); **Robert Half International Inc**
Deliveroo; **Deliveroo plc**
Deliveroo HOP; **Deliveroo plc**
Design Technical Services; **Volt Information Sciences Inc**
Dianping.com; **Meituan Dianping**
DiDi; **DiDi Global Inc**
Didi Chuxing Technology Company; **99 Technology Limited**
DiDi Consumer Loans; **DiDi Global Inc**
DiDi Driver Insurance; **DiDi Global Inc**
DiDi Finance; **DiDi Global Inc**
Digital People; **Staffmark Group**
Dollar; **Hertz Global Holdings Inc**
DoorDash Inc; **Caviar Inc**
DP World Company; **Imperial Logistics Limited**
EdgeRock Technology Holdings Inc; **BGSF Inc**
Editions; **Deliveroo plc**

INDEX OF SUBSIDIARIES, BRAND NAMES AND AFFILIATIONS, CONT.

INDEX OF SUBSIDIARIES, BRAND NAMES AND AFFILIATIONS, CONT.

INDEX OF SUBSIDIARIES, BRAND NAMES AND AFFILIATIONS, CONT.

A Short Sharing & Gig Economy Industry Glossary

3PF: See "Third-Party Fulfillment (3PF)."

3PL: See "Third-Party Logistics (3PL)."

4PL: See "Fourth-Party Logistics (4PL)."

AAA: American Automobile Association.

Accessibility: The degree to which customers can easily get into and out of a shopping center, store, home or office's various rooms and facilities. Accessibility is an issue in providing proper accommodation to the elderly and the physically challenged.

ADA Room: A hotel room designed for a disabled person, named after the Americans with Disability Act. In the U.K., such a room is referred to as a Special Needs Accommodations.

ADR: See "Average Daily Rate (ADR)."

Adventure Tour: A tour built around a sport, such as hiking, cycling or rafting. For example, Backroads, based in Berkeley, California, is a significant operator of adventure tours involving hiking, biking and other sports.

Analytics: Generally refers to the deep examination of massive amounts of data, often on a continual or real-time basis. The goal is to discover deeper insights, make recommendations or generate predictions. Advanced analytics includes such techniques as big data, predictive analytics, text analytics, data mining, forecasting, optimization and simulation.

Apollo: A computerized reservation system used for airline, cruise, tour, hotel, car and train reservations.

Applications: Computer programs and systems that allow users to interface with a computer and that collect, manipulate, summarize and report data and information. Also, see "Apps."

Apps: Short for applications, apps are small software programs designed to run primarily on mobile devices such as smartphones and tablets. Also known as "mobile apps."

ARR: Average Room Rate.

Asia Pacific Advisory Committee (APAC): A multi-country committee representing the Asia and Pacific region.

Asia Pacific Economic Cooperation (APEC): An organization established to promote investment and trade in the Pacific basin.

Association of Southeast Asian Nations (ASEAN): A regional economic development association established in 1967 by five original member countries: Indonesia, Malaysia, Philippines, Singapore and Thailand. Brunei joined on 8 January 1984, Vietnam on 28 July 1995, Laos and Myanmar on 23 July 1997 and Cambodia on 30 April 1999.

Available Rooms: The number of rooms actually available for use during a particular day in a hotel.

Average Daily Rate (ADR): In hotels, room revenue divided by rooms sold.

B&B: See "Bed and Breakfast (B&B)."

B2B: See "Business-to-Business."

B2C: See "Business-to-Consumer."

B2E: See "Business-to-Employee."

B2G: See "Business-to-Government."

Baby Boomer: Generally refers to people born from 1946 to 1964. In the U.S., the initial number of Baby Boomers totaled about 78 million. The term evolved to describe the children of soldiers and war industry workers who were involved in World War II and who began forming families after the war's end. In 2011, the oldest Baby Boomers began reaching the traditional retirement age of 65.

Back of the House: The area of a hotel or restaurant separated from the guest areas, containing administrative offices, kitchens, plant, etc.

BAR: See "Best Available Rate (BAR)."

Bareboat Charter: A charter of a boat or yacht that does not include a crew. Bareboats are typically sailing yachts used by knowledgeable vacationers.

Leading companies in the bareboat business include The Moorings and Sunsail.

Bays: Often the number of guest rooms in a hotel, but this differs from Keys because a suite with a bedroom and sitting room is counted at one key and two bays.

Bed and Breakfast (B&B): Typically, a privately owned lodging that includes breakfast in the price of a stay. A B&B can range from a small home with one spare room to a luxury inn.

Bed Night: A measure of occupancy in a hotel (one person for each bed per night).

Best Available Rate (BAR): A method of hotel room pricing that offers guests the assurance that they are paying the lowest room price available for a given night.

Bleisure: A trip that is a combination of business and leisure travel. For example, a person on a business trip to a given city during weekdays might extend the trip to stay over for a leisure weekend.

Boutique: A term used by often smaller and usually luxury independent hotels to differentiate themselves from larger branded hotels, but which has been applied to some chains to their design-led "lifestyle" brands, e.g. Starwood's "W" Hotels.

Boutique Hotel: A small hotel with enhanced levels of service, catering to affluent customers.

BPO: See "Business Process Outsourcing (BPO)."

Brand: A marketing strategy that places a focus on the brand name of a product, service or firm in order to increase the brand's market share, increase sales, establish credibility, improve satisfaction, raise the profile of the firm and increase profits. Also, see "Brand."

Branding: A marketing strategy that places a focus on the brand name of a product, service or firm in order to increase the brand's market share, increase sales, establish credibility, improve satisfaction, raise the profile of the firm and increase profits. Also, see "Brand."

Business Process Outsourcing (BPO): The process of hiring another company to handle business

activities. BPO is one of the fastest-growing segments in the offshoring sector. Services include human resources management, billing and purchasing and call centers, as well as many types of customer service or marketing activities, depending on the industry involved. Also, see "Knowledge Process Outsourcing (KPO)" and Business Transformation Outsourcing (BTO)."

Business-to-Business: An organization focused on selling products, services or data to commercial customers rather than individual consumers. Also known as B2B.

Business-to-Consumer: An organization focused on selling products, services or data to individual consumers rather than commercial customers. Also known as B2C.

Business-to-Employee: A corporate communications system, such as an intranet, aimed at conveying information from a company to its employees. Also known as B2E.

Business-to-Government: An organization focused on selling products, services or data to government units rather than commercial businesses or consumers. Also known as B2G.

CAFTA-DR: See "Central American-Dominican Republic Free Trade Agreement (CAFTA-DR)."

Cancellation Penalty: A monetary penalty incurred when a reservation or a contract is cancelled.

Car For Hire: British term for a rental car.

Central Reservation Office: Call center location at which reservations are taken for a travel services provider, such as a chain of hotels or car rental agencies.

Computerized Reservation System: Any computer system that allows instant access to airline schedules, tickets and fares.

Condominium: 1) In the travel industry, lodging similar to furnished, private apartments that are available to rent for days or weeks. 2) In real estate, a kind of property ownership in which the owner holds title to an individual unit in a multi-unit dwelling and shares ownership of common areas such as hallways or swimming pools.

Contingent Worker: A worker who works under flexible, contract relationships, rather than an employee-employer relationship. Such workers are often utilized on a non-permanent basis, and may sometimes be referred to as day laborers, freelancers, consultants, or independent professionals, depending on the nature of the service provided or work done. Also, see "Gig Economy" and "Sharing Economy."

Convention Bureau: Usually a publicly funded organization in the U.S. charged with the promotion of a town or region for conferences, meetings and exhibitions.

Corporate Rate: A reduced price for guests staying on business, sometimes through specially negotiated terms.

CRM: See "Customer Relationship Management (CRM)."

Customer Relationship Management (CRM): Refers to the automation, via sophisticated software, of business processes involving existing and prospective customers. CRM may cover aspects such as sales (contact management and contact history), marketing (campaign management and telemarketing) and customer service (call center history and field service history). Well known providers of CRM software include Salesforce, which delivers via a Software as a Service model (see "Software as a Service (Saas)"), Microsoft and Oracle.

CVB: Convention and Visitors Bureau.

Demographics: The breakdown of the population into statistical categories such as age, income, education and sex.

Destination Club: A program where wealthy travelers purchase the right to use a group of luxury vacation homes. Participants, sometimes referred to as members, purchase temporal ownership in a group of highly appealing properties. What makes this arrangement different from the standard timeshare is the fact that members buy in the right to use a variety of luxury houses (and sometimes yachts), rather than resort condos.

Destination Specialist: A person who is certified as an expert on a specific destination or region.

Digital Transformation (DX): The implementation of digital technologies into as many areas of a business as reasonably possible Goals may include: to fundamentally change how the enterprise operates: how data is gathered and tracked: how innovation is launched: and how value is delivered to customers. The hoped-for result is to create new operating efficiencies and develop new revenue or profit opportunities, while better positioning the enterprise for the future. Also abbreviated as DX or DT.

Double-Occupancy Rate: The price per person for a room for two.

DX: See "Digital Transformation (DX)."

Echo Boomers: See "Generation Y."

Ecofriendly: See "Ecotourism."

E-Commerce: The use of online, internet-based sales methods. The phrase is used to describe both business-to-consumer and business-to-business sales.

Ecotourism: A philosophy used by a hotel in design, construction and operation, generally has goals that include: conservation of electricity, water and other natural resources: sensitivity to the surrounding natural environment, ecosystem, wildlife (and sometimes native peoples): use of organic ingredients in the hotel kitchen (which may include items from a hotel's own organic garden): and a peaceful, soothing environment throughout the hotel property (which may include such elements as extensive landscaping with native plants, running water, Zen-like gardens and areas that encourage contemplation, meditation and relaxation). Ecotourism may also be used to describe sensitivity to local ecology and native peoples in tours and excursions. "Sustainable tourism" is another phrase used to describe this sector.

Electronic Data Interchange (EDI): An accepted standard format for the exchange of data between various companies' networks. EDI allows for the transfer of e-mail as well as orders, invoices and other files from one company to another.

Electronic Reservations Service Provider (ERSP): An online service such as Expedia, Orbitz and Travelocity that provides travel reservation services for airlines, car rental agencies or cruise lines.

EMEA: The region comprised of Europe, the Middle East and Africa.

Enterprise Resource Planning (ERP): An integrated information system that helps manage all aspects of a business, including accounting, ordering and human resources, typically across all locations of a major corporation or organization. ERP is considered to be a critical tool for management of large organizations. Suppliers of ERP tools include SAP and Oracle.

ERP: See "Enterprise Resource Planning (ERP)."

ERSP: Electronic Reservations Service Provider. A system that identifies airline reservations made online.

EU: See "European Union (EU)."

EU Competence: The jurisdiction in which the European Union (EU) can take legal action.

European Community (EC): See "European Union (EU)."

European Union (EU): A consolidation of European countries (member states) functioning as one body to facilitate trade. Previously known as the European Community (EC). The EU has a unified currency, the Euro. See europa.eu.int.

Experiential Travel: A phrase that reflects a desire by many travelers to deeply experience local cultures and people when they travel. In addition to connecting personally with locals, such travel may include a focus on local foods, entertainment, wines, craft beers, architecture or other features or qualities unique to a locality.

FASB: See "Financial Accounting Standards Board (FASB)."

Financial Accounting Standards Board (FASB): An independent organization that establishes the Generally Accepted Accounting Principles (GAAP).

Franchise: 1) A contractual agreement between a franchisor (for example, a company or organization owning all rights to a brand, type of business, retail operation, restaurant concept or sports league) and a franchisee (person or organization desiring to license the use of those rights for a specific purpose within a specific region) that allows the franchisee to operate a retail outlet or other type of business using a brand, trade secrets, formulas and format developed and supported by the franchisor. Typically, a franchisee pays an upfront fee and then continuing fees to the franchisor. 2) A generic term used to describe a very well established business or brand.

Franchisee: See "Franchise."

Franchisor: See "Franchise."

Full Board: A hotel rate which includes three meals a day (also known as Full Pension or American Plan (AP) in the U.S.).

GAAP: See "Generally Accepted Accounting Principles (GAAP)."

GDP: See "Gross Domestic Product (GDP)."

Generally Accepted Accounting Principles (GAAP): A set of accounting standards administered by the Financial Accounting Standards Board (FASB) and enforced by the U.S. Security and Exchange Commission (SEC). GAAP is primarily used in the U.S.

Generation M: A very loosely defined term that is sometimes used to refer to young people who have grown up in the digital age. "M" may refer to any or all of media-saturated, mobile or multi-tasking. The term was most notably used in a Kaiser Family Foundation report published in 2005, "Generation M: Media in the Lives of 8-18 year olds." Also, see "Generation Y" and "Generation Z."

Generation X: A loosely-defined and variously-used term that describes people born between approximately 1965 and 1980, but other time frames are recited. Generation X is often referred to as a group influential in defining tastes in consumer goods, entertainment and/or political and social matters.

Generation Y: Refers to people born between approximately 1982 and 2002. In the U.S., they number more than 90 million, making them the largest generation segment in the nation's history. They are also known as Echo Boomers, Millennials or the Millennial Generation. These are children of the Baby Boom generation who will be filling the work force as Baby Boomers retire.

Generation Z: Some people refer to Generation Z as people born after 1991. Others use the beginning date of 2001, or refer to the era of 1994 to 2004. Members of Generation Z are considered to be natural and rapid adopters of the latest technologies.

Gig Economy: That part of economic activity that is directed by firms like Uber that utilize independent workers as assets owned by others in order to deliver a service. The workers typically work under contract-based relationships, rather than employee-based. They may also be known as contingent workers. The firms that connect customers to these workers often are internet-based and software-driven (rather than storefront-based). These firms typically rely on technologies such as mobile apps to facilitate peer-to-peer transactions: rely on user-based online rating systems for quality control: offer workers flexibility in deciding their work hours and geographic areas of operation: and require workers to use their own tools or assets when providing service. Also see "Contingent Worker" and "Sharing Economy."

Global Positioning System (GPS): A satellite system, originally designed by the U.S. Department of Defense for navigation purposes. Today, GPS is in wide use for consumer and business purposes, such as navigation for drivers, boaters and hikers. It utilizes satellites orbiting the earth at 10,900 miles to enable users to pinpoint precise locations using small, electronic wireless receivers.

Globalization: The increased mobility of goods, services, labor, technology and capital throughout the world. Although globalization is not a new development, its pace has increased with the advent of new technologies.

GPS: See "Global Positioning System (GPS)."

Gross Domestic Product (GDP): The total value of a nation's output, income and expenditures produced with a nation's physical borders.

Gross National Product (GNP): A country's total output of goods and services from all forms of economic activity measured at market prices for one calendar year. It differs from Gross Domestic Product (GDP) in that GNP includes income from investments made in foreign nations.

Homeowners' Association: A nonprofit association that manages the common areas of a housing development or condominium project. In addition to owning and maintaining common areas, it may enforce deed restrictions and covenants.

Homeowners' Multiperil Insurance: A packaged homeowners' insurance policy that provides both property and personal liability insurance. The typical comprehensive policy covers the house, garage and other structures on the property – as well as personal property inside the house – against a wide variety of perils. The number of covered perils depends on the breadth of the policy. Trees and plants are not covered against windstorm damage. (Homeowners' insurance will, however, cover damage to a house caused by a tree that fell in a windstorm.) The typical homeowners' policy includes theft coverage on personal property, whether it is at the home or has been carried away from the home by the owner, such as luggage on a vacation. Homeowners' insurance will also reimburse a policyholder for the cost of renting elsewhere while his or her house is being repaired after a fire or other disaster. The policy's liability insurance covers the homeowner for accidental injuries to third parties (for example, if a visitor receives a broken leg by tripping on a piece of sidewalk).

Homesourcing: The use of home-based employees to perform a business process on a regular basis. A noted example is discount airline JetBlue's use of homesourced reservation agents. A sophisticated telephone call management system routes inbound customer calls to home-based employees who assist the customers. The advantages to the employer include lower office space costs. To some home-based employees, the advantages are numerous. For example, parents of young children may be able to work from home in order to keep a closer eye on the children. A related term is telecommuting.

HSMA: Hospitality Sales and Marketing Association.

IFRS: See "International Financials Reporting Standards (IFRS)."

Industry Code: A descriptive code assigned to any company in order to group it with firms that operate in similar businesses. Common industry codes include the NAICS (North American Industrial Classification System) and the SIC (Standard Industrial Classification), both of which are standards widely used in America, as well as the International

Standard Industrial Classification of all Economic Activities (ISIC), the Standard International Trade Classification established by the United Nations (SITC) and the General Industrial Classification of Economic Activities within the European Communities (NACE).

Initial Public Offering (IPO): A company's first effort to sell its stock to investors (the public). Investors in an up-trending market eagerly seek stocks offered in many IPOs because the stocks of newly public companies that seem to have great promise may appreciate very rapidly in price, reaping great profits for those who were able to get the stock at the first offering. In the United States, IPOs are regulated by the SEC (U.S. Securities Exchange Commission) and by the state-level regulatory agencies of the states in which the IPO shares are offered.

Intellectual Property (IP): The exclusive ownership of original concepts, ideas, designs, engineering plans or other assets that are protected by law. Examples include items covered by trademarks, copyrights and patents. Items such as software, engineering plans, fashion designs and architectural designs, as well as games, books, songs and other entertainment items are among the many things that may be considered to be intellectual property. (Also, see "Patent.")

International Financials Reporting Standards (IFRS): A set of accounting standards established by the International Accounting Standards Board (IASB) for the preparation of public financial statements. IFRS has been adopted by much of the world, including the European Union, Russia and Singapore.

IP: See "Intellectual Property (IP)."

LAC: An acronym for Latin America and the Caribbean.

LDCs: See "Least Developed Countries (LDCs)."

LDW: See "Loss Damage Waiver (LDW)."

Least Developed Countries (LDCs): Nations determined by the U.N. Economic and Social Council to be the poorest and weakest members of the international community. There are currently 50 LDCs, of which 34 are in Africa, 15 are in Asia Pacific and the remaining one (Haiti) is in Latin America. The top 10 on the LDC list, in descending

order from top to 10th, are Afghanistan, Angola, Bangladesh, Benin, Bhutan, Burkina Faso, Burundi, Cambodia, Cape Verde and the Central African Republic. Sixteen of the LDCs are also Landlocked Least Developed Countries (LLDCs) which present them with additional difficulties often due to the high cost of transporting trade goods. Eleven of the LDCs are Small Island Developing States (SIDS), which are often at risk of extreme weather phenomenon (hurricanes, typhoons, Tsunami): have fragile ecosystems: are often dependent on foreign energy sources: can have high disease rates for HIV/AIDS and malaria: and can have poor market access and trade terms.

LOHAS: Lifestyles of Health and Sustainability. A marketing term that refers to consumers who choose to purchase and/or live with items that are natural, organic, less polluting, etc. Such consumers may also prefer products powered by alternative energy, such as hybrid cars.

Loss Damage Waiver (LDW): Daily rental car insurance that covers vandalism, theft and damage caused by an accident. LDW is sold at considerable additional cost to travelers.

Market Segmentation: The division of a consumer market into specific groups of buyers based on demographic factors.

Metasearch: Online search platforms that search several third-party travel sites at once. They then display the combined search results in a consolidated page. Metasearch sites may also sell advertising. This type of search platform is particularly common in the travel industry.

Millenials: See "Generation Y."

OECD: See "Organisation for Economic Co-operation and Development (OECD)."

Organisation for Economic Co-operation and Development (OECD): A group of more than 30 nations that are strongly committed to the market economy and democracy. Some of the OECD members include Japan, the U.S., Spain, Germany, Australia, Korea, the U.K., Canada and Mexico. Although not members, Estonia, Israel and Russia are invited to member talks: and Brazil, China, India, Indonesia and South Africa have enhanced engagement policies with the OECD. The

Organisation provides statistics, as well as social and economic data: and researches social changes, including patterns in evolving fiscal policy, agriculture, technology, trade, the environment and other areas. It publishes over 250 titles annually: publishes a corporate magazine, the OECD Observer: has radio and TV studios: and has centers in Tokyo, Washington, D.C., Berlin and Mexico City that distributed the Organisation's work and organizes events.

Pre-Boomer: A term occasionally used to describe people who were born between 1935 and 1945. They are somewhat older than Baby Boomers (born between 1946 and 1962). Also see "Baby Boomer."

Predictive Analytics: See "Analytics."

Sharing Economy: That part of economic activity that is directed by firms like Airbnb that direct consumers to assets owned by others in order to deliver a service or temporary use of a product or property. This practice works best for items that are costly to purchase or that the consumer may want to use only on an occasional or one-time basis. Consequently, it is extremely popular in the rental of vacation properties or private homes as an alternative to commercial hotels and resorts. When sharing is done on a for-profit basis, it is essentially a rental practice that affords consumers the ability to rent or borrow everything from hotel rooms to cars to private homes. Also see "Contingent Worker" and "Gig Economy."

Software as a Service (SaaS): Refers to the practice of providing users with software applications that are hosted on remote servers and accessed via the Internet. Excellent examples include the CRM (Customer Relationship Management) software provided in SaaS format by Salesforce. An earlier technology that operated in a similar, but less sophisticated, manner was called ASP or Application Service Provider.

Time-share (Timeshare): A type of joint ownership in which a group of owners share a particular piece of property, agreeing to have use of the property only during set days each year. Typically, time-share properties are vacation properties in such areas as beach resorts or ski resorts. They typically are condominium properties in which each condominium is jointly owned by a large group of people. Each owner typically has access to one week's use per year

and pays for a proportionate share of the property's upkeep, taxes and insurance as well as management fees.

Value Added Tax (VAT): A tax that imposes a levy on businesses at every stage of manufacturing based on the value it adds to a product. Each business in the supply chain pays its own VAT and is subsequently repaid by the next link down the chain: hence, a VAT is ultimately paid by the consumer, being the last link in the supply chain, making it comparable to a sales tax. Generally, VAT only applies to goods bought for consumption within a given country: export goods are exempt from VAT, and purchasers from other countries taking goods back home may apply for a VAT refund.

Very Light Jet (VLJ): A type of business jet that is much lower in cost to purchase and to operate than commercial passenger jets. Typically seating six people, these lightweight aircraft cost from $1.5 million to $3 million, utilize high-efficiency, lightweight jet engines, and can be operated in the $2 to $3 per mile range. Many of these new aircraft will be used as air taxis.

VLJ: See "Very Light Jet (VLJ)."

World Trade Organization (WTO): One of the only globally active international organizations dealing with the trade rules between nations. Its goal is to assist the free flow of trade goods, ensuring a smooth, predictable supply of goods to help raise the quality of life of member citizens. Members form consensus decisions that are then ratified by their respective parliaments. The WTO's conflict resolution process generally emphasizes interpreting existing commitments and agreements, and discovers how to ensure trade policies to conform to those agreements, with the ultimate aim of avoiding military or political conflict.

WTO (Tourism): World Tourism Organization.

WTTC: World Travel and Tourism Council.

9 781628 316643